ISAAC'S ARMY

After working for *The New York Times* in Warsaw in the early 1990s, MATTHEW BRZEZINSKI served as Moscow correspondent for *The Wall Street Journal*. Following the September 11 attacks, he covered homeland security as a contributing writer for *The New York Times Magazine.* He is also the author of *Casino Moscow, Fortress America,* and *Red Moon Rising.* He lives in Manchester-by-the-Sea, Massachusetts.

ALSO BY MATTHEW BRZEZINSKI

*Red Moon Rising: Sputnik and the Hidden Rivalries
That Ignited the Space Age*

*Fortress America: On the Frontlines of Homeland Security—
An Inside Look at the Coming Surveillance State*

*Casino Moscow: A Tale of Greed and Adventure
on Capitalism's Wildest Frontier*

ISAAC'S ARMY

ISAAC'S ARMY

A Story of Courage and Survival
in Nazi-Occupied Poland

MATTHEW BRZEZINSKI

First published in in the United States by Random House,
an imprint of The Random House Publishing Group,
a division of Random House, Inc., New York

Published in the UK in 2013 by Head of Zeus Ltd

9 7 5 3 1 2 4 6 8

A CIP catalogue record for this book is available from the British Library.

ISBN (HB) 9781781851104
ISBN (XTPB) 9781781854471
ISBN (E) 9781781852118

Printed in Germany

Head of Zeus Ltd
Clerkenwell House
45–47 Clerkenwell Green
London EC1R 0HT

www.headofzeus.com

Title-page photograph copyright © iStockphoto.com/© Monika Lewandowska

Book design by Carole Lowenstein

To my mother, and to my wife,
who have shown me the best
of both worlds

PREFACE

To survive the Holocaust, Polish Jews had three options. They could run. They could hide. Or they could take up arms and fight. The only other alternative—to do nothing—resulted in almost certain death.

Although death also overwhelmingly claimed those who ran, hid, or fought, many still chose these paths of resistance. They refused to submit to evil, or to give up on life, and this made them exceptional individuals—not just as Jews or Poles, but as humans. Statistically, they were the "one percent," the very few who took their fate into their own hands and beat the odds.

I had been curious about these remarkable people ever since my first job in journalism as a lowly cub reporter at *The New York Times*'s Warsaw bureau back in the early 1990s. Warsaw then was so drab and lifeless, so devasted physically and spiritually by half a century of communism, that it was not hard to imagine what the Ghetto must have felt like. I often walked the neighborhood's sooty streets, where not a single prewar building had survived Hitler's wrath, and wondered what I would have done had I been one of the nearly half million people packed inside the district's walls. Since I was a Gentile—my mother was a native Varsovian—the exercise had always been academic, an arm's-length inquiry without undue emotional attachment. Perhaps that was why I always pictured myself acting heroically.

As the years passed and I moved on, to reporting stints in Moscow and then Washington, thoughts of Jewish heroes receded from my mind, replaced by more mundane concerns about marriage and mortgages, twins and tuition fees. Occasionally a newspaper article or a film set during the war would rekindle my curiosity, and I would wonder about the true nature of resistance, and about what it had taken to be part of the one percent. In popular culture, resistance figures were always portrayed as if they had been forged overnight, born defiant and wielding a grenade. The real story, I suspected, was far more interesting and nuanced, and much slower in developing.

My enduring interest was enhanced by marriage. Since my wife, Roberta, was Jewish, so, too, were our three children under both rabbinical and Nuremberg laws, which made it harder to treat the Holocaust dispassionately, like something terrible that had happened to the neighbors. It became impossible to do so in 2007, when Roberta proposed moving to Poland for a three-year posting. She had been made partner in an international private equity firm that was investing heavily in Eastern Europe. Her firm's sleek new offices were in the heart of the former Warsaw Ghetto, built over the ruins of the old Jewish Council building on Mushroom Street, which was being transformed into a soaring financial district to anchor Poland's economic rebirth.

When we settled into our rented marble McMansion in a ritzy Warsaw suburb, next door to a prewar Gothic palace with an indoor swimming pool that had belonged to a Jewish industrialist, I couldn't help but think what would have happened to my family if it were 1939 instead of 2009. Though I no longer had the luxury of detachment, I still approached my growing obsession egoistically. The question of how I would have acted was always in the back of my mind when I set out to tell this story. For purely selfish reasons, I wanted to seek out and meet the extraordinary individuals who had defied Hitler and try to discover what made them tick. Did they share common traits? A hero gene, perhaps? Or were they ordinary people who tapped some hidden reservoir of strength and courage? I knew that to get the full picture, the complete character sketch, I had to tell the whole story— not just a fragmentary rehash of a rising, but what came before and after. In other words, people's stories had to be rendered from the first day of the war to the last, and in some cases beyond. Only then would it become clear who they really were, where they came from, what their motivation was, and how they had evolved into heroic figures. I also wanted to explore the different forms of resistance: collective and individual, armed and passive, conscious and subconcious. Picking up a gun was not the only way to thwart the Nazis. While running and hiding didn't capture the public imagination in the same way as assaulting a tank, these acts of defiance also required astonishing perseverance, courage, and planning, as I discovered while researching the epic saga of the Osnos and Mortkowicz families. I came across their story by chance, in the waiting room of a decrepit Polish hospital where my son Ari was undergoing emergency surgery. I chose to write about them because they were representative of thousands of other Polish Jews who shared similar experiences, and because the related families had surviving members, one cousin living in New York, the other in Krakow.

Getting to know the protagonists personally became one of the chief determinants for selecting the main characters of the book. This was especially true in relating the tale of organized resistance, because only a handful of veterans of the Jewish Fighting Organization were still alive, scattered across continents. Some, like Mark Edelman, were well known and living nearby in Poland. Others, like Simha Ratheiser, were farther afield in Israel. I found Boruch Spiegel in Montreal, in a retirement home only a block away from the medical center where my mother had set up her family practice after immigrating to Canada in the 1960s.

I had to make one notable exception to my acquaintanceship rule. Isaac Zuckerman had passed away in Israel before I could meet him. But there was no way to tell the story of Jewish organized resistance in Poland without including him. He was too central to the narrative to omit. In fact, he was the embodiment of the underground movement, which is why his name graces the cover of this book. Fortunately, Zuckerman had written a detailed and brutally frank memoir, which he released only upon his death. The text was angry and honest, unvarnished and free of hero worship, and I found it invaluable.

The quotes in this book are drawn from a mix of interviews, memoirs, unpublished diaries, and archival materials. The data—the death tolls, roundup numbers, execution and torture tallies, starvation rates—are drawn from Polish, Israeli, and U.S. historical surveys. Source attributions are all enumerated in the endnote section so as not to disrupt the narrative flow. That flow traces the personal journeys of the main characters while also attending to the need for historical and geographic background.

Too many accounts of the Holocaust are written in a vacuum, as if sealed from the outside world. Jews were directly affected by the larger events around them: by relations with Gentiles and by shifting alliances within the fractious Polish Underground; by military developments, both victories and defeats, on the Eastern and Western fronts and by changing policies and priorities of Poland's Nazi occupiers; by cynical political decisions in London and Washington; and by the eventual arrival and agenda of new Soviet masters. These outside forces shaped Jewish destinies and decisions between 1939 and 1946, and I've tried to weave them into the plot to provide explanatory context.

I've also tried to re-create the physical landscape of wartime Warsaw, since the city no longer exists as it once was. Hitler literally erased it from the map, destroying 90 percent of the buildings in the metropolitan area. This made it frustratingly difficult, sitting at the sushi restaurant in my wife's fancy office building and staring at the million-dollar condominiums being built across the street, to picture the starving children that once lined up outside that very spot, begging for bread. Nothing was left of that world but a few dwindling memories, and it seemed important to me to paint a living and breathing portrait of the place and the time, as well as the people. That is why I chose to render location names into their English translations, whenever possible. "Mushroom Street" rolls off the tongue more easily than "Ulica Grzybowska," though both have the same meaning. Similarly, "Paul" is easier on the American ear than its Polish equivalent of "Pawel."

But ultimately, this is a book about people, about a group of individuals who experienced and accomplished extraordinary things. Alone and together, they pushed the limits of endurance and were tested like few others on this planet of seven billion. Though their stories are inseparable from the Holocaust, their appeal, and the heights to which they elevate the human condition, are universal.

CONTENTS

BOOK TWO

BOOK THREE

BOOK FOUR

BOOK FIVE

UMSCHLAG-PLATZ

LOW ST.

ZAMENHOF ST.

LOW ST.

PLEASANT ST.

DRAGON ST.

GOOSE ST.

PEACOCK ST.

CARMELITE

Peacock
Prison

Jewish
Cemetery

VALIANT ST.

TRENCH ST.

NEW LINDEN

FORESTRY BLVD.

GARDEN

COOL ST.

WARSAW GHETTO

Ghetto border on November 15, 1940

Ghetto border with expansion,
November 15, 1940–July 22, 1942

Jewish cemetery

Major parks

0   MILE   1/2

0   METERS   500

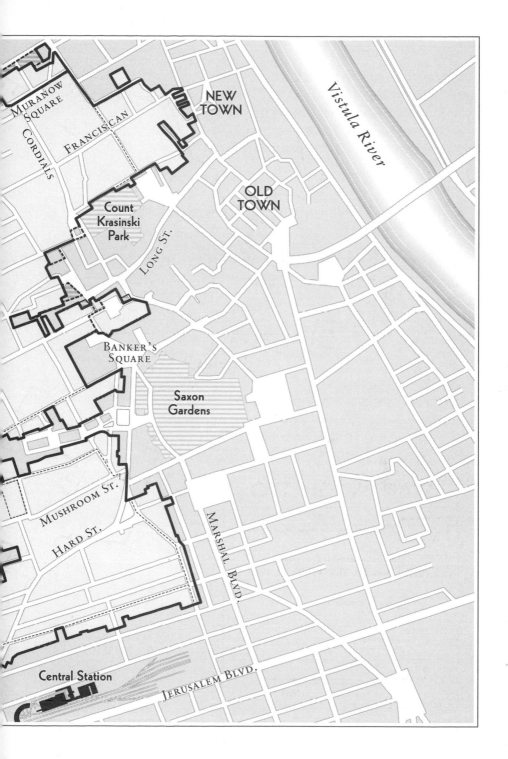

CAST OF CHARACTERS

PRIMARY

Isaac Zuckerman: Socialist Zionist youth leader, co-founder of the Jewish Fighting Organization and its leader following the Ghetto Uprising.

Simha Ratheiser: High school student. Eventually Isaac's bodyguard and lead courier.

Mark Edelman: Bundist orphan. Commander in the Jewish Fighting Organization.

Boruch Spiegel: Bundist tailor. Foot soldier in the Jewish Fighting Organization.

Zivia Lubetkin: Socialist Zionist organizer. Highest-ranking female in the Jewish Fighting Organization, and eventually Isaac's girlfriend and wife.

SECONDARY

The Osnos family: Martha, Joseph, and Robert. Assimilated upper-middle-class entrepreneurs.

The Mortkowicz family: Janine, Hanna, and Joanna. Three generations of Poland's greatest publishing dynasty.

TERTIARY

Bernard Goldstein: Bund Special Ops chief. Early architect of organized resistance.

Mordechai Anielewicz: Marxist Zionist youth leader. Led the Jewish Fighting Organization during the Ghetto Uprising.

Tuvia Borzykowski: Isaac's deputy in the Jewish Fighting Organization.

Chaika Belchatowska: Jewish Fighting Organization foot soldier, Boruch's girlfriend and later wife.

Monika Zeromska: Gentile Resistance operative. Protector of the Mortkowiczes.

Berl Spiegel: Boruch's older brother. Bund activist.

David Apfelbaum: Alleged right-wing Zionist resistance leader. His existence is disputed by historians.

BOOK ONE

Anti-Semitism is a protest against a level playing field—a protest against talent.

—MARTIN AMIS

CHAPTER 1

HANNA'S TRIUMPH

On the first morning of the Second World War the city of Warsaw slept. A willful calm reigned over the Polish capital, as if the early German incursions in the north and west of the country were minor irritants, not entirely unexpected, and best ignored.

September 1, 1939, fell on a Friday, which partly explained the initial insouciance, the reluctance to rouse to a threat that would ultimately destroy 90 percent of the city and kill nearly half its inhabitants. It was date night, and the jazz clubs, movie houses, and restaurants were packed. A comedy by the up-and-coming playwright Maria Pawlowska was premiering that evening at the New Theatre. At the Ali Baba, an encore presentation of the hit political satire *Facts and Pacts* played to a full house.

Despite the Nazi invasion, the racetrack stayed open. W. Kruk Jewelers did not cancel their autumn sale. The confectioners Fuchs, Wedel, and Blikle continued their century-old rivalry. And despite the wail of air raid sirens, the window grilles at the Jablkowski Brothers department store stood defiantly retracted, exposing the delicate stained glass landscapes that beckoned customers inside the four-floor kingdom, the Harrod's of prewar Warsaw, where the liveried staff staged puppet and fashion shows and addressed clients as "Your Excellency," regardless of age.

In Napoleon Square, at the heart of the financial district, under the shadow of the Eisenstadt & Rotberg Building and the Prudential Life Insurance Tower, billed by its architect, Marcin Weinfeld, as central Europe's tallest skyscraper, banks and brokerages awaited the latest stock market results almost as eagerly as news from the nascent front. On Marshal and Jerusalem Boulevards, it was *petite robes floues,* not panic, that were on display at the Hersh Fashion House and in the neo-Renaissance shopping arcades built by developers Karol Fritsche, Jacob Lowenberg, and Pinkus Loth, the Trumps of prewar Poland. Outside the luxurious boutiques, near the Aliyev Turkish Sweets shop and the Elite kosher restaurant next door, traffic was no heavier than usual on September 1—sparse, in fact, for a city that in 1939 was almost twice as big as Boston and nearly the size of metropolitan Los Angeles. Photos taken that day show Packards, Oldsmobiles, Fords, and Fiats idling under an enormous Chevrolet billboard, while farther uptown, near the medieval battlements and Baroque basilicas of the historic district, patrons outside the five-star Bristol Hotel could be seen reclining in elegant wicker chairs, refreshments in hand.

But there were also signs, to be sure, that all was not business as usual on that Friday. Outside the PKO State Savings Bank, depositors lined up to withdraw cash. Greengrocers, butchers, and pharmacists witnessed a spike in sales as many Varsovians stocked up on food and medical supplies. The municipal government canceled all vacation leaves, and general mobilization notices began appearing on poster columns, papering over the fall Opera schedule. And all the while, from the outlying suburbs, the distant and distressing rumble of anti-aircraft batteries could be heard.

Isaac Zuckerman needed no prompting to volunteer to fight for his country—a nation that he loved as a patriot but whose leaders he loathed as a Jew, a country he was willing to defend with his life but ultimately wanted to leave.

His dilemma was not unusual within the Zionist community, a vibrant, fractious, restless agglomeration of dreamers, loafers, activists, firebrand intellectuals, and sober realists who knew from bitter historical experience that Europe, and especially Eastern Europe, was not an American-style melting pot, and that Jews would always be treated as outsiders there, as second-class citizens, or "resident aliens" as some Polish politicians liked to say.

On the morning of September 1, 1939, Isaac Zuckerman's dilemma was particularly acute, and it had nothing to do with his hopes for the establishment of a Jewish homeland in Palestine. He wanted to enlist, yet no army unit would take him, although officers must have looked wistfully at the twenty-four-year-old volunteer standing before them: Isaac was a large and imposing individual, well over six feet tall and solidly built. He was rakishly handsome, with strong Slavic features, a square jaw, and the blond bushy mustache favored by the minor nobility. He looked like a recruiting poster for the Polish cavalry, a career he had briefly contemplated, since he could ride well, a legacy of equestrian summers at a rich uncle's estate near Vilna.

But each time he and a fellow Zionist presented themselves to the authorities, the answer was the same. "We reported to the officer, a pleasant young man," Isaac later wrote, describing their second attempt to enlist, "who told us he wished he knew what to do with his own soldiers, let alone civilians."

That Poland's armed forces were in such disarray astonished Zuckerman. The Polish government, the Fascist-leaning Sanation regime, which had seized power in a quasi-coup, supposedly to cleanse the republic in a sanitary sweep, was essentially a dictatorship run by generals. Diplomatic tensions with Berlin had boiled throughout the spring and summer, with threats and counterthreats leaving little doubt that conflict was imminent. In July, state radio had begun issuing instructions on how to black out windows and use gas masks. Patriotic fund drives had been launched, urging citizens to donate to rearming the nation. Even the anti-Semitic vitriol of the right-wing press had been suspended during the campaign, which stressed unity and a newfound tolerance toward minorities. Newspapers praised Jewish entrepreneurs for their generous contributions toward the purchase of tanks and artillery pieces, and the entire country feted the "wonderful news" that students at Public School Number 166 in upper Warka had raised 11.75 zlotys, or roughly $2.00, for ammunition. The war did not come as a surprise to anyone, it seemed, other than Poland's authoritarian military leaders.

Enlistment aside, Isaac faced an even more pressing problem on the morning of September 1. He needed to get back home to Warsaw. He had been delivering a series of lectures at a Zionist training seminar in the town of Kleban, not far from Rovno in present-day Ukraine, when the Nazis struck. He felt certain the authorities would have a more sophisticated view of events in the capital than they did in Kleban, a shtetl of a few thousand impoverished Jews in the equivalent of the Polish Appalachians. Isaac had no intention of wasting away in this speck on the map 220 miles southeast of Warsaw while the Germans marched on the capital. The defense would surely be far better organized there than it was in the provinces, where the chain of command seemed diffuse, the order of battle confused, the officers visibly frustrated. In Warsaw, the largest urban center in Central Europe, the cultural and political center of world Jewry, the situation would be clearer.

Just before dawn on September 1, Adolf Hitler had staged a Polish invasion of Germany. German convicts dressed in Polish uniforms were forced to "storm" a Reich border post. Photos of the convicts' bullet-riddled bodies served as evidence of Polish aggression and were the official pretext for the war Hitler had just launched in response.

The ruse was so blatantly farcical that many Poles doubted that the accompanying campaign would be any more serious, that the whole thing would be regarded as anything but staged theater, a few shots fired in another of the Führer's famous antics. "Not everyone understood what war with the Germans meant," Zuckerman would later say.

Whether the war was real was a topic of much discussion and little agreement in the Polish capital on the morning of September 1, 1939. At the Landed Gentry Café, outdoor tables buzzed with speculation. The fashionable eatery was a liberal bastion in a city that had turned rightward in lockstep with Germany and so many other European nations in the 1930s, and one of the few places in Warsaw where Jews and Gentiles still socialized outside of work.

The Landed Gentry only started filling up around eleven that morning, since its principal clientele—writers, poets, and journalists—tended to be late risers, and lived in the northernmost part of the city, in leafy Jolie Bord, an upper-middle-class enclave anchored around Woodrow Wilson Square. But already heated debate raged, and that morning's newspapers were thrust from hand to hand like intellectual batons amid a breathless relay of theories and conjecture. The hostilities would last only a few weeks, posited the optimists. Hitler was making another limited land grab. He probably wanted the Pomeranian Corridor, the coastal landmass awarded to Poland in 1918 that cut off West Prussia from the rest of Germany. Naturally, he'd demand Danzig—the disputed Baltic port that President Wilson's League of Nations had declared a Free City following World War I, when Poland reemerged on world maps after more than a century of foreign dominion. Maybe the Führer would also seek some of the Silesian lands that Berlin had lost in the Versailles Treaty. A territorial price would have to be paid. Then peace would return.

Martha Osnos later compared the hopeful assertions to "blind people discussing colors." But she, too, had felt optimistic that September morning, when she was thirty-three years old, a confident and worldly woman who had lived in Paris for several years. A biochemist by training, she spoke six languages, though pointedly not Yiddish, and could hold her own in any of the high-minded discussions that usually accompanied the signature plum cake at the Landed Gentry: from the latest developments in the romantic poetry movement to the latest outrages of the Sanation regime. Osnos's smile was wide and effortless. Her cheeks glowed, and her dark hair, which she kept short, cut above her ears, gave the impression of a person at ease with herself.

Martha's cousin Hanna was more troubled by the rumblings of war. Hanna Mortkowicz-Olczak and Martha Osnos were frequent dining companions at the Landed Gentry, as famous in prewar Poland as Elaine's in its heyday in New York. The café owed its lettered clientele to Osnos's uncle, the publisher Jacob Mortkowicz, whose flagship bookstore was next door, and whose stable of writers—cultural stars

in the pre-television age, many of them Jews—had permanently reserved tables on elevated platforms that denoted their celebrity status.

Hanna was Jacob Mortkowicz's thirty-six-year-old daughter, a
stately dark-haired woman with hypnotic, hooded eyes, a doctorate in
fine arts from the University of Warsaw, a gift for foreign languages,
and a failed marriage to a Gentile geology professor. There were many
such mixed marriages among the Warsaw intelligentsia, but Hanna
had converted to Protestantism, the first person to abandon Judaism
in a family that traced its Talmudic heritage to great-grandfather
Lazar Horowitz, one of the leading rabbis of Vienna, himself the son
and grandson of rabbis dating back to seventeenth-century Bavaria.

Hanna had inherited the financially troubled publishing empire
after her father's suicide in 1931. Though a visionary—a man who
had introduced the paperback to Poland, founded a nationwide chain
of kiosks to sell mass-market books, and nurtured some of the country's brightest literary talents—he had been an indifferent money
manager, and the 1929 stock market collapse wreaked havoc on his
affairs. It had taken Hanna eight years to nurse the business back to
health, and as the war was about to begin, she finally had reason to
celebrate. A few weeks earlier, she had paid off the last of the J. Mortkowicz Publishing House debts, which meant its printing presses and
the beautiful building that housed them in Old Town Square were finally free of liens. A further sum equivalent to around $100,000 had
just been deposited at the PKO State Savings Bank to fund the autumn
advertising budget in expectation of a big Christmas season.

September 1939 should have been a triumphant month for Hanna.
She had saved her father's legacy. She had won the admiration of Warsaw's elitist intellectuals. She was arguably the most influential female
publisher in Eastern Europe, and perhaps on the entire continent,
since the field was not crowded with women. And while her marriage
had unraveled, in part due to her success, she had a lovely and intelli-
gent five-year-old daughter, Joanna, a strong and supportive mother in
Jacob Mortkowicz's vivacious widow, Janine, and a future that at last
seemed secure.

Instead she was worried about the plume of smoke rising menacingly to the west of the city, from the airport, where German bombs
were said to have fallen at dawn. Martha, she suggested, should send

her eight-year-old son, Robert, to join little Joanna at the Mortkowicz country house, south of Warsaw, safely out of bombing range. At least for a few days, until the politicians settled their differences.

And calm would return, the city's widest circulation daily confidently declared in its September 1, 1939, special edition. The Sanation regime, its editors insisted, had the situation well in hand. The *Warsaw Courier* had always been sympathetic to the strongmen who ruled Poland with increasingly rabid anti-Semitic pomp since the 1935 death of the country's beloved leader, Joseph Pilsudski. That Friday, however, the conservative paper outdid itself—both in sycophancy and in misleading its readers. Coverage of the Nazi invasion was relegated to the bottom half of the first page. In the prime journalistic real estate "above the fold" were patriotic headshots of Poland's authoritarian leaders: the puppet president Ignatius Moscicki, resplendent in white bow tie, tuxedo, and aristocratic whiskers, and the de facto ruler Marshal Edward Smigly-Rydz, his gold-braided uniform straining under the combined weight of the nation's highest honors. Wedged between them, an official statement from President Moscicki pledged: "The entire Polish nation, blessed by God in its Holy and Righteous cause, together with the Army, will march arm in arm to battle and total victory."

The portraits said it all. They projected such arrogant authority, such confidence and power, that the message couldn't be clearer: Poland's government would deal with Hitler with the same forceful dispatch they had hitherto reserved for unruly Ukrainians and overly enterprising Jews.

CHAPTER 2

SIMHA'S FIRST DAY OF SCHOOL

Reassured by their leaders' confident declarations, Warsaw's 1.3 million residents thus permitted themselves one more day of near normalcy.

By midmorning on September 1, 1939, the Saxon Gardens and Count Krasinski Park, a few blocks north of the Landed Gentry Café, rang with the laughter of Jewish children running along its warm pebble paths, splashing in the round white marble fountain, flinging chestnuts, and climbing the circular oak girders of the Summer Amphitheatre, where a performance of *A Divided Heart* would be given that evening. Their parents were hard at work on Nalewki, or Cordials, Street, which bordered the park's ornate wrought iron fence, running north of Marshal Boulevard, Warsaw's main artery, into the heart of the congested Jewish neighborhood above the city center.

Boruch Spiegel, like thousands of others in the Jewish Quarter that Friday, at the height of the sweater-knitting season, one of the busiest times of the year, was seated in front of a sewing machine. It was a prized Singer, far superior to models like Pfaff or Kempisty-Kasprzycki, or the larger industrial-sized Adlers, and it had been a parting gift from an uncle who managed to emigrate to the United States despite the hated Johnson-Reed Act, which had all but slammed shut America's doors to Eastern European Jewry after 1924.

Spiegel's motions that morning, like every morning, were mechanical, already the unthinking product of endless repetition, though he was barely twenty, and technically still an apprentice. With one hand he fed a piece of felt into the rapidly plunging spear of a whirring needle. With the other he deftly guided the emerging seam along contours and curves, overlapping the soft material in some places, leaving excess to be trimmed off in others, all the while adjusting the speed and pitch of the process with foot pedals. His father sat next to him, holding shears, chalk, and a wooden template, which he used to pre-cut sections from the rolls of black and brown felt that Boruch sewed into spats. Between them they could make five or six dozen pairs of the fashionable shoe covers in a good day.

But September 1 was not a good day. News of the German offensive and air raid sirens were distracting Spiegel, a short and slim youth with round, sensitive features and large, expressive eyes that could look deeply wounded in one moment, indignantly angry the next, pleading a few seconds later. He could not sit still. He made an excuse to his father about running an errand and set off for Cordials Street, the commercial hub of the large Jewish Quarter, to find out what was happening.

Ironically, an earlier German onslaught, during the First World War, had brought the Spiegel family to Warsaw from a small town near Plotsk, where Boruch was born. The Quarter was a way station for new arrivals in the capital, much as New York's Lower East Side was a gateway to the American middle class; except that Cordials Street was more prosperous and had remained largely unchanged since it was first cobbled in 1783. Wave after wave of eastern migrants, the so-called Litvaks, had passed through its busy tenements over the years, some escaping Tsarist repressions and pogroms, others fleeing the poverty and limited opportunity of the shtetls. By the 1930s the Quarter had already produced several generations of attorneys, university professors, and doctors—two-thirds of Warsaw's prewar physicians were Jewish, as were 37 percent of its lawyers—and though the predominantly Yiddish-speaking district had lost many former residents to assimilation and upward mobility, its fundamentally ambitious and hardworking character had stayed the same.

The mood on the streets that morning was uneasy, Spiegel later recalled, but there was no greater sense of urgency in the Quarter that Friday than in the rest of Warsaw: no panic, no preparations for mass flight, no visible deviations from the usual routine. The prevailing atmosphere seemed to be one of heightened tension, "collective nervousness." Radios in shops were all tuned to the show of Zbigniew Swietochowski on Warsaw One, the main state broadcaster, who assured listeners that "we are strong, united and ready," and customers—both Gentile and Jewish—anxiously awaited bulletins and updates, asking one another for the latest news.

As always, Cordials Street teemed with frenetic activity before the Sabbath. Porters, horse-drawn delivery vans, *droshki,* bicycle rickshaws, trucks, and saloon cars clogged the broad road, bisected by the dual tracks of tram line 17. Pedestrians jostled one another on sidewalks lined with all manner of goods; hats, lamps, ladders, barrels of nails, pickles, pungent sauerkrauts, and umbrellas—Cordials alone boasted 28 umbrella factories. Street vendors stabbed the smoky air with their long skewers of bagels, neatly speared on sticks. Carp wallowed in murky tubs, waiting to be sold, clubbed, and cooked. And the Dubicki refreshment stand offered its famous lemonade, served either sweet with "pure sugar" or bitter and "doubly saturated."

The three- to five-story buildings that lined Cordials were equally crowded with billboards, advertisements, and multilingual signs bearing the names of small businesses and their proprietors: Jacob Stein, S. Goldstein, M. Grubstein, Lancev, Leningradter, Tyrman, Pik. Shops occupied the ground floors: opticians, tobacconists, pharmacists, and florists; haberdashers, factors, and travel agents; shoe stores, hardware stores, and bookstores. The artisans and craftsmen—tailors, cobblers, upholsterers, and radio repairmen—were generally relegated to the second floors, where rents were cheaper, while the wholesalers, small leather-goods factories, furniture and curtain makers, basket weavers, tinsmiths, and sweatshops filled out the garrets and cellars. Narrow passages tunneled through some buildings, where informal secondary markets for promissory notes thrived. Most small manufacturers around Cordials were paid with IOUs by "jobbers," who resold their products in stores throughout Poland. "Speculators who had money would walk in the courtyards that ran from Cordials to Zamenhof Street, and they would buy notes at a discount," one participant in the trade recalled. The notes were discounted depending on their term and the reputation of the jobber, and they formed the backbone of a back-alley banking system in the Jewish Quarter.

Rear courtyards were the real hubs of economic activity throughout the district, and enterprising landlords like Abraham Kalushiner rented out stalls for mini interior shopping plazas, over which apartments doubled as workshops. The Spiegel family rented such dual-use accommodations three blocks west of Cordials, at 30 Peacock Street. Their atelier occupied the front parlor of the ground-floor apartment, and Boruch, his two sisters, his parents, and his older brother shared three small back rooms. It was crowded and loud, and privacy was nonexistent. But it was a typical living arrangement in the Quarter, which housed more than half of Warsaw's 380,000 Jews.

When Boruch returned from his putative errand, his mind had still not settled, and his thoughts meandered from talk of war, and the probability of victory, to girls, and to the opera, his other great passion. He had inherited his love of music from his father, whose most prized possession, a violin, stood carefully wrapped in a closet. And while Boruch did not have his father's gift with instruments, he had developed a fine ear and a keen appreciation for opera. The fall season, as always, brought Boruch mixed feelings. There would be new performances—*Faust* was already being advertised—but also the obligatory paid coat check that accompanied the chillier temperatures. That would add to the price of admission, an unwelcome burden on Spiegel's very meager resources. Many years later, he would reflect with wonder how such a seemingly trivial concern competed with the German invasion in his list of worries on September 1, 1939.

For Simha Ratheiser, and for every school-age child in Warsaw, the first day of the Second World War coincided with the commencement of classes, an unhappy date even at the best of times. In Poland, September 1 signified the traditional conclusion of the summer break, of sailing in the Mazury lake region, hiking in the Tatra Mountains, and camping in the primeval forest of Bialowieza, where wild bison roamed among the ancient pines. September 1 meant no more visits to distant and gift-laden relatives, no more picnics in ruined castles. It brought an abrupt end to those carefree August afternoons in the sand dunes of the Hel Peninsula, with kites fluttering in the maritime breeze and the sun warming the frigid Baltic waters just enough to splash around in the waves.

On this particular September 1, the ring of school bells competed with air raid sirens throughout the city, followed by radio announcements of "All Clear." No doubt the more reluctant returnees cursed their bad luck that classes had not been canceled as a result of the outbreak of hostilities. Simha Ratheiser was too distracted by the sight and sound of planes buzzing over the capital to think much about school that morning. The fifteen-year-old was entering his sophomore year. He was a good and generally attentive student and an excellent athlete, a gifted striker who played soccer with Gentiles in the Christian suburb where he lived. With his pale blue-green eyes and light chestnut hair, he fit in with his Slavic neighbors.

School was a forty-five-minute commute from Simha's home near the Vistula River. Catholic public schools in his district were much closer. But his parents, like the parents of half the Jewish children in Poland, had insisted he attend a private Jewish academy. "My father was an observant Jew, and he wanted me to study at a Jewish institution," Simha would later explain.

Ratheiser's school was in the southernmost part of the Jewish Quarter at 26 Mushroom Street, an imposing neoclassical edifice that also housed the offices of the Jewish Community Council, the modern administrative successor of the Kehila self-governing bodies that had existed in Poland since the fifteenth century. Large oil paintings of long-deceased community elders decorated the building's cavernous halls, their gaze scrutinizing future leaders as they trudged between classes.

Simha was popular. It was not just his good looks, or the fact that the girls, both Gentile and Jewish, thought him intriguing. He was in fact unusually cool: blessed by some inner regulating mechanism that lent him the ability to stay calm when others grew agitated. Perhaps that helped explain why his neighborhood bullies—the *sheygetzes,* as

Gentiles were called in Yiddish—didn't bother trying to get a rise out of him. He certainly wasn't big or intimidating. He didn't curse, or talk tough, like some of his Polish neighbors, and other kids at school. But he carried himself in the sort of detached, casual manner that suggested he belonged in whatever environment he found himself in.

Like Isaac Zuckerman and so many other young Polish Jews, Simha Ratheiser had been captivated for a time by Zionism's dream of a Jewish homeland. The previous summer he had gone to a camp run by Akiva, one of the dozens of Zionist youth organizations in Poland, and he had been captivated by stories of daring kibbutzniks, of camels and exotic Bedouins, of fearless settlers turning parched desert into blooming orchards. But the fervor had passed. Simha, by his own admission, "was never overly political." And there was a monastic, cult-like atmosphere in some Zionist groups that left him cold. In the meantime, the usual teenage interests—soccer, girls, the movies—had replaced Palestine.

Those teenage preoccupations kept Simha from cracking the books on September 1. The sound of sirens and airplanes were distracting him, and he and his schoolmates stared at the cloudless sky, trying to guess whether the unsettling aircraft circling overhead were Polish or German. They were not alone. Most of Warsaw was gazing skyward. "Those are our planes," people on the streets said, pointing excitedly. "No, they are not," others countered. "Those are exercises," some reassured. "No, they aren't." The debates raged. The planes were in fact antiquated Polish P-6s retrofitted with British Vickers engines, and ungainly P-11s, or Bumblebees, as the slow and bulbous machines would become known, part of a squadron of fighters that had been redeployed to defend the Polish capital. But like most Varsovians, Ratheiser could not yet distinguish the distinctive sound and silhouette of enemy bombers. Nonetheless, he was intensely curious about them. Much like any fifteen-year-old, he had longed to see a dogfight—the real-life, swooping version of the World War I duels shown in the American movies that played at the Napoleon Theater in Three Crosses Square.

His wish would be granted shortly after the lunch bell.

————

At 3:30 that afternoon, steam whistles sounded throughout Praga, the smokestack district on the eastern, unfashionable bank of the Vistula River—a tough, mixed neighborhood where 40 percent of the residents were Jewish. The day shift had ended, and 3,870 workers streamed out of the Lilpop, Rau & Lowenstein plant. The forty-acre facility assembled Buicks, Chevrolets, and Opel Kadetts under license from General Motors, as well as locomotives, trams, heavy trucks, and armored vehicles. It was one of Warsaw's largest industrial concerns, a joint venture between Belgian Jews and ethnic Germans who founded the conglomerate in the mid-nineteenth century to build rail ties for the tsar, after Poland's annexation into the Russian empire had opened vast new markets and attracted great sums of foreign investment.

Next door, thick pale fumes billowed from the vents of the Schicht-Lever soap and laundry detergent plant, an Anglo-Dutch concern that would morph into global giant Unilever, while the three hundred workers of Samuel and Sender Ginsburg's BRAGE Rubber Works poured out onto November 11 Street, a road that commemorated the date of a failed uprising against tsarist dominion.

Nearby, Joseph Osnos, Martha's tall and elegant thirty-five-year-old husband—an urbane businessman and fastidious dresser who bore a passing resemblance to Errol Flynn—was also letting his employees out for the weekend. He had raised his start-up capital as a diamond broker in France and Belgium, and now his plant, Karolyt Incorporated, produced toasters, electric irons, and kettles. During the long run-up to the invasion, he had introduced a new line of hermetically sealed food containers to protect against the mustard gas attacks that figured prominently in every newspaper report about German arsenals and tactics. Sales shot through the roof, and the plant operated at full capacity throughout the summer of 1939 to meet the media-driven demand. Gas masks and duct tape also sold out, because if the Nazis struck, the Sanation government had repeatedly warned during its incessant military fund drives, it would surely be with chemical weapons.

Years later, Joseph's family would not remember how many workers he had employed. But as they streamed out of his plant that Friday, those workers had reason to be anxious. In the distance, rising hundreds of feet in the air, beyond the huge Koneser Vodka distillery with its production capacity of a million liters a month, a black, noxious cloud swirled over the Pea Town Oil Reservoir—Warsaw's first industrial casualty of the war.

Watching the reservoir blaze, Osnos made a mental note to contact his notary and attorney on Monday morning. He would put the factory in Martha's name, and put a few financial matters in order. As a precaution, in the unlikely event the situation spiraled out of control and something happened to him. At least Martha and Robert would be protected and provided for.

As dusk descended on the first day of the Second World War, the quasi-normalcy that still prevailed over the Polish capital assumed its typical nocturnal features. In blue-collar Praga, the drunken bar brawls that inaugurated the launch of every weekend flared up, even as firefighters fought in vain to douse the raging inferno in Pea Town. Across the Vistula, Simha Ratheiser's father, Zvi, locked up his store early, as was his custom every Friday, and set off on foot to synagogue, skirting the Royal Gardens, Warsaw's stunning central park, where the shrill, lustful cries of free-ranging peacocks and swans echoed over the ponds, amphitheaters, and manicured lawns.

The elegant, tree-lined district bordering the park had once been King Stanislaw August's private hunting preserve. It now was home to imposing government ministries and high officials, high-ceilinged apartments with elaborate plasterwork, and the gated villas of minor aristocrats and the city's financial and industrial elite; a mixed neighborhood where Jews and Gentiles shared gardeners and stock tips, but rarely socialized.

On Belvedere Street, whose principal palace would later adorn bottles of high-end vodka, black Citroën limousines with headlights doused raced past Zvi, shuttling between the presidential residence and the gleaming white façade of the Ministry of Defense, where the anti-Semitic commander in chief, Marshal Smigly-Rydz, was issuing the Sanation regime's first official communiqué of the war.

Blue Chevy trucks with loudspeakers on their roofs and the swirling logo of Polish State Radio on their sides carried Smigly-Rydz's triumphal announcement throughout the city center. "Today a total of 16 enemy airplanes were destroyed. Our own losses—2 aircraft," the taped message proclaimed in a continuous loop. "We have captured prisoners at many points. . . . In [Danzig], three enemy attempts to storm Westerplatte were repulsed."

Martha and Joseph Osnos caught the happy developments on Warsaw One, the main state broadcaster, that evening, while Helen, their Gentile nanny, packed young Robert's bags so he could join his cousin Joanna at the Mortkowicz country house the next morning— although now, apparently, there was less urgency in getting him out of the city.

The Osnoses usually went out or entertained on Friday evenings, and their guest lists conformed to the prevailing norms and degrees of social segregation in prewar Warsaw. "My parents only associated with other assimilated Jews," their son Robert would later recall. "Yiddish was taboo in our house." That Friday, however, there was no dinner party, and dark blackout drapes shaded the Osnos home—a spacious art-filled apartment with a baby grand piano in the parlor and white oleanders blooming on the balcony. The Sanation's battle communiqué might have been comforting, but Joseph was not entirely convinced.

Across town, Boruch Spiegel and his family heard the glorious news from a passing sound truck because like many other poorer residents of the Jewish Quarter, they did not own a radio. The Jewish neighborhood that Friday was as still and silent as on any Sabbath, with the notable exception of the crowds milling around the marble pillars of the Great Synagogue near Banker's Square, and the raucous Theater District a few blocks west, where reassured patrons devoured the late edition of the *Evening Times*-7: TO COMPLETE VICTORY, its banner headlines jubilantly declared.

And so, as the sun set on September 1, 1939, the city's restaurants and theaters slowly filled. The bars and cafés on New World Street resounded with cheers and celebratory toasts. And Warsaw's four hundred synagogues and prayer houses reverberated with relief.

CHAPTER 3

WOLSKA STREET IS COVERED WITH BLOOD

On the evening of September 6, 1939, the Sanation regime fled Warsaw. Boruch Spiegel was stunned by the ensuing pandemonium. He had never witnessed such chaos before—a national government dismantling itself overnight and running for dear life, so all that remained of once-powerful ministries were the charcoal embers of hastily burned documents, along with trailing declarations that Poland's strongmen held "the firm resolve of returning once the war has been won."

The Spiegels, like countless other Varsovian families, weighed the rapidly deteriorating situation and debated their options. Marshal Smigly-Rydz, before decamping, had called on all able-bodied men to withdraw to the east, where the Polish armed forces were to regroup and launch a counteroffensive. Boruch, like many other Jews, did not put much stock in Smigly-Rydz, who had distinguished himself more in rhetorical campaigns against mythical Hebraic cabals than on any real battlefield. Boruch's brother Berl, however, insisted they go. The German juggernaut, he argued, had already overrun much of Western Poland. "Warsaw was going to surrender," Berl declared. "There was no point in staying."

Despite misgivings, Boruch respected his big brother's judgment. At twenty-two, Berl was only a few years older than Boruch. But he was a bookkeeper, the first member of the Spiegel family to finish high school and to earn a living with his mind rather than his hands. Boruch himself had left school in seventh grade, the educational norm for Warsaw's working class. In spite of his own love of opera and high culture, he viewed his older brother as his intellectual superior and an authority figure. Berl was also an active member of the Bund, one of the two competing forces that divided Polish Jewry—Zionism's great rival and antithesis. Bundists believed that Jews had to carve out a future in Poland—*der hoym*, or "the homeland," as they called it— and fight for their political, linguistic, and economic rights there, rather than waste time and energy on unrealistic expectations of creating a Jewish state in some distant future and far-off place. To Poland's three hundred thousand registered Bundists, Zionism was nothing more than a fairy tale, "a utopian illusion," in Boruch Spiegel's words, while the Bund was a real political force. The Bund could negotiate better social and working conditions, combat fascist groups (who on occasion found their Warsaw offices mysteriously torched), sway public officials, even shut down entire cities with strikes, as the Bund had done in Warsaw in 1937 to protest anti-Semitic violence.

To Boruch, the Bund "was about Jewish pride and dignity." It was also the biggest Judeocentric political entity in Poland, having received an outright majority of all Jewish votes cast in the 1938 nationwide elections that the Sanation had permitted for city legislatures. That Berl was rising in the ranks of the organization conferred additional status in Boruch's eyes, and if Berl said that the Bund's beloved co-leaders, Hersh Erlich and Victor Alter, were evacuating east to join Smigly-Rydz, then they, too, should leave at first light.

In the early morning hours of September 7, Isaac Zuckerman had no idea that Warsaw was leaderless. He was literally mired in mud, frantically digging an antitank trench. It was 2 A.M., and he was working along with several hundred other civilian volunteers under the glare of portable sodium lamps, desperately trying to shore up the Polish capital's western defenses.

Four days had passed since the battered cab Isaac hired in Kleban had finally delivered him to Warsaw, rattled, dusty, and raw. He had spent much of this time, and expended a great deal of his considerable charm, trying to mobilize the youngsters in the left-leaning Zionist youth group he led. He was bothered by their apathy, which he tried to shake by stoking anti-German resentment and appealing to Polish pride. While young Zionists were eager to defend their families, it was understandably difficult for them to rally under a patriotic banner—to overlook, as Isaac acknowledged, "the injustices and hatred of the Polish state against the Jews."

Yet many of his Young Pioneers were there with him that night, shovels and picks in hand, toiling alongside the Gentiles, gouging out deep troughs to impede the passage of tracked vehicles. They were in Wola, a blue-collar Catholic neighborhood flanking a major industrial zone that was home to breweries, armament factories, and the sprawling steelworks that made Poland the world's eighth-largest producer of steel in 1939, and a high-tech corridor where multinationals like Philips, Telefunken, and Marconi had large electronics plants.

Wola lay due west of the Jewish Quarter and was judged to be the most likely initial target of any German ground assault. All day, while he dug, Isaac saw refugees pouring into Wola from the cities of Lodz and Kielce, Kalisz and Serock, and many of them brought horrifying tales of mass executions, of children burned alive, of Polish forces in disarray, and of an enemy that did not seem to distinguish between civilians and combatants.

By 4 A.M., Zuckerman was filthy and exhausted. He had been digging all day, and the effects of his labors showed in his blistered hands and shredded clothes. Yet he was also elated. It felt good to see Gentiles and Jews working together in harmony. Relations between the two communities had deteriorated sharply in the decade following the Great Depression, arguably reaching a five-hundred-year low. Animosity toward Jews spiked all across the European continent during the troubled 1930s. It even breached the relatively tolerant shores of the United States, as pollster Elmo Roper reported in 1938: "Anti-Semitism has spread all over the nation, and is particularly virulent in urban centers." But Poland had been among the worst offenders, and it was good to see mutual animosities momentarily forgotten. "We worked hard and the Poles were nice to us," Zuckerman recalled. "We didn't sense a whiff of anti-Semitism."

His spirits sank, however, when, just after daybreak, he returned to the Young Pioneers' communal clubhouse on Goose Street, in the heart of the Jewish district. With its oversized wall maps of Palestine, dog-eared agricultural manuals, and portraits of Theodor Herzl, the clubhouse should have been full of slumbering teenagers and the stirrings of breakfast. Instead there was an unearthly silence. Where was everyone? What could have happened overnight?

By dawn a frenzied river of humanity was pushing and shoving across the three bridges that offered the only eastward passage out of the metropolis.

Some three hundred thousand people fled Warsaw on the morning of September 7, 1939, all in the space of a few hours. Traffic was so impregnably dense that Boruch Spiegel worried the groaning spans would collapse into the Vistula under the weight of the exodus. Every manner of conveyance had been pressed into service: fire trucks, police cars, taxis, ambulances. Even the distinctive blue Chevys that carried Polish Radio's mobile loudspeakers were evacuating eastward because the retreating Sanation regime had ordered the 800-foot transmission mast for Warsaw One, central Europe's tallest structure, disabled.

The disorganized civilian horde was not limited to men of military age responding to the Sanation government's appeal. Entire families had taken their cue from the commander in chief and were running for safety: Women, children, the elderly, and couples wrestling with strollers completely overwhelmed the columns of retreating troops, blocking all the roads leading east, bogging down military traffic, and swamping any possibility of an orderly withdrawal and redeployment. Most evacuees were on foot, like the Spiegel brothers, or on bicycles, and had brought only what they could carry, which in Boruch's case was a spare set of clothes, toiletries, and a few apples and boiled eggs his mother had put in the backpack that now drooped from his small frame. "It was crazy, it was chaos," he remembered. "We barely moved. Cars were constantly honking. Army drivers were screaming to clear the way. It took hours just to get through Praga [on Warsaw's east bank]."

Somewhere in the heaving throng around Boruch, Joseph Osnos rode in a borrowed British sports car, blaring his horn impatiently. Osnos, like Isaac Zuckerman, was big and fit and not one to sit still, and also like Zuckerman he had been trying to join the fighting ever since he signed the power of attorney for his factory over to Martha. His brother Zano, a doctor and reserve army officer, was already in the east tending to Marshal Smigly-Rydz's wounded. Joseph, too, wanted to do his duty. "Go, I will stay with Robert," Martha had urged, when the call for able-bodied men had gone out the night before. "Join the army. We are safe. The radio says so. We will just be a nuisance. Besides," she added, "how can I leave my job?"

Simha Ratheiser was too young to answer the call to arms. He had desperately wanted to go east, to continue the heroic struggle. But his father, Zvi, would not hear of it. Simha was barely fifteen. Bar mitzvah notwithstanding, he was still a child. War was no place for him to discover his manhood.

Simha glared at his father but did not press his case. The two had a complicated relationship at times, and its strains went beyond the usual teenage rebellion against authority. The generation gap between Simha and Zvi was even wider than that of the typical father and son because they were the products of two very distinct eras—pre- and post-independence Poland. Many young Jews born or reared after 1918, when Poland reappeared on maps and Polish replaced Russian or German as the country's official language, experienced a similar gulf—a phenomenon that was also documented among the children of immigrants in America. Simha, as a product of the new generation, was bicultural. He spoke Polish fluently, thanks to public elementary school, and looked and dressed like any Gentile. Had he lived in America, with his fair hair and athletic frame, he would have been described as a surfer kid. Zvi Ratheiser, on the other hand, wore a dark beard, a skullcap, and the black suits favored by the pious. His Polish was poor, since had come of age under tsarist colonial rule, when the Cyrillic alphabet graced street signs in Warsaw and a neo-feudal order still largely segregated Jews as a separate commercial caste self-governed by learned rabbis. Zvi was a kind and loving parent, and he did not press his religious views on his son. He knew instinctively that secular twentieth-century forces—Bundism, Zionism, Communism—were replacing faith-based isolationist movements like Chasidism as the driving cultural forces among Jewish youth. But it was also crystal clear to him that in this yawning gap between Jewish generations, he did not fully understand Simha, just as Simha found his father's old-fashioned ways equally baffling at times.

So Simha reluctantly stayed, glumly shuffling around the family compound just southeast of the Royal Gardens Park, where the city petered out, cabbage fields sprouted between dwindling housing tracts, and gypsy caravans camped in the low brush. There was little to do but putter around the garden—a lifelong passion of Simha's—and listen to Warsaw Two, the less-powerful backup broadcaster, relay ominous bulletins about the approaching German army, the deployment of gas masks, how the smell of mustard and garlic could signify a chemical attack, and how the French and the English, who had declared war on the Nazis, had still not fired a shot.

Simha felt frightened and helpless. It was the waiting that was most intolerable, and the certain knowledge that the Germans were coming.

They struck the following day. Shortly after noon on September 8, four Panzer armored divisions stormed Warsaw's westernmost outer suburbs. By 3 P.M. they had seized the airport, a critical installation that allowed the Luftwaffe to refuel and rearm locally rather than lose valuable time and fuel flying to and from distant airfields. At 5 P.M. the surging columns of tanks reached the inner districts of Ochota and Wola, where a thin line of defenders cowered behind the trenches that Isaac Zuckerman had helped dig.

"Wolska Street is covered with blood," one combatant said, describing the scene. "There are dead horses, burnt hulks, and pulverized corpses crushed by tank treads. An uninterrupted wall of fire precedes the Germans; a hurricane of bullets. The sound is deafening. They are massacring civilians, mowing down running refugees, indiscriminately clearing a path straight toward our barricade. Before our eyes, it seems as though every rule and custom of civilized warfare is being violated. They are only a hundred meters away now. . . ."

CHAPTER 4

ROBERT'S PAPER AIRPLANES

Twenty miles east of the carnage, surrounded by sunflower fields and the weathered, bucolic huts of small farming villages, Isaac Zuckerman raced to catch up to his Zionist friends on September 8, 1939. He had not slept or eaten in two days, and his pride still felt the sting of being left behind. "I don't know why they went off and left me," he lamented. "I think it was because of the general panic and chaos." For Isaac, who like many charismatic men was sensitive and not immune to vanity, this was the second perceived slight in as many weeks. The first occurred when he had not been selected as a delegate to represent his He-Halutz youth group at the 21st Zionist Congress, held in Geneva just days before the invasion of Poland. His omission from that prestigious gathering had hurt. He was, after all, a professional Zionist, not merely a dabbler like hundreds of thousands of other Polish Jews who dreamed of Palestine. He was a salaried career man within the fractious movement, who opted to devote himself to preparing Polish Jews for immigration to Palestine rather than attend university and enter a traditional profession like law or medicine, as his parents had wanted.

The evacuation traffic had thinned this far from Warsaw, though it still stretched as far as Isaac could see down the rows of telegraph poles that lined the country road. These were crowned, every few hundred feet, with giant stork's nests, and the huge white birds served as an early warning system whenever an aircraft approached and they fled their nests. Panic would then ensue, with refugees scattering in every direction and Isaac herding the group of very young Zionists he had stumbled across into a nearby forest or ditch.

The Germans strafed almost all the roads. Boruch Spiegel also recalled these moments of sheer terror, which punctuated hours of shuffling monotony, of aching forward movement. First came the sight and sound of a distant plane. Then a split second of uncertainty: Was it was friend or foe? Then shouts, screams, and a mad scramble for cover. The staccato of machine gun fire and the roar of propellers drowned out all other noise. Where the bullets struck, clumps of earth and pavement burst loose, gouging a double line down the median. And then, just as quickly, it was over—except for the anguished cries of those whose loved ones had not gotten out of the way fast enough. "There would always be a dozen bodies lying on the road," Spiegel recalled. "You tried not to look at them as you walked past."

The German pilots didn't distinguish between Jew and Gentile, adult and child, civilian and combatant. "They flew so low you could sometimes see their smiling faces," said Boruch.

That the Luftwaffe, by September 8, had near total control over Poland's skies was partly a result of Marshal Smigly-Rydz's order to withdraw all squadrons to the rear, behind the Bug River, where he was raising what some skeptics were already calling a "phantom army." Fighter pilots had been particularly furious at the relocation order and had argued against abandoning the capital, which they had defended with remarkable success up until then. Though their rickety P-11s flew at only half the speed of the far more advanced Messerschmitts and Junkers, carried only one-quarter of their armaments, and could climb only half as high, the Warsaw Fighter Brigade had knocked out 72 German craft while losing 38 of their own planes in the first week of the war.

All told, the Luftwaffe had lost six hundred planes that week, a quarter of all its squadrons, and now that it no longer had the pesky

P-IIs to contend with, it seemed intent on exacting retribution by strafing civilians.

Country roads provided little cover for the Spiegels, Joseph Osnos, Isaac Zuckerman, and the tens of thousands of other refugees. Even forests offered little refuge from the vengeful German airmen, as Zuckerman discovered on the night of September 9, when he and his followers camped next to a Polish military unit. "They began bombing the woods. Trees fell right before my eyes," he recalled. "It went on for hours, and it was extraordinary luck that we weren't hit. The Polish army group was hit."

Zuckerman's Zionists suffered their first casualty the following day—from friendly fire. The youths he was leading were German refugees. They belonged to the Berlin chapter of Zuckerman's Young Pioneers, and their parents had arranged for them to go to Poland to escape Nazi persecution. Since they spoke only German and Yiddish, Isaac ordered to them to keep their mouths shut and stay close to him. "I didn't know whether to walk at the head of the line or bring up the rear," he recalled of shepherding the group. "These were youngsters and you had to watch them."

One of the lads wandered off and was stopped by a Polish military patrol. Because he could only respond in German, and because it was widely known that Germany had agents on the ground equipped with radios to call in the location of military targets for air strikes, a soldier mistook him for a spy and shot him on the spot.

While Isaac and Boruch dodged German planes, an astonishing development fifty miles to the west was styming Hitler's plan for the rapid conquest of Poland. After a week of virtually unimpeded progress, the vaunted Wehrmacht had run into a solid wall of unexpected resistance in Warsaw. "No one gave any thought to serious fighting," General Eric Hoepner, commander of the 16th Panzer Corps, later recalled of the assault on the Polish capital. "Many [tank crews] already envisioned themselves in the best hotel rooms, lords of the city."

But Warsaw mayor Stephen Starzinski apparently had not understood that his beloved town was supposed to surrender without a fight. The youthful former banker (who, unlike his Sanation superiors, had never engaged in baiting Jews or any other form of populist politics) could not stomach the notion of capitulation. During the desperate days when Poland seemed devoid of national leaders and the tough-talking ultranationalists had fallen uncharacteristically silent, he almost single-handedly rallied the city.

Surprised, the Germans regrouped and tried a second assault, with an even greater force of 250 Panzer tanks. And once more they were compelled to retreat—with only 194 Panzers left intact. Their armored behemoths, after advancing hundreds of miles with little or no opposition, had suddenly encountered an inhospitable landscape. The urban setting offered little room to maneuver, with claustrophobic lanes and blind alleys, potential traps around every street corner, and countless vantage points for adversaries to hide. Here the line drawn by Starzinski and 82,000 civilian and military defenders simply would not budge.

On September 10, 1939, the German High Command changed tactics. They were going to bomb the city into submission. Adolf Hitler could not afford to wait.

He had counted on a quick victory to forestall fighting with Britain and especially France, which had nearly one hundred battle-ready divisions sitting behind the Maginot Line. The Führer had only twenty-five divisions on his western frontier, and they were third-rate reserves, since his best troops were busy pounding Poland. He was thus exposed and vulnerable. If the French attacked, they could easily overwhelm his temporarily weakened western flank. But if German troops could take the Polish capital before Paris committed its hundred divisions to the conflict, Hitler thought there might still be a chance to avoid all-out war.

On Sunday, September 10, three divisions of heavy Junker bombers, totaling several hundred aircraft, flew seventeen sorties over the city, unleashing "a rain of bombs." Joseph Osnos's small plant, Karolyt, was hit, though without loss of life or significant damage to the assembly line. His notary, however, was not so fortunate. The rush to sign all those documents before Joseph left had seemed "so urgent and important." Now Martha's power of attorney had gone up in flames, along with the notary, his office, and all his papers.

Her cousin's famous bookstore next door to the Landed Gentry

Café had fared only marginally better. Hanna Mortkowicz-Olczak's then five-year-old daughter, Joanna, saw piles of books shaken from the shelves by the concussions from the blasts. "Paintings and beautiful color prints had been ripped from the walls and lay strewn on the floor, their frames shattered, their canvases tattered, dirty, and covered with ash, dust, and glass."

The youngest heir to Poland's greatest prewar publishing dynasty, Joanna was still too immature to grasp what was happening to Warsaw. "This new reality offered certain attractions, a world of wonder. There was no longer any glass in the front display windows and I could jump straight through into the street, which was so unexpected. So were the military horses that now whinnied in what used to be the Landed Gentry's outdoor terrace."

Like Joanna, eight-year-old Robert Osnos also marveled at the new landscape of rubble and twenty-foot-deep craters, at the smoke and sirens. "I don't recall once being scared, not of the bombs or the burning buildings," he would say. "Maybe I was repressing my fear. I do remember very clearly, however, playing paper airplanes. Making them and having dog fights with my cousin [Joanna]."

Simha Ratheiser was not only old enough to understand the gravity of the situation, but could see that the Sanation regime had made a serious strategic error in withdrawing air support from the besieged capital. Ratheiser no longer confused Polish and German planes. He could by now tell Junkers and Heinkls and Dorniers apart. "The planes swooped so low over the Royal Gardens that soldiers next to me were shooting at the cockpits with their rifles."

The Royal Gardens Park was uncomfortably close to Simha's home in the southern suburbs of Warsaw. Their house, with its garden and barn and his father's store, was also a mile or so from a Polish military base and residential compound for ranking officers, which was being targeted by the Luftwaffe. So Simha's father, Zvi, decided to move the family to the center of the city to stay with friends in the Jewish Quarter. Simha didn't initially agree, reasoning that the more wide-open suburban spaces offered better protection than the congested heart of the city. But thousands of Varsovians relocated every day, depending on which part of the city was being bombarded. After a few close calls in her predominantly Gentile neighborhood, even

Martha Osnos moved to the Jewish Quarter, to her brother-in-law's spacious apartment on Hard Street. It was empty, since Zano Osnos was with the medical corps in the east, and it had the additional recommendation of being on the ground floor, which was judged safest, in one of the more upscale parts of the Jewish district that had not yet been hit.

Unfortunately for the Ratheisers and for Martha and Robert Osnos, by September 17 the Wehrmacht had reached Wawelberg Street, a road in neighboring Wola named after the Jewish philanthropist and banker Hipolit Wawelberg, who had built hundreds of units of affordable housing in the working-class district. From its new vantage point, the Wehrmacht launched a devastating artillery barrage. That day, five thousand shells fell on the Jewish Quarter and Midtown.

Many of the city's greatest landmarks vanished in a fiery instant. The majestic dome of St. John's Cathedral crumpled in a heap of medieval red brick. The Parliament disappeared in a choking pile of white plaster dust. The Opera burned so hot that its massive steel doors melted. The Philharmonic Building—erected in 1909 thanks to the then astounding donation of $15 million by another Jewish philanthropist, Leopold Kronenberg, the Polish Rockefeller—lay in ruins, its columns of imported marble pulverized.

On Hard Street, Martha Osnos saw only "an ocean of flames." Next to her brother-in-law's intact apartment building, "several furniture stores were burning, with tables, beds, mattresses spread on the pavement." There were grisly body parts in the rubble, and structures collapsing while residents frantically scrambled to douse the flames. "Young Poles and Jews performed miracles of heroism. I saw how the young Jews of the block at 13 Forestry Street kept on fighting the fires that broke out endlessly. There was no water. The fire was smothered with sand and put out with water collected from the toilets of individual flats. These young people were competing with German pilots, who were dropping incendiary bombs from a height of tens of meters. When the pilots saw the tenants trying to put out the fires, they machine-gunned them."

———

By the close of the second week of the war, Isaac Zuckerman reached the Polish town of Kovel, in present-day western Ukraine. The Spiegel brothers, by coincidence, were also there, along with thousands of other refugees and military personnel milling around Kovel's main market square, impatiently waiting for Marshal Smigly-Rydz to launch his great counteroffensive.

"There were no weapons, no uniforms, no trucks, nothing," Boruch Spiegel recalled of the general disappointment that greeted would-be volunteers. Amid the disorganization, and the glaring lack of orders or fighting infrastructure, it was becoming increasingly obvious to all that there would be no westward march to repulse the invaders. Joseph Osnos had come to this realization earlier than most others. Poland, he decided, was "kaput." He avoided Kovel and other rendezvous points where Polish officers might try to commandeer his sports car, and instead headed straight for the Romanian border in the hope of escaping the country before it was too late.

Kovel, meanwhile, like countless other eastern Polish hamlets, sagged under the burden of so many new arrivals. The town had had a prewar population of 33,000 and was half Jewish. It had swollen remarkably over the past few days, more than doubling in size with the influx of so many refugees. The lack of accommodations was such that Boruch Spiegel slept in the lobby of a Jewish-owned bank on Legionnaire Street. Zuckerman was luckier. He secured a cot in the apartment of a local Zionist. Hundreds of others camped in a tent city pitched beneath the onion domes of several Ukrainian Orthodox churches or slept on long benches inside the town's big rococo railway station.

The station and the spur linking Kovel to Warsaw had been built in the late nineteenth century by the Jewish industrialist Jan Bloch, Poland's "railroad king." The construction of the line had transformed the sleepy shtetl into a transportation hub and a center of light manufacturing, brewing, and leather processing by the beginning of the twentieth century. That same rail and road network made it a major transit point for tens of thousands of refugees in 1939.

Only now, Kovel seemed more a terminus than a way station. To Boruch Spiegel, it was obvious that "no one knew what to do, or where to go. There was a lot of confusion and meetings and different opinions." Once people realized that the Polish Army had no real plan, they began thinking of their own welfare. In various corners of the town, Bundists and Zionists huddled in separate circles and weighed their options. The two groups had no contact, however, and made no effort to coordinate. The war had not changed the fundamental fact that the two movements were still essentially at cross-purposes, much as they had been in peacetime. Zionists, now more than ever, were focused on finding ways out of Poland and into Palestine. Zuckerman planned to head north on horseback—since he could ride well and had somehow procured a stallion—through Lithuania. Many of his colleagues had already been dispatched to the south to look for an escape route through Romania.

For Bundists like the Spiegel brothers, however, escape was not an option. The Bund was committed to Poland and therefore duty bound to assist the Sanation regime in any way possible. That Marshal Smigly-Rydz's largely anti-Semitic staff did not want their help, nor seemed to be in any position to help itself, only made the Bundist dilemma greater.

Boruch was not privy to the discussions at the Bund's top level, where Victor Alter and Hersh Erlich reigned supreme. Both were in Kovel, but Boruch felt he was too "junior, and not important" enough to introduce himself to the great men, even though his brother knew some of the Bund's "aristocracy." Several of the group's lesser leaders had been sent back to Warsaw once word had spread that the city was holding out. The Bund still had tens of thousands of rank-and-file members in the Polish capital, and Mayor Starzinski was amenable to working with Jews. The organization could help man the civilian defense force the mayor had cobbled together. What it could do in the eastern backwaters of Poland, far from the front, to help the war effort was a more difficult question. "I don't think anyone had any clear ideas," Boruch recalled.

The Bund's dilemma was rendered moot on the morning of September 17. At dawn, planes darkened the skies over Kovel. In the panicked scramble to take shelter, only a few people initially noticed something different about these aircraft. They were green rather than gray and they had red stars rather than black crosses on their fuselages. The Soviet Union had just invaded Poland.

CHAPTER 5

HIS BROTHER'S HAND

By the time Radio Warsaw Two announced that Stalin had joined Hitler in dismembering Poland on September 17, 1939, the Red Army had deployed a million and a half soldiers and six thousand tanks across the border, and Warsaw had officially run out of coffins. Makeshift graves began appearing everywhere in the Polish capital as access to the main cemeteries was cut off by advancing Panzer divisions. Ammunition and medicine were running out. Warsaw's predominantly Jewish physicians struggled valiantly to cope with nearly fifty thousand critically wounded patients even as hospitals were systematically leveled. Miraculously, the Jewish Quarter's Berson and Bauman Children's Hospital—the pediatric center built by the family foundations of banker Meyer Berson and real estate developer Solomon Bauman—stood unscathed.

Just before Radio Two was knocked off the air on September 21, Mayor Starzinski made one of the most memorable of his twice-daily addresses. "I wanted Warsaw to be great," he said, as the sound of detonations echoed in the background. "I believed she would be great. Along with my municipal co-workers, we drew plans. We pored over blueprints. We sketched Warsaw's future greatness. And I thought it would take fifty or a hundred years to accomplish. But as I speak to you today, looking through the window I can see in the haze of smoke and red flames that Warsaw is already great—a magnificent, indestructible, undaunted, fighting spirit. And though in places where there were supposed to be brand-new orphanages, there are now ruins, where there were supposed to be beautiful parks there are now torn barricades littered with corpses, though our libraries burn, though fires rage in our hospitals, it is not in fifty or even a hundred years, but today that Warsaw has reached the pinnacle of her greatness defending the honor and pride of the entire country."

That speech was the last that residents of the besieged Polish capital heard from their courageous mayor. The next day, the city lost all electricity; telephone and telegraph communications went out the next day. The day after that, the main pumping station was obliterated, and water ceased running from taps. Hundreds of fires now raged uncontrolled, threatening to engulf the entire town. Simha Ratheiser's family fled back to their suburban compound. Aside from the growing inferno, Zvi Ratheiser also worried about epidemics in the congested city center, a danger now rising exponentially with the worsening sanitary conditions. Food and medical supplies were critically low, and the drinking water people had stored in their bathtubs was dwindling. Joanna Olczak recalled a severe tongue-lashing her cousin Robert Osnos received from her Gentile nanny, Miss Anne, for playing in the tub and wasting the precious liquid. "She has the right to be stupid because she's still little." Miss Anne angrily pointed at Joanna. "But you?" she snapped at the eight-year-old Osnos. "Don't you know what water means?"

Hopes of being resupplied from the east dwindled when news reached the capital that Marshal Smigly-Rydz had left Poland entirely and taken refuge in Romania, where the authorities promptly detained him. Varsovians spat in disgust; never had a Polish government fallen so low so fast in the esteem of its people.

The city was now completely on its own, surrounded by enemy forces on all sides, down to less than twenty rounds of ammunition per gun, and increasingly hungry. But still it would not yield. Mayor Starzinski's Worker Brigades, anchored by volunteers from the Bund, threw up earthworks and toppled trams to block German access to the city center.

On September 24, Hitler's patience ran out. He ordered the Wehrmacht and Luftwaffe to unleash a firestorm over Warsaw. Nine hundred howitzers and four hundred heavy bombers, mostly Junkers, pounded the Polish capital in a merciless forty-eight-hour barrage—explosives poured from the sky on what sardonic Varsovians later dubbed "Rainy Monday."

Three of those bombs, each weighing half a ton, landed on the Ratheisers' apartment complex south of the central park. The first hit an open field next to a neighboring warehouse that Simha's grandfather used to store the agricultural produce he imported. The next two blasted the roof off the family's three-story house, buckled the brick walls, and shattered floors. In the convulsive, deafening split second it took for the structure to collapse on itself, Simha was knocked unconscious. When he came to, "there was dead silence." He found himself trapped under a pile of rubble, electrical lines tangled around his torso and neck. Dazed, he could barely breathe, and his legs were pinned under the debris. Blood and dust caked his face, and as he struggled to untangle himself, his scratched hands felt an odd object sticking out of this throat. It was a wood splinter and it had pierced his windpipe. He felt himself choking. Slowly, agonizingly, he pulled out the splinter, spitting out blood. Luckily, the wooden projectile hadn't ruptured any arteries, and with great effort Simha was able to extricate himself from the rubble and stumble into the street, where a neighbor slung him over his shoulder and carried him to a shelter.

It was only two days later, as he lay on a stretcher recuperating, that the enormity of the devastation struck him. His apartment building was gone. His grandparents, his aunt Hanna, his aunt Zissl's husband, a cousin, and his fourteen-year-old brother, Israel, were all dead. But his parents and two sisters survived, and they collected the parts of their relatives' bodies they could find. There was no time for a proper funeral, so the family buried their dead temporarily in the small flower garden Simha had tended outside their now smoldering home.

Nearly twenty thousand similar graves dotted Warsaw—black, rectangular earth mounds, marked by sticks, primitive wooden crosses, or little pyramids of rock and red brick. They covered courtyards, front and back yards, patches of grass between sidewalks and roads, public parks and town squares—anywhere that was not cobbled or paved over.

Once the city finally fell—it had negotiated a formal capitulation on September 28—the populace raced to unearth these temporary graves. The Nazis, according to the terms of surrender, were to make their triumphal entry into the vanquished Polish capital and hold celebrations and victory parades in the first week of October. But before then, Warsaw faced the grim task of exhuming its decaying corpses and moving them to proper resting places.

Simha found the disinterment shocking. His relatives' remains had all been jumbled together, and some were missing limbs. "I caught sight of a hand separated from a body, and was told it was my brother's hand. It was buried next to his grave."

Simha Ratheiser saw a great deal more death in the years to come. In time, he even became inured to it. But the sight of his brother's small, shriveled hand, pale and purple and blackened with dirt, would stay with him forever.

CHAPTER 6

WHERE IS YOUR HUSBAND?

On October 1, 1939, the makeshift barricades that had blocked the main arteries into Warsaw were dismantled and German troops formally took possession of the city, ceremonially cutting a white ribbon that marked the official capitulation line.

The streets of the capital were too littered with debris for the Wehrmacht to march in proper formations, so Varsovians were put to work carting away rubble and filling in craters. Jews were disproportionately selected for these cleanup crews, and Nazi newsreels aired propaganda footage of elderly men—their dark caftan frocks and beards covered with pale dust, their hands bloody from the jagged rubble—laboring to pave the way for an official victory parade that was to be held on October 5. Hitler himself was to attend the triumphal ceremony and confer medals on the worthiest field officers—many of whom did not wait for their Führer to begin celebrating.

Throughout the first night of German occupation, the sound of revelry punctuated an otherwise silent and dark city. There was still no electricity, water, gas, or heating, but pockets of light blazed from the five-star hotels—the Bristol, the European, the Hotel Vienna—where portable generators were installed and the finest wines were pried from locked cellars to toast the victory. Nightclubs and cafés that had survived the bombings were also pressed into service—with or without their owners' consent—and these establishments resounded with song and dance and slurred toasts to the feminine qualities of Warsaw's newly inexpensive prostitutes, Poland's currency having lost four-fifths of its value in four weeks.

In the month since the inception of the Second World War, Warsaw—a city that compared itself to Prague, even Paris in parts—had been horribly disfigured. Seventy-eight thousand apartment units had gone up in flames. Fifteen percent of all structures and almost a quarter of the city center, where the bombing was heaviest, had been completely destroyed. Nearly every building had suffered damage. And even those few that had escaped unscathed were covered by a thick layer of pulverized brick, mortar, and stone that created a choking brown haze when whipped up by the autumn wind.

Now a great migration occurred, as some people returned to their old neighborhoods and apartments from the places they had taken shelter, while others, whose homes had been destroyed, searched in vain for new lodgings. Martha Osnos walked into her flat after leaving her brother-in-law's to discover that in her absence, eighteen people had moved into her place. "The door was broken; a stranger was shaving on my baby grand piano." He was a neighbor from the fourth floor, and apologetically he explained that he had been afraid his own place was too elevated and exposed. Many others, apparently, had used Martha's more secure first floor apartment as a refuge in her absence. The toilet with filled with excrement, which could not be flushed since there was no water, and her pantry was empty of provisions. "We tried to clean up the place—the shit hidden in the rolled-up carpets we only found after the smell in the dining room became fierce."

As more and more occupying troops poured into central Warsaw, bringing bureaucrats and civilian administrators in tow, preparations for Hitler's October victory parade reached fever pitch, and the city began to experience a different form of transformation.

The first and unmistakable signs of this alteration were the flags.

Every Polish banner, every red and white pendant, and every White Eagle that had graced any building, flagstaff, home, or business was removed. In their place, swastikas were hoisted by the hundreds. Nazi standards now flew over ministries and outside the university gates. They hung from bank porticos and from every Art Deco lamppost on Jerusalem Boulevard. They even flanked the entrance to the Julius Meinl coffee shop on New World Street—the Starbucks of its day, with more than a thousand prewar outlets throughout central Europe.

Poland itself had ceased to exist. The Soviets took the east; the Third Reich appropriated the central and western parts of the country. The new demarcation line, ironically, ran along the same geographic points that Marshal Smigly-Rydz had chosen to raise his now notorious phantom army. But Varsovians, in their gloomy soul-searching and bitter recriminations—*How could we have been so ill prepared? How could we have lost so quickly? How come the British and French didn't help us?*—didn't need to be reminded of their government's shocking collapse. They cursed their former commander in chief, who, along with President Ignatius Moscicki, resigned in disgrace from the safety of their Romanian internment camp. A new, non-Sanation coalition government was hastily formed in Paris and recognized by the Allies, whose passivity was eagerly exploited by German propaganda.

ENGLAND! THIS IS YOUR DOING screamed Nazi-designed posters slapped up on the teetering walls of roofless buildings leaning precariously over sidewalks throughout Warsaw. In the placards, a Polish officer, bandaged and bleeding, pointed accusingly at the hulk of a burning house, while Prime Minister Neville Chamberlain, formally attired in tails, aloofly crossed his arms, his back turned to the devastation.

Varsovians tried to ignore the offensive posters while two of the 1,863 people executed in the weeks following Warsaw's capitulation were shot for ripping them down. But the Germans had touched a nerve. Poles, both Gentile and Jewish, felt let down by the English and the French. Hitler gambled that the Great Powers would not fight for Poland, and he was right.

To celebrate his conquest, the Führer flew into Warsaw on the morning of October 5, his first and only visit to the Polish capital. The entire city was locked down in anticipation of his arrival. A general curfew was announced, and the residents of every apartment building and high-rise along Hitler's route were ordered to vacate their homes to thwart potential assassins. "Anyone approaching a window or the street will immediately be shot," advance teams with megaphones called out, as troops with sniper rifles deployed along rooftops.

Simha Ratheiser had been locked down by his own parents, who feared that his curiosity could land him in trouble. Already he had sneaked out of his infirmary bed, face and neck covered in bandages still seeping blood, to watch German troops march into Warsaw: "They made an incredible impression on me. All those helmets, the gleaming steel, the sheer discipline. I'll never forget it."

Sensing that his recuperating son would not be able to resist escaping again to catch a glimpse of the Führer, Zvi did not tell him of the October 5 visit. "Really! He was there?" Ratheiser exclaimed seventy years later in Jerusalem when informed about the victory parade. "I had no idea."

Meanwhile, the Führer's huge six-wheeled Mercedes convertible toured the emptied city center, pausing for photo opportunities two blocks from the Jewish Quarter, at the heavily damaged Pilsudski Square. The square was named after the Polish military hero who had beaten back Joseph Stalin from the gates of Warsaw in 1920, saving Central Europe from Communist dominion in a battle known as the Miracle on the Vistula. It was now to be rechristened Adolf Hitler Platz, in recognition of the miracle that did not take place this time.

The victory parade—a flawless, endless, single-minded organism that flowed without interruption for several straight hours—slowly wended its way through Three Crosses Square, past the mansions and Italianate palaces of tree-lined Horsebreaker Avenue, to the elegant cross section of Chopin Street, where the Führer himself stood on a platform, his ankle-length leather coat tightly buttoned, his right arm rigidly raised, his favorite filmmaker Leni Riefenstahl immortalizing the moment.

Unbeknownst to the beaming German leader, five hundred pounds of dynamite was set to rain on his parade.

The bomb that might have changed history and saved fifty million lives never detonated under Adolf Hitler's feet. Contrary to popular belief, it was not buried beneath the Führer's reviewing stand near Chopin Street. Security had been too tight there; no Pole was allowed within two blocks of the heavily restricted area. Instead the explosives were planted on the corner of New World Street and Jerusalem Boulevard, a busy intersection on the southern edge of Midtown that Hitler's motorcade would have to cross on its way to the reviewing stand. Sappers had secreted TNT under paving stones and run a buried cable several hundred yards to a ruined building where a pair of demolition experts with a detonator waited for the Führer's motorcade.

Alas, at the right moment, they thought Hitler was General von Blaskowitz, the senior Wehrmacht commander in Warsaw, who was riding in another vehicle, and did not plunge the detonator for fear of missing their intended target. "He passed right under our noses," the man in charge of the operation would later lament, with equal measures of disgust and disbelief.

Oblivious to their leader's narrow escape from death, Warsaw's new masters resumed their principal activity the moment Hitler's plane lifted off the ground: looting. The systematic theft, which netted ten thousand train-wagon loads of booty in October and November 1939 alone, was initially undertaken under the guise of a citywide hunt for hidden weapons. Jewish households and businesses were particularly subject to such searches, and Simha Ratheiser recalled the hammering on their door as a pair of German soldiers gruffly pushed his mother aside to examine the contents of their home. His family had moved across the street from the shell of their old building, and their household offered slim pickings since their valuables had all been destroyed. The Germans made a show of looking for grenades or ammunition, poking their heads inside the oven, and left cursing the Ratheisers' lack of material possessions.

In Martha Osnos's case, the Nazis didn't even bother with the weapons charade.

She ran into trouble on a visit to her pediatrician's house in an exclusive part of the Mokotow district to pick up medication for a Gentile neighbor. She was surprised to see a large moving van parked outside the doctor's office and two SS officers on the stairs. They were "very tall, very slick," she recalled, and their pitch-black capes and tall, polished boots lent them an ominously "elegant" air.

"Where are you going?" one demanded, as workers carried out

select pieces of the doctor's furniture. Responding in German, one of six languages she spoke, Martha tried to slip past them with an innocuous comment about purchasing medicine. "Are you single?" they persisted. "Where is your husband?" This question Martha could not honestly answer, because like nearly a million other Polish women, she did not know where her husband was; whether Joe was in a POW camp, or in Siberia, or dead like his older brother Zano, who along with twenty thousand other Polish officers was murdered by the Soviet secret police in the Katyn forest. She had no way of knowing that he in fact had made it safely across the border into Romania and that a kind Jewish family in the small town of Cernauti had taken him in. Since all communication with the outside world was disrupted, Martha did not know that Joe Osnos had managed to use his business acumen to make a few desperately needed dollars trading currencies, exploiting the wild cross-border fluctuations in the crashing Polish zloty, and that he had earned enough money to pay his way to Bucharest.

SS men were always interested to learn of a lost husband. With so many Polish women home alone, an underworld fraternity of fraudsters, confidence men, and thieves, both Polish and German, had sprung up to prey on war widows and the wives of Poland's eight hundred thousand imprisoned servicemen. "Where do you live?" the SS officers immediately asked Martha. "You must have very good furniture. How far is your house? We will drive there with you."

How many such "visits" took place in Warsaw in the early months of the occupation is impossible to say. But the expropriation started at the very top. The first thing Warsaw's newly appointed district governor, Dr. Ludwig Fisher, did upon assuming his post was to go villa shopping in the resort suburb of Konstancin, Poland's Beverly Hills. He selected the Art Deco mansion of industrialist Gustav Wertheim, which was known as Villa Julia after Wertheim's Jewish wife, the art collector Julia Kramsztyk. Villa Julia had been famous before the war for the concerts and charity balls held there, parties that attracted a who's who of Warsaw's cultural elite, including many of the bestselling writers published by Martha's cousin Hanna Mortkowicz-Olczak. Julia Kramsztyk had been a formidable social doyenne and a much-admired hostess. Her support could launch a young artist's career, and an invitation to Villa Julia could propel ambitious guests up the social ladder. It was unheard of for Julia Kramsztyk to be turned down, and she was not a woman who was easily intimidated. When she protested the confiscation of her 14,000-square-foot home, Governor Fischer's henchmen dragged her out onto the garden terrace and shot her through the head.

Homes, cars, pleasure craft—nothing was off-limits. Most of the antique furnishings and art stolen by the Nazis simply vanished, only to reappear, in rare cases, decades later in the most improbable locales. A painting looted in October 1939 from the Zacheta National Gallery, for instance, resurfaced in 2007 at a garage sale in Lexington, Kentucky. A few months later in 2007, a seventeenth-century canvas by the Dutch master Pieter de Grebber taken from the Cool Street shop of antiques dealer Abe Gutneyer showed up at Christie's auction house in London, placed there by an anonymous Lithuanian seller.

Many prominent Jewish collectors did not wait for the Germans to knock on their doors. They surreptitiously donated their paintings to the Zacheta National Gallery in the hope that the art would be hidden by the Underground and not fall into German hands. (A number of pieces were indeed saved. Seventy years later, dozens of priceless paintings, along with the impressionist collections of Jacob and Alina Glass, the Zacheta Gallery's most prominent prewar patrons, adorn the National Museum on Jerusalem Boulevard.)

When Martha Osnos arrived at her apartment with a pair of SS officers in tow, her eight-year-old son, Robert, froze at the sight, which he never forgot. He stared in terror at the towering black figures; at their death's-head insignias, the metallic hussar skulls that rested between the silver piping of their visor bands; at the SS eagles on their sleeves, with their extended talons embroidered in bullion wire; at the twin lightning-bolt runes on their thick wool collar patches. "It was one of the only times during the war that I can remember being truly scared," he later recalled.

Martha rushed to embrace her son. "Don't be afraid," she soothed. "They mean no harm." The SS men, paying no heed to the cowering child, "ran around the house making noise and a commotion not like two men but twenty." They banged at the keys of Martha's baby grand piano, trying their musical hand, poked around her closets, and zeroed in on a white marble bust she kept on her writing desk. "Who is this?" they asked.

It was a likeness of Voltaire. Martha had bought it in Paris, where

Robert was born, during the three years she and Joe had spent in the French capital. "We returned to Poland because my mother missed her friends and family, she missed Warsaw," Robert recalled.

"Voltaire," Martha repeated. "Oh," said one of the Germans, a flicker of sudden recognition. "Madame Imaginaire?"

"No, that was Molière," Martha corrected.

"Aha," said the SS man, losing interest.

The disappointed Germans departed soon after, grumbling that Martha did not have a double bed, which had apparently been high on their shopping list. They took a camera and a box of chocolates, according to Robert, but left behind the bust of Voltaire. It was a priceless sculpture by Jean-Antoine Houdon, whose works today are exhibited at the National Gallery of Art in Washington, at the John Paul Getty Museum in Los Angeles, and in countless other museums throughout the world.

CHAPTER 7

MARK'S VOW

The Polish capital's grotesque transformation was most jarring for those who had missed the siege, who had answered the Sanation regime's misguided call to evacuate east and were now trickling back throughout October and November 1939. One of those early returnees was a young man who was to play a major role in the future Jewish resistance, along with Isaac, Simha, and Boruch. His name was Mark Edelman (or "Marek" in Polish), and like Zuckerman and the Spiegel brothers, he had left Warsaw during the September 7 evacuation and spent a fruitless month aimlessly wandering through Poland's eastern townships before returning to the Jewish district. At age eighteen, he was rail thin, with a pronounced Adam's apple, and he bore the pinched, pale features of someone for whom nutrition was a secondary consideration. He had been homeless and unemployed when the war broke out, living at a girlfriend's and in no hurry to find a job. That June, he had just barely finished high school, which was no small feat given one expulsion, many prolonged absences, and a general lack of interest in formal education. An orphan, he was a transplanted "Litvak," which meant he hailed from the far eastern borderlands, specifically from a town called Gomel near Minsk, placing him at a social disadvantage in the snobbish Polish capital. Litvaks occupied the lowest rung in Warsaw's Jewish hierarchy, and their Yiddish was markedly different from the rapid-fire urban dialect spoken in central Poland, as out of place as a southern drawl in New York City.

Along with the Spiegel brothers, whom he vaguely knew, Edelman was a Bundist. The Bund was pretty much the only thing he took seriously at the time, and it was partly out of gratitude, because after his mother's death some of the Bund's leaders had more or less adopted him. It was Bund bosses who had gotten him into good schools and used their connections to smooth over some of his academic ruffles. He played with and befriended their children, who tutored him in Polish, since he was a native Russian speaker, taught him the *Polaykin* Yiddish used in Warsaw and Lodz, and afforded him access to a world that would otherwise have been denied to him.

Edelman had not gotten very far east during the evacuation, and he was one of the first to make his way back home. He was shocked at how his adopted city had changed. "It was terrible," he said, describing the once prosperous Jerusalem Boulevard, a street that only weeks earlier had teemed with French fashion boutiques and Martini umbrellas shading diners at expensive restaurants. "Now it was full of soup kitchens with long lines, and people on the sidewalk selling anything they could—pots, pans, bed sheets, household appliances— anything to raise a few [pennies] so they could eat."

Nazi newsreel crews filmed the crowds waiting for free soup and bread. The handouts had been supplied by the Hilfzug Bayern "help trains" that arrived as part of the capitulation agreement to alleviate food and medical shortages. And though the trains supplied only a small fraction of the capital's needs, footage of the Wehrmacht dispensing aid to Poles made good propaganda. Many of the shots, alas, were marred by the grim faces of the recipients of German largesse, and frustrated camera operators had to resort to snatching back the bread to elicit forced smiles.

But for Edelman, it was a sight in the Jewish Quarter, where, outside the benevolent spotlight, drunken soldiers accosted pedestrians demanding *"Sind Sie ein Jid?"* (Are you a kike?), that left the most lasting impression. "I saw a crowd on Iron Street. People were swarming around this barrel—a simple wooden barrel with a Jew on top of it. He was old and short and he had a long beard," Edelman recalled of the scene, one of the seminal moments in his life. "Next to him were two German officers. Two beautiful, tall men next to this small bowed Jew. And those Germans, tuft by tuft, were chopping this Jew's long beard with huge tailor's shears, splitting their sides with laughter all the while."

The surrounding crowd was also laughing, despite the fact that many of them were also Jews. "Objectively, it was really funny: a little man on wooden a barrel with his beard growing shorter by the moment. Just like a movie gag," Edelman explained. "After all, nothing really horrible was happening to that Jew. Only that it was now possible to put him on a barrel with impunity."

For Mark Edelman—up until then a feckless youth, a grown child without purpose or direction—the scene was transformational. "At that moment, I realized that the most important thing on earth was going to be never letting myself get pushed onto the top of that barrel. Never, by anybody."

The humiliation that Edelman witnessed in the fall of 1939 was repeated throughout Warsaw as the Germans set about dividing the conquered in addition to robbing them blind.

Jews and Gentiles had closed ranks to a remarkable degree during the siege. The rapprochement that began during the buildup to the war, and that Isaac Zuckerman had witnessed while digging ditches, only strengthened once the shelling started. The two communities fought side by side, manned barricades together, and shared bomb shelters. Jewish women fed Gentile soldiers and helped tend their wounds while Christian housewives carried water to parched Jewish combatants in the trenches. Martha Osnos fondly recalled the initial shock of a Gentile co-worker, a fellow chemist, whom she brought home during a bombardment that happened to fall on Yom Kippur. "She had never even spoken to a Jewish person before she met me," Osnos said of the woman, who for the first time in her life was exposed to Judaic rituals. "The wailing of the tallis-clad men was for her as frightening as the constant bombing." Despite the cultural chasm, powerful bonds formed during the siege. Religious and linguistic differences were largely overridden by shared life-and-death experiences, by the personal connections forged in trenches and air raid shelters.

Not surprisingly, the newfound unity and uncharacteristically cordial state of affairs did not sit well with the Nazis. Almost immediately, the Third Reich's propaganda machine set out to stoke the mutual suspicions that were more typical of relations between the Catholic majority and the large Jewish minority in the Polish capital. Nazi newsreels and newspapers like the *New Warsaw Courier*, which began publication under German editorial control in the second week of October, began disseminating stories about Jews collaborating in the Gestapo's hunt for hidden weapons. Varsovians woke to front-page photographs (staged, as it turned out, by Arthur Grimm of the Waffen-SS Propaganda Company) showing individuals with distinctly Semitic features pulling heavy-caliber machine guns from unearthed coffins while others pointed to the hidden location of ammunition stores.

Though such shots were blatantly phony, they found a receptive audience among certain segments of Polish society, as did similarly ludicrous newsreels of German police officers saving Poles from mobs of violent Talmudic students, or of Jews greeting Soviet troops with flowers, cheering as Polish soldiers were led away to Siberian camps.

"German propaganda agencies worked ceaselessly," Mark Edelman recalled. "We also started hearing about how Jews were turning in Poles [to the NKVD Russian secret police in the Soviet Occupation zone]," he added. "But we now know that German propaganda was behind many of these tales."

What was remarkable was how little effort the Nazis needed to expend to erode the goodwill that had built up between Jews and Gentiles during the siege. Driving a wedge between the two proved far easier than many Poles would later care to admit.

Like a great many Poles, Edelman took his first step toward conspiracy during this period of propagandizing and looting, under the cover of the ghostly darkness that still permeated the Polish capital at night in December 1939.

Electricity, gas, and water supplies had not yet been fully restored to large swaths of the battered city. Every evening after the 9 P.M. police curfew, Warsaw plunged into a dark and barren wasteland patrolled by German gendarmes who enforced the mandated blackout by shooting at any window emitting light. Most windows were boarded up with plywood because there was no replacement glass for the hundreds of thousands of panes that had been shattered during the siege; Warsaw was quite possibly the darkest metropolis on the planet.

That suited Edelman just fine, for almost every night he crept out to his old school on Carmelite Street, in the heart of the badly damaged Jewish Quarter, where a hand-cranked mimeograph machine was hidden in the basement. There, the Bund printed pamphlets and newsletters in defiance of the German media monopoly.

The underground press was the first manifestation of organized resistance in occupied Poland. Virtually every prewar group, ranging from the Boy Scouts to major political parties, set up small printing operations designed to counter German propaganda, disseminate accurate information, and boost morale.

Edelman had eagerly signed up to help print the Bund's clandestine pamphlet largely for that reason. He and his Bundist friends needed to do something, anything, "to overcome our own terrifying apathy. To force ourselves to the smallest spark of activity, to fight against our own acceptance of the generally prevailing feeling of panic."

This sensation was unnatural to Edelman, who unlike the humble and self-effacing Boruch Spiegel did not usually suffer from self-doubt. Edelman, before the war, might well have been an underachiever— "lazy" in his own words. His sloth, however, had been of his own choosing. Now, under the Nazis, no Jew was master of his own destiny, thanks to the stream of ever more restrictive anti-Semitic edicts issued by the *General Gouvernement*—the new colonial administrative body that had been given the mandate to rule central Poland. It was led by Hans Frank, Hitler's longtime legal adviser and personal attorney. From his headquarters atop a massive medieval castle in Krakow, Frank already issued a torrent of decrees freezing all Jewish bank accounts, barring Jews from many industries and trades, and subjecting them to daily humiliations and onerous forced labor requirements.

So for the free-spirited eighteen-year-old orphan, participation in the underground press was as much about exercising control over at least one aspect of his life as it was about lifting the sinking spirits of his fellow Bundists. "Considerable effort went into the publication of these papers," Edelman recalled. Printing supplies were not easy to come by. Paper and ink had to be acquired on the burgeoning black market and discreetly delivered to the school, which like all other educational facilities in Warsaw had been closed by the Nazis.

The printing was done with a cumbersome hand crank by the harsh light of homemade carbide lamps, which were used because of the kerosene shortage. They consisted of two small metal pots mounted over each other. Lumps of calcium carbide were placed in the lower container, while water dripped through a pinhole in the upper chamber. When the drops came into contact with the carbide, they released acetylene gas, which fueled a flame. "Working by carbide light proved extremely strenuous," Edelman remembered. By 2 A.M. everyone's eyes burned, but the printing went on until seven in the morning, when the exhausted printing crews had to go to their day jobs. "We averaged two or three sleepless nights a week," he recalled.

The riskiest aspect of the process also started in the morning, when the five hundred copies Edelman had printed overnight were sent out for distribution. To lessen the potential for capture, a system of "fivers and tenners" was instituted, whereby activities were divided among different groups—cells—comprised of no more than five or ten individuals. Mark Edelman's nocturnal printing operation was one such fiver. It received its materials—the essays, articles, and proclamations—from another fiver, and then handed off the finished copies to the leader of a tenner, who distributed them to ten others, stratifying the process in such a way that if someone was caught with an illegal pamphlet, the entire chain was not at risk.

The only publication officially permitted in Warsaw was the *New Courier,* which featured Nazi notices and poorly translated articles whose German authors all worked for Joseph Goebbels's propaganda ministry. All other forms of mass communication were banned, and their disseminators subject to arrest, interrogation, and execution. The prohibition included ownership of radios, which Varsovians had been ordered to relinquish on pain of death lest they listen to the BBC's new Polish language service, or Radio Paris, where the Polish government in exile under a new leader, General Wladislaw Sikorski, a career soldier and centrist, broadcast daily. Eighty-seven thousand of the estimated 125,000 transistor radios in the Polish capital were confiscated by late 1939, and the Germans were conducting sweeps to search for the remainder.

The *Courier* itself was an unexpected publishing success. It had a daily circulation of two hundred thousand copies and was almost always sold out at newsstands. Varsovians read it mostly for its obituaries, to learn the names, for instance, of the ten people sentenced to death for tearing down a German flag, or of the eighty shot for tampering with a telecommunications cable. The paper was also scoured for formal announcements like the arrest of Mayor Stephen Starzinski, the hero of the siege of Warsaw, who was sent to Dachau, where he would be executed for daring to defy Hitler.

It was in the pages of the *Courier* that Edelman and the rest of the Jewish community were informed that as of December 1, 1939, "All Jews and Jewesses within the General Government who are over ten years of age are required to wear on the right sleeve of their inner and outer garment a white band at least 10cm. wide, with the Star of David on it. Jews and Jewesses must procure these armbands themselves, and provide them with the required distinguishing mark. Violations will be punished by imprisonment."

CHAPTER 8

JOANNA'S RHYME

Publisher Hanna Mortkowicz-Olczak read the December 1939 armband decree with anxiety. The new regulation condemned her mother and her cousin Martha Osnos to wear the identifying mark. But as a convert to Christianity, as a Protestant, did the edict apply to her? And what of her daughter? As a five-year-old, Joanna was exempted by virtue of age. But on racial grounds, was she Semitic? Her father, Hanna's ex-husband, was a Gentile. Hanna's conversion had also predated Joanna's birth. Was this sufficient to spare the child a Jewish classification?

Such anguished questions were posed in thousands of homes throughout the Polish capital by those who had switched faith, or intermarried, or were themselves the products of mixed marriages. The list included descendants of the biggest Polish banking and industrial dynasties, the country's Carnegies, Rockefellers, and Mellons; the Baumans, the Bersons, the Blochs, the Epsteins, Kohns, Wawelbergs, Rotwands, Nathansons, and Kronenbergs, who were among the many nineteenth-century oligarchs who adopted Christianity to circumvent tsarist restrictions. Would they, too, be affected? How far back would the Nazis search for Jewish genealogy? And what of mixed marriages? Would these spare spouses? Or would there be a rash of divorces and nullifications in the coming months, as there had been in Germany in the mid-1930s?

A rush to obtain legal interpretations, not to mention baptismal certificates, both genuine and forged, accompanied the promulgation of the armband law, and confusion reigned until the General Government issued clarifications to the racial code. These were based on the notorious Nuremberg Laws of September 15, 1935, which stated unequivocally that mixed marriages were "forbidden and invalid" and subject to annulment. Wedding bands therefore offered no protection in the new German colony. The adoption of Christianity was addressed by an amendment to the Nuremberg Laws passed on November 14, 1935, which stipulated "A Jew is a person descended from at least three grandparents who are full Jews by race," regardless of current faith. All of Hanna's grandparents were Jewish, so in the eyes of the Nazis, her conversion was moot. Little Joanna's case was slightly more hopeful. Legally, she was classified a *Mischling* in the first degree, a person of "mixed breed," who had only two Jewish grandparents. Under the Nuremberg Laws, *Mischlings* could remain full citizens if they were born before September 15, 1935. Fortunately, Joanna had just celebrated her fifth birthday. She predated the Nuremberg Laws by a full year.

If this spared her, she was blissfully oblivious—too young to comprehend the implications of the new racial code or the anxiety it was causing her mother and grandmother. The three generations of Mortkowicz women had moved into Old Town after the siege. Hanna's elegant riverside apartment, with its sweeping views of the Vistula, had been damaged during the bombardments, and the housing shortage forced her to take up residence in the historic quarter, in the musty old edifice where her late father had maintained his printing presses and bookbinding operations. The sixteenth-century structure that the Mortkowiczes owned was on the main market square, a cobbled expanse that stretched the length of several football fields and was lined on all sides by large baroque townhouses with steeply pitched tile roofs. This was Warsaw's future tourist district, and Hanna's building would one day house an Italian restaurant and corporate apartments.

But in 1939, Old Town's medieval charm had not yet been realized, and the cramped and crumbling neighborhood had an unsavory reputation that was eloquently captured in Sholem Asch's *Motke the Thief*:

"In a corner of the great Warsaw there still stands a remnant of the medieval city. The Old Town consists of tall, narrow old houses that our ancestors built hundreds of years ago. The outer wall of each house is built into that of the next, so if you barely touch one, its neighbors will fall down. These houses have no courtyards, no windows, no light. Each one is like a labyrinth. Long dark corridors lead one along secret paths into the rooms of the houses, and only the longtime inhabitants know how to follow them. Someone who chances into such a house might think that he has gotten lost in an ancient church, the walls of which smell of the Inquisition. A terror comes over him as he regards the high rounded rafters that arch above his head, and the heavy black walls that surround him, and he stands stock still, frightened in the darkness."

For Joanna—who, like her mother and grandmother, was tiny, almost elfin—Old Town was a wonderland. There was nothing scary about its church-steeple skyline, or the long curving shadows that the spires of its Gothic cathedrals cast in the early winter sun. She ran wild through its maze of narrow, musty streets, her raven curls spilling out of her bonnet, her little pumps slipping and scuffing on cobblestones, as she tried to keep up with the older, rougher neighborhood kids. Together, they scaled the Barbakan Gate and scampered along its crenellated brick ramparts. They played hide-and-seek along the drained and grassy moat that still encircled parts of the ancient settlement. They teased the peddlers and swiped apples from their pushcarts, and Joanna laughed loudest as they all skipped through Market Square singing "Jew, Jew, crawl under your shack. Now the shack is creaking. Now the Jew is shrieking!"

It was Vincent, the Mortkowiczes' Gentile caretaker, who finally put an end to the fun and games. Hearing Joanna mindlessly spout the offensive singsong, he led her home by the ear and gave her a lecture. "It was then that I found out what was the real and macabre meaning of the rhyme. And that it was about us," Joanna recalled. The revelation was shocking on many different levels.

Joanna had been raised in a secular household where the emphasis had always been on assimilation. Despite the Mortkowiczes' rabbinical Viennese roots, religion had never played a role in their lives. "My grandfather wanted to be more Polish than the Poles," Joanna recalled of the patriarch Jacob Mortkowicz, who in the world of Polish publishing occupied a lofty position similar to that of Alfred Knopf in New York. "He would stay up late into the night, almost each night, poring over the dictionary in search of ever more esoteric words." These linguistic exertions were partly a matter of pride: Jacob Mortkowicz traveled in notoriously elite intellectual circles and he wanted to be the most eloquent person in the room. But the word games also reflected a deep-seated insecurity that might have been instantly recognizable to any American immigrant: "He practiced pronunciation," Joanna explained. He wanted to ensure that his elocution left no trace of his own father's heavy Yiddish accent, of "the Hebraic-German garble and the traditional mutilation of Polish speech," as his star writer, Julian Tuwim, himself an assimilated Jew, put it, less delicately.

As with the Osnos family, Yiddish was pointedly not among the vast reservoir of languages—French, English, German, and Russian—spoken around the Mortkowicz dinner table. Nor was the Sabbath celebrated. And Joanna passed each Christmas in the Polish tradition: opening her presents under the mistletoe after supper on December 24.

So the news that she was Jewish was shattering. "It's not true!" she shouted, running into her mother's arms. "I'm not Jewish. I don't want to be Jewish," she kept repeating. Joanna wailed and pounded her little fists, until her grandmother Janine finally had enough. "And what is so terrible about being Jewish?" she snapped, wresting the startled child from her mother's soothing embrace. Joanna trembled. She lived in fear of her grandmother. "She was a very proud and strong-willed woman. In many ways she was much stronger than my mother."

Despite her diminutive stature and matronly appearance—even with her gray hair coiled up in a bun, she barely reached five feet—Janine had always been the power behind the Mortkowicz throne. Her husband had built the publishing empire on the strength of his relationship with writers. But his artistic and sensitive personality had not lent itself well to the harsher business side of publishing. And Hanna had inherited her father's delicate personality, along with his corporate debts. "She was not well suited to bear the burdens after my grandfather's suicide. In practice, my grandmother ran things."

In her anger at that moment, Joanna recognized a tragic feature of Polish assimilation that would take her decades to understand when she was an adult. "I was so upset at being Jewish because assimilation was based on identification with Polishness, which was based in part on anti-Semitism," she later explained. "I was being taught to hate myself."

Ironically, Joanna's family had spearheaded the literary assault on anti-Semitism in Poland by publishing writers like Tuwim, Antoni Slonimski, Jan Lechon, and Boleslaw Lesmian. Collectively known as the "Skamander Group," they were mostly poets and mostly Jews, all household names in a poetry-crazed culture that built monuments to its dead bards and elevated the living to a celebrity status just shy of movie matinee idols.

The Skamanders battled bigotry through parody and allegory while laying siege to the chauvinist proponents of "Poland for Poles" by ridiculing the far right's misguided notions of nationalism. Tuwim and Slonimski are one hundred percent Jews screamed headlines in conservative newspapers, seething with outrage that Poland's national poets, men whose works would later be required reading in every high school and who would have streets named after them in virtually every major Polish city, were neither Catholic nor Slavic.

So despite their own strong personal preference for assimilation, the Mortkowiczes professionally strove for social tolerance and did not see themselves as self-loathing Jews. In the days that followed the armband proclamation, when Joanna spotted a pair of Magen David cloth strips in the vestibule, it was once again Vincent, the old and wizened Catholic caretaker, who intervened. He had been with the Jacob Mortkowicz Publishing House for as long as anyone could remember, looking after its ink-stained presses and dusty storerooms filled with first editions. Often drunk, and always surrounded by a cloud of cigarette smoke, he possessed a peasant wisdom and a keen devotion to his employers. The armbands were thrown to the floor, spat on, and trampled by the indignant caretaker. "I will never permit my Ladies to follow such a despicable order," he vowed.

CHAPTER 9

ISAAC ON MEMORY LANE

While Jews in Warsaw grappled with the implications of the armband edict, Isaac Zuckerman and the leaders of the Zionist left were meeting in the waning days of 1939 in the Galician provincial capital of Lvov, which was now under Soviet occupation.

Since he fled Warsaw in the opening week of the war, Zuckerman's wanderings had initially taken him north to Vilna, or Vilnius, as it would become known. He'd arrived there on September 19, the same day the Red Army had captured the provincial Baltic city, and he planned to hire a professional smuggler to sneak him across the nearby Polish-Lithuanian border, guarded now by trigger-happy Soviet troops. At the last moment, however, a stroke of diplomatic luck changed his plans. Moscow, for inexplicable reasons, announced that it would cede the entire Polish province of Vilna, including "321,700 Poles, 107,600 Jews, 75,200 Belarussians, 31,300 Lithuanians, 9,000 Russians, and 1,100 Germans," to Lithuania as part of a newly signed Treaty of Friendship and Non-Aggression. So instead of risking a dangerous crossing, Zuckerman decided to wait for the transfer.

Many others had the same idea. In anticipation of the handover, fifteen thousand Jewish refugees flooded into Vilna, including members of virtually every Zionist faction, ranging from the Marxist Hashomer Hatzair on the far left through Betar and the Revisionists on the far right, and every shading in between.

As in Kovel, housing was problematic. Isaac roomed with relatives, for Vilna was his hometown, where his parents and siblings lived. He had gone to school there, learned to swim and ride a horse there. It was where he had picked up his Vilnoese Polish accent, as distinct as a Boston brogue, and where he had kissed a girl for the first time. It was the place he associated with the bloom of his Uncle Simon's orchards, and the damp, comforting smell of the family flour mill. Yet it also held darker memories: of fear and fire, and of Isaac as a five-year-old trembling before the Polish troops that had seized the city from the Red Army in 1920 and stormed through the Jewish neighborhood, looting, burning, and beating. No one in Zuckerman's family had been hurt during the rampage, but sixty-five Jews were murdered for allegedly collaborating with the Bolsheviks. The false accusations were supported by the sole U.S. military observer on the scene, Colonel William F. Godson. In his report to Washington, Godson justified the actions of the units under the command of Edward Smigly-Rydz, then a mere general, noting that "Jews constituted at least 80% of every Bolshevik organization," murdered Polish civilians, and were "extremely dangerous."

The experience remained "engraved" in Isaac's heart. It had taught him that the Poles could be just as bloodthirsty as the Russians, who orchestrated many of the nineteenth-century pogroms on Polish soil. In fact they had given the world the word "pogrom," from the Russian verb *pogromit,* to destroy.

Now, nineteen years later, Isaac was staying with his sister while waiting for the city's transfer to Lithuanian hands. She had married well but was widowed. She owned a large two-story house on Ponary Street, near Old Town—in the baroque heart of what would one day be the tourist district. His parents and his ninety-year-old grandfather, whom he had not seen in some time, were staying there, too, and Isaac was taken aback at how the family patriarch had aged. "What's new, *Dyedushka?*" Isaac called out in Yiddish, using the Russian diminutive for "grandpa." "The French have entered Vilna," his grandfather replied, confusing Stalin with Napoleon, who had liberated the Polish city from tsarist dominion in 1812.

Isaac was deeply affected by the visible deterioration of a man he had always admired as a rebel and maverick. He viewed his grandfather, Rabbi Yohanan Zuckerman, as "a rabbi who didn't want to make a living at it," who preferred worldly to spiritual pursuits. It was from his grandfather that his own father inherited a rebellious streak. At one point, he had run away from home, marrying without permission and apparently absconding with some family funds. It had caused quite a stir in Vilna's tight-knit Jewish community, where a good scandal was relished. "My father had been something of a hippie," Isaac would later write with evident pride. Zuckerman, in turn, had inherited his father's good looks, imposing height, and penchant for defiance.

Isaac was not prone to insubordination, however, when it came to instructions from his Zionist superiors. And new orders soon arrived from the organization's temporary headquarters in Kovel. Zuckerman was not to go to Lithuania to search for a northern passage to Palestine after all. It was now clear that the overwhelming majority of the more than one million Polish Jews trapped in the Soviet zone would not be able to escape. And the total was likely much higher, because no one knew how many of the 2.3 million other Jews in the German part of Poland had already crossed the Nazi-Soviet demarcation line. The boundary between the two occupying powers was still open and would remain unguarded until October 26, 1939, when the frontiers were formally set. Every day trains carrying refugees east encountered trains moving west. "Are you insane, where are you going?" the eastward-bound passengers gasped as they passed the occasional trainload of Jews returning to Warsaw. "You are insane. Where are you going?" retorted westbound travelers fleeing the Soviets, with equal astonishment.

It was presumed that many senior Zionist leaders in Soviet-occupied Poland were well known to the NKVD because the dreaded security service that had murdered millions of Russians during Stalin's purges was hastily compiling dossiers on hundreds of thousands of potential Polish troublemakers in preparation for mass arrests. Younger, more obscure activists like Isaac, however, might still be able to operate under the NKVD's radar and take their place. Zuckerman's instructions were to travel deep into the Soviet occupation zone and form an underground network. What precisely that entailed, he did not know. He had no relevant experience, and only the vaguest notion of where to start. But he did not hesitate, despite his father's admonition that leaving Vilna just as it was about to be handed over to neutral Lithuania made no sense. "He would have understood if I had gone closer to Eretz Israel. But to go further away! I couldn't tell him that I was going to do clandestine work. Mother did not know anything. I went to the kitchen, came up from behind her, kissed her and told her I was leaving. She started weeping." Isaac would later be haunted by his quick departure. "I didn't know that it would be the last time I would see my parents."

After leaving Vilna, Zuckerman wandered Soviet-occupied Poland, trying to revive local Socialist-Zionist chapters in towns including Kovel, Lutsk, and Bialystok, before finally settling in Lvov, the largest urban center in the Carpathians. All along this geographic corridor the Russians were pressuring young, left-leaning Zionists to join Komsomol, the Leninist youth organization, and Zuckerman was fighting a rearguard action to stem the defections. "There were cases of members leaving the movement to join the communists," he later acknowledged. "Even teachers in Hebrew schools forgot their learning overnight."

Actively undermining Komsomol recruiters was a very dangerous undertaking. Jews, though initially less targeted by the NKVD than aristocrats or former Sanation officials, were hardly immune to arrest. Many belonged to the bourgeois capitalist class, which was equally viewed as an enemy of the people in Marxist dogma. Of the 330,000 Galician Poles sent to Siberian camps in 1940, 21 percent were Jews—twice the Jewish representation in the population. Isaac had seen enough of those bedraggled prisoner transports at rail stations to be free of delusions. "Some day they'll probably lead me away like that too," he thought.

But still he took unnecessary and what he would later call amateurish risks. "I was such a great conspirer that my room," at the apartment in Lutsk where everyone knew he was staying, "was famous and people would come and go. In time," he added, "I learned that you couldn't behave like that."

To his credit, Isaac was a quick study. What little he knew about conspiratorial work he had read in spy novels. But his instinct for self-preservation was strong. "I began acting increasingly through contacts. If I could avoid any trip, I didn't travel. I withdrew . . . I learned not to meet with people unnecessarily, not to appear in public." He also learned to buy train tickets directly from corrupt Soviet conductors rather than at rail stations, which were under surveillance. The silence and goodwill of doormen and building superintendents—traditional NKVD or Gestapo stooges—could be purchased with generous bribes. And thanks to his Aryan looks and cavalryman's mustache, Zuckerman discovered that he could blend in like a chameleon—be Jewish or Gentile, depending on the circumstances.

He was learning clandestine tradecraft on the go, and his growing familiarity with subterfuge was already evident at the big conference he convened in Lvov on December 31, 1939. The date had not been chosen idly. It was New Year's Eve, a night of parties and celebrations for Russian soldiers, when a gathering of young Jews would attract little attention. Most of the senior NKVD officers would be at a gala at the Opera House, a magnificent Austrian-built music hall whose neo-Renaissance façade was decorated with Italian sculptures and bas-reliefs and crowned with three giant winged angels. Many of the Soviet secret policemen posted in Lvov hailed from Central Asia and had never seen such European delights. Some of their giddy wives paraded in nightgowns up the marble steps of the Opera, mistaking the sleeping garments they had appropriated from Polish noblewomen for ball gowns.

Lvov's Jewish Quarter stood just behind the Opera, at the tail end of the tree-lined pedestrian promenade that housed some of the city's top hotels—the George, the Grand, the Napoleon—where rooms were now double- and triple-occupied and the gilded corridors crammed with the overflow cots of Jewish refugees. A third of Lvov's residents had been Jewish before the war, but their numbers soared from 110,000 to 160,000 by year's end, so great was the flood of refugees.

Isaac chose to stay away from the Jewish neighborhood when he got to Lvov because it sat on the slope of a small escarpment close to the bars and restaurants frequented by Lvov's new Soviet masters. The city itself was laid out like a landlocked San Francisco, with steep and meandering cobblestone streets that snaked through topographical districts—Castle Hill, Bare Hill, Sandy Hill, St. George's Hill, Citadel Hill, Kortum Hill—undulating through Jewish, Armenian, Catholic, Protestant, and Ukrainian neighborhoods.

Lvov, like Vilna, also lay on a volatile geopolitical fault line where empires collided and suppressed ethnic tensions erupted in bloodshed with historical regularity whenever power shifted or one side made a bid to unseat the other. Ukrainians, a minority in the city but a long-suffering majority in the countryside and surrounding regions, took up arms against the Poles as soon as the Nazis entered Poland. Partisan bands attacked and ambushed retreating columns of Polish soldiers and refugees during the September 1939 campaign, and their dreams of independence that had been brutally quashed by the Sanation regime were rekindled.

But as the province was incorporated into the Soviet Union, many dejected Ukrainians sat glumly in their Polish- and Jewish-owned apartments, reflecting bitterly that they had traded one landlord for another. With smoldering resentment, they awaited the next liberator to promise them freedom.

It was in such an unhappy Ukrainian district, on the unfashionable northern edge of Lvov, that Isaac held the conference that formally founded the Labor Zionist Underground. Since the address of the safe house was secret, participants gathered at a café and were taken to the meeting in small groups. Alcohol and snacks were laid out and dance music blared to maintain the outward appearance of a New Year's Eve party. The fifteen "guests" in attendance represented senior organizers from the main Zionist factions that would eventually form Mapai, or the Labor Party—the dominant political force in Israel until the mid-1970s. Absent from the gathering were representatives of Hashomer Hatzair, the Marxist Zionist group, who declined Zuckerman's invitation on the grounds that the mainstream Zionist left refused to accept the primacy of Moscow. "They had more faith in the Soviet regime," Isaac recounted. "We didn't." Two other significant Zionist youth organizations, Akiva and Gordinia, both centrist and belonging to the more moderate General Zionists, also passed up invitations, much to Zuckerman's dismay. The war, thus far, had done little to unite the notoriously quarrelsome Zionists, whose dogmatic disputes could prove baffling to outsiders, like "medieval monastic debates," as Zuckerman would later concede.

The Lvov Conference, as the faux New Year's Eve celebration came to be known, laid the foundation for the fragmented Labor Zionists to begin structuring a cohesive underground. Amid toasts and cheers, the Soviet zone was divided into five sectors and group leaders were appointed to run each geographical quadrant. The question of what to do about the more than two million Jews stranded in German-occupied Poland proved more problematic. Many of those present that night had escaped from Warsaw in early September, leaving colleagues behind, and there was a general sense of guilt that their organizations had been left rudderless in the largest Jewish population center—a place where Jews were now most at risk and where leadership was most needed.

That uncomfortable sentiment was prevalent throughout the refugee community and crossed all ideological lines. The young rightist Betar leader Menachem Begin, for instance, in a series of letters penned in Vilna at the time, deflected accusations from fellow rightwing Zionists that in abandoning Warsaw during the siege he had acted "like a captain who had been the first to leave his sinking ship."

"Do you really believe that I did not have these thoughts?" the future Israeli prime minister responded in a January 1940 letter. "And that before I decided to leave Warsaw, I did not consider and question myself and my friends?" "I will return to Warsaw," he pledged in another letter the following month, shortly before his arrest by the NKVD and deportation to Siberia.

Likewise, the Bundist Boruch Spiegel, who was still in the Soviet zone, languishing in relative safety while his family faced ever growing hardships in Warsaw, struggled with his conscience. His older brother Berl had decided to return home to Warsaw and was pressuring him to do the same, not just to participate in the Underground but to safeguard their parents and sisters. As a Bundist organizer, Berl was more exposed behind Soviet zone lines than his less active little brother and thus had a stronger incentive to leave. The NKVD was actively hunting Bund leaders on ideological grounds. The Bund was socialist but staunchly anticommunist, and already co-chairs Victor Alter and Hersh Erlich had been arrested, destined for execution. Perhaps Berl feared arrest as well. Boruch, who was too low in the organization to worry about the NKVD, wanted to stay put. In the end Berl left for Warsaw without Boruch. "We had a fight about it and I'm not ashamed to say that I was too frightened to go."

The idea also terrified Isaac Zuckerman. "Warsaw under the Nazis scared me to death," he recalled. "In comparison to the information we were getting from [Warsaw] we were really living in paradise." A courier had come in the waning days of December 1939 from the beleaguered capital, bearing horror stories of Nazi maltreatment and a plea from rank-and-file activists that someone senior return to start an underground resistance organization for the Zionist left in Warsaw.

That someone, it was decided at the Lvov Conference, would be Zivia Lubetkin, the same person who had been chosen instead of Isaac to attend the 21st Zionist Congress in Geneva the previous summer.

CHAPTER 10

ZIVIA

Zivia Lubetkin and Isaac Zuckerman could not have had more different personalities. While Isaac was gregarious, an extrovert who stood
on tables and dominated most meetings he attended, Zivia was naturally shy. To strangers, she could appear "unapproachable," cold,
hard, and "tough" in the words of one old acquaintance, while Isaac
played the boisterous bon vivant. But those who knew Zivia well said
that her self-possessed standoffish demeanor masked a deep-seated
insecurity.

"Introverted and modest" as a child, a family member would later
say, she would often "blush and be embarrassed" whenever company
arrived. To force young Zivia out of her shell, her family made her
stand on a chair and deliver a speech whenever guests came to the
house, and though she eventually got over her fear of public speaking,
Zivia always preferred to sit in a quiet corner at Zionist gatherings
while Isaac talked up a storm. Isaac had always been more of a political animal within the Zionist movement, launching himself into debates and squabbles that Zivia pronounced "unproductive"—the
endless chattering of "do-nothings" and "squares," as she put it.

While Isaac was flamboyant and spontaneous, Zivia was methodical and unwavering. He often changed his mind. She never did. His sense of humor was legend. Hers "bordered on skepticism." He was a city boy; she was a small-town girl. "Zivia and Isaac only had two things in common," one of their fellow future combatants later said. "Zionism and alcohol. Both liked to drink. But only Zivia knew how."

Lubetkin came from a Polish shtetl with a few thousand inhabitants deep in the marshlands of what is today southwestern Belarus. The place was called Bytem, and residing there was "like living on a small Jewish island surrounded by a foreign and alien world of Gentiles." The Gentiles worked the soggy soil and lived in huts with "straw and mud roofs." Bytem's Jews clustered around the only street wired for electricity and made a living as merchants, tradesmen, and legal and medical professionals, servicing the largely illiterate Christian peasantry. "In sociological terms, most of the Jews were middle class," an Israeli historian described the economic conditions in Zivia's hometown. "However, this term is relative."

Like most of Bytem's Jews, the Lubetkins were far from prosperous, even by the impoverished standards of the Ukrainian, Polish, and Belarussian peasants who subsisted on meager farms in the surrounding swamplands. But Zivia's father owned a grocery store, and the business did well enough that he was able to send her brother to yeshivas in Vilna and Warsaw, hire a private tutor for her older sisters, and later, at Zivia's insistence, pay for a younger sister to study in Palestine.

Zivia herself got involved in the Zionist Socialist pioneering movement as a teenager, in a kind of youthful rebellion against the stifling isolation of the shtetl and the social inequalities she witnessed growing up in rural Poland, "where Gentiles did the manual labor while Jews worked in the white-collar professions."

Like Isaac, she became a full-time activist by her early twenties, helping prepare young Polish Jews for a life on the kibbutzes, the communal farms being established in Palestine. This role involved making public speeches, but while Zivia lacked natural oratorical skills, she possessed an inner strength that won many converts. During one such address, held around a bonfire on the outskirts of a town, a large group of Gentiles descended on the Zionist trainees gathered around

Zivia. The Christians heckled the Jews, brandished sticks, and started throwing rocks. Zivia's trainees fled, and when they gathered together at the Zionist clubhouse in the city they noticed Lubetkin was not there. Fearing that something had happened to her, a few of them went back to the field to look for her. When they reached the site of the bonfire they found Zivia sitting quietly on the same rock where they had left her. They were amazed and asked her: "Tell us, didn't they do anything to you?" She gave them a piercing stare and said: "I sat and looked them straight in the eye . . . and they went away."

Zivia's nerves were about to be put on trial once more. Tall and imposing, with neat dark hair that she often pulled into a tight bun, she was twenty-five years old in January 1940, when she set out for Warsaw.

Her route took her to the large eastern city of Bialystok, in the Soviet sector, where she had been given the address of a professional smuggler who took groups across a forested stretch of the border in exchange for a fee. A for-profit cottage industry had sprung up there, guiding people through the Soviet-Nazi frontier. It could cost as little as a few zlotys to be rowed in a crowded dory at night across the Bug River. But some smugglers robbed their clients, leading them deep into the woods and stripping them of all their belongings at gunpoint. Though Zivia's guide was a Gentile, he came highly recommended. The same courier who had come from Warsaw bearing the request for the Labor Zionists to send a senior emissary to the Polish capital had vouched for him.

In Bialystok, Zivia waited at a safe house for her appointed departure. The various Zionist factions were all well represented in the predominantly Jewish city. After a few days, Zivia's guide made contact. They would leave the following morning. He was also taking a handful of university students across, and together the group boarded a rickety old commuter train to a village near the new border. The students, like many Polish Gentiles, naïvely believed they would be safer in the General Government than under the Communists. While the Poles were afraid of what would happen if the Bolsheviks caught them, Lubetkin "was terrified of what the Germans would do to me." As they hiked through the snow and pine trees under the cover of darkness, braving temperatures of 13 degrees below zero, Zivia noticed a remarkable change in the students' behavior. On the Soviet side, they had been polite and respectful, but as dawn approached and they crossed the forested frontier into Nazi territory, their demeanor changed. "It was as if they suddenly remembered that I was a lower being, and that as a Jewess I had to be treated accordingly."

Lubetkin's discomfort grew as the group made its frigid way to the first train station inside German territory. It was called Malkinia, and it was located about fifty miles northeast of Warsaw, near a branch in the line that led to a tiny logging station called Treblinka. On the platform, a large crowd was waiting for the locomotive, she recalled. "There were a few Jews cowering in one corner, hoping not to be noticed." Suddenly a German leaped on them, screaming, kicking, and hitting them in the face. "The platform is for Aryans," he shouted, brutally shoving them out of the station.

"She's also a Jew," someone pointed to Lubetkin, and her heart sank. Zivia's dark, attractive features were distinctly Semitic; unlike Zuckerman, she would never blend into a Christian crowd. And in Poland, anti-Semitism was sufficiently widespread that in any large crowd there was almost a statistical certainty that at least one individual wished Jews ill.

Zivia gritted her teeth. But she didn't move. She didn't budge. She didn't breathe. She stood her ground, much like the time she had stared down the bullies around the campfire. Just then the train arrived, the throng pushed forward, and in the rush for seats she managed to board. Lubetkin was safe but deeply shaken, and suddenly unsure of herself now that Warsaw was the next stop. She was a proud woman, accustomed to holding her head high. But from the moment she crossed the border, she felt defeated and drained. "Do I have the strength," she wondered, "to do this?"

BOOK TWO

Gone now are those little towns where the Shoemaker was a poet,
The watchmaker a philosopher, the barber a Troubadour.
Gone now are those little towns where the wind joined
Biblical songs with Polish tunes and Slavic rue,
Where old Jews in orchards in the shade of cherry trees
Lamented for the holy walls of Jerusalem.
Gone now are those little towns, through the poetic mists,
The moons, winds, ponds and stars above them
Have recorded in the blood of centuries the tragic tales,
The histories of the two saddest nations on earth.

—ANTONI SLONIMSKI

CHAPTER 11

WHY DOES HITLER LIKE MRS. ZEROMSKA?

Good Friday was a national holiday in Poland. Every year, solemn processions led by white-robed altar boys would wend their way past Hanna Mortkowicz-Olczak's sixteenth-century townhouse in Old Town to kneel before the Gothic altar of St. John's Cathedral, while large crowds bearing candles and religious banners congregated outside the towers of St. Florian's Basilica, across the Vistula River in Praga.

On March 22, 1940, the ceremonies commemorating the crucifixion of Christ were muted, by Poland's pious standards. Warsaw's German masters kept factories working, and the press-gangs that snatched Poles to work as slave laborers in Germany continued, unaffected by spiritual considerations.

Around noon that day, the Bundist Mark Edelman made his way to New Linden Street from the Berson and Bauman Children's Hospital, where he had taken a job as an orderly. It paid barely enough to buy a few dozen loaves of bread at the nearby Mirowski Market, where food prices had tripled over the harsh winter, along with the value of the U.S. dollar, now trading at thirty times its prewar exchange rate. Most days during his lunch hour Edelman walked the dozen blocks from the hospital to New Linden Street to visit the Bund's security chief, Bernard Goldstein, a major figure in the earliest incarnations of the Jewish resistance movement.

On his way to Goldstein's, Edelman cut through tiny False Street, which was aptly named since it zigzagged confusingly through a warren of back alleys linking the neon-lit department stores of Forestry Street to the far quieter New Linden, where he passed the elegant Hotel Britannia. The hotel had been eminently respectable before the war, hosting traveling representatives of the big textile mills in Lodz, salesmen from foundries in Radom, and metals traders from Silesia. But German officers had turned it into a brothel. The sound of their merriment carried for blocks in the evenings, as the curfew requiring Varsovians to stay indoors after 9 P.M. plunged the city into an eerie silence, interrupted only by bursts of German mirth.

Each day, Edelman brought Goldstein food, cigarettes, and news, and collected messages and instructions to relay to other activists, since Goldstein had to lie low owing to his particular duties within the Jewish Labor Union, as the Bund was formally known in Yiddish.

In Bundist circles, Goldstein was an icon. He was the closest thing the Jewish Labor Union had to a defense minister, and he had run the Bund's "black ops" before the war. It was largely because of him that the thugs from violent fascist fringe groups like the ONR, the Falanga, or the notorious Sword and Ploughmen—the prewar equivalent of skinheads—had never dared to cross Count Krasinski Park and the Saxon Gardens, the border in Warsaw between the Jewish and Gentile districts. It was Goldstein, a large and gruff forty-nine-year-old trade union boss with connections to the underworld, who organized special units of burly Jewish porters, Poland's Teamsters, to disrupt fascist demonstrations. And it was Goldstein, a survivor of many bouts of fisticuffs, evidenced by the long scar etched on one cheek, who was said to have been behind the series of mysterious explosions that rocked the offices of anti-Semitic organizations in Warsaw in the late 1930s. He had been jailed many times for his union activities, and his escape from a Siberian prison camp had further enhanced his reputation. To young Bundists like Edelman and Spiegel he was a living legend. "We worshipped him," Boruch said.

The Bund's security chief rarely ventured outdoors, for fear of being spotted by the Gestapo or its henchmen in the hated Polish Blue Police, a puppet force formed by the Nazis. Goldstein had grown a thick tangled beard to disguise his appearance, and he passed the time playing cards, often with Abrasha Blum and other Bund central committee members. Sometimes, if they were missing a fourth, the Bund bosses would invite their brash errand boy to play with them, an honor that Edelman deeply cherished since he considered himself "a nobody and they were great men."

Mark had known the security chief since childhood, when he had played with his son, and the two boys used to steal Goldstein's cigarettes and smoke them on the balcony when he wasn't around. Over the years, the admiration grew to verge on hero worship, with Mark praising Goldstein's "lightning reflexes and good nature" and a sense of humor "that masked steely nerves and courage."

On Good Friday 1940, a sunny but chilly day with frost still icing much of Warsaw, Goldstein's lunch-hour card game was interrupted by reports of disturbances two blocks east on Banker's Square. The Square, near Saxon Gardens, at the foot of Cordials Avenue, had been a traditional demarcation line between Jewish and Gentile neighborhoods. A band of hoodlums was attacking people at random in Banker's Square, screaming that the Jews had killed Christ. They started looting stores, smashing windows, and chasing Jewish shopkeepers, who were easy to identify because all Jewish property in Warsaw now had to be clearly marked with white hand-painted *Juden* placards. Businesses throughout the Jewish district quickly shuttered their storefronts as word of the disturbances spread. The Good Friday rampage did not set off panic at Bund headquarters, since Goldstein was no stranger to violent confrontations with anti-Semitic mobs. Before the war, his militias had developed an ingenious weapon to deal with such thugs: a series of spring-loaded small pipes that telescoped outward at the push of a button to form a long steel truncheon. The Bund's fascist opponents also had a prewar weapon of choice—a wood board attached to the thigh just above the knee and studded with razor blades. A kick from it would slice up victims.

The following Monday it became clear that Good Friday had not been a one-off incident. The looters and rioters returned in greater force—one eyewitness put their numbers at around a thousand—and the attacks spread to the neighboring Forestry, Mushroom, and Dragon Streets, to Iron Gate Square and Haberdasher's Row, and as far west as Cool and Wolska Streets. Once more Jewish residents fled indoors, barricading themselves in their apartments and cellars. Stores whose front windows were not protected by retractable metal grille curtains were pillaged, as roving bands of club-wielding youths shouted "Kill the Jews" and tried to force their way into people's homes.

The Blue Police stood passively by while the attacks gained momentum, intervening only when a Jewish victim got the upper hand on his Gentile assailant. Most Varsovians also turned a blind eye to the brutality, with the notable exception of Polish intellectuals, who, according to the historian Yisrael Gutman, were "enraged by the pogrom in March, and especially by the fact that it was perpetrated by a mob of Poles."

Exactly who made up this mob became more evident when German army buses were seen delivering large groups of ruffians to the edge of the Jewish Quarter, many of whom were later spotted lining up to receive money from laughing men in Luftwaffe uniforms. Edelman quickly deduced that Germans were recruiting thugs from "the fringe elements of Polish society," busing them into Banker's Square, and paying them four or five zlotys to beat up Jews.

Once the Bund learned that it was dealing with many of its old prewar skinhead adversaries, Bernard Goldstein sprang into action and quickly rounded up his former militiamen. "The guys in the Bund's Self-Defense Force were not shrinking violets," Mark recalled. "They were strong, strapping lads: porters and water carriers, and the coal men from Bird Street. Armed with long pikes from their hand wagons and stout clubs, they had been more than a match for the ON-Rites before the war."

The acronym stood for *Oboz Narodowo-Radykalny,* or the Radical Nationalist Camp. The extremist group had been founded at the height of the Great Depression, on a platform of eliminating all Jews, liberals, communists, and homosexuals from Slavic society. Their message was so hateful that Joseph Pilsudski, the centrist war hero who had defeated Stalin, had banned the nascent fascist party and thrown its leaders in jail when he seized power. After Pilsudski's death in 1935, when the Sanation regime shifted dramatically rightward, the ONR's founders were quietly released from prison, and their activities had been tolerated as an outlet for social unrest among disaffected urban youth. It was the young and mostly unemployed ONRites, predominantly poor and poorly educated, who had attacked Jewish students at the University of Warsaw in 1937 and thrown bricks through Jewish-owned storefronts in 1938, threatening shoppers who dared enter. It was the Falangists and other ONR bully-boys, with their distinctive green armbands depicting a truncated swastika pierced by a sword, that Goldstein's teamsters had beaten to a pulp in a famous 1938 brawl on Banker's Square. And now they were back, spoiling for revenge.

The Bund's Self-Defense Force started to prepare. "We decided to fight back with 'cold weapons'—iron pipes and brass knuckles, but not with knives and firearms," Goldstein recalled, since any deaths resulting from the defenders' actions would almost certainly bring collective punishment on the Jewish community. "Every fighting contingent was mobilized—slaughterhouse workers, transport workers, party members. We organized them into three groups."

Just before curfew, the detachments were discreetly deployed to different spots, a tactic Goldstein had used successfully in the past to make his units seem more numerous and omnipresent. Boruch Spiegel's older brother Berl, who had returned to Warsaw from the Soviet zone following their dispute in December, was among those lying in wait for the Polish thugs.

"When the pogromists appeared in these sections on the following morning, they were surprised to find our comrades waiting for them. A bloody battle broke out immediately. Ambulances rushed to carry off wounded pogromists. Our own wounded were hidden and cared for in private homes to avoid their arrest by Polish or German police," Goldstein recalled. "The battle kept shifting to various parts of the city. Our organized groups were joined spontaneously by other workers. In the Wola district, our comrades received help from non-Jewish Socialist workers to whom we had appealed for aid. Many Christians tried to persuade the pogromists to stop," Goldstein added. "Many Jews, afraid of the dangers of 'collective responsibility,' tried to keep us from hitting back."

Fighting that day lasted until just before curfew and resumed the next morning, though the Polish fascists appeared less numerous and seemed to have lost some of their enthusiasm now that someone was striking back. Four or five zlotys apparently were not worth the risk of having one's head split open by a burly slaughterhouse worker, and by 1 P.M. the Blue Police, perhaps sensing the shifting tide of battle, dispersed the combatants. The pogrom ended on March 29, as abruptly as it had begun.

Miraculously, no one was reported killed during the weeklong assault on the Jewish district, and the feared German retaliation for this first act of physical Jewish resistance never materialized.

The Osnoses, their cousins the Mortkowiczes, and Simha Ratheiser's family had not been affected by the Easter pogrom, since they all lived in predominantly Catholic neighborhoods. But they were all subject to another, equally perfidious form of German persecution during the winter and spring of 1940.

Ratheiser's facial wounds had healed by then, and only a small scar remained from the wood splinter that had pierced his neck when his apartment building collapsed. Fortunately for the Ratheisers, Zvi's store had been unscathed during the siege, and the family could still earn a living. Warsaw's economy had been devastated, contracting by an estimated 40 percent as a result of the war. Some 270,000 men and 63,470 women had lost their jobs. Electricity, when it was finally restored, was available only on alternating days, so that one side of the street had it on Monday while the other side received it on Tuesday, because the Germans had cut Warsaw's coal deliveries in half in order to power their own industries. Hyperinflation raged and "young men of land-owning families," as one observer noted, "were sweeping the streets in fox-fur caps and bearskin fur coats reaching down to their ankles," while society women worked as waitresses and students stood on street corners selling used clothes.

Simha's family had thus far escaped the worst of this economic cataclysm, thanks to his father's store. It occupied a small stand-alone structure only a few yards from the ruins of their former home, near the elegant military stables where officers kept their parade horses, and Zvi had been able to reopen it in October. The shop was what was known in Polish as a *mylnia*, a type of general hardware store popular before the war, where people could buy all manner of household goods: paraffin lamps and kerosene, small ladders and lightbulbs, cleaning solvents and shaving cream. The store itself was not big, less than a thousand square feet, and Zvi Ratheiser ran it alone. Until the invasion, Simha's mother, Miriam, a beautiful blue-eyed blonde, had her own business arranging credit lines and layaway plans for the wives of the senior Polish officers who lived in a nearby colony of luxurious villas reserved for colonels and generals. She was quite successful, Simha recalled: "I think she made more money than Father."

Simha was much closer to his mother, from whom he had inherited his fair good looks. She was more of a free spirit than his remote, orthodox dad. She was also far more integrated into the wider Polish society, with many Gentile friends in the neighborhood, and she spoke accent-free Polish. In fact, on occasions when she relieved Simha's father behind the cash register, customers would sometimes lower their voice and ask how such an attractive Polish girl could have married an Orthodox Jew. Miriam's response, that she, too, was Jewish, would astonish the customers, who remained fond of her nonetheless. It was possibly largely due to Miriam's high standing in the community that Zvi's store was never looted or harassed by the likes of the ONR.

"We were not rich, but we were comfortable," Simha recalled. The family employed a Gentile housekeeper, and they managed to hold on to a semblance of their prewar middle-class existence. Everything changed, however, the day a Volksdeutsche walked into the store. The Volksdeutsche were ethnic Germans living outside the Third Reich. They were scattered throughout central Europe and the Baltic states, and as far east as central Asia. In Poland there were several million individuals of German descent, residing mostly in the western territories that Germany annexed directly in 1939. Most had been Polonized and considered themselves Polish patriots, but a small minority had signed a loyalty oath to Hitler after the Nazi invasion, volunteering to act as the spearhead of a larger German colonization program in the captured lands. Some hundred thousand Polish Volksdeutsche were now doing the bidding of the Nazis within the boundaries of the General Government, and one of them was at Zvi Ratheiser's door. "He was a *Treuhander,*" Simha said of the ethnic German.

The Treuhandstelle Ost, or Main Economic Trustee Office East, as the institution was formally known, was the invention of Reichsmarshal Hermann Goering, and its stated purpose was to confiscate Polish property. The Nazi agency was already fully operational in the western part of Poland, where it had seized 112,000 small businesses, 9,120 large enterprises, 76,000 small artisan shops, 9,000 medium-sized factories, and 216 large industrial concerns such as power plants, steel mills, and coal mines.

The Treuhandstelle was now setting up shop in the General Government, and Simha's father's store was about to become another statistical entry in its bloated ledgers. "The Volksdeutsche demanded the keys, and that was that." Ratheiser shrugged. In an instant, the business his father had built up over the years was taken away by a complete stranger. Shock set in first, then resignation, then fear. How would the Ratheiser family live? Where would money for food, clothes, rent, and heating coal come from?

The same anguished questions were being posed by owners of thousands of expropriated businesses across Warsaw. According to prewar commercial records, 57.5 percent of all medium-sized and small enterprises and 40 percent of large industrial concerns in the capital were Jewish-owned, including the city's largest employer, automotive giant and GM licensee Lilpop, Rau & Lowenstein. Its Chevrolet plant, one of the largest in Europe, was now officially rechristened Hermann Goering Works in honor of the architect of the mass theft.

Publisher Hanna Mortkowicz-Olczak's bookstore also bore a new German name: A. Zeromski Buchhandlung und Antiquariat. But the shop had not really changed hands. Hanna had refused to give it up and had shrewdly exploited a provision in the Treuhandstelle regulations that allowed Gentiles to keep their businesses. At the behest of Janine, her strong-willed mother, she had arranged to put the store in the name of a trusted friend, the widow of Poland's most popular writer, Stephen Zeromski. Jacob Mortkowicz had discovered him, nurtured his talent, and helped turn him into a Polish Hemingway. Along the way, the two families became very close, and now Zeromski's widow volunteered to repay those former acts of kindness.

Five-year-old Joanna, however, didn't understand her mother and grandmother's subterfuge and reacted furiously. "I didn't realize that Mrs. Zeromska was really saving our lives, ensuring that we would have money to survive," she recalled seventy years later, sitting at a table in her family's old bookstore, now a high-end martini bar filled with yuppies and leggy waitresses. "At the time I kept screaming, 'It's our store, give it back! Why does Hitler like Mrs. Zeromska better than Grandma?' "

Joanna's cousin Robert would not remember what happened to his father's appliance factory. But it did not matter, because his mother, Martha, had finally heard from his father. Joe Osnos was safe in Bucharest, Romania. And he was arranging exit visas for his son and wife. All at once, it dawned on Robert that his father had not abandoned them in September 1939, as he had recently begun to fear. Robert, like Joanna, had been too young to comprehend adult machinations. "I didn't understand why he left us behind," he recalled. "And I had been hurt by it." But all along, Joe Osnos had had a plan.

"We are going to get out," he recalled his mother's joyful shout after receiving the doubly good news. "We are going to leave Poland."

CHAPTER 12

AM I WILLING TO DO THIS?

On the morning of April 1, 1940, workers began excavating a series of long trenches around the Jewish Quarter. Large poster boards were erected along these earthworks, warning *Seuchensperrgebeit,* or Area Threatened by Typhus. The signs depicted a skeletal image of an old and stereotypically Semitic face crawling with hairy, oversized lice.

The new trench excavations were foundations for a series of walls "to protect Jews against Polish excesses," like the Good Friday riots, the Germans explained to stunned Jewish officials. Christians were given another explanation for the need to wall off the Jewish neighborhood. Jews were "spreaders of diseases," Warsaw's chief Nazi physician, Dr. Kurt Schrempf, announced. "For sanitary reasons, their district has to be cut off from the rest of the city."

The first cases of typhus in Warsaw were reported in December 1939: 88 among Jews and 5 among non-Jews. By February the numbers had increased to 214 among Jews while remaining steady at 5 among non-Jews. By April 1940, 407 Jews had contracted typhus versus 28 cases among Christians, who constituted 72 percent of the city's population and historically had a life expectancy that ranged between

7.5 years and a full decade less than their traditionally healthier Jewish neighbors.

The destitution, growing malnutrition, and resulting health problems among Jews were incremental and therefore not very noticeable for those who had been in Warsaw since the September siege. But for Bundist Boruch Spiegel, who had finally succumbed to his older brother's pleading letters and returned from the Soviet zone at the beginning of April, the deterioration of the Jewish community was shocking. "I could not face Mama," he recalled. "My mother was not the same person." In just over six months, she had gone completely gray. She was listless and stared out the window for hours on end. Boruch's father had fared only slightly better. He no longer made spats because felt could not be found in Poland. It used to be imported from England, but with the war, the large rolls of material that were shipped from Manchester through the Baltic port of Gdynia became virtually unobtainable. For a while, Boruch's father had been able to purchase the remaining stocks that wholesalers from Franciscan Street had hoarded, but at prices that became less and less economically viable. He then managed to find alternate suppliers: top hat makers, who also used felt but who no longer had customers since formal wear was not needed under German occupation. By winter's end, the market for spats had withered as well, as Poles no longer had discretionary income to spend on a relative luxury like shoe covering. Shoes, in fact, had all but disappeared from store shelves because the Germans had appropriated Poland's entire rubber supply for their military plants. Those sold had wooden soles.

Eventually, Boruch's father was forced to sell his prized Singer sewing machine, and it was from the proceeds of that machine and from his very meager savings that he was supporting his family. "We could now only afford to eat one decent meal a day. Meat maybe once a week," Boruch recalled.

For Zionist Zivia Lubetkin, the situation was equally horrifying. Since returning from the Soviet zone in January, Isaac Zuckerman's fellow activist had focused almost exclusively on promoting the physical well-being of young left-leaning Zionists. "We had to first and foremost provide the hungry with bread and a hot meal," she recalled. Printing underground newsletters and organizing rallies were not priorities when the teenagers in Zionist youth clubs lacked basic food staples. Poland's agricultural output, like its coal, was being diverted to Germany, and the official daily food ration allotted to Varsovians totaled 669 calories for "Poles," 184 calories for Jews, and 2,613 calories for German colonial administrators and their Volksdeutsche collaborators.

Much of the city was subsisting thanks to charitable soup kitchens, and Zivia, with money she had raised in part from the American Joint Distribution Committee, set up a network of free cantinas, where any member of her movement could get a bowl of borscht, some boiled potatoes with a little *shmaletz* (chicken fat), and, as the weather improved, vegetables she started growing on a large scale in window-ledge planters on rooftops and balconies.

Lubetkin was also deeply shaken by the increasingly violent nature of the German occupation. Labor Zionists had no self-defense force, unlike the Bund or the right-wing Zionists, who had also participated in the street fighting during the Easter pogrom. Realizing she needed able-bodied men to lead such a force, Zivia sent word for Isaac to join her in Warsaw. By then, the Zionist left had refined a system of smuggling people across borders and no longer had to rely exclusively on paid and potentially untrustworthy Gentiles.

Zuckerman's guide, Yehuda Mankuta, lived in the border town of Zaromb, between Bialystok and Malkinia, where Zivia had crossed over. He specialized in taking refugees from the General Government to the Soviet zone and then to free Lithuania. But this was his first trip going in the opposite direction.

Like Zivia before him, Isaac and his young guide trudged by moonlight through the dense, dark forest, still heavy with the winter's wet, melting snow. Though Isaac was strong and fit, he could barely keep up with his guide. "I was amazed at Yehuda's senses: how he would bend down over the ground to listen to rustling; how he knew every tree, every bush. He was shorter and thinner than me. I wanted to stop and rest. But he didn't let me . . . I begged him to let me sit down for a minute and he absolutely refused. He kept moving constantly, indefatigably toward the border."

Barbed wire demarcated the frontier, and Yehuda found a small hole in the fence. "Now the German danger began," Zuckerman recalled. As they walked on, every house near the boundary lay in charred ruins, as if the Nazis had depopulated the area with flamethrowers.

At the Malkinia train station, Yehuda decided that it would be too dangerous to wait at the platform as Zivia had done. The risk of running into an army patrol or gendarmes was too great. Instead, they asked a Gentile to buy their tickets, and they planned to jump on the moving train as it pulled out of the station from a spot a few hundred yards away on a curve in the track. The only problem was that the Gestapo had its local headquarters at that very spot, which Isaac and Yehuda only discovered as they rounded the corner in pursuit of the moving train. Sure enough, they were spotted. Shots rang out as Isaac grabbed the door handle of the railcar. A Polish railroad worker called out "Throw away your bundle."

Isaac dropped his bag and pulled himself up into the carriage, lying flat on the floor as more shots were fired. Looking back, he saw bullet holes at the spot where Yehuda's head had been. His guide was gone. (Yehuda Mankuta would survive the war, emigrate to Israel, and change his surname to Manor.)

As Zuckerman picked himself up off the floor, his heart pounding, sweat running down the small of his back, he asked himself once more the question that had been nagging him ever since he received Zivia's summons: "Am I willing to do this?"

Isaac Zuckerman's return to Warsaw was eclipsed by much larger and more significant events. Just before dawn on April 9, 1940, Germany invaded Norway and Denmark. The unprepared Danes surrendered after two hours. The Norwegian forces, after suffering devastating casualties in the opening day of the Blitzkrieg, regrouped in the sparsely populated north of the country and held out for a month, by which time German armored brigades, on May 10, 1940, had rolled into Holland, Belgium, and France.

The Second World War had now begun in earnest. In Warsaw the news was greeted with joy and great hope. Now that the British and French had finally entered the fray, the belief was widespread that Germany would not be able to match the combined firepower of these two military giants. One measure of the growing optimism was the black market value of the dollar. After climbing to 150 zlotys during the harsh winter, it plunged to 90 zlotys in late May on rumors that the first British bombing missions had struck German soil.

Emboldened by the prospects of an Allied victory, the Polish Underground stepped up its sabotage activities, targeting the transport trains that hauled fuel from the Soviet Union to the Third Reich. These crude oil shipments, part of Stalin's pact with Hitler, transited through the General Government, and the Polish resistance developed an ingenious method of disrupting the deliveries without exposing the Polish public to mass retaliation. A specially prepared chemical was added to the lubricating oil in the grease and gearboxes of locomotives. This was done by Polish workers in rail yards during stops to reload coal. When the trains later broke down, the Germans blamed what they believed was mechanical failure owing to the shoddy design and construction of the Polish- and Soviet-built locomotives. Several hundred trains were disabled in this manner before the Germans caught on to the sabotage and retaliated with a flurry of executions. At the same time, the first Underground courts and execution squads were being created to sentence and eliminate known Polish informers, and a nonviolent campaign to thin the ranks of the equally traitorous Volksdeutsche was launched by sending forged letters to Wehrmacht recruiting offices. "The Führer has awakened in me the consciousness of the German community," the bogus letters, signed in the name of individual Volksdeutsche, would state. "I cannot continue any longer to stand by while German brothers are heroically dying. I wish to contribute my services to the glorious German army and herewith solicit the privilege of immediate induction into the Wehrmacht."

As the quality of underground activity improved, a newfound pride and swagger could be perceived in the demeanor of some clandestine operatives. "Their gait and their whole appearance seemed to proclaim to all and sundry, 'Look, I'm a conspirator,'" one partisan recalled. There was a noticeable spike in the defacement of German proclamation posters, particularly of the dreaded red-bordered wanted notices for fugitive conspirators, and walls boasted a proliferation of painted Zs, the Polish first initial of the Union of Armed Struggle, the central underground organization. As for Jewish and

Gentile clandestine publications like Mark Edelman's *Bulletin,* their total numbers skyrocketed to sixty separate titles by the spring of 1940. The largest of these, *Poland Lives,* saw its print run soar from six thousand weekly copies in December 1939 to forty thousand by the time the Gestapo arrested its editor in late May 1940.

The rise in resistance activity had not gone unnoticed in Wawel Castle, the towering medieval fortress perched high atop Krakow where Governor General Hans Frank issued orders for an Extraordinary Pacification Action, Nazi newspeak for a terror campaign intended to crush the rebellious spirit of the Poles.

The crackdown coincided with a massive increase in demand for forced laborers. Now that the fighting had resumed in Western Europe, munitions plants, steel mills, and factories producing tanks, aircraft, and all manner of weapons were operating at full tilt and were in constant need of workers. Since racial laws prohibited the shipment of Jews into the Third Reich, labor quotas had to be filled from the ranks of Gentiles. The Arbeitsamt Labor Office, which occupied the former headquarters of the Agricultural Land Credit Bank across the street from Hanna Mortkowicz-Olczak's bookstore, became one of the most feared addresses in Warsaw. It would process some three hundred thousand Varsovian slave laborers in the coming years, most ripped from their families, shaved bald, affixed with a purple *P* sewn onto their clothes, and sent without warning to distant factories in a foreign country. The German war machine's appetite for workers was so insatiable that the Nazis took to randomly stopping trains and trams and grabbing every able-bodied man on board from the ages of fourteen to sixty. "Horrifying night," the Zionist historian Emmanuel Ringelblum noted in his diary on May 8. "At twilight Poles were seized in every street. Jews had their papers checked to make sure they weren't Christians."

"Some Poles are beginning to wear Jewish armbands" to avoid deportation to the Reich, another diarist wrote in his journal a few days later. So many Christians were suddenly trying to pass themselves off as Jews that German gendarmes began demanding that anyone wearing a Magen David armband speak Yiddish to prove they were not Gentiles.

The far more feared Gestapo, meanwhile, launched its greatest dragnet to date, arresting tens of thousands of potential resistance members over a six-week period. They targeted lawyers, doctors, journalists—all educated "thought leaders." In one day alone in May 1940, sixty-five hundred were snatched from their Warsaw homes and places of work. On another single spring day in 1940, the toll in Warsaw alone was three thousand. Fifteen hundred of those unfortunate detainees were herded into the Light Horse Regiment Barracks and Stables near Simha Ratheiser's house, just south of the Royal Gardens. "Hundreds were lying in the sawdust," one underground member recalled. "SS men marched up and down with whips in their hands, which they used unsparingly."

Boruch Spiegel had a prime window, literally, on the wave of terror. His family's apartment in the Jewish Quarter faced the notorious Peacock Prison, a sprawling tsarist edifice designed in 1835 by Henry Marconi, the same architect who had built Warsaw's most ornate merchant palaces and bank headquarters during the gilded age of the mid-nineteenth century. The Russians had used the huge structure to lock up rebels and political prisoners, and publisher Jacob Mortkowicz had been among the thousands of pro-independence protesters jailed there prior to World War I. After Poland won its independence, Peacock Prison housed common criminals. Now the Gestapo had taken it over, and an endless stream of black vans and tarpaulin-covered gray trucks raced in and out of its gates delivering suspected resistance members. Outside its barbed wire walls, which spanned an entire city block, Boruch saw huge crowds staring desperately at the six-story prison's barred windows, hoping to catch a last glimpse of their relatives. "You could hear them calling. 'I see you, I see you.' Or 'I have the papers.' And from the cell windows, you could hear back, 'Don't stay here. Keep moving. I love you.' "

It was usually a last glimpse. Of the hundred thousand Poles imprisoned at Peacock (almost all of them Christians), thirty-seven thousand were shot on the spot or at Palmiry, the old ammunition depot just north of Warsaw that had been turned into a killing field, while sixty thousand were shipped to various concentration camps, where half of these also perished.

To deal with the growing flow of political prisoners being funneled through Peacock and other detention centers throughout the

General Government, a large new camp two hundred miles south of Warsaw opened in May 1940. It occupied a former military base originally built to quarter Austro-Hungarian troops and stood just outside a small town of twelve thousand inhabitants from which it took its name. The town, like many in southern Poland, was one-third Jewish and had two synagogues, the oldest of which had been built shortly after the arrival of the first Jews to settle there in 1564. The place was called Oswiecim, or in its new, Germanized appellation, Auschwitz.

CHAPTER 13

MARTHA AND ROBERT RUN

In the late spring of 1940, as construction on the walls around the Jewish Quarter quickened, Martha Osnos prepared to be baptized. The Christian cleansing ritual was the final step in obtaining the Gentile travel documents that she and nine-year-old Robert needed for their imminent departure from Poland. Martha had thought of nothing else since her husband, Joseph, contacted her from Bucharest with word that he had arranged a *promessa* from the Romanian government. A *promessa* was a diplomatic promissory note guaranteeing the recipient a permanent visa—if the recipient was allowed to get to the issuing country's nearest embassy. Since Poland no longer legally existed, the nearest Romanian consulate was in Berlin. The *promessa* thus amounted to a request that German authorities allow the bearer of the note to transit through the Third Reich.

*Promessa*s were rarely granted, and were usually reserved for VIPs or the very rich. Martha had no idea how Joseph had managed to obtain one. In fact, it was through a combination of dumb luck and brazen chutzpah. Since arriving in Bucharest in October 1939, Joe Osnos had focused on earning the money he would need to get his family out of Poland. Just as he had initially made a few dollars trading currencies with evacuees along the Polish-Romanian frontier, he used his salesman's talent and gift of gab to go into the used car business in Bucharest, where refugees were selling their vehicles to raise funds.

Joe did well enough trading automobiles that with his first big payout, he was able to hire a tailor to make him an expensive suit of high-quality fabric. Osnos had always been a smart dresser in Warsaw, perhaps even somewhat vain about his appearance. Now he had a plan, and for that plan to succeed, he needed to make a strong first impression.

Looking like an oligarch in his new suit, Joseph marched confidently into the Polish embassy in Bucharest and managed to procure (perhaps through a discreet donation) a difficult-to-obtain *note verbale* formally recommending that the Romanian Foreign Ministry assist him in obtaining exit visas for his family. Armed with the all-important *note verbale,* his fluent French, and a determined, arrogant attitude that matched his finely tailored clothing, Joe Osnos then bluffed his way into the Romanian Foreign Ministry, past gruff security guards and through several layers of protective secretaries, into what he thought was the office of the head of the visa department. But in fact Joe had been too convincing in his displays of self-importance, and he found himself face-to-face with the foreign minister himself. Taken aback by the intrusion, Romania's top diplomat politely but coolly informed Joseph that he was in the wrong office, and called an assistant to remove him. "Another elegant secretary took Joseph to the right place and explained that 'Monsieur le Ministre' was sending Mr. Osnos," Martha later explained in her unpublished journal. "That was understood as 'Mr. Osnos is recommended by Monsieur le Ministre,' and the visas were granted at once. No place in the world thrived on bribery like prewar Romania," she added. "No friends, no fellow refugees in Bucharest would believe that only sheer luck helped in this endeavor."

Joe's unexpected coup, however, still obliged Martha to procure a passport and emigration permits from the German authorities, a nerve-racking process that took months and required large sums of money. A shadowy network of intermediaries and charlatans occupied this fraud-ridden niche, and Martha fell prey to one particularly odious document fixer in Warsw who claimed to have connections with the Gestapo. "He looked like Mephisto himself," she recalled. "Tremendous black eyebrows, everlasting little smile, very well dressed in Tyrolean hat and camel hair coat. He would come every few days assuring me that everything is proceeding fine."

To pay for Mephisto's services, Martha rented her apartment to a prosperous family of assimilated Jews who had fled from Western Poland. The influx of refugees from Western Poland, which had been incorporated directly into the Reich and was being systematically depopulated, had swollen Warsaw's Jewish population from 357,000 in October 1939 to just under 400,000 by mid-1940, and many of the new Jewish arrivals sought out flats in predominantly Gentile neighborhoods, which seemed safer than the Jewish Quarter. For one, there was a far smaller chance of being attacked by pogromists. And the labyrinth of walls being erected around the Quarter made daily life there increasingly inconvenient. By June 1940, after several months of construction, twenty sections of the ten-foot-high barrier had been completed. Some parts were only strung in wire; some were still theoretical, plans on paper. At other points, like the area between New Linden and Forestry Boulevard, the wall meandered unpredictably so that going to a store directly across the street now required a five-block detour. Traversing from Mushroom Street, where Simha Ratheiser had attended high school, to neighboring Electoral Avenue necessitated exiting through one gate and reentering through another, adding twenty minutes to what was otherwise a few minutes' walk.

Life in the Jewish Quarter also involved the constant specter of delousing baths, and their attendant financial costs, which the Nazis now used as the latest means of shaking down the Jewish community. In the name of disease prevention Jews were routinely required to be deloused—or pay bribes not to be deloused—a humiliating process that often involved public nudity.

So Martha had little difficulty finding willing tenants in her Gentile neighborhood. The problem was that the tenant family had moved in with the expectation that she would soon be leaving the country. But as Mephisto's excuses became increasingly improbable, living conditions became increasingly difficult. "One kitchen, one bathroom, and all those people just waiting for me to leave."

Finally, Martha's patience ran out and she went to Mephisto's house to confront him about the lack of progress with her documentation. "[His] home was one room in an otherwise empty and bombed-out apartment: A straw sack in one corner, a string with drying socks and underwear across the room, one chair where the camel hair coat and Tyrolian hat were hanging." Mephisto was a con man. He had no connections with the Gestapo, and had simply been pocketing Martha's money.

Ironically, it was Martha's increasingly impatient tenants who turned out to have connections to the authorities. "By a miracle," she recalled, "they discovered that a cousin of theirs was married to a German girl." He was able to use his influence to get Martha her passport and travel permit. Now all Martha needed was two contradictory documents. To leave Poland, she needed a certificate stipulating that she had paid her emigration dues to the Jewish Community Council; and to transit through Germany, she needed written proof that she was not Jewish, since Jews could not travel on trains or enter the Reich. This Kafkaesque pair of transactions was accomplished first at the *Judenrat,* the German-appointed governing body in the Jewish Quarter, and then at a small private chapel, where in exchange for a few zlotys Martha was sprinkled with holy water and baptized Irene.

By June 5, 1940, as German forces outflanked the vaunted Maginot Line and advanced on Paris, Martha Osnos had circumvented the final bureaucratic barrier to her departure. Emigrants from the General Government were permitted to take only a few clothes and ten Reichsmarks with them when they left the colony. Martha had jewelry that she would later need to sell to finance her travels, including a 1.5 carat diamond engagement ring. While she would never leave something so valuable behind, she was afraid of being searched and arrested for smuggling at the border. So she invited customs officers over to her apartment for a private viewing. Such prescreenings were common during the corrupt Nazi occupation, and always accompanied by gifts. "I prepared a lot of vodka Wyborowa [the premium brand made by the huge Konesser plant in Praga], pickles and kielbasa, set the table and packed my few possessions," Martha recalled. "Everything went very well." The stuffed and pickled customs men happily stamped and sealed her suitcase, obligingly leaving a narrow slit through which she slid her jewels.

On Sunday, June 9, 1940, the day before the French government evacuated Paris and Italy declared war on Britain and France, Martha and Robert Osnos bade a tearful farewell to Janine, Hanna, and little Joanna Mortkowicz and boarded their train to Berlin.

"Berlin was full of sunshine, flowers, decorated with flags," Martha recalled of the German capital, so starkly confident and well kept in comparison to occupied Warsaw. Martha had an elderly uncle in Berlin who had just taken a much younger wife. He lived in the upscale district of Wilmesdorf-Charlottenburg, in the western part of the city not far from the Olympic Stadium built for the 1936 Games. Many Jews used to reside in Wilmesdorf, which was known for its cafés, cabarets, and rich cultural life. Most had fled, however, by the time Martha and Robert arrived at Uncle Mendel's door in the summer of 1940. Mendel remained because his new bride "didn't want to part with her lovely apartment, grand piano and oriental rugs," Martha recalled. "Just a few weeks prior to my arrival she had had face-lifting by surgery, which was rather amazing considering the circumstances."

The welcome Martha and Robert received from their relatives was frosty. "I'm sorry to say that the stay in Berlin was painful and difficult mostly because of the lady of the house," Martha would later comment in her unpublished journal. "She wanted to know if I had brought enough food with me to last through the few days I was supposed to stay."

That Warsaw was being starved to feed Berlin had apparently been lost on Mendel's pampered wife, who examined the few boiled eggs Martha had packed in Poland with evident disdain. Martha was stunned by the pettiness of her relatives, but she was even more worried about the reception she would get from Romanian officials. Romania, after all, was an openly anti-Semitic state, and its government, though professing neutrality, enjoyed friendly relations with the Third Reich.

To Martha's surprise and relief, Romanian consular officials proved gracious and accommodating. "The Romanian consul with whom I spoke French was charming and helpful. He knew immediately that I was Jewish."

The promised visas were ready and issued without delay. Perhaps Joseph Osnos's accidental brush with the foreign minister had expedited the process. The Romanian consul chivalrously announced that he would treat Martha as his "special protégée."

Martha and Robert's Romanian travel documents were all in order. But to get to Bucharest they needed to cross Yugoslavia, and the Yugoslav authorities were not issuing transit visas to Jews. Not a problem, Martha's new diplomatic protector declared gallantly. He called his counterparts at the Yugoslav embassy and assured them over the phone that Martha was Catholic, winking at her "humorously at the same time."

Martha and Robert's Polish passports now held Yugoslav transit stamps. All that remained was to purchase a pair of train tickets with the money Joseph had wired from Bucharest. Martha thought their troubles were over. But when she and Robert went to a Berlin travel agency to inquire about the tickets, an unexpected and potentially serious accounting problem arose: "You couldn't have brought money from Poland for your ticket," the German travel agent said suspiciously. All Poles, including Gentiles, were allowed to take no more than ten marks out of the General Government, and Martha feared that the travel agent suspected that she was either a runaway slave laborer, or, worse, a Jew. Either way he would call the Gestapo. "My husband deposited the money for me with the Romanian consul," Martha lied in a panic. "I will know," the nosy German snapped, reaching for the phone.

"This is the end," Martha whispered to Robert in Polish. "The consul will never say he has the money for me." The chivalrous Romanian not only vouched for Martha, but he also offered to give the suspicious travel agent a letter to that effect and to wire the funds personally.

Martha's euphoria that the Romanian consul had unexpectedly backed her story soon turned to concern. She needed to reimburse him for the tickets, but she had only ten marks. Other than her smuggled jewelry, she was without means. The money Joseph Osnos had wired her from Bucharest for tickets had apparently been lost or stolen in transit. Reluctantly, Martha turned for help to her uncle Mendel, who only weeks earlier had paid for his wife's cosmetic surgery. "There is a war on, money is scarce," her uncle responded.

Martha exploded. She threatened to humiliate Mendel in front of all his neighbors by screaming from the balcony that he was a miser. She would make a scene at the afternoon tea party his haughty wife was organizing. She would never let either of them live down this uncharitable moment. Uncle Mendel grudgingly lent her the fare—albeit only for the cheapest possible seats and on the condition that Joseph Osnos repay him via bank transfer the moment Martha landed in Bucharest.

Thirty-six hours later, having bade farewell to "poor uncle," whom they would never see again, Martha and Robert were in a crowded train compartment full of working-class Germans. Martha's nerves were frayed, her emotions swaying between relief and resentment.

But her belief in humanity was soon restored. "In the evening we went to the dining car, and when I asked for one mark worth of food for my child, they brought two full dinners, and refused even that one mark." At the Yugoslav border, "Robert was promptly sick all over the white uniform of the customs officer." The food and the fright had taken its toll on the boy's digestive system. But they were safely out. "We left Germany!"

Near Zagreb, while transiting through Yugoslavia, Martha found herself once more the beneficiary of generosity. Other passengers gave Robert chocolates and cookies and bought enough snacks for them at the Zagreb station to last through the rest of the journey. The Balkan hospitality continued at the Romanian checkpoint, where Martha wanted to send Joseph a message announcing her impending arrival. "I couldn't find a telegraph office at the frontier station so I asked one of the officials who [spoke] some French whether he could somehow send a telegram for me." Martha had saved her last five marks for this purpose, and she was surprised when one of the border guards refused the money but agreed to wire ahead nonetheless.

Martha had no idea whether the Romanian border guard would keep his promise and cable ahead to Joe. As the train pulled into Bucharest, she scanned the crowds anxiously for her husband. Nearly ten months had passed since she had seen him last. Had he changed? Had he aged? Had he lost any of his swagger and supreme self-confidence? Robert, too, stuck his head out the third-class compartment window, straining for a glimpse of his towering father. And there he stood, tall, tanned, resplendent in a tailored suit, waving a bouquet of white roses.

The Osnoses, at long last, were together again. But their troubles were far from over. As the days turned into weeks and the weeks into months, Martha began to realize what Joseph already knew: They were stuck in Romania—a nation flirting with joining Hitler's cause— with nowhere to go. By autumn 1940, thousands of other Jewish refugees shared their plight, desperately trying to arrange immigration and transit visas to virtually any country that would take them: India, Brazil, Australia, Palestine, Canada.

The United States was notably not among the prime destinations, in spite of being every European refugee's first choice. The United States in 1940 had closed its doors on immigration in general and on Jewish refugees in particular. The very month that Martha had arrived in Bucharest, Breckenridge Long, the assistant secretary of state in charge of visa policies, had issued a classified interdepartmental memo that outlined how U.S. diplomats could circumvent their own government's immigration quotas. "We can delay and effectively stop for a temporary period of indefinite length the number of immigrants into the United States. We could do this by simply advising our consuls to put every obstacle in the way and to require additional evidence and to resort to various administrative devices which would postpone and postpone the granting of the visas."

Jews were singled out by Long's office as a potential threat to U.S. national security. "The Department received information from reliable confidential sources indicating that the Gestapo is using the Jewish Refugee Organization HICEM in getting their agents into the United States. . . . It is suggested that any application for visas of persons to whom this information applies be examined in the light thereof."

Because of Breckenridge Long's policies, the number of Jewish immigrants to the United States fell from 43,450 in 1939, to 23,737 in 1941, to 10,608 the following year, and 4,705 in 1943—a roughly tenfold decrease. Among those whose visa requests were "postponed and postponed" was a Dutch applicant by the name of Otto Frank. Unable to wait, he and his family were forced to go into hiding in Amsterdam, where his daughter Anne began keeping a diary.

Martha and Joseph Osnos also could not afford to wait indefinitely. Romania was rapidly changing. It was still nominally neutral in the summer of 1940, but its territory was being systematically carved up by Hitler and Stalin, and its weak monarch, King Carol II, was under increasing pressure to join the German alliance or find his country partitioned like Poland. In July, the Soviets took most of Bessarabia and Bukovina in the east—provinces that would become modern-day Moldova. Tightening the screws, Hitler cut off half of Transylvania in the north, awarding it to Hungary, and ceded large swaths of Carol II's southernmost territory to Bulgaria.

By September 1940, the Romanian king was forced to abdicate in favor of a pro-Nazi regime that included senior ministers from the virulently anti-Semitic Iron Guard. Martha and Joseph, still without travel documents, helplessly watched as Romania's new fascist rulers passed decree after decree discriminating against Jews. Within a month, half a million German troops were stationed on Romanian soil. In late November 1940, Romania formally joined the Axis powers.

For Martha, Robert, and Joseph Osnos, time had run out. They either had to flee immediately or risk being trapped in Nazi-controlled Romania.

CHAPTER 14

HANNA AND JOANNA HIDE

In late fall 1940, as time was running out for the Osnoses in Bucharest, Warsaw's Jewish community braced for the dreaded announcement that a fully enclosed ghetto would permanently separate Jews and Gentiles. In anticipation of the formal declaration, Isaac Zuckerman, Zivia Lubetkin, and several hundred other young Zionists huddled together in a clandestine conference.

The meeting took place at Isaac's headquarters at 34 Valiant Street, on the other side of the Peacock prison from Boruch Spiegel's apartment, opposite "Serbia," the huge jail's southwestern section reserved for female prisoners. Officially, the Valiant Street premises housed one of the soup kitchens Zivia had established. In reality, the distribution of free daily meals provided a perfect cover for conspiratorial meetings and an illegal school.

"Nowhere else but Valiant Street could we seat forty people for classes," Zuckerman proudly recalled. By classes, he meant high school courses complete with grades and exams and eventually graduation diplomas. Almost all of Poland had moved its educational system underground, to circumvent Nazi edicts that capped formal learning for Gentiles at the sixth grade and banned schooling entirely for Jews. Doctorates, high school diplomas, medical degrees, law and engineering certificates were all still being issued in basements and abandoned factories. The price of this continuing education was paid with the lives of 274 teachers and faculty members tracked down and shot by the Gestapo. But that didn't stop Isaac from holding classes on September 1, 1940, a date that marked not only the traditional commencement of the school year but also the first anniversary of the German invasion of Poland. Enrollment quickly grew to 120 pupils, and the entire operation was financed through the care packages sent by Labor Zionists in free Vilna—sausages, coffee, chocolate, and canned goods that were resold on the black market.

In the early evenings, before the 9 P.M. curfew, the classrooms at Valiant Street turned into training centers for activists from Lublin, Kielce, Krakow, and smaller towns in the General Government. "Holding a seminar next door to Peacock [prison] held an air of the romantic," Zuckerman recalled. "Our guards were stretched out on the balcony, and informed us if Germans passed by."

The seminars served not only to coordinate future activity between cells in various cities and towns, but also to disseminate information and establish policy. This particular meeting was important because it was the first time that the Marxist Hashomer Hatzair ("Young Guard" in Hebrew) had agreed to joint discussions with Zuckerman's Socialist faction. The Young Guard had five hundred members in Warsaw, while Isaac had eight hundred. Together, Isaac proposed, they could be a formidable force. The unification talks were held on October 12, 1940, which fell on Yom Kippur. "Our dining room on Valiant was packed," Zuckerman recalled. "They were sitting on top of one another and on the floor." At a particularly contentious stage of the discussions, when German intentions were being debated, a courier burst into the room. "A ghetto," she cried. Loudspeakers outside—the so-called Barkers affixed to lampposts—had just announced the decision. By month's end, every Jew in Warsaw would be required to move into the walled district.

There was no longer any discussion about German intentions. "They intend to starve us," Zivia Lubetkin declared.

———

As the deadline for all Jews to relocate into the Ghetto approached, the city of Warsaw plunged into chaos. A fifth of the capital's population—113,000 Gentiles and 138,000 Jews—had been served with eviction notices and sent packing. The massive dislocation clogged streets and back alleys and created impassable traffic jams along all the main arteries leading in and out of the condemned Jewish district.

Every rickshaw, taxi, truck, and horse-drawn cart in the city had been hired for the mandatory move, and peasants from distant farms drove their wagons to Warsaw, lured by the exorbitant prices they could charge to transport household goods. Their fees rose daily, then hourly, as the October 31 deadline loomed. Technically, only Gentiles could remove all their belongings. For Jews, a complex set of guidelines limited what could be taken: a fifty-kilogram suitcase for each adult and a thirty-kilo bag for each child, one woolen blanket per person, food and drink for several days, and cooking implements. Those vacating their apartments had to ensure that "a) Open fires are to be extinguished; b) Water and gas supply is to be turned off; c) Electrical fuses are to be disconnected; and d) The keys to the apartment are to be tied together and provided with a tie-on label with the name, city, street, and number of the house of the owner."

The trade in apartments reached such a frenzy that the Germans were forced to extend the relocation deadline to November 15. People frantically searched classified ads and notice boards for any sort of last-minute accommodations. "Reliable, discreet mediation in the exchange of all types of apartments in the Aryan district and behind the walls," the A.S. Consulting Company advertised in the *New Courier*, inviting customers to visit their offices at 26 New Grodzka Street, Suite 1.

All this rendered the real estate market anything but free and unfettered. For crooks and unsavory speculators—the same shady operators who had shaken down war widows and tried to swindle women whose husbands were in POW camps—opportunities for quick profits were nearly boundless. Jews owned 40 percent of what was described as "Category A" property in Warsaw, the best buildings in the choicest locations. Now, on pain of imprisonment, they had to swap their dwellings for dingy walk-ups in the working-class sections of the ghetto being vacated by Gentiles.

Simha Ratheiser recalled the shock of seeing his new living arrangements for the first time. "It was terrible," he said of the apartment his father had sublet on St. George's Street, in the northeastern quadrant of the Ghetto opposite Count Krasinski Park, which was now walled off, its chestnut trees and white gravel paths visible only through the barbed wire coils that capped the red brick dividing barrier. "It was tiny, and dark," he remembered. "There was one room for all of us."

Statistically, the Ratheisers fared slightly better than most Ghetto residents. There were five of them—Simha, his parents, and two sisters—sharing a bedroom, which was one and a half fewer occupants per room than the new Ghetto average. Already four hundred thousand people, and eventually nearly half a million, would be squeezed into the Ghetto's 730 livable acres. As a comparison, in neighboring Jolie Bord, a northern middle-class enclave favored by intellectuals, fifty thousand inhabitants were spread out over an area more than twice that size. In Wola—the big blue-collar district just west of the Ghetto—140,000 residents occupied 4,000 acres.

Simha felt angry and frustrated. He had not wanted to move in the first place. He had wanted to disregard the order, just as he had refused to wear the Magen David armband whenever possible, while his father, who always "followed the crowd," donned the hated vestment, just as he always obeyed all the rules. His mother also balked at moving to the ghetto. Many of Miriam's Gentile friends and neighbors— swayed perhaps by her beauty, perfect Polish, and vivacious personality—had advised her not to go. But Zvi, with his dark beard, yarmulke, and Orthodox wardrobe, could never pass for a Christian. The Ghetto, he argued, echoing a common refrain in the Jewish community, would almost certainly be open. Jews would still be able to leave the ringed district to conduct their affairs, so long as they returned by the 9 P.M. curfew. In the end Zvi prevailed. He was the head of the family, and tradition dictated that the decision was his. Before they left, however, one of the Ratheisers' Gentile neighbors took Miriam aside. "If you are ever in trouble and need help," the neighbor said, "get in touch with us."

———

Janine Mortkowicz never even contemplated moving to the Ghetto. The sixty-five-year-old matriarch had not waited for the November 15 deadline to act. The moment the Nazis announced their intention to seal off the Jewish population, she began to plan. "I don't think it ever crossed her mind to follow the [relocation] order," recalled Joanna. She was not alone. The Germans issued 11,130 arrest warrants for Jews who disobeyed the ghetto decree, including for twelve members of the extended Mortkowicz clan.

"I don't know if there had been a family-wide discussion about it. But everyone decided to stay on the Aryan side," said Joanna, employing the widely used German nomenclature for the Christian parts of Warsaw.

Two factors weighed heavily in favor of staying put: "We had money and we had [Gentile] friends," both of which would be essential for survival. Joanna herself had not initially been subject to the Ghetto relocation order. But the Germans had just tightened race regulations and the criteria by which the Nuremberg Laws determined Jewish origin. Under the new restrictions, Joanna's status as a *mischling,* an individual of mixed parentage still classified as Christian, had been changed to Jewish.

Staying put, however, could not mean remaining at their current address in Old Town Square. The SS knew that Jews lived there, because they had hauled Janine Mortkowicz in for questioning in August. She had packed a toothbrush then, as everyone in Warsaw invariably did when summoned to Gestapo headquarters on Szuch Avenue, because so few people ever walked out freely again.

Janine's Gestapo troubles had apparently stemmed from an innocent housecleaning. Janine had ordered Vincent, their devoted caretaker, to throw out some of the old unsold inventory when they moved into the former printing facilities, and the discarded books had found their way to one of the open-air markets in the Jewish district. Unfortunately, the castoffs included 1905 volumes by Karl Marx—now considered seditious propaganda.

"As she was entering Gestapo headquarters, the doorman insulted her with some anti-Semitic abuse," Joanna recalled. Far from cowering, Janine opened her own interrogation by going on the offensive and berating the investigating officer for the doorman's offensive re marks. "She stood up and in a loud voice proclaimed that she was proud of her heritage, that her father was from Vienna, that he held a doctorate, and that she was unaccustomed to such rude treatment." Perhaps it was her fluent German, or the sight of such a tiny, gray-haired grandmother daring to admonish him, but the amused Gestapo officer was obviously taken aback. Janine was not sent to Serbia, the women's section of the Peacock prison. She was released and returned home, more determined than ever not to bend to the will of the Nazis.

Remaining on the "Aryan" side would not be easy for Janine, Hanna, and little Joanna. Jews in hiding needed to invent new identities and find new places to live. They required a constant source of income to support themselves. And they had to rely almost entirely on the friendship and protection of Gentiles.

The outlines of the newly formed Ghetto formed a squat T with a large notch carved into its wide base. Its surface area covered just under a thousand acres, roughly the size of New York City's Central Park. On the morning of November 16, 1940, its four hundred thousand inhabitants discovered to their shock and horror that the Ghetto's twenty-two gates would not be open, as they had been led to believe. They were now permanently shut, guarded by German gendarmes and the despised Polish Blue Police, who permitted only special pass holders to exit on official business.

Panic spread throughout the sealed district that morning, with neighbors waking one another to deliver the grim news, and word quickly reached Zivia Lubetkin and Isaac Zuckerman. Zivia was not surprised. She was by nature less hopeful than the gregarious and perennially cheerful Isaac. But even to Zuckerman, the move had not been entirely unexpected. Together, they called an emergency meeting to address the situation. In some ways, the Ghetto made clandestine life easier: There was no longer a need to post lookouts on balconies and straircases since there were no Gentiles snooping about. The expulsion of Christians had also left Zuckerman free to hire a loyal Jewish building superintendent in place of the Gentile who had previously occupied the position. Isaac no longer had to worry about being denounced to the Gestapo, who frequently kept doormen and concierges on the payroll. The new man was a Zionist. "As soon as the Poles were sent out we grabbed that job," Zuckerman recalled. "The porter kept a list of residents so we knew everything. On the top floor," where Isaac and Zivia lived, "was a bell attached to the concierge's lodge by a concealed string, and a ring for me meant an alarm."

The new isolation and the lack of potential Gentile informants made security arrangements easier in the Ghetto, but contact with the outside world became far more difficult. "We cannot allow ourselves to be cut off," Zuckerman warned. Until then, communicating with other Zionist cells throughout Poland had been relatively easy. Isaac himself had toured the German-occupied western territories extensively, and delegates from smaller towns had routinely come to Warsaw. This was no longer possible, as closed Ghettos now trapped Jews in all the major population centers.

"We need to know what is happening to our brothers and sisters in the rest of the country," Zivia declared. This was important not only out of concern for the fate of fellow Jews and Zionists, but for their own safety as well. Events in other cities often presaged the future in Warsaw. The capital tended to follow Lodz, because that big industrial center, now renamed Litzmannstadt, was annexed directly to the Reich, fast-tracked for Germanization. The hated *Treuhandstelle* had started its confiscatory work in Lodz, seizing the 2,300 mostly Jewish-owned textile mills that had given the city its nickname, the "Manchester of the East." The Lodz ghetto had also been established and sealed months ahead of Warsaw. If one could keep abreast of events there, one could predict what lay in store for the former Polish capital.

To stay connected, Zivia proposed forming a team of couriers who would travel surreptitiously from ghetto to ghetto maintaining links. For this purpose she would employ women almost exclusively. Women traveling alone were less likely to arouse suspicion in Nazi-occupied Poland, since so many men were now absent, having been relocated to Siberian gulags or German POW, concentration, or labor camps. And in a part of the world where most males were uncircumcised, female liaison agents could not be betrayed by the surgical cut that distinguished all Jewish men. So Zivia, who would be in charge of recruiting the "liaison women," set out to search for potential couriers.

"They had to have an Aryan appearance, speak Polish well, and act a certain way," she recalled, "and we did not have many candidates that fit those criteria."

Few Jews "looked good," the expression widely used in the Ghetto to denote those with Slavic appearances. And fluency posed another serious issue. In the last census conducted before the war, only 5 percent, or 19,300 out of 353,000 Warsaw Jews, classified themselves as native Polish speakers. While many of these may have been proficient, "most Polish Jews could not speak Polish well," according to the American Holocaust scholar Nechama Tec, herself a native of Warsaw and a Holocaust survivor.

Zivia's recruitment difficulties were not restricted to physiognomy and language. They were also cultural, relating to a lack of familiarity with prevailing customs and mannerisms. "These differences permeated all aspects of life," explains Tec (whose many works on the war include *Defiance,* the story of Polish-Jewish partisans that became a Hollywood blockbuster starring James Bond actor Daniel Craig). "For centuries Poles and Jews lived apart and in different worlds. Whatever contacts there had been between them were commercial rather than social. Partly because of this, each felt like a stranger in the world of the other."

Just as the Polish Underground might find it challenging to locate agents who could pass as Jewish, converse knowledgeably with a rabbi, set a kosher table, or discuss Zionist politics, Zivia struggled to find candidates able to field innocent questions about the Catholic catechism, Polish politics, or literature.

Zivia herself was disqualified by her appearance. Her features were Semitic, her hair and skin tone too dark—unlike Isaac, who was often told by fellow Zionists, "Your Aryan face is worth its weight in gold, worth a hundred thousand zlotys."

Isaac's problem was his accent. "It was terrible," one of his fellow combatants recalled. Zuckerman's Polish was inflected with heavy traces of both Yiddish and Vilnoese, the lilting, drawn-out dialect from his native Vilna. The Vilnoese helped mask the Yiddish, but Isaac had to be constantly vigilant, like an actor permanently onstage, since one mispronunciation, one slip of the tongue, could give him away.

So far, the only couriers Zivia had been able to find with any experience were the Plotnicka sisters, Frumka and Hancia. It was Hancia who had been sent by her older sister Frumka to Lvov in December 1939 to plead for Zivia's return. And it had been through Frumka as well that Isaac had learned a few months later that Zivia needed him back in Warsaw. Frumka was fair and light-haired, tall and leggy—she "looked good." Her biggest drawback was that she didn't "sound good." "Her Polish wasn't fluent," worried Isaac.

There was one final obstacle in Zivia's courier plan: travel documents. Up until now, Zionists had used either no identification papers whatsoever or very crudely forged ones. For the courier plan to succeed, their amateurish operation would have to become far more professional.

CHAPTER 15

SIMHA AND BORUCH PAY THE BILLS

The most immediate effect of sealing the Ghetto was an astonishing spike in the cost of basic foodstuffs. Overnight, the price of a kilo of potatoes tripled, coal more than doubled, and every other staple rose by at least 100 percent. "There are long queues in front of every food store, and everything is being bought out," the historian and Ghetto archivist Emmanuel Ringelblum wrote on November 19, 1940. "On the first day after the Ghetto was closed, many Christians brought bread for their Jewish acquaintances and friends. This was a mass phenomenon," he noted—which ended abruptly three days later, when the Germans shot a Pole for transferring a sack of flour over the wall. The message of that public execution was clear: The sealed district was to be cut off from the city's meager food supply, just as Zivia Lubetkin had predicted.

The Jewish community reacted instantaneously, in near-universal defiance of the food import ban. In just a few days a massive smuggling industry sprang up, incorporating thousands of people on a full-time basis on both sides of the wall. Some acted individually, others collectively. Some were organized around tightly knit family units, others in sprawling and sophisticated for-profit ventures that reached deep into the countryside and produced huge fortunes. These smuggling networks provided an estimated 80 to 90 percent of the food consumed in the Warsaw Ghetto over the next two years.

Simha Ratheiser, like many other Jewish children and teenagers, who were naturally more adept than adults at scaling walls and squeezing through narrow openings, turned to smuggling to help his family survive. This assumption of responsibility was perhaps his first act of adulthood. Until then he had never worked—even in his father's former store. And he had never apprenticed for a trade, like spats maker Boruch Spiegel. He had not needed to. His parents were sufficiently well off that he had received a small allowance, like many ordinary middle-class teens: new pants or shoes when his old ones wore out, pocket money for the movies, or perhaps a bike for his birthday.

"It was not at all uncommon for ten- or twelve-year-olds to support entire families," Ratheiser recalled of the part kids played in the burgeoning ghetto black market, where markups could be thirty-, forty-, or fiftyfold from prewar prices, and two to three times the rate charged in the rest of Warsaw.

"Getting out of the Ghetto was not that difficult," Simha explained—at least not initially. The district was not hermetically sealed; the wall was actually quite porous. It ran through a great many buildings, where windows and doors had been sloppily bricked up, or where the preexisting fire walls between apartments acted as makeshift boundaries, leaving gaps in cellars and attics or between structures. "At Goat Street smuggling is through a door in a wall bordering on the Aryan side," Emmanuel Ringelblum noted in his journal. "It costs 5 zlotys to pass through. The Jewish owner of the apartment is making a fortune." Alternatively, trams traversed the Jewish Quarter, and for a few zlotys' bribe one could board any of the municipal lines that ran through the Ghetto. With money, the gates were effectively open.

In the subtle generational power shift that began with the closure of the Ghetto's twenty-two gates, it was the child smugglers who made the most significant mark early on. Often they were simply catapulted over the wall, or pushed through some narrow crack, with a shopping list and money or articles of value to trade. How parents felt about entrusting the family finances to sixth or seventh graders is hard to imagine. Most of them never went farther than a few blocks into so-called Aryan territory, but some, like Simha, traveled by commuter train far into the countryside to obtain better deals.

Seventy to 80 percent of the food sold in Warsaw outside the Ghetto was already smuggled, with hefty risk premiums priced in—a consequence of German decrees barring the free flow of all perishable goods in occupied Poland. Poland's role was to feed Germany, not itself, and the General Government's colonial overseers had set ruinous requisition quotas on all farming districts. Peasants had to relinquish their crops and their dairy, pork, and poultry production to Nazi agencies for export to the Reich, and anyone caught hoarding grain or eggs faced arrest and sometimes summary execution. The delivery of food to Polish cities was strictly controlled through ration cards issued monthly, and it could fluctuate wildly. During one brief and bountiful month, for instance, Ghetto residents were allotted a daily high of 400 calories, while Gentiles were given far more generous rations equivalent to 1,377 daily calories. In other months Jews got next to nothing, while the rest of Warsaw's 1.3 million residents received a mere 385 calories each.

At official ration rates, the entire city would soon have starved. Fortunately for the inhabitants of Poland's metropolitan regions, farmers proved adept at concealing food from the rapacious Germans and sneaking it into towns. Thanks to the thriving black market, food was widely available in all Polish cities. It was just incredibly expensive. A kilogram of sugar, for instance, purchased with ration cards, retailed for 1.6 zlotys at official prices. On the black market the same kilo sold for 65 zlotys. In the Ghetto—where the wall now added another level of risk, an additional transport and payoff premium, and one more set of intermediaries—it could easily cost twice that sum. Meat cost the most because animals had to be brought in alive, to conform to kosher butchering laws. This was accomplished by placing mobile ramps on either side of the wall. Cattle were walked over the wall while the Blue Police or German gendarmes were paid to look the other way. Milk was relatively cheaper, since it was pumped—by the cisternload—through reconfigured plumbing or drainage pipes in buildings that straddled the boundary. Dairy products thus benefited from both economies of scale and discretion, requiring fewer bribes.

The peculiarities of the underground agro-economy quickly became apparent to Simha. To cut out the middlemen, he started traveling to outlying villages and buying directly from farmers. "I'd jump on and off moving trains to get there," he recalled. His parents opposed this activity, especially since his mother was getting food from her old neighborhood friends. Like hundreds of others, she bribed guards at the gates to let her out and then back in. Simha's smuggling route was riskier, but it saved the cost of the bribe. "I'd wait for the forced labor gangs to march in or out of the ghetto," he recalled. Every day hundreds of Jews were taken out to clean streets, clear snow, fill in potholes, or work at construction sites on the other side. Simha would wait for the right moment, when the guards were distracted, and melt into the moving groups. His Slavic appearance, ironically, often worked against him in these instances. "The other Jews would think I was a Polish smuggler, and threaten to denounce me to the police. I would have to recite a prayer in Hebrew to prove I was one of them."

Taking trains was also far riskier than shopping in Warsaw, but Simha felt comfortable in the now exclusively Gentile milieu. "I don't remember being frightened or nervous. I was used to being among Poles. It was not a big deal to me."

Though he did not fear being exposed as a Jew, there was still the constant danger of being robbed or caught up in one of the Arbeitsamt's forced labor roundups, which often targeted trains whenever the Labor Office fell short of its human export quota. By the end of 1940, 798,000 Poles—all Christians—were already working as slave laborers in Germany, in conditions resulting in ever greater death tolls. To slow the brutal deportations, the Polish Underground launched a concerted campaign against the Arbeitsamt. Labor offices across the General Government were torched at night. The agency's headquarters in the former Land Credit Bank building across the street from the Mortkowiczes' bookstore was firebombed in an unsuccessful attempt to destroy the central labor registry records. Huge billboards enticing labor draftees to COME WITH US TO GERMANY were defaced to read DON'T COME WITH US TO GERMANY. And tens of thousands of false identity papers were issued to people dodging the draft.

The rebellion led the Nazis to redouble their efforts to catch evaders, and every time Simha boarded a train, he faced the prospect of being herded into a cattle car. Still, the rewards outweighed the risks. Going to the source of food saved considerable sums. "I remember the smell of the huge round loaves, freshly baked," he recalled of the bread he bought from peasant bakers, which was fresh, free of the sawdust often found in Warsaw's bread, and a hefty two feet in diameter. "One [loaf] was enough to feed a whole family." What Simha's family did not eat could be resold inside the walls at a substantial profit, which could finance further trips to the country and put more food on the table.

"Apparently I was rather successful," Ratheiser recalled of his smuggling expeditions. "Friends and relatives used to come to our apartment for a bowl of soup, a sign that there was at least some food in our house."

Simha did not give much thought to his trips to the "other side." He was just doing what he could to help his family. The handsome sixteen-year-old did not realize that he had become the man of the house and that he was gaining invaluable training that would soon serve a greater Jewish cause.

A deceptive calm reigned in the newly isolated Jewish Quarter as the winter of 1941 set in. Jews, for the first time since the invasion, were left relatively unmolested. Germans had little reason to enter the sealed district, other than to deliver inmates to Peacock Prison, trips they used as opportunities to run down pedestrians with their trucks. But the random beatings, the petty harassments and daily humiliations, had significantly decreased now that Jews were being left largely to themselves. The community was even policing itself, thanks to a newly created law enforcement agency staffed entirely by Jewish police officers.

Smuggling continued in ever more sophisticated forms, and the underground economy rapidly grew to encompass virtually every branch of commerce that operated outside the Ghetto walls. Christian entrepreneurs smuggled raw materials—leather, textiles, dyes, tobacco leaves, sheet metal, cocoa—into the ghetto, and smuggled out finished products—chocolate, shirts, shoes, cigarettes and cigarette lighters, canned goods, watches, even jewelry—for resale on the black market. The scale of these illicit enterprises soon became mind-boggling, involving not only mom-and-pop shops but entire tanneries and canneries and factories with delivery trucks and hundreds of employees. Insurance companies offered policies on the safe delivery of goods, with premiums based on distance covered and delivery location and depending on the degree of bribability of the relevant officials. These indispensable payoffs lubricated every stage of the operation, and bribes were earning corrupt German overseers the equivalent of hundreds of thousands of dollars monthly.

For Boruch Spiegel and his family, the clandestine work offered a lifeline. They had been in desperate straits when the market for spats dried up following the 1939 invasion. While Boruch and his older brother were in the Soviet zone, his father had survived by selling everything of value—the Singer sewing machine, the Persian carpets—everything but his most prized possession: his violin. Upon the brothers' return to Warsaw, the Bund had helped feed the Spiegel family through its network of soup kitchens. These were open only to Bundists, Boruch explained. "The Zionists had theirs. We had ours. All the groups looked after their own."

Around the time of the creation of the Ghetto, Boruch's father was contacted by a prewar business acquaintance, a Gentile by the name of Stasiek, the Polish equivalent of "Stan." Stan had a proposal. He would provide Boruch and his father with wood blocks, which they would carve into clogs that Stan would smuggle out and sell on the black market. Clogs were in high demand in Warsaw because they were the only form of footwear, other than the knee-high military boots worn by the rich, being produced under Nazi occupation.

The pay Spiegel and his father received for each pair of clogs was small, but it was enough to buy a small piece of chicken once every few weeks, a kilo or two of *kasza gryczana,* the buckwheat cereal that was the staple of the Varsovian wartime diet, and occasionally a little lard to fatten the thin soups they ate as most main courses. The items they bought were almost all smuggled, as was nearly 90 percent of all the food in the Warsaw Ghetto. As a result, the average Ghetto resident, according to *Judenrat* (Jewish Council) calculations, actually consumed 1,125 daily calories in early 1941 instead of the allotted 184. Middle-class Jews had an average intake of 1,400 calories a day. The poorest subsisted on only 785.

It was hardly a time of plenty, but Boruch, like many others, would remember this early ghetto period with melancholy fondness; in Isaac Zuckerman's words, it was a time "of flourishing autonomy." The phones worked. Mail was delivered. Shops were open. And prewar billboards, advertising shampoo, floor wax, "Carmel" Palestinian wines, and Wrigley's spearmint gum, lent the district an air of normalcy. "The innumerable confectionery stores that have sprung up lately," the resident historian Emmanuel Ringelblum remarked in early 1941, "give a distorted picture of the Ghetto."

The crowds on the streets were now denser, and more shabbily dressed. But people seemed more relaxed, more willing to linger at a shop window or stop and converse with a neighbor. The change in attitude in the Ghetto could even be heard. The Yiddish that reverberated throughout the district was no longer hushed and halting, but louder, brasher, more confident and rapid-fire—impenetrable to outsiders once more, as it had so famously been before the war. "It would take even a fluent Yiddish speaker coming from the more distant parts of Poland to Warsaw quite a bit of time to get acquainted with the extremely fast and economical way of speech in which sentences were reduced to single words, single words to syllables and syllables to phenomes," Ewa Geller, a philologist at the University of Warsaw, explained. "Their speech reflected the pitch and marrow of Jewish Warsaw, its very busy, hasty and pragmatic way of life."

Warsaw's Jews were trapped, and yet many felt paradoxically freer within their walls, within their "Garden City," as the wits had sardonically dubbed the district because not a blade of grass grew inside the walls. "Things were better," Boruch recalled. "We even thought that perhaps the worst was behind us, that we would be left alone."

Boruch was unusually upbeat during this period, in large part because he had met someone who would play a major role in his life. Her name was Chaika Belchatowska, and she was exceedingly pretty, with dark bangs, high cheekbones, and almond eyes. She lived on Dragon Street in the poorer northwest quadrant of the Ghetto, closer to the main Jewish cemetery and the Skra Stadium. Chaika was twenty-one, the same age as Boruch, and also a Bundist, though she was more active in the organization than he was. She was part of a "fiver," a cell that distributed underground newsletters like the *Bulletin,* printed by Mark Edelman.

"Dating in the Ghetto was different," Spiegel recalled. "I obviously couldn't afford to go to dinner and a movie. But we had a very rich cultural life." Many of the theater district's two dozen prewar playhouses, almost all located inside the Ghetto, had reopened to cater to the newly rich smugglers and other well-off residents. On Valiant Street, not far from Isaac Zuckerman's headquarters, the Eldorado featured a musical comedy called *The Rabbi's Little Rebecca,* starring Regina Sugar, or Cukier, as she was known in Polish. The twelve-hundred-seat Yiddish Artistic Theater, built in 1913 by the legendary stage star Ester Rachel Kaminski with money she earned from an American tour, put on some subsidized Molière plays and a dramatic adaptation of *The Brothers Karamazov,* also at cut-rate prices. The Azazel on New Linden Street premiered a new play, *Got Fun Nerume,* directed by and starring Adam Samberg.

But what Boruch, the lifelong music lover, looked forward to most were the free concerts. More than eighty former members of the Warsaw Philharmonic, the Opera Chamber Orchestra, and the Polish Radio Orchestra were in the Ghetto, accompanied by some of Poland's most celebrated prewar composers and conductors, two winners of the Chopin prize, awarded annually to the nation's top pianist, and solo violinists like Ludwig Holtzman, twice recognized as Polish concertmaster of the year. The musicians formed the Jewish Philharmonic Orchestra, under the patronage of Jewish Council chairman Adam Czerniakow, and staged concerts at venues such as the Femina movie theater on Forestry Street, the Melody Palace on Rymar Street, and the Great Hall, near the Children's Hospital on Sienna Street. "At those concerts, you temporarily forget that there was a war, a ghetto," Spiegel recalled. "To me they were an escape."

CHAPTER 16

JOANNA CAUSES TROUBLE

Resistance, like crime, tends to capture the public imagination when it is organized. But in Warsaw in the winter of 1941, individual acts of defiance best defined the fighting spirit of the Jewish community. Within the eleven miles of walls that ringed the Ghetto, tens of thousands of people participated in the massive underground economy, actively undermining Gestapo attempts to deprive them of a livelihood. They educated their children in secret schools, printed and distributed clandestine newspapers, and thwarted Nazi efforts to starve them by engaging in near-universal smuggling.

Beyond the walls, thousands more sabotaged the German master plan; some, like the Osnoses, ran as far and as fast as providence would allow; others, like the three generations of Mortkowicz women, refused to submit to Ghetto decrees.

Hanna, Joanna, and Janine had gone into hiding at the suburban estate of a family friend. It was unobtrusively located about ten miles west of Warsaw, in what was then the sparsely populated countryside. The property was large, spanning several hundred acres, with a main manor house, many outbuildings and dependencies, a large barn, animal pens, apple orchards, and a small church whose belfry dominated the rolling bucolic terrain. Joanna, who was now almost seven years old, vividly remembers sledding on those hills throughout the long winter and running through wildflowers when the snow finally melted in the spring of 1941 and the marshy land came to life. She remembers the nuns who rented part of the estate, and going to church for the sake of blending in, saying grace and reciting daily prayers that soon became as natural to her as to any Catholic child in Poland. Seventy years later, she could still recite them all from memory.

The hideout had been arranged by Monika Zeromska, the daughter of Poland's Hemingway, who along with her mother now ran the renamed Mortkowicz bookstore, fronting for Hanna and Janine. Every few weeks Monika brought money from the store, which was doing shockingly well. Varsovians were traditionally big readers, but during the war, with curfews, no radio, and precious little outside entertainment, books became one of the sole means of escape. People pooled their money to purchase copies they then shared among friends or neighbors, and the Mortkowicz bookstore flourished. (It helped that its biggest prewar competitor, Gebetner & Wolff, had been Germanized and served Nazi and colonial officials, selling only German-language books.)

Monika Zeromska resembled Hedy Lamarr, with dark doe eyes that hinted at innocent mischief. This was fitting because Zeromska, like many Poles, led a double life, as Joanna eventually discovered. The dawning realization that there was more to Monika and to the estate where the Mortkowiczes were hiding occurred over many months and a series of small incidents. Joanna, like most kids her age, was insatiably curious and prone to exploration, which brought her into conflict with the estate's severe caretaker, Thaddeus Glaser. "I was mortally afraid of Mr. Glaser," she recalled. "He was often angry with me, especially when I peeped into the barn."

The ill-tempered caretaker kept chasing Joanna away from the barn because a series of tunnels and secret chambers ran underneath it. "Conspirators, underground agents, and saboteurs used it," Joanna later learned. "So it was not surprising that he got mad when I was jumping around above their heads, or when I romped through the attic, where clandestine documents were stored." The estate, as it turned out, was a major hub of the Polish Resistance, which like its Jewish counterparts was slowly coalescing in 1941, still fractious and divided along prewar political lines but making strides toward centralization and unification. One joint body, the Foreign Affairs Department, met regularly at the estate to coordinate policy with the government in exile in London, and there were enough weapons cached about the property to arm a battalion.

"Not bad for a hideout," Joanna would later laugh about the place she called home for the next year.

Luck, like resistance, takes many forms. A chance encounter, an unconscious decision, a reflexive motion or misperception could spell doom or deliverance.

For Joanna's cousins, salvation came in the unlikely form of an earthquake. The Osnoses had been stranded in Romania with no real prospects for emigration, fighting a losing battle against time and the looming anti-Semitic crackdowns promised by the pro-Hitler authorities. Like thousands of other Polish Jews in Bucharest, they were ready to go anywhere.

All roads, however, seemed to lead through Turkey. Every other potential escape route was controlled by either Berlin or Moscow. The Turks were still nominally neutral, theoretically in a position to grant Jews transit visas through their sovereign territory. But they weren't particularly inclined to do so—at least not at a price that Joseph could afford. He had tried repeatedly to get an audience with Turkish consular officials and had been rebuffed on every occasion. Not easily put off, Joseph came up with a different strategy. He rented a room in a villa next to the Turkish embassy and moved there with Martha and Robert. The proximity, he hoped, might lead to a chance encounter: bumping into a diplomat on the street, or in the garden—any opportunity to strike up a neighborly conversation and to achieve socially what could not be done officially. To a large degree, Joseph made his own luck. But his plan did benefit from a little "help from God himself," in Martha's opinion.

At 3:30 in the morning on November 10, Joseph, Martha, and Robert were rocked from their beds by an earthquake that measured

7.7 on the Richter scale. The quake lasted five terrifying minutes, leveling large parts of Bucharest, and its shock waves were felt as far east as Kiev and as far west as Marseilles. The city's tallest building, the thirteen-story Carlton Hotel, collapsed, killing 267 guests, as did the roof of the Royal Palace, home of Romania's recently deposed monarch. Fires from oil reservoirs and burst pipelines raged uncontrollably, while soldiers raced to extract thousands of injured residents trapped in the rubble.

The Osnoses escaped unhurt, running out into the street in their pajamas, where the disheveled Turkish ambassador had also fled, wearing little more than a bathrobe. In the dusty chaos, with gas explosions echoing in the background, Joseph shrewdly made sure that the traumatized Turkish envoy was well attended to in his time of need. "Two days later we had a transit visa," Martha said.

They departed from the Romanian port city of Constanta, on the shores of the Black Sea, southwest of Odessa. The tramp steamer that ferried them to Istanbul was crammed with Polish refugees, both Jewish and Gentile. The weather was torrid, the waves high, and the choppy twenty-four-hour crossing felt endless to the seasick passengers. In Istanbul, a boat carrying a group of illegal Jewish refugees had sunk in the harbor, and irate port officials were searching the stormy waters for survivors to arrest. When the ship carrying the Osnoses docked, angry customs officers checked for illegal Jews. Joseph and Martha had legitimate papers, but their transit visa was valid for only twenty-four hours. If they remained in Turkey any longer, they were told, they would be deported back to Romania. "It seemed impossible to accomplish in a few hours all we had to do," Martha recalled. "We wanted to go to Palestine or be able to stay in Istanbul, but everything had to be arranged immediately."

They were exhausted, in the midst of a strange and alien town whose language they did not understand and whose warren of winding streets invited disorientation. And every path to assistance was proving a dead end. The Polish consulate, representing the London government in exile, was apologetic that it could not help. The Jewish Relief Agency provided a meal at the luxurious Park Hotel but was otherwise occupied with fishing bodies of drowned refugees out of the harbor. They could arrange for young Robert to go to Palestine on a so-called *kinder* (children's) transport, but the family would have to split up, and Martha would not contemplate such a separation.

The Osnoses were running out of options. It was pouring rain and after midnight—with only a few hours left before their enforced 6:00 a.m. departure deadline—by the time they were directed to a seedy nightclub, where help could be purchased. It was "known for all kinds of guides and *machers*," Martha recalled, so Joseph would have to place their last hopes in the hands of unsavory fixers and smugglers.

The Osnoses wanted to go by boat to Cyprus and then Palestine, like countless other Jewish refugees. But at the seedy bar, a cursory negotiation had all but eliminated any hope of buying the required British visas. The documents were far too expensive to purchase on the black market. That left a land crossing as their only option, and Iraq as the closest British protectorate. Iraqi visas were far easier to obtain legally, because London was less fearful of an Arab rebellion there, whereas in Jerusalem, the Grand Mufti was stirring up popular resentment against Jewish immigration, communicating openly with Nazi agents who were promising aid from Berlin if the Palestinians switched sides and rose up against the English.

Reaching Iraq posed its own difficulties. It required traveling through Syria, which was under the control of the Vichy regime, the French Nazi puppet government that deported Jews. The Osnoses could get around that hurdle; they all carried forged baptismal certificates. What they couldn't falsify were their Polish passports, and for Joe Osnos this was a serious problem. "Since Joseph was a Pole of military age, we would not be allowed to have a transit visa," Martha explained, "because [once in British territory] he would be able to reach England and join the free Polish army."

The only other way from Turkey to Iraq was the smuggler's route: a weeklong raft trip down the Tigris River to the town of Mosul. It was dangerous and costly, and the Tigris was temperamental at that time of the year, prone to floods and bouts of roiling whitewater. Martha envisioned ten-year-old Robert being swept away by currents, her raft capsizing, breaking up into a thousand pieces. She would not risk it. Better to take their chances on the Syrian train, Martha argued. At worst, they would be turned away at the border when their lack of visas was discovered, which was certainly still preferable to a watery grave.

And so with only hours to spare before their Turkish transit visas expired, the Osnoses made their way to the train station, hoping to bluff their way onto the Syrian-bound Taurus Express. As luck would have it, the French colonial commissioner was on the very train they boarded. Syrian officials were so preoccupied with fawning over the Vichy representative that no one paid attention to the Jewish family huddled in the dark, windowless third-class compartment at the unfashionable end of the Taurus Express. They crossed the Syrian border unnoticed and no one challenged them when the train continued on its journey to Iraq. Martha, Joseph, and Robert arrived in Baghdad twenty-four hours later, overwhelmed by the generosity of their Arabic fellow travelers. "They constantly would feed Robert and me by stuffing us with their fat fingers, either from their own provisions or buying at the stations little baskets with colored and decorated hard-boiled eggs. They didn't even let us peel them," Martha fondly recalled. "They would peel them and then only feed us."

Baghdad, Martha recalled less fondly, "was the most miserable capital we ever saw: the dirt, the smell of open urinals, mutton grease and cooking turnips on streetcorners; crowds of fierce looking men, especially Kurds whose matted hair mixed with the long fringes of their enormous turbans; women covered completely with their black robes. Robert said 'Everyone is in mourning here.'"

Baghdad may not have been beautiful. But it was beyond Adolf Hitler's reach. For the first time since the war began, Martha, Robert, and Joseph Osnos could relax. They were safe on British soil.

Back in Warsaw, the relatively mild winter had passed, but the spring of 1941 brought a renewed chill. The measure of autonomy that residents of the Jewish Quarter enjoyed during the initial period after the Ghetto's formation was over. The Nazis and their various proxy organs—the Blue Police, the new Jewish Police—once more resumed tormenting Jews.

The Jewish Police stormed Isaac Zuckerman's Zionist clubhouse on the last day of Passover, in mid-April 1941. The raid took place in the evening, just after curfew, and caught everyone by surprise.

Dozens of Jewish police officers dressed in civilian garb, with their peaked black caps topped by a blue Star of David and the identifying orange armbands that constituted their makeshift uniforms, suddenly burst through the gate of the Valiant Street tenement.

Fanning out through the courtyard, they sealed all entrances and staircases, using the stubby truncheons that served as their only permitted weapons to trap everyone inside. The young Zionists on the third floor of the large apartment building had no time to escape. They had not anticipated trouble from the relatively benign Jewish police agency, formally known as the Order Service, or *Judischer Ordungsdienst* in German.

The law enforcement body had been created by German fiat during the 1940 Ghetto closure. It answered nominally to the Jewish Council chairman, Adam Czerniakow, a portly, urbane engineer and polyglot who favored bow ties and read classics late into the night to ward off insomnia. He was a gentle, cultured, and well-intentioned man, bald and bespectacled, "the picture of bourgeois respectability," as were most senior Jewish police officers, many of whom were attorneys before the war. Most of the sixteen-hundred-strong force hailed from an upper-middle-class background. "Many used bribery and influential connections to obtain a prized appointment to the force," noted one Ghetto chronicler. "People with college educations, professional men, former white-collar workers, idle and sheltered sons of the wealthy rushed to get into the precious uniform."

Like many other Ghetto residents, Zuckerman had not initially viewed the Order Service as a threat. The agency had enjoyed widespread support early on under the principle that it was better for Jews to police themselves than to have the Gestapo rampaging through the sealed district. Jewish officers provided a protective buffer between the populace and their German masters and acted as conduits for greedy German guards, funneling millions of dollars in bribes that kept the Ghetto's lifeline flowing. The temptation for Order Service employees to participate in this institutionalized corruption proved powerful. Jewish police officers soon began dressing in expensive tailored suits and demanding "contributions" from smugglers, factory owners, and homeowners wishing to avoid delousing and disinfection. They took to wearing the newly fashionable knee-high military boots that were the most ostentatious mark of war profiteers in Warsaw, and their reputation as honest brokers began to erode.

Isaac Zuckerman was not present at the Valiant Street clubhouse when the raid took place. He and Zivia Lubetkin had stolen off to another apartment that evening so they could spend some time together alone. The two had fallen for each other, which was not unusual in conspiratorial circles, with so many teenagers and college-age leaders sharing secrets and close quarters. What was unusual about their budding romance was that both initially seemed intent on keeping their affair discreet—not an easy task in the overcrowded Jewish district.

When Zuckerman got word of the raid, he rushed to Valiant Street, where the police were herding young Zionists into the courtyard. "I heard cries and shouts. They gathered about ten people from our commune." The sweep, Isaac already suspected, had nothing to do with any of the conspiratorial activity that went on at the clubhouse, or the Gestapo would have been there. The Jewish Police were not tasked with rooting out the Underground. Instead, Isaac's Young Pioneers were being led off to the Jewish Council's Labor Department, another extremely controversial institution whose reputation was rapidly deteriorating. Like the Jewish Police, it had been established at the behest of the Germans to supply manpower for the colonial administration. The Nazis provided the Jewish Council with daily requests for laborers, and the Council supplied the specified number of workers, drawn from a draft lottery of Ghetto inhabitants. Wealthy residents could pay a special labor avoidance tax to have their names struck from the lists, which did not sit well with socialist groups like the Bund or the Labor Zionists. But the imperfect system was preferable to having the Germans randomly snatching people, terrorizing the entire community in the process.

The Nazi appetite for forced labor, after a brief lull, had once more become ravenous. By spring of 1941, well over a million Polish slave laborers had been shipped off to work in munitions plants in Germany—a number that would peak at 1.6 million by war's end—and nearly a hundred new labor camps had been created within the General Government, most near the Soviet border. The spike was so alarming that the Polish Resistance notified British Intelligence that Hitler could be preparing for some major offensive that summer. It also meant that the Jewish Council, through its enforcement arm, had to resort to the same sort of ambush tactics the Germans themselves employed. "These snatchings were done in streets and in houses, and at night with a system of manhunts," Zuckerman recalled.

Isaac had mistakenly thought his Young Pioneers were exempt from forced labor because the Zionist left had good connections at the Jewish Council, which to date had spared them. But when he went to complain at the Labor Department offices on Forestry Boulevard, where several hundred anxious Jews rounded up that night awaited shipment to various camps, not only were his pleas ignored, but he, too, was added to the group of captives when the count proved short.

It took three of the inexperienced policemen to wrestle the furious and towering Zuckerman into submission, and he spat in their faces until a German soldier finally put an end to the scuffle by pointing a pistol at his head. He was now headed for a labor colony.

"Before dawn, we were led through the streets of Warsaw and the suburb of Praga, to the railway station," he would later reproach himself. "I had two opportunities to escape, and twice I wrestled with myself: I was used to this sort of thing, and I thought I could escape at the bends in the roads. I was experienced by then, and thought I would succeed. But I was in a group."

Zuckerman was loath to leave his young Zionist comrades behind. While being loaded onto a cattle car, however, he realized that he had made a terrible mistake.

CHAPTER 17

ISAAC AND BORUCH GLIMPSE HELL

The Jewish Police came for Boruch Spiegel at almost the exact same time as they came for Isaac. As with the Zionist clubhouse raid, the police arrived just after curfew, when all Ghetto residents were required to be home. Only Boruch's older brother Berl was not home. He had been tipped off by friends in the Bund that his name had been drawn in the labor draft, so he stayed away from his apartment. Unlike Isaac Zuckerman's Zionist faction, the Bund had a policy of actively resisting forced labor. The two groups, though both socialist in political orientation, had vastly different philosophies about cooperating with the Judenrat. While Zuckerman and the Zionists tended to view the Judenrat as the lesser of two evils and its chairman, Adam Czerniakow, as a good man in an untenable position, the Bund was less charitable. Czerniakow was "weak," according to Mark Edelman, someone who served "German rather than Jewish interests." The Judenrat was rife with corruption and collaborators, claimed Bund Special Ops chief Bernard Goldstein. Czerniakow may have been honest, but he was surrounded by "scoundrels, vipers, and louses," as he himself decried, and the fact that he "spoke Polish exclusively" rankled the Yiddish-centric Bund, as did his Zionist sympathies.

The Bund and the Judenrat had experienced an early and acrimonious rift, dating back to the first German attempt to create a ghetto in late 1939. At the time, the Bund's ranking official in Warsaw was Arthur Ziegelbaum, a trade union leader from Lodz, who had been appointed to serve on the Jewish Council. But he resigned in disgust and organized a large civic protest when Czerniakow proposed a motion—forced on him by the SS—to create a "Jewish residential district." The SS had had to back off, because the Wehrmacht was then still in charge of Warsaw, and the Gestapo vengefully issued an arrest warrant for Ziegelbaum. He fled Poland, with help from a socialist faction of the Polish Underground, and made his way to Belgium, where the Socialist foreign minister Paul-Henri Spaak (the future secretary general of the United Nations) arranged for his passage to New York. In the spring of 1941, Ziegelbaum was back in Europe as a representative of the Bund in the Polish government in exile in London.

Boruch Spiegel, like most Bundists, viewed Ziegelbaum rather than Czerniakow as the legitimate leader of the Jewish community. Boruch was not, however, as fiercely critical of the controversial Judenrat chairman as some of his Bund colleagues. "He was in an impossible position," Spiegel reasoned. "Maybe he should have quit. But I think he meant well, and tried to lessen Jewish suffering by going along." Indeed, had the Bund known of the toll that governing the Ghetto was taking on its soft-spoken chairman, they might have dampened their criticism. "Vomiting at home," Czerniakow recorded in a typically anguished diary entry. "At 2 A.M. I begin to fret. And so on until 5 or 6 in the morning when I get up," he wrote in another.

Nonetheless, it was Czerniakow's police force that came to Boruch's door, looking for his brother Berl. Boruch had hidden under a bed as soon as he heard the knock. He didn't know at first if the Order Service was after him or Berl, so he had acted on impulse. The Jewish officers hauled him out and checked his papers before resuming their search. The Spiegels' ground-floor apartment was sufficiently cramped that it did not take long for the intruders to determine that their quarry was missing. "When they found out he wasn't there, they said 'we'll take you instead.'" Boruch was stunned. His mother started screaming that the police couldn't do that. His younger sister clutched him protectively. His usually tranquil father began cursing, letting loose a flurry of Yiddish invective since he spoke virtually no Polish, the preferred language of most Jewish policemen.

The protests fell on deaf ears. The Order Service had a quota to meet, and one B. Spiegel was as good as the next. An officer took Boruch aside and intimated that if the Spiegels had money, the cops could look elsewhere. Unfortunately, the family's material situation had markedly worsened by spring 1941. The piecework carving clogs that Boruch and his father did for Stan, their Christian business partner, was becoming increasingly irregular. Stan was delivering wood supplies less and less frequently, complaining that access to the Ghetto for Gentiles was becoming too difficult. Nearly half of the district's initial twenty-two gates had been closed to restrict traffic, and bilingual signs warned in German and Polish that Ghetto entry for Christians was *Streng Verboten*, or strictly prohibited. The punishment for Jews caught outside the Ghetto was growing harsher by the month and the number of exit passes issued to Judenrat officials was being drastically reduced. The steady and systematic constriction of the knot around the Jewish community had its most profound effect on the quantity, quality, and cost of basic foodstuffs. For the poorest Ghetto residents, those clustered around the crumbling tenements in the northwest section of the district where Boruch's girlfriend lived, it meant a starvation diet that officially allotted 196 calories a day, consisting of a watery gruel distributed by aid agencies that was derisively known as a "spitter soup" because recipients were just as likely to spit it out as swallow it.

The forty to fifty thousand additional refugees who had arrived in the Ghetto throughout the harsh winter as the Nazis emptied surrounding towns of Jews fared even worse. Dumped inside the gates, the terrified latecomers had found every available accommodation already occupied. With nowhere to live and with the temperatures well below freezing, thousands crammed into unheated synagogues or deserted factories. "They remain all day on their filthy straw mattresses, with no strength to rise," Edelman reported. "The walls are green, slimy, mildewed. The mattresses usually lie on the ground, seldom on wooden supports. A whole family often receives sleeping space for one. This is the kingdom of hunger and misery."

Not only did the unfortunate new arrivals have nowhere to live, but the vast majority had nothing to live on. As strangers to Warsaw, they had no local support network—no former neighbors like Miriam Ratheiser's to turn to for food, no prewar acquaintances like Boruch's wood clog supplier through whom to earn money, no old business partners with whom to continue to trade. "Very rapidly they started to die," Spiegel recalled. "At first, it was a few a day. Then a few hundred a week. Then by the thousands."

For the Spiegels the clampdown meant dramatically less money in family coffers. The sum mentioned by the policeman was far beyond their financial means.

"So they took me."

The blood on Isaac Zuckerman's face had coagulated, forming a crusty patina on his temple and cheek. One eye was swollen shut, and his ribs throbbed with every breath. He lay in a detention cell at the bottom of a mud pit in the Kampinos labor camp, twenty miles northwest of Warsaw.

Between the iron grates of his cell, Isaac could see the long rows of wooden barracks and the emaciated Jewish workers, their damp clothes tattered and filthy with bog stains, filing out to morning roll call around the gallows in the camp's square. Shovels and spades were stacked in neat pyramids next to wagons that would deliver the workers to the nearby swamps they would drain. Ukrainian guards, still drunk from their past evening's revelry, lurched through the ranks, flailing haphazardly with their whips, shouting in their slurred and heavily accented Polish.

Isaac shivered uncontrollably, fighting fever and chills. He lay half-naked, immersed in the muddy water that filled the bottom of the fenced pit, water stained red with his own blood. The guards had beaten him all night, trying to get him to talk. "Who was that woman?" they demanded. "Why was she asking about a Yid?"

The woman, Isaac knew, was among the cadre of couriers that Zivia Lubetkin had trained. Her name was Lonka Kozibrodska, and she was a blond-haired former philology student at the University of Warsaw who spoke six languages fluently, including German and Ukrainian. As soon as Zuckerman was abducted at the Labor Office,

Zivia dispatched Lonka to find which work colony he had been sent to, and to determine if his freedom could be bought. Lonka's Polish disguise, however, had been too convincing. When she approached one of the guards patrolling the Kampinos barbed wire perimeter to ask about Isaac, the camp commander grew suspicious. She must be from the Polish Resistance, he reasoned. That meant that Zuckerman must somehow also be connected to the Gentile Underground.

"So, who was she?" the interrogation resumed. Isaac shrugged. The more the guards beat him, the less pain he felt. He was numb, and stuck to his story that Lonka was just an old classmate, a Christian friend. The guards finally sighed and left. "For three days his body will hang as a warning to the entire camp," the commandant ordered, pointing to the gallows.

Waiting for the sentence to be carried out was more painful than any beating Isaac would ever endure. "I was a hundred percent sure that they were about to execute me," he recalled. "I said farewell. I tried to stand tall with my head held high." But the hours passed and Zuckerman did not hang. He started wavering, begging his tormentors to get it over with.

When they finally did come for him, he was shocked to find himself dragged not to the noose, but back to barracks, where other inmates gave him bread and watery soup. For three days, he was allowed to rest, and on the fourth day, the camp commander courteously informed him that he would be working as a clerk on the soft duty detail.

Zuckerman was dumbfounded by his reversal of fortune. "I have only one explanation," he later speculated. "The Germans were keeping an eye on the Polish Underground; they suspected I had contacts with them and this wasn't just some Jew you could execute and get rid of."

This may have been the case. The Gestapo had tortured to death so many suspected Polish Resistance members without gleaning useful information from them that they were now adopting more subtle tactics, trying to turn people, or discreetly observing them in the hopes of uncovering their networks. For the camp's Volksdeutsche manager and his senior Polish staff, there was likely a second motivation for treading softly with Isaac: They "were afraid of the vengeance of the

Polish Underground and didn't want to get into trouble because of a Yid," Zuckerman speculated. The Resistance had orchestrated a series of assisted "suicides" among the nine thousand Volksdeutsche Polish-Germans working on behalf of the Nazis in Warsaw. Bogus farewell notes were left at the scenes, alleging that the victims had killed themselves out of guilt for betraying Poland, which prevented the Gestapo from executing the customary one hundred Poles in retaliation for every German murdered. For ethnic Poles collaborating with the Nazis there was no need for such subterfuge. The Resistance assassinated them in broad daylight, without fear of German reprisal, and as an example to others.

Sensing that he had been singled out for special treatment due to his suspected Polish Underground ties, Isaac decided to press his advantage. "I hinted that I would be willing to pay" to be included in a group of sick inmates who were about to be returned to the Ghetto because they were too weak to work. The Polish camp managers readily agreed, anxious to be rid of a potential source of trouble. They even permitted him to telephone Zivia to have her send money for the release of five other Zionists held at Kampinos.

The camp was about a four-mile walk from the nearest rail station, and many of the released laborers died on the way. A wagon followed the bedraggled procession, collecting the corpses of the fallen, who had literally been worked to death. Of the roughly 250 men sent to Kampinos with Zuckerman, fifty-three died in camp, and another fifty died shortly after their release. The living made such a sorrowful sight that peasants from surrounding villages, not usually known for philo-Semitism, took pity. "They behaved wonderfully toward us," Zuckerman recalled. "They tossed us bread and bottles of milk." The Ukrainian guards beat the generous peasants back and tried to prevent the prisoners from reaching the food. "I saw a bottle break and people ran to lick the milk from the ground."

At the station, as the train to Warsaw pulled in, Isaac asked the commander a question that had been nagging him for days: "When you set up the gallows, and said you were going to execute me, did you mean that seriously?"

"Absolutely," the man replied.

Unlike Isaac, Boruch Spiegel could not count on underground connections (either real or perceived) to save him from the labor camp. Isaac, after all, headed one of the largest Zionist factions in the Ghetto. He had more than a thousand members behind him and was dating his second in command. It was not surprising that Zivia had used the Zionists' funds and their network of couriers to try to spring her lover.

Boruch had no such luck. He was only peripherally involved with the Bund. His new girlfriend, Chaika, was merely one of dozens of "fivers" and "tenners" who distributed the organization's newsletters. Neither she nor Boruch's big brother had direct contacts with the Bund's inner circle, who might have been capable of mounting a rescue effort. So Spiegel was on his own, forced to spend the full three to four months in camp.

The labor colony to which he was sent was forty miles southeast of Warsaw, near a little town called Garwolin. Like Kampinos, this was a new installation. But already it had earned the dreaded nickname "Garwolin Hell."

The place, Spiegel soon realized, had no obvious purpose other than to torment Jews. There was no factory to assemble armaments; no mine to extract mineral deposits for the war machine; no logging operations to harvest wood; no road-building crews. "I didn't understand what we were doing there. It seemed pointless."

The swamp draining and mound building that went on six days a week did in fact have a purpose: It was part of defensive fortifications the Germans were excavating along the entire Soviet frontier. But to Spiegel, who had no military experience, it looked largely like an exercise in cruelty, an experiment in exhaustion and malnourishment. "They fed us a bowl of soup a day and two hundred grams of bread. That's a few slices," Boruch explained. "And on that [sustenance] we had to work around ten hours."

Very quickly, often within days of arriving in Garwolin Hell, people began to collapse. Since the poorest Ghetto residents tended to be drafted for forced labor, they were also the least prepared to withstand the hardships. Many arrived in camps already emaciated, their immune systems weakened, their strength long ebbed. "It was awful," Boruch recalled. "Our clothes never had time to dry so we were wet and cold the whole time. At roll call in the morning, when we sometimes had to stand at attention for an hour, people would faint or fall to the ground. The guards would leap on them, kick them, beat them with clubs, or whip them."

As in the Kampinos camp, the guards at Garwolin were ethnic Ukrainians. The SS began actively recruiting Ukrainian nationalists that winter and spring—a fact that didn't go unnoticed by Polish Resistance members, who relayed the potentially meaningful intelligence to London. Why the Germans had developed a sudden interest in Galician natives from western Ukraine—now under Soviet occupation—was not immediately evident. But many Galician Ukrainians despised their Polish colonial masters, and the SS exploited the long-standing ethnic grievances to attract recruits. For SS chief Heinrich Himmler, this was critical because Poland was one of the only countries in occupied Europe without locally staffed SS detachments or a quisling puppet government. These existed virtually everywhere on the Continent, from Vichy France and the Balkans all the way to the Baltic, where a small and traitorous minority of Danes had formed a local SS force. In Poland, the hated Blue Police was the closest the country came to institutionalized collaboration, and the Blue Police was so corrupt and infiltrated by the Resistance that the Germans could not rely on it.

"I thought the Blue Police was bad, but they were nothing compared to the Ukrainians at Garwolin," Spiegel remembered. "If someone fell while working they beat him. If he couldn't get up afterward they shot him."

Soon the makeshift cemetery next to the camp began to fill. The burial pits that Boruch and other inmates were forced to dig grew larger, from single graves to shallow holes that could accommodate a dozen corpses each.

As the weeks passed, the lack of food and merciless pace of work began to take their toll on Boruch. He had never been physically fit like Isaac Zuckerman, and even the stores of baby fat around his cheeks had long since melted away. His legs began giving him trouble. At first they just ached and cramped, but then they started swelling up. "I could barely walk." One inflated to nearly twice its normal size. An oozing, pustulent scab formed on the shin, a scar that was visible seventy years later, and the pain became excruciating. But still Boruch mustered the strength to stand at roll call, to try to go through the motions of working. The sick bay at Garwolin was nothing more than a way station to the cemetery.

Much as he tried, Boruch could not keep up with the murderous tempo set by the Ukrainians. He felt the stinging lash of their whips on his back, and at one point, something in him snapped. "You know," he shouted at one especially brutal guard, "when they finish with us, they'll move on to you." The other inmates instinctively drew away from him. "Shut up," one whispered. "You're going to get yourself killed."

But Boruch, who was mild-mannered by nature, like his father, had reached a breaking point. He dropped his shovel and kept shouting. The guards pounced on him, hitting him with their rifle butts, kicking him with their heavy boots. When he fell and curled up into a protective fetal position, the guard he had insulted sat astride him and began punching his face. The blows fell one after another, jerking his head from side to side with such force he thought his neck would snap. And all the while Boruch pleaded with himself, repeating over and over: "Don't faint. You can't faint."

If he did, he was certain he would never get up again.

CHAPTER 18

THEY DIDN'T DESERVE SUCH A PARTING

It took Isaac Zuckerman a week in May 1941 to recover from his brief stay in Kampinos. He lay in bed the entire time as "the pampered child of Valiant" Street, with Zivia Lubetkin and the other Zionists fussing over him and nursing him back to health.

When his sores and scabs had healed and he was strong enough to resume command, Zuckerman convened a meeting. He'd been wrong about the camps, and about cooperating with the Judenrat, he said. "For the first time, I had seen with my own eyes what a labor camp was. Before that, we used to distinguish between labor camps and concentration camps, but now I knew it was all the same," Isaac explained. They were both "death camps," and Zionists throughout the General Government needed to be warned about them and instructed not to obey Judenrat orders to go.

Couriers must be dispatched immediately to Krakow and Lublin to spread the word, Isaac directed. He himself would travel to other towns with large Jewish populations and advise local Zionist leaders that they should actively resist the labor draft. Zuckerman could have delegated the responsibility, but he was restless after being confined in bed and wanted to stretch his legs on "an extended tour." It was May, the best time of the year in Poland, when the gray shroud of near-permanent cloud cover that descends on the country each September finally lifts and the sun makes its welcome reappearance for the summer.

As usual, Isaac left the Ghetto through the Municipal Courthouse Building. The structure, which served the legal needs of both the Jewish and Gentile communities, straddled the border and was a favored smuggling route. Jews would enter from Forestry Boulevard, where the Courthouse had had its main entrance before the war. Inside, they would remove their armbands, pay off a guard, and exit through the back door onto tiny White Street. From there, it was a short walk through Iron Gate Square, near the Saxon Gardens, and along Marshal Boulevard, Warsaw's busiest thoroughfare, to Central Station on Jerusalem Boulevard.

The relative taste of freedom Zuckerman experienced whenever he left the Ghetto was always leavened by the risk of random violence that existed on the Aryan side. "I saw how the Germans beat the Poles there at the station, really beat them. By chance, I didn't get beaten myself, but I saw the humiliation of the Poles."

Passenger train traffic on Isaac's tour in early June 1941 was irregular because the Wehrmacht was requisitioning all available locomotives for military service. This, too, was dutifully communicated to London by the Polish Resistance, and British Intelligence concluded that there could be only one reason for the Wehrmacht to be massing troops and armament along the Soviet demarcation line: Germany was preparing to attack the USSR.

The June 22, 1941, invasion of the Soviet Union surprised no one but Joseph Stalin himself. The Soviet leader had refused to heed all the early warning signs that Hitler was going to abrogate the Molotov-Ribbentrop Pact. In his megalomania, he couldn't believe that anyone would dare double-cross him.

News of the huge offensive electrified the Warsaw Ghetto. "We were sure of a quick victory by the Red Army," Zuckerman recalled. The celebrations were quickly dampened by the triumphal announcements that issued almost hourly from the "barkers," the loudspeakers strung up across Warsaw through which the General Government communicated decrees. It was the Wehrmacht scoring victory upon victory against the Soviets. The Red Army was in full retreat, and Stalin was in a paralyzed funk, refusing to see anyone in his Kremlin apartment.

The most distressing news was that the Germans had taken Zuckerman's hometown of Vilna, a mere two days into the invasion. Isaac was haunted by the way he had left his family in 1939, when he had received his first assignment to set up an underground. "I left in a few minutes, and I could have stayed for another twenty-four hours to prepare my parents," he remembered sadly. "They didn't deserve such a parting."

Through his underground network, he had kept tabs on his parents and his sister Lena, always making sure couriers checked in on them. Now, as the weeks passed and communication with Vilna was cut off, Isaac became increasingly desperate. A Gentile contact told Zuckerman that the Polish Boy Scouts, known in the Underground as the Gray Ranks, were sending a messenger to Vilna to find out what had happened there. He would travel by bicycle because all train traffic had been diverted to the Eastern Front, and Zuckerman was told that if he helped finance the mission, the Boy Scout courier would carry correspondence on behalf of the Zionists.

Summer was over by the time the Boy Scout returned. Isaac's family, he said, was safe. But he had not been able to deliver the letters that Isaac had posted with him for the Zionist cell in Troki, an exurb of Vilna. He couldn't find any Jews in Troki, or in neighboring Landwarowo, or in Ponar, a closer suburb of Vilna. They had all been taken to a pit in the forest and shot.

News of the Vilna massacre spread rapidly through the Warsaw Ghetto. "We were shocked," Zivia Lubetkin remembered. Zivia and Isaac called together young Socialist Zionists to their headquarters to discuss the troubling reports. Perhaps they were exaggerated, some skeptics posited. "We must assume that this was an awful act of revenge," Isaac recalled someone speculating. "We know that some Jews welcomed the Red Army and made themselves hated by their neighbors." The Lithuanians might have been incited to violence by the

Germans. Besides, others questioned, how reliable was this information? The account was, after all, secondhand, relayed by a non-Zionist and a non-Jew. Could it even be trusted?

Zivia decided to find out for herself. She dispatched two of her most reliable couriers to Vilna, Frumka Plotnicka and Lonka Kozibrodska, the same messenger who had located Isaac at the Kampinos camp. "There was nowhere Lonka would not go. Nothing was impossible for her," Zivia recalled admiringly. And Frumka was Zivia's most trusted lieutenant. Hearing from them would be like seeing with her own eyes.

The Bund also convened an emergency meeting of its central committee to discuss the situation. "The craziest rumors were circulating," Mark Edelman recalled. Alas, Bundists had even less to go on than Isaac and Zivia's Zionists: What was the extent of the slaughter in Lithuania? Was it a pogrom? Or had the Germans committed the killings in reprisal for some perceived offense such as supposed Jewish loyalty to the Soviets? Was it a one-off event, the tragic by-product of ethnic tensions that flared up whenever the borderlands violently changed hands, as had been the case during the First World War? Or were there larger, more ominous implications for Jews in general?

"A lot of people refused to believe that this was anything more than an isolated incident," Edelman recalled. He had been allowed to sit in while the central committee met, a rare honor for a twenty-two-year-old who was half the age of most other members and still "prone to childish bouts of fantasy and enthusiasm," in the words of one superior. The privilege, however, did not extend to voicing any opinions, which proved frustrating. Perhaps it was the impatience of youth, but Edelman didn't agree with the cautious skepticism of party elders like Maurice Orzech, Leon Feiner, Abrasha Blum, and, surprisingly, special ops chief Bernard Goldstein. While these colleagues counseled against jumping to conclusions or making any rash decisions, Edelman and some of the younger Bundists were already convinced that Hitler sought the annihilation of all Jews.

The elder and younger members of the Bund did agree on one thing, however—to delay action until they had gathered reliable information of their own. Asking the rival Zionists to share the report they had received from the Polish Boy Scouts was out of the question. Even the more impatient and impetuous Edelman, who, at the time, lived on the same street as Isaac and Zivia, never contemplated knocking on their clubhouse door to ask for help. "We were ideological rivals." Instead the Bund chose to duplicate the Zionists' efforts to try to get a clearer picture of what was happening in the east. Non-Jews were free to travel into the newly seized territories being incorporated into the General Government, so Bernard Goldstein reached out to a former trade union colleague, a man by the name of Runge, who had served as head of the Polish Federation of Labor before the war and was now active in the Polish Underground. In the past, Edelman would have acted as a go-between for this sort of message. His job at the Jewish hospital gave him a coveted Ghetto exit pass so he could deliver contaminated blood samples to laboratories on the Aryan side. This made him an ideal courier for the Bund, despite his pronounced Semitic features. He could legally leave the sealed district, and because he carried typhus samples, no one dared approach him on the streets of Warsaw for fear of infection—not even the police or anti-Semitic thugs; "I was like a leper." Unfortunately his hospital pass had been recently revoked, and he had been relegated to cleaning up after autopsies of typhus victims. The disease had reached epidemic proportions by the fall of 1941, spreading from the horrifically overcrowded refugee shelters to the rest of the Ghetto. It would claim 14,449 lives by year's end. Overwhelmed hospitals gave up on treating the ill and could only helplessly study the dead. "Their organs were translucent," Edelman recalled. "My job was to sew up body cavities and dispose of the corpses."

So with Edelman sidelined, the Bund had to find other ways of getting its message out. Leaving the Ghetto without a pass beame infinitely more perilous on October 10, 1941, when Warsaw district governor Ludwig Fisher announced that henceforth any Jew caught outside the walls would be summarily executed. The death penalty, Fisher added in a statement published in the New Warsaw Courier two days later, would also apply to any Gentile harboring or lending assistance to Jews. "I instruct the entire population of the Warsaw District to draw careful attention to this latest decree because it will be administered with merciless severity," he warned.

Despite the new death threat, Goldstein's trade union friend agreed to gather the requested information and deliver his report in person. "Runge was smuggled into the ghetto with great care," Goldstein recalled, and a meeting was arranged on Goose Street, near the district's newly opened Jewish prison. Goldstein was hiding out in a safe house because the Gestapo had recently raided his apartment building on New Linden Avenue. While the two labor leaders talked, shots rang out from the nearby prison. Jews caught outside the Ghetto were being executed.

The rumors of widespread atrocities in the east, Runge reported, were true. In Vilna, a special pogrom unit of Lithuanians called the *Ipatingas,* or the Elect, had been created by the Germans. It was staffed with relatives of victims of Soviet repression, many of whom were told by the Germans that Jewish Bolsheviks were responsible for their family's sufferings. In "revenge," they killed, or helped the Germans kill, nearly a third of Vilna's sixty thousand Jews. In other Lithuanian towns, the SS released violent criminals from jails and put them to work murdering Jews. In the Lithuanian capital of Kaunas, or Kovno as it was then also known in Polish, meting out "rightful punishment to collaborators and traitors" had become a spectator sport, according to eyewitnesses, complete with large crowds, "cheering and clapping." Lithuanian children were lifted onto the shoulders of their parents to catch a glimpse of the famous "Death-dealer of Kovno," a sight that one German regular army officer later described as the most frightful event he'd witnessed in the course of two world wars.

"On the concrete forecourt of the petrol station a blond man of medium height, aged about twenty-five, stood leaning on a wooden club, resting," the disgusted officer, a colonel in the Wehrmacht's Army Group North, recounted. "The club was as thick as his arm and came up to his chest. At his feet lay about fifteen to twenty dead or dying people. Water flowed continuously from a hose washing blood away into the drainage gully. Just a few steps behind this man some twenty men, guarded by armed civilians, stood waiting for their cruel execution in silent submission. In response to a cursory wave the next man stepped forward silently and was beaten to death with the wooden club in the most bestial manner, each blow accompanied by enthusiastic shouts from the audience."

Once the mound of Jewish bodies at his feet had reached fifty, the

Death-dealer fetched an accordion, climbed to the top of the pile of corpses, and played the Lithuanian national anthem.

The wave of brutality was not confined to Lithuania. It ran the length of the old Pale of Settlement, the historically volatile border-lands between Poland and Russia, where Himmler had ordered local killing squads to be recruited "from the reliable non-Communist elements among Ukrainians, Estonians, Latvians, Lithuanians, and Bye-lorussians." In Galicia, leaders of the Organization of Ukrainian Nationalists, the partisan group that had been long repressed by Pol-ish authorities, went on Radio Berlin to declare "Death to Jews, death to Communists, death to Commissars, exactly in that sequence." Then they went on a rampage, murdering seven thousand Jews in Lvov, 1,100 in Lutsk, 600 in Ternopol, and progressively spreading the terror to ever smaller towns until blood had been spilled throughout all of western Ukraine.

The absence of Poles from Himmler's recruiting directive did not mean that the SS couldn't count on Polish pogromists. In the town of Radzilow, Germans incited Polish peasants to murder eight hundred Jewish inhabitants on the worn pretext that Jews had denounced Gen-tiles to the Soviet secret police. In nearby Jedwabne, the same ploy was used to drive the hamlet's entire Jewish population into its lone syna-gogue, which was then set ablaze.

For Edelman, who had already convinced himself that a wider campaign against the Jews was afoot, confirmation of the mass kill-ings "was not shocking." Runge's report did not, however, conclu-sively answer the question that still racked senior Bundists: Was this orgy of violence fundamentally different from past waves of pogroms, which had flared in the east with tragic regularity for centuries? "That was part of the German genius," Edelman later noted ruefully.

The Bund decided to form and begin training a five-hundred-member militia in the event that the Nazis tried to incite another, more lethal pogrom in Warsaw. Both Edelman and Berl Spiegel eagerly joined the fledgling self-defense organization. The unit was "mostly theoretical" at this early stage, Boruch Spiegel recalled; a list of names, a few lecture meetings, no real training to speak of. The only arms at the Bund's disposal were truncheons and knives. These had always kept petty local thugs from the fascist Falanga and ONR at bay, but they clearly no longer sufficed.

In light of the scale and barbarity of the eastern atrocities, Bernard Goldstein had one additional request for his Gentile trade union colleague. Could he help the Bund get guns?

Boruch Spiegel wanted to join the Bund's newly formed militia, but he was in no condition to do so. When he finally returned to the Ghetto after nearly four months in the Garwolin camp, his mother barely recognized him.

His face and neck were covered in boils. His hair was falling out in clumps. His body was so bloated that it stretched his worn-out clothes to the ripping point. He could hardly walk and barely had the strength to speak. By all statistical measures, he should not have been alive. He should not have survived the beatings at the hands of the Ukrainian guards. And he should not have been capable of returning to work in his injured and starving state. But somehow he had mustered hidden reserves of energy and tapped into an inner strength he had not known he possessed—just enough to get him through his mandatory ninety-day stay in "Garwolin Hell." Once safely back home, he completely collapsed.

"I didn't get out of bed for a month," he recalled. He slept almost the entire time, and the period of convalescence became a hazy blur. Only the occasional distorted image lodged in his memory: his mother applying cream to his blistered lips; his brother Berl playing the violin by his bedside; his girlfriend Chaika blowing him a kiss; his sisters arguing and being shushed by his father.

At first he was unable to eat. His depleted organs could process only tiny amounts of food because Boruch was suffering from ascites, or the "wet form" of severe malnutrition—fluid in the abdominal cavity bloating him like a balloon. His mother had to be very careful feeding him, as any sudden caloric surge could overwhelm Spiegel's metabolism. It would go into overdrive, causing his weakened heart to go into cardiac arrest, laboring to pump the extra blood various organs needed to process increased digestive activity.

Because malnutrition was becoming so prevalent in the Ghetto, Boruch's mother probably heard many cautionary tales of starving people dropping dead after eating a single large meal. Once Boruch's system started responding to food, his body began jettisoning excess fluid. This was known as the diuretic phase of starvation treatment, a critical excretion period, when the balance of minerals and electrolytes in the body must be kept in check or death becomes a possibility once again. Boruch's mother probably understood little about biochemical ratios and could not have monitored her son's sodium, potassium, and calcium levels even if she was aware of the delicate equilibrium her patient needed to maintain. Instead, she trusted a higher order. "For her, everything was 'God's will, God's will,'" Spiegel explained. "She was very religious."

Slipping in and out of consciousness, Boruch was blissfully unaware of his continued danger. Once the excess fluids had flushed themselves from his system and the swelling subsided, Spiegel, like all starving patients, underwent a startling transformation. Like a deflated balloon, he instantly shrank, his bluish, stretched, almost transparent skin hanging grotesquely from what must have seemed an impossibly frail frame. He was literally skin and bones: almost no subcutaneous tissue was left.

For the Spiegel family, Boruch's skeletal condition presented a serious financial burden. They desperately needed to fatten him up but had no money to buy food on the black market. Stan had stopped smuggling materials for clogs in and out of the Ghetto. It had simply become too dangerous. The October 10 announcement setting the death penalty as punishment for leaving the district or harboring Jews wreaked havoc on the underground economy. For many Gentiles, the price of doing business with Jews became too high. Moreover, many of the corrupt Polish Blue Police officers who had facilitated the illicit trade were being replaced with Ukrainian and Lithuanian auxiliaries. These new Ghetto guards immediately distinguished themselves with acts of shocking brutality. They showed particular zeal in a cracking down on illegal trade. The Ghetto's lifeline, the all-pervasive smuggling operations that kept food flowing and tens of thousands of residents employed, was severed. In November 1941, the Nazis dealt a final blow to the underground economy: They shut off almost all electricity to the Ghetto. Lights flickered only in the wealthy southernmost quadrant of the district, near the elegant townhouses of Sienna Street, where thanks to bribes "in the evening you could see welldressed women, wearing lipstick and rouge, strolling calmly down the street with their dogs, as if there was no war," the Ghetto chronicler Emmanuel Ringelblum recalled. Meanwhile, hundreds of clandestine factories and mills that had formed the backbone of illicit trade shut down.

To feed Boruch, Berl sold the one item of value the family still possessed: their father's prized violin. "He had had it for eight or nine years," Boruch recalled. "He played beautifully. Our house was so full of life and love and music even though we were poor."

Now their apartment, like countless others, was virtually empty, stripped of everything that could be traded for a meal: furniture, kitchen appliances, floor coverings, clothes. When Boruch eventually learned that the food he ate had come from the sale of the treasured violin, he was struck by guilt. "I didn't know if I could bring myself to swallow that bread." What Boruch also didn't realize was that his father had stopped eating so that Boruch could recover. "There was not enough food, so he started giving his share to me and to my sisters." By the time Spiegel understood what was happening, it was too late. "I watched him fade, day by day. It was terrible," he said, the guilt still overwhelming him to tears seventy years later. "Starvation is the worst possible death."

CHAPTER 19

SIMHA LEAVES ZIVIA TO HER PROPHECY

When Boruch's father passed away, the family carried his naked body out onto the street. They covered him with newspapers weighted by rocks—because "bedsheets could be traded for half a kilo of bread" and would immediately be stolen, as would any clothing on a corpse—and left him there. Eventually the sanitation department would collect him in a wheelbarrow and bury him in a communal grave at the Jewish Cemetery, along the far western wall of the Ghetto. Paying the exorbitant fees charged by undertakers like Model Pienkert or Nathan Wittenberg's Final Journey Funeral Parlor was only possible for the very rich. By the end of 1941, forty-three thousand people had died of hunger and disease in the Ghetto and the streets were littered with decaying corpses. "Dead bodies had become part of the landscape. At first it was shocking. But soon there were so many that you stopped paying any attention to them," explained Simha.

Like the Spiegels, the Ratheiser family was faring progressively worse. Simha's mother, Miriam, could no longer venture outside the Ghetto to collect food from her Catholic friends and former neighbors. She was still a head turner, blond and statuesque, but she smiled less now. Her features were grayer and worry lines creased her once flawless skin. It was as if she had aged a decade in the course of one year.

Her husband Zvi's dark beard had also grayed prematurely, and he had visibly lost weight. But Simha's pious father was in reasonably good spirits. He prayed a great deal, even more than before the war, and seemed content to entrust his family's fate to God. Miriam was of a different mind. She felt the situation was spiraling out of control and that the Ratheisers needed to do something.

Miriam worried most about Simha, who often sneaked out of the Ghetto to trade for food. Smuggling had become mortally dangerous even before the October death penalty decree. German and Ukrainian guards took to shooting smugglers for sport, and one guard earned the nickname Frankenstein because he developed a lethal routine of killing two or three Jews with his morning coffee. Child smugglers were particularly vulnerable to German cruelty. One such child was walking across the bridge from the farmer's market in Praga when he encountered an SS patrol. "I could only guess that this was a Jewish boy. He was around ten years old, very thin, and dark haired," a witness, who was also Jewish and posing as a Christian, recounted. "The little boy was now nearer the SS man, who suddenly without uttering a word, without asking the boy any questions, seized him by the collar and threw him into the dark and turbulent waters of the Vistula."

Another Jewish witness reported seeing a child from the Ghetto begging on bustling Jerusalem Boulevard. "A little skeleton, four or five years old, as in India. People wouldn't give him money, but would put a bun in his hand. An elegant German came by, opened a sewer grating, took the child, and threw him into the sewer."

Given the rising dangers associated with smuggling, Miriam had forbidden Simha to go to the countryside to buy food anymore. He wasn't pleased, but he did not rebel against his parents' decision. For a while, he tried to earn money by hiring himself out as a replacement forced day laborer, taking the place of older Ghetto residents willing to pay to avoid cleaning Warsaw streets. "I was almost seventeen and strong, so substituting was a good way to make a few zlotys," he explained. But that, too, had its inherent dangers. At any time, Simha could be snatched and taken to a labor camp. "My parents didn't like it. They were scared of what might happen and looked for something else for me."

Simha's life was still largely dictated by his mother and father, even though many other boys his age had effectively become heads of their households, supporting extended families through smuggling. As with any teen, part of Simha longed to break free of the parental cocoon. Although his father increasingly took a backseat as a provider, in the evolving family dynamic, Miriam emerged as more of the authority figure, and Simha still deferred to her on major decisions. "We were very close."

Miriam was the one who thought of sending Simha out of the Ghetto for good. Since he could pass for a Gentile, she reasoned, he would be safer on the Aryan side, away from the typhus, the snatchings, the starvation. "My mom had relatives who lived in a tiny village deep in the countryside," Simha recalled. The place was near Radom, about three hours south of Warsaw by train. Its principal appeal was isolation; it was small enough not to figure on any map, and there were no Germans permanently posted there. It was also a farming community, which meant food was plentiful and strong hands were always welcome to toil in the fields, especially given the chronic labor shortages. In short, it was the perfect hideout to stash Simha while Miriam figured out what to do with his sisters and her Orthodox husband. "I was very eager to leave," Ratheiser recalled. And not just because he would be out of harm's way. More important, he would be on his own, an adult fending for himself. In fact, this would be the last decision his parents would ever make on his behalf.

Simha Ratheiser's December 1941 departure from Warsaw coincided with a distant event that had immediate ramifications for the roughly 430,000 Jews trapped inside the city. The Japanese attack on Pearl Harbor finally pushed the United States to declare war on Germany and Japan, and the news was greeted with great joy followed by deep consternation in the Ghetto. At first, people rejoiced at the prospect of Hitler's facing such a formidable adversary, an industrial giant with seemingly endless reserves of manpower and armament. But within days, the care packages that arrived regularly via Switzerland from relief organizations in New York stopped coming. The Germans were no longer letting them through, and another critical food source had dried up.

On hearing of the U.S. entry into the war, Zivia Lubetkin shuddered. Far from making her hopeful, it immediately reminded her of a speech that Hitler had given, warning, "If international Jewry, in Europe and outside of Europe, once again pushes nations to world war, the result will be the extermination of the Jewish race in Europe."

When she first heard that declaration, Zivia had dismissed it as the "barking of a mad dog." Only now, with America mobilizing, did it fill her with dread, like a dark premonition she could not shake. She suddenly had an uncontrollable urge to hear from Lonka and Frumka and prayed that her prized couriers would return with tidings from the east.

When some news finally reached her, shortly after New Year's Eve—which was celebrated with abandon by smugglers and gangsters at the Eldorado, the Melody Palace, the Arizona, and other champagne-soaked nightclubs frequented by the new Ghetto elite—the reports were far worse than she had imagined. They were all the more terrifying because they came not from the wild and pogrom-prone east, but from the west, from the orderly industrialized territories long incorporated into the Reich. There, on the very day that Japanese aircraft had struck the American fleet in Hawaii, the Germans had opened what could only be called an extermination camp. It occupied an abandoned castle near Chelmno, forty miles northwest of Lodz. The following day, December 8, Jews from surrounding villages were brought to the camp, according to a terrified eyewitness who described the scene to Lubetkin. "A fat German officer greeted them politely," the witness recalled. "We have treated you unfairly and would like to make amends," the corpulent SS officer said in a soothing voice. "You have suffered," he continued, puffing on a cigar, and he assured the gathered families that their torments were over. "You will all go to work, but first you must wash yourselves. Here's a place for women and here for men," he waved nonchalantly to separate entrances with his cigar. "Undress and go take a shower and you will be issued new clothes."

Once the Jews were inside the building, the tone and demeanor of the Germans changed abruptly. Instead of being led to showers, the naked and unsuspecting victims were crammed in groups of fifty to sixty into large trucks. The doors were sealed, the engines were started, and carbon monoxide exhaust fumes were vented into the sealed rear cabins while the trucks drove to a nearby wood. When the screaming and pounding ceased, the doors were opened and the bodies of victims, some still alive and writhing in agony, were buried in huge pits, according to the eyewitness, a Jewish prisoner who had managed to escape while digging the mass graves and made his way to Warsaw.

"Nobody believed him," Lubetkin recalled. "Nobody wanted to believe him." His story was entirely outside the Jewish experience. Pogroms, Jews could understand. They had ample historic precedent: the Cossack Rebellion of 1648, which claimed a hundred thousand lives; the 1881 assassination of Tsar Alexander II, whose aftermath left ten thousand dead; the 1903 and 1905 outbursts in Kishinev, Edelman's hometown of Gomel, and Zhitomir that resulted in nearly a thousand murders; and the awful wave of killings during the Bolshevik Revolution, where in Ukraine and Belarus alone, fifteen thousand Jews lost their lives.

What the grave digger described was not a pogrom. It was far more sinister, cold and clinical in its lack of emotion and reliance on technology. "People were unable to believe that they could be killed like that," Edelman remembered.

The grave digger was brought before an assembly of skeptical Ghetto elders, Judenrat members, and senior relief agency managers to relate his tale. "Impossible," Zivia recalled one indignant speaker declaring, dismissing the account. "Something like this could never happen in the heart of Europe, in Warsaw." Even if the story was true, others said, Warsaw was not some insignificant shtetl that could be made to disappear without a trace. It was central Europe's largest urban agglomeration, the biggest city east of Berlin—still considered by its residents as the cultural and economic heart of world Jewry, despite New York City's recent gains. The Wehrmacht didn't have enough trucks to kill all of the Jews in Warsaw. They would never dare.

Zivia listened to the cacophony of raised voices as, all at once, the Ghetto elders began shouting one another down, arguing, denouncing, denying what to her was glaringly obvious. "I closed my eyes," she recalled, "and I saw all these people as corpses."

Zivia realized then and there what her Zionist faction, Dror, had to do. "We are going to defend ourselves," she resolved. Isaac Zuckerman and the other Dror leaders were in agreement. "There was only one question: How and with what?"

Weeks passed before the answer to that question became clear. In the interim, the abnormally cold 1942 winter claimed thousands more lives, littering the unheated Ghetto with frozen cadavers whose torsos had to be pried from the pavement with shovels in the mornings, while at night street urchins with pliers pulled out gold fillings to trade for bread.

Another miraculous escape from Chelmno corroborated the grave digger's account the following month. The camp not only existed; it was being expanded. In mid-January 1942, Chelmno began "processing" Jews from the Lodz ghetto, and not merely by the hundreds, as before, but by the thousands.

The couriers Lonka and Frumka, meanwhile, returned from their mission to Vilna. The news they brought was horrifying. Three-quarters of Vilna's Jews were now dead, buried in the Ponary pits on the outskirts of town. The toll included Isaac Zuckerman's entire family. "I remember sitting in silence," stunned, he recalled. Zuckerman thought of his parents, cousins, uncles, aunts, nieces, in-laws. "The whole clan" was gone. He couldn't believe it.

The couriers had one other significant development to relay, but Isaac wasn't listening. He was numb, racked with guilt and regret. For months, ever since the Nazi invasion of the USSR and the first whispered mentions of Ponary, Zuckerman had feared that his family—his mother, his sister, his father, his beloved granddad—would not survive the war. Many times he reproached himself for leaving them so abruptly to begin his conspiratorial journey back in October 1939. He could have spent a few more days at home: hugged his mom, Rivka, some more, stayed up late talking to his dad, Simon, and humored his gentle and senile old grandfather. But he had been in such a rush to start his underground activity, to do his own thing, that he had put his own selfish needs above those of his relatives. And now he would never get a chance to make amends.

"Those were the hardest weeks of my life," Zuckerman recalled of the deep funk he fell into after hearing of his loved ones' death. "A depression that went on all day and all night. Thoughts of the end. Isolation." The charismatic extrovert withdrew into himself and into successive bottles of vodka. Isaac had always been an enthusiastic social drinker—already unusual within the generally abstemious Jewish community. But now alcohol became a crutch he would lean on with increasing regularity.

For a time, the anguished Zionist leader contemplated leaving the movement that he blamed for causing him to abandon his family. At one low point, he thought of running away to Switzerland to tell the world what was happening in Poland. He even talked to Lonka about enlisting her help. She had befriended a German officer, a common ruse among female Polish Underground operatives, who often slept with the enemy to elicit information or assistance. Lonka was fairly certain that "her German" could get Isaac across the border.

Zuckerman eventually found an outlet to expiate his guilt: revenge. As Zivia kept reminding Isaac, a template already existed for a Jewish fighting force. Lonka and Frumka had told them about it when they returned from Vilna. In response to the Vilna carnage, Jewish youth groups of all political stripes had joined together and pooled their resources to form one cohesive combat unit. It was called the United Partisan Organization, and although it was anchored by Zionists from the Marxist Young Guard, it included virulently anticommunist Bundists and Betarists from the Revisionist Zionist far right, General Zionists from the center, and moderate Socialists from Zuckerman's own left-leaning Dror Young Pioneer faction. Together these ideologically disparate groups had issued a common manifesto, penned by the partisan poet Abba Kovner. "Brothers," it exhorted all Jews. "It is better to die fighting like free men than to live at the mercy of murderers. Arise! Arise with your last breath!"

"Let's face facts," Zivia declared at a February party meeting that included Mordechai Tennenbaum and Tuvia Borzykowski, newly arrived Dror leaders from Vilna. "We have no weapons, no instructors that could teach us how to use them, and we know nothing about military tactics."

The Polish Resistance, on the other hand, had access to guns, as well as experienced army officers. But they almost certainly would not help or trust strangers. "We are completely unknown to them," Lubet-kin acknowledged. "We have no contacts." That was not the case, she said, for other Jewish groups. The Young Guard, despite its dogged atheism, had a surprisingly good prewar relationship with the de-voutly Catholic Boy Scouts, with whom they had often shared sum-mer campgrounds, and whose underground arm, the Gray Ranks, had become a highly successful sabotage unit. The Bund, for its part, had close and long-established ties to the Polish Socialist Party, the only mainstream political organization in Poland that could even remotely be called philo-Semitic. The Socialists and the Bund had adjoining headquarters on Long Street before the war. The Socialists had backed the Bund in prewar strikes to protest rising anti-Semitism and had joined in some street battles against fascist thugs. They had been help-ful during the 1940 Easter pogrom attempt, and some of their leaders now occupied prominent positions within the Polish Resistance.

"We must make contact with other Jewish groups at all costs," Zivia concluded. "We are all sentenced to the same fate. Today, it's Chelmno and Ponary—tomorrow, Warsaw and the rest of Poland."

CHAPTER 20

JOANNA AND THE TERRIFYING MR. GLASER

By the time Zivia and Isaac realized that Jewish groups needed to unite in March 1942, Joanna, Hanna, and Janine Mortkowicz had passed a year in their idyllic suburban refuge without seeing a fellow Jew. Though the sprawling estate in which they were hiding was only ten miles west of Warsaw, its tranquillity seemed far removed from the death and disease of the Ghetto and the Gestapo roundups that terrorized the rest of the city.

For the three generations of Mortkowicz women, time beat to a different rhythm; one marked hourly by the gentle peal of church bells, and seasonally by the gradually changing landscape. For Joanna, the winter of 1942 passed in a snowy blur of sled rides and wild tobogganing runs—the pursuits of a childhood not yet interrupted by the horrors of war.

Joanna was now almost eight, an intensely curious and stubborn child, and an avid reader who showed every sign of following in the family's literary footsteps. She was still short for her age, but, like her equally diminutive grandmother Janine, a tiny bundle of hyperactive energy. Throughout her stay at the Zbikow estate, Joanna had remained blissfully ignorant of Ponary, and Chelmno, and the mounting human catastrophe inside the Ghetto. She wasn't even fully cognizant of the conspiratorial activity taking place under her feet, in the estate's labyrinth of secret tunnels crammed with guns and sophisticated long-range radios provided by British Intelligence. She remained terrified of the mean and mysterious caretaker who always shooed her away from the big main barn, where strangers would sometimes materialize as if out of thin air.

Janine and Hanna both knew better. They made it a point never to ask any questions of their hosts, to stay away from certain parts of the property, and to keep to the grounds subleased by the nuns from the Order of the Immaculate Conception who were responsible for their care. Though Hanna and Janine had not left the estate for over a year, they managed to stay reasonably well informed about the war. From Underground newspapers they knew that the first American troops had arrived in Europe, landing in Northern Ireland; that the RAF had launched an ambitious new bombing campaign on German industrial targets; and that the Red Army, under a new commander, General Zhukov, had launched a massive counteroffensive in the east against the Wehrmacht. From German propaganda, they also learned that General Rommel was still holding off the British in Libya, that Singapore had fallen to the Japanese, and that General Douglas MacArthur had been ordered by President Roosevelt to abandon the besieged Philippines.

Joanna's mother and grandmother were not aware of the massacres of Jews taking place in Vilna, Lvov, and elsewhere, but events in the Ghetto were harder for the Germans to hide from ordinary Varsovians. From their friend and protector, the beautiful Underground operative Monika Zeromska, they heard horror stories of starvation and disease, of hundreds of Jews dying daily—and this only reinforced Hanna's determination to stay among Gentiles.

That the Polish Resistance kept tabs on developments in the sealed Jewish district was not unusual. Useful intelligence could be gleaned there. For instance, when the Germans ordered Jews to relinquish all fur coats remaining in the Ghetto during one of the coldest spells of the 1942 winter, the cruel requisition was relayed to London. British Intelligence was interested in the military rather than the humanitarian aspects of the seizure, since the furs were needed to line the uniforms of Wehrmacht soldiers fighting on the frigid Eastern Front. To the British, who were increasingly funding the Polish Resistance, the report on fur requisitions hinted at materials shortages and deteriorating conditions on the German front lines—both important pieces of the war puzzle.

Monika Zeromska's specific role in the Polish Underground was unknown to the Mortkowicz women. "My mother and grandmother would not have asked about it," Joanna said. Their beautiful benefactor, who bore a remarkable resemblance to the pinup queen Hedy Lamarr, came to see them every few weeks, bringing news from the outside world and money from their bookstore, which continued to flourish under the famous Zeromski cover name. (The publishing arm of the firm had ceased operating when the Nazis confiscated all the printing presses in Poland.) Hanna, ever the businesswoman, kept careful tabs on their daily expenses and biweekly receipts in a little black ledger dotted with dates and balances. There was always enough left over at the end of the month to send to their cousins, the Beylins, who were hiding under false identities on the "Aryan side" in Warsaw.

As for their other relatives, Hanna and Janine could only hope that they were alive and well. They had no way of knowing what had become of the Osnoses. All contact had been severed after Martha's 1940 departure for Berlin. Sometimes Joanna asked after Robert, whom she had always looked up to, since he was a few years older. The answers she received were comfortingly vague: "He's far away, traveling."

Joanna's recollections of her yearlong stay at the Zbikow estate were equally vague and nostalgic, until the day in early April 1942 when she vividly remembers being rousted from bed by her frightened mother.

"In my next memory we are slogging through mud in the middle of the night, running in panic, God knows where." In the rush to escape, Joanna's favorite doll, Michael, fell from her arms, and there was no time to retrieve it in the darkness. "Dragged along, I kept running. We had to hurry or they would catch us."

It was the Gestapo. The Germans had been tipped off that Jews were hiding at the estate, and the Resistance managed to warn the nuns housing Joanna, Janine, and Hanna that a raiding party was on its way.

In later years, Joanna often wondered who betrayed them and why. "Was it for money? Out of servile loyalty to the occupiers? Or because of anti-Semitic dogma?" she would reflect. That night, though, she blamed herself. She thought the nasty caretaker, Mr. Glaser from the Polish Underground, had driven them out because she had recently bitten his daughter during an argument and he was cross with her. So Joanna's eight-year-old mind reeled with irrational guilt as she and her family fled. It was her fault that her stern grandmother, who was nearly seventy, was now gasping for breath, lugging a hastily packed suitcase through dark, marshy fields.

Where they ran and for how long, Joanna would not remember. "In my hazy recollection of events, we knocked at the lighted window of a cottage we chanced upon in a side road, and someone invited us in without any questions or hesitation," she later recalled. "But that is impossible. The good Sisters would not have driven us out into the dark night without anyone to look after us. They must have sorted out a place for us to go, our arrival must have been prearranged, someone must have agreed on that address with someone in case of misfortune, and someone must have escorted us," Joanna speculated. "The terrifying Mr. Glaser may have been our go-between for that hiding place, and maybe one of his liaison officers escorted us through the muddy darkness."

Glaser, of course, would have had his own reasons for helping the Mortkowiczes escape. The presence of Jews at the estate risked compromising his clandestine operation. That Hanna, Janine, and Joanna had been brought there at all was a serious breach of security protocol, an amateurish mistake. If the Gestapo, while searching for them, stumbled upon any of the weapons, archives, communications equipment, or saboteurs that also hid at the estate, it would spell disaster: torture and the dreaded gas chambers at Auschwitz, which by 1942 had already claimed the lives of sixty thousand suspected Gentile rebels, many of them murdered with an experimental new cyanide-based pesticide known as Zyklon-B.

The mysterious Mr. Glaser was anxious to protect his network and to wash his hands of the troublesome Mortkowicz women, who had been forced on him by Monika Zeromska's contacts. Now that they were endangering his entire operation, they had to go. For the Mortkowiczes, this was a frightening prospect, one for which they were entirely unprepared. For young Joanna, the nocturnal flight proved a transitional moment. Until then she had largely been sheltered from the realities of Nazi occupation. While other Jewish children fought for a crumb of bread, she romped through blooming orchards, attended school with Christian kids, and reveled in "daredevil sledge rides," innocent of the larger world around her. That carefree existence was now over, and even as an eight-year-old she sensed that her life was about to change. "So without shedding any tears I left Michael in a puddle, and along with him my childhood."

Joanna, Hanna, and Janine were not the only ones being hunted by the Gestapo in the spring of 1942. On the night of Friday, April 17, trucks crammed with German soldiers and SS officers stormed the Warsaw Ghetto. They poured through several gates simultaneously, fanning out through the locked-down district, which was dark and silent, no lights or movement being permitted after curfew. Within minutes the deserted cobblestone streets echoed with the clatter of jackboots, while portable searchlights scanned buildings and doors were hammered down with rifle butts. Shots soon rang out, along with the occasional staccato of machine gun fire.

One of the tenements targeted during the raids was Isaac Zuckerman's Valiant Street headquarters. His startled janitor-lookout barely had time to pull the makeshift alarm bell before Gestapo agents were pounding up the stairs. On the third floor, in the Young Pioneer clubhouse, panic erupted and there was a mad dash for the attic, where an emergency exit had been cut through the wall into an adjacent building. In the ensuing scramble one of Isaac's most trusted deputies, Tuvia Borzykowski, was shot in the leg, but he still managed to escape. Two other Young Pioneers were not so fortunate. They were dragged to the ground-floor courtyard, and, with all the residents looking on in horror, each was shot in the head.

Before executing them, the Gestapo posed only one question to the victims: Where were Isaac Zuckerman and Lonka Kozibrodska?

That the SS knew about Isaac was not surprising. His involvement with the Socialist Zionist youth movement was not a secret. But Lonka was a different story. Very few outsiders were aware of the clandestine role the beautiful blonde played in linking the Young Pioneers to the outside world.

This could only mean that the Nazis had Jewish informants, a suspicion that was borne out when the homes of almost all the Bund's central committee members were also raided that evening. Sonya Nowogrodska, the only woman in the Bund underground leadership, narrowly cheated death, as did Bernard Goldstein by switching hiding places at the last minute. Mark Edelman and the Spiegel brothers were not targeted, perhaps because they were not senior enough to warrant Gestapo interest. Nonetheless, the Bund lost nearly a dozen operatives that night. All were shot on the spot, their bodies left to bleed out where they fell. In total, fifty-two people were killed on April 17, which became known variously as Bloody Friday, Night of Blood, or the Sabbath Massacre.

Bloody Friday revealed a shift in Nazi tactics. Until then, the Gestapo had focused its brutal counterinsurgency measures almost exclusively on Gentiles. (Indeed, earlier that very day, the Nazis had conducted a series of separate raids in the Christian quarters of Warsaw, deporting 461 suspected Resistance members to Auschwitz.) Prior to Bloody Friday, no evidence existed to suggest that the occupation authorities either knew or cared that Jews were forming conspiratorial cells. Occasionally, the Gestapo inquired about the likes of Bernard Goldstein, since he was a well-known agitator from before the war. But there had never been mass arrests or Gestapo dragnets in the Jewish Quarter on the scale that routinely decimated the Polish Resistance. The question was: Why now? What prompted the raids? Had the Germans, through their network of spies, gotten wind of the unification talks between Zionists and Bundists? Had they heard of the intensified efforts to acquire weapons? Did they know about the newly formed youth militias and their growing chorus of calls for self-defense?

The sad fact remained that the Bund, to date, had not managed to procure a single gun. The vaunted militias, in Boruch Spiegel's opinion, "were not very serious." Spiegel, after he recuperated, had demanded to join the defense unit, and he quickly became disillusioned by its lack of structure, discipline, adequate training, and, most of all, arms. Boruch had become far more militant since his father's death and his own near-death experience. His older brother Berl, who used to nag him to become more involved with the Bund, now had to restrain him. Boruch was volunteering for every possible assignment. He joined his girlfriend Chaika Belchatowska's "fiver" in distributing underground newsletters. He did gofer duty for Bund bosses, relaying messages and parcels from the main section of the Ghetto to what was now known as the Little Ghetto. This was the smaller, more prosperous southern part of the district, where display windows were still stocked with wines and luxury goods and the wives of the Ghetto's new "aristocracy"—Judenrat officials and smugglers—shopped. The Little Ghetto had effectively been cut off from the northern section when the Germans extended the Cool Street corridor in January 1942. The deep Aryan incision that provided Gentile access to the municipal courthouse and several churches was elongated to cut all the way through the Ghetto, connecting Midtown to the western working-class neighborhood of Wola. A new wooden bridge was erected over the Aryan passage, providing the only tenuous link between the northern and southern parts of the divided Jewish district.

Boruch was not content with gofering, however. What he really wanted was to learn how to fight. Physically, he was not a large man, unlike the gruff porters and coal carters from Bird Street who made up the Bund's prewar militias. But he had survived Garwolin Hell, and he had mustered the will to withstand the beatings by its Ukrainian guards. So despite his gentle temperament, his height deficiency, his delicate features, and his love of opera, Boruch possessed a reservoir of inner strength, a hidden toughness that he had never been aware of until he was pushed to his limits. Perhaps it was only natural that he wanted to push back and, in the process, expiate the guilt of having exchanged his father's life for his own. Boruch himself could not explain the reasons behind his newfound militancy; he only knew that it was there, and that he was frustrated about his inability to act on it. That frustration ran deep throughout the younger generation of Bundists, particularly after the failed unification talks with the Labor Zionists.

Isaac Zuckerman and Zivia Lubetkin's plan to form a joint defense force within the Ghetto encountered surprisingly stiff opposition. An initial pitch to Jewish Council leaders and relief agency heads prompted "a vehement reaction," in Zivia's words. "We were accused of being dangerously irresponsible" and of playing with people's lives. "If the Germans get wind of even the barest hint of what you propose," the Elders admonished the young Zionist hotheads, "the reprisals will be catastrophic. Are you ready to take responsibility for the massacre of tens of thousands?"

Undaunted, Zuckerman next approached the Bund. The Bund's elder statesmen, however, were not entertaining notions of immediate combat, as Isaac discovered to his dismay. When Isaac made his case for the establishment of a Jewish fighting force, an argument he buttressed with fresh reports of renewed atrocities in the east, Bund boss Maurice Orzech was not impressed. "You are quite young," Isaac remembered him responding. "And your assessment of the situation appears somewhat rushed and unseasoned." Orzech was fifty, twice Isaac's age, and a trained economist from a very wealthy industrialist family, who carried himself with the authority of one born into money. "It's impossible for the Germans to kill us all. Three and a half million Polish Jews!" he proclaimed. "You're spreading panic unnecessarily, young man."

Jews were not the only ones dying, Orzech argued. In Auschwitz, almost all the victims were still Gentiles at this stage, and the camp's capacity was vastly expanding with the construction of a satellite site in neighboring Birkenau. "Thousands of Poles are also being murdered," he insisted. When the Gentiles rose up, the Bund would join in the national rebellion, Orzech declared, but not before. "Our struggle is linked with the Polish working class," he ended the discussions. "We will not participate in any pan-Jewish organization."

Isaac was dumbfounded. "I was ready to kill my Bundist colleagues for their blindness," he vented to Zivia Lubetkin and several other dejected Zionists. They had counted on the Bund's connections with the Polish Resistance, but not on its baffling solidarity with Polish workers. Unbeknownst to Isaac, many younger Bundists like Boruch and Mark Edelman shared his view. Orzech's rejection of a joint fighting force stirred considerable rumblings within the Bund's lower (and less ideological) ranks. "Many of us were not happy with the decision," Boruch recalled. "It was a mistake," Mark Edelman agreed.

Though rebuffed, Zuckerman would not give up. Like the Spiegel brothers, he had lost family members, and that hardened his resolve to fight. So when a charismatic Communist operative contacted another big Zionist group, the Marxist-leaning Po'alei Zion Left, and its youth arm, the Young Guard, with a proposal to forge an antifascist alliance, Isaac set aside his ideological misgivings and listened. The man's name was Pinkus Kartin, and he was a veteran of the Spanish Civil War, a flamboyant Jewish adventurer who had spent years in Polish jails and Parisian exile because of his Leninist beliefs. Kartin did not promise access to the Polish Resistance, because the Polish Underground actively barred Communists. He offered something better: the backing of the Red Army. Kartin was a Soviet agent. Trained in guerrilla tactics by the NKVD, he had been parachuted into Poland in late 1941 to launch a network of Communist partisan cells that would disrupt German lines from the rear.

While his affiliation didn't bother the Po'alei Zion Left—its leader, Dr. Adolf Berman, had a younger brother in Moscow also being schooled by the Soviet secret police—Isaac Zuckerman and Zivia Lubetkin were neither Marxists nor particularly enamored of the USSR. "We had serious reservations," Lubetkin recalled. "There was a lot of dissension at that meeting," Isaac added. But there were very few other options. "This was after our great failure with the Bund, and we were grabbing at anything that could shape a force."

The offer Pinkus dangled before them was too tempting to ignore: unlimited supplies of Red Army–issue weapons, access to trained military instructors, intelligence reports—in short, everything Isaac and Zivia lacked, and desperately needed. "We feared that by the time all the other Jewish groups united in a common front, it would be too late," Lubetkin explained. "So we joined."

CHAPTER 21

THE RIGHT OPTION

Zuckerman's professed lack of unification options was not entirely accurate. A little-known but relatively well-armed resistance group already operated in the Ghetto in the spring of 1942. That group was the Jewish Military Union. Had Isaac bothered to inquire, he would have been astounded to discover the full extent of the JMU's clandestine web.

The JMU had tunnels burrowing under the Ghetto's walls. It ran an underground railroad that smuggled people out of Nazi-occupied Poland, and it had subterranean shooting galleries for target practice. Its gunsmiths made machine guns and its headquarters had sophisticated radio equipment.

Isaac knew none of this for the same reason the JMU would all but disappear from postwar history. The organization was politically toxic in left-leaning Jewish circles, and Zuckerman would sooner have made a deal with the devil than with right-wing Zionists.

So great was the animosity toward the JMU across much of the Jewish political spectrum that the organization was virtually expunged from the historical record by the Labor Party in postwar Israel. Only much later, with the rise of the right in Israeli politics, were concerted efforts made to revive the JMU's historical fortunes. But by then, it would largely be too late, because scant information survived.

From what little is known, the JMU may have been founded in December 1939 by Lt. David Apfelbaum, a highly disputed historical figure. He was supposedly then a thirty-eight-year-old reserve army officer, a veteran of Joseph Pilsudski's famous Legions, and a member of an elitist prewar organization called *Brit Hechayal,* or the Ex-Soldiers League, a secretive right-wing association of Jewish retired servicemen who tended to be supporters of the Sanation regime. Like most members of the Ex-Soldiers League, Apfelbaum, according to several narratives, hailed from an upper-middle-class background, from a "well-off" family that had achieved success both in business and within the medical community. His uncle was said to be the chief of cardiology at the Jewish General Hospital on Clean Street. Little else is known about David Apfelbaum; no photograph or physical description survives. There is no record of what he did for a living before the war, and few clues as to his personal habits, other than the fact that he was a bachelor and an admirer of Ze'ev Jabotinsky, the militant founder of the right-wing Revisionist Zionist movement that spawned the Likud Party of Israel.

Apfelbaum apparently fought with distinction during the siege of Warsaw, and in late 1939 he presented himself to his former superiors with the intention of going underground, like countless other Polish combat veterans who were beginning to organize resistance cells. "We don't want to go to the *Oflag,*" he told his ex-battalion commander, Captain Henry Iwanski, referring to prison camps being set up at the time for Polish army officers. (Iwanski is another deeply controversial figure.)

Three other Jewish officers—men who, like Apfelbaum, were described as "cultured and well off" and had conservative political views—attended the meeting. It was held in the infectious disease ward of St. Stanislas Hospital on Wolska Street, not far from where the first Panzer assault on Warsaw had been repulsed (and where a small square would be named in Apfelbaum's honor by right-wing Polish politicians in 2004). The unusual location was not accidental. St. Stanislas was one of the earliest hubs of Polish resistance because typhus and tuberculosis offered protection from German inquisitiveness. Nazi officials in Warsaw were notoriously sensitive to germs. Their fear of contracting a local ailment bordered on paranoia, and the Poles eagerly exploited this phobia to hide weapons in isolation wards and to organize resistance activities from behind doors marked WARNING: CONTAMINATED MATERIAL.

The thirty-seven-year-old Iwanski, a self-assured, formal man with blond hair and piercing blue eyes, was an equally unusual candidate to assist in the formation of a Jewish underground. Some historians would brand him a liar and he would prove a thorny embarrassment to Yad Vashem and problematic to Righteous Gentiles. A staunch nationalist, he was a National Democrat, or *Endek,* as Poland's largest right-wing party was more popularly known before the war. Its philosophy could be distilled, in the words of Warsaw writer Wladyslaw Broniewski, as "Hurray patriotism combined with primitive anti-Semitism." Under the motto, "God, Nation, State," the party preached love of country while practicing the politics of resentment. "Anti-Semitism was not merely an addendum to the Endek program," Alina Cala of the Jewish Historical Institute in Warsaw would later comment. "It was a principal pillar."

Despite his presumptive prejudices, Iwanski said he had been deeply impressed with Apfelbaum during the 1939 siege of Warsaw. "I must confess that I had never expected to find such a brave soldier as you among the Jews," he told him.

"There are many like me," Apfelbaum supposedly replied. "Thousands even better than me."

A bond formed between the two warriors, and trust—a very precious commodity for someone in Iwanski's position—overrode whatever political or philosophical misgivings he may have had in dealing with outsiders from an embattled minority. So when Apfelbaum and the three Jewish officers who accompanied him sought out Iwanski's counsel, he was receptive.

"Help us organize the Jewish youth and train them to fight the Germans," Apfelbaum pleaded. "The campaign against the Jews has already begun. We can't just stand back and watch this oppression be imposed on us. We have to act."

"It's a fact that you Jews are on the front line," Iwanski acknowledged, according to the postwar testimony of one of Apfelbaum's three fellow conspirators. "But before we get down to practical matters, I just want to say that whoever wants to fight the Germans is our brother. We'll help you as much as we can."

The first order of business was discretion. "Forget the name Iwanski," Apfelbaum was instructed. "From now on call me Sharp." Everyone in the nascent Polish Underground used pseudonyms; Apfelbaum was given the code name Blacksmith, and he and his three Jewish co-conspirators each received a 9 mm semiautomatic VIS handgun and a spare ammunition clip. They were told to recruit like-minded individuals from similar backgrounds—bourgeois, militarily trained, conservative; no socialists from the ideologically suspect Bund or Zionist left—and to wait for further orders.

Incongruous as it may have seemed, there was a historical precedent for the Judeo-Christian conservative alliance. Throughout the late 1930s, the Sanation regime helped train a radical offshoot of the Revisionist Zionist youth movement Betar. It was known as the *Irgun Zvai Leumi,* or National Military Organization in Hebrew, and it would later be labeled a terrorist organization by the British for its violent tactics in Palestine, including the notorious bombing of the King David Hotel in Jerusalem. In 1937, the Sanation government forged an agreement with the Irgun commander (and Polish émigré) Avraham Stern, later the leader of the Stern Gang, to provide Jewish recruits from Palestine with large arms caches, military instruction, and seminars on how to conduct guerrilla warfare. Training facilities at Polish army bases in the Carpathian Mountains near Lvov were opened to the Irgun in the hope that future Zionist military successes in Palestine might eventually encourage greater emigration. The Sanation regime's motives were self-serving—to reduce the number of Jews in Poland. But since Revisionists also shared that ultimate goal—"it is in your interest and in ours," as Ze'ev Jabotinsky said to convince Sanation officials—the marriage of convenience stuck. Valuable relationships between army officers and young right-wing Zionists were forged, and a precedent for wartime alliance was established.

During the siege of Warsaw, the Polish military had reaped rewards from its prewar association with the Irgun. On the eve of the Nazi invasion, the Irgun's Warsaw representatives had received a thousand rifles and ammunition clips from Polish army arsenals intended for shipment to Palestine. When the Germans attacked, local Irgun coordinator Ila Sztrasman voluntarily turned over the weapons to the

Warsaw military district commander, who in turn distributed the guns to the capital's defenders during the siege.

From a practical point of view, continuing the partnership made sense. Nearly a third of Poland's urban population was Jewish, and through its right-wing Jewish allies, the Polish Underground gained eyes and ears in places that might otherwise have been off-limits to Gentiles, such as Warsaw's large Jewish Quarter. The cooperation was very limited, however. Just as the Sanation regime kept its arrangement with the Irgun from the general public, Iwanski's superiors did not burden the Polish Resistance's central coordinating body with the details of the deal struck with Apfelbaum.

By the time Iwanski allegedly made contact again shortly before Christmas 1939, Apfelbaum—or Blacksmith, as he was now called—and his co-conspirators had found thirty-nine individuals, including five women, who met Iwanski's criteria. The group gathered at the home of an engineer named Urbach, where a formal ceremony was convened to induct the new members into the Resistance. The induction was held in a partly destroyed building on the corner of Valiant and Carmelite Streets, on the same block where Mark Edelman printed the Bund's news bulletins. Candles burned as the new members took an oath. "I receive thee among the soldiers of Freedom" was the standard Polish Underground wording. "Victory will be thy reward. Treason will be punished by death." As all underground members had to swear loyalty "before God the Almighty," a rabbi was present to bless the newly formed unit.

It was formally named the Jewish Military Union, and was supplied with twenty-nine handguns.

The early years of the JMU's development are not well documented, since—as the *Jerusalem Post* mourned in a 2006 headline—information about this organization was the first casualty of war. The dearth of historical documentation on the resistance group was actually a deliberate casualty of postwar politics in both Communist Poland and Labor-dominated Israel, according to the Holocaust historian Yisrael Gutman. For ideological reasons, the role of the right was ignored "almost to the point of total omission in an effort to write rival camps out of history."

So little is definitively known about the Jewish Military Union that the left-leaning *Haaretz,* another leading Israeli daily, asked in a skeptical 2007 article "what to make of the story of David Moryc Apfelbaum," noting that the only authenticated archival reference to him in either Polish or Israeli official documents is a listing in the 1938 Warsaw telephone book. The paper questioned whether or not Apfelbaum ever existed, claiming that he was an invention of the Polish and Israeli right.

Mark Edelman is equally dismissive of the JMU. "They were smugglers and thieves backed by a bunch of [Polish] nationalists," he angrily declared, between puffs of an unfiltered cigarette at his Lodz home in 2007. "They were never a real resistance movement."

The bitter divisions between the right and left ran too deep in both Jewish and Gentile circles for there to be any kind of effective cooperation. This was reflected in the Jewish Military Union's own "elitist recruitment policies strongly weighted toward those better-off Jews who were most integrated into Polish culture and society," according to Apfelbaum's cousin Marian, who at the time was a toddler in Warsaw. Their members had to be "bourgeois and right-leaning," and able to pass as Poles because the Jewish Military Union's conservative Polish patrons, like Captain Henry Iwanski, would not have welcomed unassimilated Yiddish speakers into their midst. As a result, the organization had only expanded from roughly forty initial inductees in December 1939 to almost a hundred by the fall of 1940.

During that time, the group had not been given any missions of note by Captain Iwanski or its other Gentile overseers. It had set up an underground railroad to smuggle people into the Soviet zone, which the Polish Resistance is known to have used. And it had been charged with the rather pedestrian responsibility of monitoring foreign radio broadcasts for the Poles and producing written transcripts similar to Mark Edelman's *Bulletin.*

Neither smuggling people nor transcribing radio broadcasts was a particularly prestigious assignment, and perhaps reflected the relatively low standing Jews held within the Polish Resistance's fractious hierarchy. Still, the Jewish Military Union had guns: at least three dozen Polish army-issue VIS-35 9 mm semiautomatic pistols based on a Colt design. Founding member Kalmen Mendelson, a thirty-eight-year-old former second lieutenant, had set up a firing range in the basement of a residential building at 5 Carmelite Street, a block away from Mark Edelman's nocturnal printing press. When the Ghetto was decreed, David Apfelbaum moved to the same street, according to Mendelson, which offered good cover because it was one of the busiest through-traffic roads in the Jewish Quarter, running from bustling Forestry Street in the south to Valiant Street three blocks north, abutting the east gates of Peacock Prison.

Apfelbaum's move into the Jewish Quarter and the closure of the Ghetto drastically altered the makeup and mission of the Jewish Military Union. Within a few months, membership in the group soared to over 250 inductees. The influx of new candidates during the winter of 1941 was partly the result of a change in philosophy by Apfelbaum, Mendelson, and some of the other early leaders. Up until then they had largely viewed themselves as subordinate to the Polish Resistance. But the forced segregation of Jews had altered their perspective, and they began to act more like an independent Jewish combat organization, now only loosely affiliated with outside forces. This gave them far greater leeway in recruiting and led to what effectively became a merger with the Zionist right.

The Revisionist Zionist Party and its youth arm, Betar, were natural partners for the veterans from the Ex-Soldiers League who dominated the earliest incarnation of the Jewish Military Union. Betar, through its militant offshoot the Irgun, already had a long-standing association with the Polish military, having been trained and armed by the Sanation regime, and of all the Zionist groups—dozens of dogmatic factions spread along the entire political spectrum—its ideology most closely mirrored that of the Jewish Military Union.

For the Revisionists, forging an alliance with Apfelbaum's unit made sense because they were virtually pariahs in the generally left-leaning Zionist community at this point and had nowhere else to turn. "We became Fascists, Hitlerites," David Wdowinski, the ranking Revisionist in Warsaw in 1941, recalled of the accusations hurled at his party from the Left in retaliation for founder Vladimir Ze'ev Jabotinsky's position that Jews "cannot serve two gods, Zionism and Socialism."

Revisionists held certain doctrinal positions that were heretical to the Zionist left. They favored heavy industry and big business over organized labor and the communal kibbutz at the heart of Labor Zionist philosophy. And, more important, they advocated the use of force if necessary to achieve Jewish statehood in Palestine, accusing the rest of the Zionist community, which pushed for negotiated diplomatic settlements, of complicity with the British to maintain the status quo. As a result of the rift, the two wings were not on speaking terms when the Second World War broke out. Revisionists boycotted the World Zionist Congresses, and Congress chairman David Ben-Gurion labeled the hawkish Jabotinsky "Vladimir Hitler," declaring that "the fight against Revisionism is a fight unto the death in the strongest sense of the word."

Betar was similarly isolated. Its members were derided by the left as "Brown Shirts" because of the color of their Scout uniforms. Just before the war, Menachem Begin had been appointed head of Betar in Poland. But the charismatic Warsaw University Law School graduate was now in Soviet custody, having been arrested by the NKVD in Vilna before he could make good on his promise to return to Warsaw. Young Betarists in the Polish capital were leaderless and eagerly looking for direction.

The Jewish Military Union provided that direction. How the groups first connected is not known. Perhaps they initiated contact through Apfelbaum's uncle, who was chief of cardiology at the same hospital where Revisionist leader David Wdowinski worked as a neuropsychiatrist. Whatever the case, in the winter of 1941, Betarists began to flood into the ranks of the Jewish Military Union.

One of these new recruits was a young man by the name of Paul Frenkel. He almost certainly did exist, was around twenty-two years old, and "was among the most beautiful, the most honest, the most modest people I have ever met in the course of a long political life," David Wdowinski later wrote. "He was the personification of *hadar*— dignity."

Frenkel was dark and delicate-featured, of slim build and refined appearance, according to Wdowinski. Already the young Betarist was establishing himself as a promising commander with an independent streak, "a rare combination of steel and silk." Acting on his own, outside formal party structures, he had rallied a group of like-minded Betarists in late 1940 and begun to train fighting units. His teenage followers were required to leave their families as a condition for joining his band, and Frenkel demanded that all recruits live communally and hew to near-monastic self-discipline. They practiced hand-to-hand combat, conducted seminars on partisan warfare, and adhered to a strict regimen of physical exercise. What they lacked was guns, and that was one area where the rapidly expanding Jewish Military Union could help.

"The [Polish Underground] became aware of this influx of volunteers and wanted to take advantage of the as yet relatively unhampered access to the ghetto," Kalmen Mendelson later explained. "They sent two combat rifles, two carbines, two machine guns, ten pistols, and dozens of hand grenades."

The shipment was relatively insignificant by Polish Underground standards. But it represented far and away the largest single store of weapons in the Warsaw Ghetto in the spring of 1941.

By 1942, the JMU boasted nearly three hundred registered combatants, split into two companies of four platoons whose commanders had all received advanced military instruction on the "Aryan side"—that is, from the Polish Resistance. Its organizational chart was rigidly martial and modeled on that of the Polish Underground, with separate department heads responsible for information and propaganda, transport and supplies, and technical, legal, financial, medical, military, and rescue operations, as well as a chief armorer.

A three-man general command staff presided over the secretive group. At its head stood Apfelbaum, or so some claimed. He was forty-one by now, and no longer a lowly lieutenant. In recognition of the JMU's numerical growth, his Polish Underground patrons had promoted him to captain. Despite the rise in rank, he faced a strong challenge to his leadership from twenty-two-year-old Paul Frenkel. Leon Rodal rounded out the triumvirate. Like Frenkel, he had no combat experience and had also joined the Military Union late. An independently wealthy twenty-nine-year-old journalist from Kielce, Rodal was the ranking Revisionist in the JMU. As the main editor of several Revisionist underground publications, he was the party's chief ideologue, the man in charge of disseminating Ze'ev Jabotinsky's founding philosophy of Jewish empowerment and self-defense. In the JMU, Rodal had found the perfect vehicle for his message, and his organizational skills and access to Revisionist Party funds gave him outsized influence.

Between them, Rodal and Frenkel started displacing the apolitical army veterans who had initially formed the JMU as a subordinate unit of Security Corps, a nationalist faction of the Polish Underground. Though still nominally attached to Battalion V of the Security Corps, the JMU by 1942 was begining to operate quasi-independently, more under the sway of Revisionist ideology than of its Polish patrons.

Apfelbaum still relied almost exclusively on his Gentile superiors for weapons supplies. But the training of his troops took place inside the Ghetto, in two underground shooting galleries on Cordials and Franciscan Streets which also housed clandestine gunsmith shops and grenade manufacturing facilities. The arms the JMU had acquired—a small number of large-caliber carbines and rifles, a few machine guns, perhaps as many as a hundred pistols, some in poor working order, and several hundred homemade grenades—were cached in a half dozen safe houses.

To smuggle weapons and maintain links with Security Corps officers, the JMU's Technical Department dug a tunnel in December 1941 on the corner of Trench and Goose Streets, in the northwestern sector of the district. Its entrance was beneath the ruins of a burned-out building next to the wall, and it ran fifty feet outside the adjacent Jewish cemetery, exiting discreetly under a morgue on the Aryan side.

The JMU thus had far less incentive to forge links with Jewish groups from across the political spectrum. Revisionists did not need to join a left-leaning coalition to gain access to Polish Resistance units or their weapons stores. They were already well supplied. For the JMU, moreover, there was substantial risk in crossing ideological lines: heightened exposure to potential Gestapo moles who might have infiltrated other underground organizations. That, more than any doctrinal disagreement, was a risk Apfelbaum, Rodal, and Frenkel were not willing to take.

Although the various Jewish underground groups were still bitterly divided in the spring of 1942, the Germans were not taking any chances. It was not a coincidence that the Gestapo rampage on Friday, April 17, 1942, followed so closely on the heels of the failed unification talks between the Bund and the Labor Zionists and the subsequent formation of the Communist-led Anti-Fascist Bloc. The Nazis wanted to ensure that the Jews remained divided.

"Bloody Friday has had strong repercussions," the Ghetto chronicler Emmanuel Ringelblum noted in his journal. "Since the slaughter was the result of tattling by Jewish informers, people tremble to speak a word. The illegal press has stopped publishing. There has been a significant weakening of political activity."

Fear and paranoia gripped the Jewish community. The Germans shrewdly exploited the mounting anxiety by staging smaller raids every few nights throughout May 1942 to keep the lid on underground activity. "I became a pariah," Isaac Zuckerman recalled. Word spread throughout the Ghetto that the Gestapo was searching for him. "My landlord heard about it immediately and insisted we leave his apartment." Isaac started changing flats every few days, avoiding Valiant Street headquarters, and dealing only with trusted intermediaries, just as he had once done in the Soviet zone. He was far from alone in lying low. Some formerly active conspirators quit. Others went "deep underground," dispersing into sleeper cells that would never re-form. And others still left Warsaw altogether, vowing in disgust to search for braver Jews in other ghettos. Pinkus Kartin, the flamboyant Soviet agent behind the newly formed Anti-Fascist Bloc, also refused to bow to the Gestapo terror tactics. He was denounced by an informant and tortured to death by the SS. The short-lived Anti-Fascist Bloc that Isaac Zuckerman and Zivia Lubetkin had joined only a few weeks earlier died with him.

In this atmosphere of suspicion and fear, trust almost completely evaporated, wiping out any chance for competing groups to find common ground. The Underground was atomized, once more reduced to its basic elements. In its place, a paralyzing obsession with informants arose. "There were not many," Mark Edelman recalled. "But they did a tremendous amount of damage."

That the Ghetto would eventually spawn a homegrown league of traitors was a statistical certainty. Any agglomeration of nearly half a million people will have its bad apples, regardless of ethnicity or religion. "People don't like to hear that we had Jewish prostitutes, criminals, or collaborators," Edelman explained. "But that was the reality."

In the Ghetto, this intrinsically human phenomenon could be seen at any of the district's sixty-one nightclubs. "The clientele of these places consisted principally of Jewish Gestapo agents, Jewish police officials, rich merchants who did business with the Germans, smugglers, dealers in foreign exchange," Bernard Goldstein recalled. "The worst nest of drunkenness and vice was the Britannia. The curfew did not apply to the habitués of this establishment. They made merry all night. Feasting, drinking, and carousing went on to the rhythm of a jazz band. At dawn, when the revelers left, the streets were already strewn with naked paper-covered corpses. The drunkards paid little attention, tripping unsteadily over the obstacles in their path. Around them hovered human shadows, swollen with hunger, who trailed after the well-fed drunks, begging for scraps. They were usually angrily pushed aside."

The Britannia, with its champagne-and-caviar-fueled revelry, became a symbol of the excesses of this small class of morally indifferent survivalists. The once respectable four-star hotel on New Linden Street had been turned into a brothel by German officers before being taken over by Abraham Gancwajch, the most notorious Gestapo-backed gangster in the Ghetto. He headed a Nazi-sanctioned extortion ring known as the Thirteen, dabbled in all manner of smuggling and illicit affairs, and was said to be one of the richest war profiteers in all of Warsaw.

"Gancwajch is turning into a regular Maecenas," Ringelblum, the underground archivist and member of Po'alei Zion Left, wryly noted. "He arranges receptions for Jewish writers and artists, where there is plenty of food—nowadays the important thing. A short time ago he threw an all-night party at the El Dorado night spot. . . . The party was opened with the dedication of an ambulance, named Miriam (after Gancwajch's wife at home)."

There was one other small group of Jews that earned near-universal scorn. They began arriving in Warsaw in May 1942 in American-made Pullman railcars, toting their matching leather luggage sets and dressed in expensive fur-trimmed coats. "The new arrivals would have nothing to do with Ghetto Jews," Goldstein derided the wealthy German Jews deported from Berlin. "They still talk about *unser Fuehrer* [our leader, Hitler]," Ringelblum marveled in astonishment, "still certain, despite everything, that they will return to Germany." Among them, almost certainly, were Martha Osnos's uncle Mendel and his shallow young wife.

BOOK THREE

It burns, brothers, it burns.
The time of anguish–God forbid–now churns
When the village and you in blow
Turn to ashes, to flames all aglow,
Nothing will remain at all–
Just a blackened wall
And you look and you stand,
Each with folded hand.
And you look and you stand,
At burned village and land.

It burns, brothers, it burns.
To you alone this agony turns.
If you love your town, its name,
Take the vessels, quench the flame.
Quench it with your own blood too:
Show what you can do.
Brothers, do not look and stand,
Each with folded hand.
Brothers, do look and stand
While the town burns and the land.

—JEWISH RESISTANCE ANTHEM

CHAPTER 22

SIMHA PLAYS SHEPHERD AND EDELMAN PLAYS GOD

In June 1942, as U.S. naval forces battered the Japanese fleet in the Battle of Midway, rumors circulated through Warsaw that the Germans were planning to deport tens of thousands of Jews to the east.

Simha Ratheiser, who had been isolated and in hiding for eight months, knew nothing of these developments: neither of the stunning American victory, which had turned the tide in the Pacific, nor of the growing anxiety in the Polish capital, where the implications of a massive resettlement campaign filled the entire Jewish community with dread.

For Ratheiser, the known universe had shrunk considerably since he had fled the Ghetto the previous fall. Very little information filtered through the dense forests enveloping the secluded hamlet where his mother, Miriam, sent him to stay with distant relatives. The little town was roughly halfway between Warsaw and Krakow, a two-hour walk through wooded trails from the nearest train station. It was called Klvov, and it derived its unusual name from its medieval status as a feed station for horses on a long-abandoned trading route to Lvov. Several hundred families still lived there, in old, dilapidated log cabins with earthen floors, amid their geese and goats.

Many teenagers accustomed to the bustle of the big city might have balked at getting stuck in a town whose twenty Jewish households clustered around the only street. But Ratheiser, who was almost eighteen by now, his boyish Slavic features still brimming with innocent mischief, welcomed the tranquillity. "It was heaven on earth" to him.

Klvov was too small and too far off the beaten path for a ghetto or a permanent German garrison. Its one-hundred-odd Jews were required to wear identifying yellow stars on their outer clothing, in accordance with Nazi law, but were otherwise free to come and go as they pleased. Occasionally, a German patrol passed through the village, but mostly the people of Klvov were left to their own devices.

Simha had never worn the Magen David armband in Warsaw, and he refused to heed his relatives' stern admonition that he sew one on now. His cousins were even less pleased when Ratheiser announced that he wanted to find work outside the tightly knit Jewish community. "My relatives were religious Jews and didn't like the idea of a Jew working for a Gentile," he recalled

Simha, however, instinctively grasped that even in isolated Klvov he would find greater safety among the Christian majority. Perhaps he was also eager to exercise his newfound freedom from parental control. Legally, he was almost an adult, and no doubt wished to make his own decisions. Simha overrode the objections of his relatives and asked them to introduce him to any local peasants in need of farmhands.

One agreed to take him on. "The peasant knew that my relatives were Jewish and concluded that I was a Jew too. Nevertheless, I was hired to herd cows, even though Jews usually didn't do such work."

Simha's new position was certainly unusual. According to prewar surveys, only 4 percent of Polish Jews made their living off the land, mostly in milling and food processing. Sixty percent of Poland's non-Jewish workforce, on the other hand, engaged directly in farming. Ratheiser's new employer either had not heard of the death penalty decree for assisting Jews, or, just as likely, didn't care. Polish peasants had a long-standing reputation for stubbornness and defiance.

The job had some significant perks: "Every morning I would go to the peasant's house, where I ate my fill of bread, potatoes, and lard, and drank milk," Simha recalled. He would then corral half a dozen cows from the barn and lead them out into the open fields, where they grazed until evening. "I'd lie in the meadow all day long, with the summer sky above me, listening to the birds singing," he recalled of his undemanding cowboy duties.

After the horrors of Warsaw, the abundance and serenity of Klvov were almost intoxicating. Simha's strength and carefree spirit quickly returned. His frame regained its athletic form, and the sun bleached his hair wheat-field gold. Only thoughts of home intruded on his bucolic paradise: "I was haunted by the idea that people in the Ghetto were suffering from hunger and disease while I lay between the green grass and blue sky."

This nagging remorse was compounded by the fact that Simha had not heard from his parents or sisters in the more than eight months since he'd left Warsaw. Not a scrap of news from the Polish capital had reached rural Klvov that entire summer. The isolated village had no radios, no access to newspapers, virtually no links to the outside world. Simha thus had no inkling that on July 22, 1942, the dreaded deportation order to liquidate the Warsaw Ghetto had finally been issued.

"All Jewish persons living in Warsaw, regardless of age and sex, will be resettled in the East," the decree read. "Evacuees" were instructed to prepare a three-day supply of food, and pack no more than thirty pounds of luggage, including, notably, "all valuables such as gold, jewelry, money, etc."

They were not told where they would be taken.

During the next seven weeks, through the course of what became known as the *Gross Aktion,* or Great Deportation, Mark Edelman emerged as a leading figure in the underground. The brash Belorussian orphan had until then played a peripheral role in the Bund, running errands and hanging around bosses like Abrasha Blum and Bernard Goldstein, who appreciated his cocky attitude and entrusted him with minor missions. The *Gross Aktion* changed everything, however, turning the Ghetto's power structures upside down.

Twenty-two-year-old Edelman was the Bund's gatekeeper, tasked with rescuing the doomed during the deportations. His role as a savior was unwittingly made possible by Nazi duplicity and his job as a hospital orderly. To maintain the fiction that all "evacuees" needed to be in good health in order to resettle in the new labor colonies, a field hospital had been set up at a large railroad siding where freight trains arrived each day. The new clinic was staffed with doctors, nurses, and orderlies from the Ghetto hospital where Edelman worked. Mark was among the medical personnel in crisp white frocks who were posted at this transfer station to further the illusion that deportees were being sent east to work. He saw his duties differently, however: to liberate members of the Underground before they were crammed into the cattle cars that departed the transfer station every morning and late afternoon.

The station, or *Umschlagplatz* in German, was the Ghetto's main cargo terminal and rail depot, where food and raw materials were legally imported from the "Aryan side" and where finished products from Ghetto factories were exported, mainly from German military contractors who had set up shop in the Jewish district to exploit cheap skilled labor.

To accommodate the new human traffic, the Umschlagplatz had been expanded to incorporate four large buildings off Zamenhof Street, the large diagonal avenue that slashed across Pleasant, Goose, Peacock, Valiant, and New Linden Streets, forming one of the Ghetto's main north-south arteries.

Deportees were led to the station along Zamenhof, a dense corridor of four- and five-story buildings whose upper floors had traditionally housed dentists and denture manufacturers. Edelman's job was to screen them when they arrived. "My task was to stand at the gateway to the Umschlagplatz and select out 'sick' people," he recalled. On the first day of the deportations it rained, he remembered, and a large crowd of onlookers lined the narrow sidewalks on Zamenhof in front of Teperman and Morgensztern's bakery to watch the Jewish Police shepherd the first batch of evacuees to the Umschlagplatz. They formed a heart-wrenching parade: skeletal survivors from the typhus quarantines, ragged refugees from homeless shelters and poorhouses, emaciated inmates from the Goose Street jail, the Ghetto's relatively small but hardened group of convicted criminals—all shuffling unsteadily on their feet, their skin pale as parchment, their bony limbs poking through torn clothes.

The staggering procession moved in an orderly silence that astounded Edelman, until he overheard some of the whispered conversations. "If they intended to kill us, they wouldn't feed us so much," the usually cynical thieves reasoned. "When will we be given the bread?" asked a child of about five, too weak to walk, perched on his father's thin shoulder. "Soon," the father promised, as they approached the gates. "It is already very, very near."

A promised travel ration was eliciting the extraordinary compliance. The Germans had offered six pounds of bread and two pounds of jam to every volunteer for relocation. This was more food than most had seen in weeks. "Do you have any idea what bread meant at the time?" Edelman asked. "In this way, even the most rebellious elements in the Ghetto, the hard cases, the pimps, thieves, and gangsters from Krochmalna Street, this whole underworld segment, lined up meekly at the ramps, saying that if they're feeding us we must be going to work."

Edelman soon realized that the transports were not departing on lengthy journeys to distant labor colonies. The locomotives were numbered, and the same engines, often driven by the same engineers, returned on a daily basis. "We didn't know where people were being taken, but we knew it could not have been very far." To find out, the Bund dispatched one of its most daring couriers, Zalman Friedrich. "He was a strong, well-built, athletic, handsome young man," Bernard Goldstein, who employed him frequently, recalled. "He looked like the German propagandist's dream of the blond Aryan." Goldstein arranged for him to make contact with a Socialist Party acquaintance in the Polish Resistance. Within the Resistance, the Socialists specialized in sabotaging trains because their trade unions had controlled maintenance and rail yards before the war. Inside knowledge allowed them to launch diversionary operations that ultimately damaged 6,930 locomotives and 19,058 railcars, disrupting raw material shipments and Wehrmacht supply schedules. Their derailing activities had vastly increased in the summer of 1942, but the heightened sabotage had nothing to do with the *Gross Aktion*. They were acting on British orders to hamper munitions deliveries to German troops attacking Stalingrad, where Hitler, on July 17, 1942, had launched one of the biggest offensives of the war.

The Socialists were dragging their feet on their earlier pledge to arm the Bund, but they promised to help uncover the destination of the Ghetto transports. Disguised as a mechanic from the Danzig station, Zalman rode the Warsaw–Malkinia line some fifty miles northeast of the capital, near where Isaac and Zivia had crossed back into Poland in 1941. There, the track branched onto a newly built spur, where trains from the Ghetto were diverted. The spur traveled through boggy fields and disappeared into a thick pine forest. Since the new line was closed to all other traffic, this was as far as the Polish railwaymen could take him. He observed, however, that the trains entering the forested area would reemerge a few hours later, empty. No food was ever carried into the woods. All Friedrich could learn initially was that the Germans had opened a small but particularly brutal detention facility in the vicinity for Polish political prisoners in the summer of 1941. It was called Treblinka I, and thousands of Gentiles had already lost their lives there.

Back in Warsaw, the Ghetto split into two distinct communities by early August: those who held *Dienstausweis* identity papers listing them as "productive" members of society, and those who did not. Holders of the so-called "life-tickets," which had been distributed to employees of the German-owned factories and to Judenrat and Sanitation Department officials, relief agency staff, medical personnel, and the Jewish Police, were exempt from initial deportation. All others—some sixty to seventy thousand people—were deemed nonproductive and subject to expulsion.

Edelman, meanwhile, continued his lonely vigil at the Umschlagplatz gates, trying to save fellow conspirators. "I had a hard rule. I only rescued those I knew personally from the Underground," he recalled. It was painful, and felt like playing God, but only a few dozen of the six to seven thousand evacuees that passed through the Umschlagplatz each day could be saved. Friends, neighbors, and former schoolmates had to be sacrificed. When they filed by him, Mark looked away. He pretended not to see them, pretended he didn't know what awaited them. "I was merciless," he said. "I had to be, because if I wavered I would not have saved a single soul."

Those he did select, he discreetly redirected to the field hospital emergency room. "In order to pull someone out of the lines it was necessary to prove to the Germans that the person was seriously ill." This was part of the cynical German charade that played out daily at the Umschlagplatz. "Only a healthy person could work, right? So these girls from the emergency room, those nurses, would break the legs of those people who had to be saved. They would wedge a leg up with a wooden block and smash it with another block."

Edelman tried not to resort to such incapacitating measures. He kept extra lab coats hidden in the field hospital and he would smuggle out Bundists dressed as hospital staff after the transports had departed. Sometimes Jewish Police officers helped him. "They weren't all sons of bitches," Edelman recalled. But every Jewish policeman, no matter how well intentioned, had a deportation quota to fill, and if the day's allocation was not met, the shortfall had to be made up from within his own family. This was a powerful incentive that explained the zeal with which some members of the Jewish Police performed their duties, snatching pedestrians from the street and hauling people from their homes.

"People—your friends, your neighbors, your co-workers, your family—just disappeared," Boruch Spiegel recalled. "Every day someone you knew was taken." For Boruch, it was his older brother Berl. "He had gotten into an argument, a fight, with a Jewish policeman, the son of a rich man who had owned printing presses before the war. I don't know the details, but a few days later he went out and didn't return. I never saw Berl again."

Boruch had no time to mourn. He himself had been caught twice in roundups. It was only by sheer luck that he managed to escape: once when a fellow Bundist intervened with a friendly Jewish policeman, and a second time when the Germans waved him off because they had just filled their daily quota. "Mostly I was hiding on the roof now in case they raided our building," Boruch explained. "My hands and pants were so blackened and torn from sliding on the tin that Chaika joked that she wouldn't be seen with me."

The popular theory that the expulsions would end after the seventy thousand "nonproductive" residents had been resettled was proving disastrously false. "Street by street, building by building, they were emptying the Ghetto," Spiegel said.

The dragnets became particularly savage after courier Zalman

Friedrich returned in mid-August with an eyewitness who had escaped from the newly opened camp at Treblinka II. The Bund began to paper the Ghetto with handbills describing Treblinka's gas chambers. "Do not be deceived! You are being taken to death and extermination. Do not let them destroy you! Do not give yourselves voluntarily into the hands of your executioners."

At the Umschlagplatz, heavily armed Ukrainian, Latvian, and Lithuanian units were called in by the SS to control increasingly uncooperative and hysterical crowds. "Everybody's eyes have a wild, crazy, fearful look," Edelman later described the scene in his memoir. "People beg for water and mothers cry for their separated children. The stench is unbearable. There are no latrines, and people must lie in their own feces for hours on end. The Ukrainians and Latvians rob and kill at will. In this crowded square," Edelman continued, "all the continually nursed illusions collapse. This is the moment of revelation that soon the worst, the unthinkable, the thing one would not believe to the very last moment is about to happen. A nightmare settles in one's chest, grips one's throat, shoves one's eyes out of their sockets, opens one's mouth to a soundless cry. One wants to yell but there is no one to yell to; to implore, to argue—there is no one to argue with; one is alone, completely alone in this multitude of people."

Edelman, too, wanted to yell with helpless rage as he watched "six, maybe eight" Ukrainian guards rape a young girl. "They held her by the hands and legs, suspended in the air. She hung there, bleeding as they took turns. This was in front of hundreds of people," he said. "What did I do? Nothing. What could I do?"

CHAPTER 23

ONE GUN

Whether it was horror or helpless rage, disbelief or despondent resignation, the mass deportations of June and July 1942 affected each Ghetto resident in a different way. The relief of having been spared each day was accompanied by the grief for lost friends and relatives and the terrifying realization that tomorrow would bring another roundup, another forced march up Zamenhof, past Edelman and the other white-frocked angels of death who stood vigil by the gates of the Umschlagplatz.

Fear and fury mixed equally in the minds of surviving Ghetto residents, and if Bundists like Mark or Boruch harbored any fantasies of revenge, these were tempered by the fact that the Bund still had no weapons, despite repeated promises from their Socialist allies that a shipment was expected any day. The lack of guns was the main reason Bund boss Maurice Orzech refused another entreaty from Isaac Zuckerman and the Zionist left to form a fighting alliance. The idea was proposed at an emergency meeting of Ghetto leaders in the opening days of the expulsions. Edelman was present at the high-level discussions, though more by accident than by invitation. "I was accompanying Abraham Schneidmel," the head of the Bund's self-defense militia. "Suddenly some Ukrainians started shooting at us. Abraham, a former [Polish army] officer, immediately sized up the situation and bolted. I stayed and went to the meeting in his place," Edelman recalled. "It surprised me that such a great figure would run away. But I was a kid. Abraham didn't believe in the organized resistance that we young people so desperately wanted because he was an adult. As a professional soldier, he knew that realistically we had no chance."

"You can't shoot from two fingers," Maurice Orzech lectured Zuckerman in a similar vein. Isaac countered by suggesting that they attack the unarmed Jewish Police while waiting for the weapons the Communists had promised him. At least they would be doing something, he insisted. His bearing and forceful manner made an impression on Edelman, who had never seen Zuckerman before. "He looked like a nobleman," Mark recalled, "tall and handsome, and self-assured." But that didn't alter the fact that Bundists "didn't know the Zionists, didn't trust the Communists, and saw no point in cooperating until we had something to shoot with anyway."

So once more no agreement was reached on a common Jewish defense force. What Orzech did not tell Zuckerman during the meeting, however, was that the Bund was on the cusp of acquiring a large batch of weapons, perhaps because they did not want to share it. After months of frustrating delay, the Socialists were finally about to deliver. Through a trusted prewar contact, Orzech had been informed that a Wehrmacht freight car loaded with rifles destined for the Eastern Front had been diverted by the Polish Underground to one of hundreds of sidings at the busy Eastern Cargo Terminal Station. It could sit there for a maximum of two days before the Germans would notice it was missing, so the Bund needed to act fast. "I don't believe [it will be] a whole wagonload, but we'll get something out of this," Orzech promised Edelman before setting out for the Aryan side. "He said that I should wait by a phone at eight A.M. for his call," Mark recalled. By then, very few telephones were still operational in the Ghetto. Fortunately, Sonia Nowogrodzka, the only woman in the Bund leadership, had a working line in her apartment on New Linden Street. Almost seventy years later, Edelman could still remember the number: 11-92-28.

At the appointed hour, Mark arrived at Nowogrodzka's apartment above a coffee shop. He climbed the five flights of stairs to Sonia's spacious top-floor flat and waited. "I sat by the phone," staring at the blank spots on the wall where paintings by Mane Katz, a contemporary of Picasso, had hung before the war. The hours passed. Mark chain-smoked to ward away hunger, eyeing the jars of marmalade in the kitchen. Nowogrodzka had probably bought them from Sztykgold's, the famous preserves shop a few doors down across the street. But she was gone on an errand and he could not help himself without permission. By midafternoon, she hadn't returned, and Orzech still hadn't called. Edelman grew worried. Something was wrong.

"Suddenly I saw a large mob on the street below being driven toward the Umschlagplatz," Edelman recalled. The screaming and shouting was deafening. Commands of *Raus! Weg! Los!* were accompanied by curses in Ukrainian, Yiddish, and Polish and the retort of the occasional shot. Among the panicked faces, he recognized Sonia Nowogrodzka's dark, elegant features.

"It was four o'clock P.M. There was nothing one could do. At that hour you couldn't get anyone out of the Umschlagplatz because people were loaded directly into trains." New Linden Street was cordoned off. Front doors had all been sealed shut by the Jewish Police, so Edelman was trapped in Sonia's building. The Ukrainians and Germans were checking for anyone left in emptied apartments—and, more important, for anything of value left to steal. Edelman crouched in a corner of the kitchen, shuddering involuntarily. Soon he heard German voices barking in the stairwell. Would they ransack the apartment and find him? It was late, and that may have saved him. The Germans, in a hurry to make the last deportation train at 6 P.M., could not loot at leisure. Just in case they returned, Edelman spent that night hidden in the back of a closet. Orzech never called. The guns never materialized. And Edelman finished off all the marmalade.

When the Ghetto's elder statesmen rebuffed Isaac Zuckerman for a second time, the Zionist youth leader decided to go it alone. Isaac and Zivia Lubetkin convened a meeting at their Valiant Street headquarters on July 28 and founded the Jewish Fighting Organization, or ZOB, as it became more popularly known by its Polish acronym.

At first, only the Marxist Young Guard joined, as well as one representative from the centrist Akiva, a youth arm of the General Zionists. The lone Akiva recruit was disproportionally important, however, because he was an officer of the Jewish Police, and Isaac had decided that the ZOB's first objective would be to assassinate the chief of that traitorous force.

The mission was heartily endorsed by Joseph Kaplan and Samuel Braslaw, the co-leaders of the Young Guard, and it was entrusted to Israel Kanal, the Akivist cop. Kanal was twenty-two years old and hailed from a good family in western Poland. He had signed up for police duty thinking he would be in a position to help Jews. But like many others, he had become disillusioned by the corruption and complicity that pervaded the force. The deportations were the tipping point for Kanal, and he had resigned. Isaac, however, persuaded him to don the hated *Ordungsdienst* police cap one last time because only a member of the Order Service could get close to their target, Joseph Szerynski.

Szerynski was a career law enforcement officer, a careful man and fastidious dresser who seemed to have let power, money, and women go to his head after the occupation began. He had been a district police commander before the war, and it was largely because of his reputation as a stickler for detail and for doing things by the book that Judenrat chairman Adam Czerniakow had appointed him head of the Ghetto police. A Catholic convert who had polonized his surname from Shinkman in order to win promotion in the Polish civil service, Szerynski had no particular affinity for his abandoned faith. In that regard, he proved himself an ideal choice to do the Nazis' bidding, unlike Czerniakow, who committed suicide on the first day of the *Aktion* rather than sign the deportation order presented to him by the SS.

The decision to kill Szerynski was both symbolic and politically expedient. It was a way for Zuckerman to buy time, because his fledgling fighting organization faced the same problem as the Bund: It had no weapons with which to launch an uprising, and a slew of impatient young members itching to attack the SS with nothing more than switchblades. Zuckerman talked to the rash and rebellious teenagers in much the same way Orzech had spoken to him. A Ghetto-wide revolt, he explained, could not be accomplished with the one gun that currently constituted the ZOB's whole arsenal. But one pistol was sufficient to kill Szerynski and send a message to the entire Jewish Police.

The hit was planned for the night of August 20, a Thursday. It turned out to be a blistering day, with thermometers at the Umschlagplatz registering 80 degrees even after dark. Nearly two hundred thousand Varsovian Jews, over half the Ghetto's inhabitants, had been sent to Treblinka by then. Valiant Street, like many other large sections of the district, was completely empty, a ghost town of ransacked apartments, where white feathers from shredded pillows and mattresses swirled in the deserted courtyards like summer snow. "There wasn't a single Jew on Valiant," Zuckerman recalled. Ironically, that made it safer for the ZOB to operate out of the Dror clubhouse, since the danger of unexpected raids had decreased dramatically. The Germans and Ukrainians had already pillaged the vacant buildings and were now focused on the remaining, inhabited parts of the Ghetto.

Szerynski was with his mistress in one of the populated areas that evening, guarded by a pair of Jewish Police officers posted outside his luxurious apartment building. Israel Kanal rode up to the edifice on a motorcycle and breathlessly informed the guards that he had an urgent message from police headquarters. They may or may not have recognized Kanal—the Order Service had two thousand members—but they let him pass. A woman answered the door when Kanal knocked. While she fetched Szerynski, the young Akivist removed the revolver from his waistband. The gun had been supplied by the Young Guard, one of two they had received from the Polish Boy Scouts.

When Szerynski's large frame filled the doorway, Kanal pulled the trigger. The pistol jammed. Frantically, he cocked the firing pin again, and this time a shot rang out. Szerynski must have been so stunned that his jaw literally dropped, because the bullet entered one cheek, grazed his tongue, and exited the other cheek without so much as dislodging a molar. Kanal was too stunned to fire again and fled into the night.

Word of the assassination attempt spread rapidly through the Ghetto, but to Zuckerman's frustration, it was widely presumed to be the work of Gentiles from a Socialist faction of the Polish Resistance.

"It didn't occur to a Jew that Jews would use weapons, that they had weapons."

Acquiring those weapons now became the ZOB's overriding priority. To that end, Zivia Lubetkin dispatched courier Frumka Plotnicka to join the Young Guard's top runner, Ari Wilner, on the Aryan side. Wilner, a veteran of the Vilna ghetto, was blond and blue-eyed, and he looked like a regular *sheygetz,* in the pejorative parlance of one contemporary. He was apparently so convincing at playing the *sheygetz* that the Mother Superior of a Dominican convent where he took refuge during the 1941 massacres in Vilna rechristened him George in honor of her late brother, who she swore was his spitting image. The name had stuck, and in the waning days of August 1942, Frumka Plotnicka sent a message to Zivia that she and "George" were returning to the Ghetto with a package.

The package consisted of eight hand grenades and five handguns that Wilner procured through fellow Marxists. It was hardly the Red Army arsenal that the Communist underground had promised, and Isaac was disappointed. Smuggling the meager weapons haul into the Ghetto was Zivia Lubetkin's responsibility, since she was formally in charge of couriers. She would use the same method Simha Ratheiser had employed to sneak back into the Ghetto after his shopping expeditions: try to blend into a column of forced laborers returning after a day's work on the Aryan side. These labor details still operated, despite the expulsions. The danger was that now, whenever the Germans were behind on their daily deportation quota, the captive laborers were marched straight to the Umschlagplatz instead of being released.

Forced laborers often bought food while on the Aryan side, so Frumka packed the hand grenades and pistols in the bottom of a sack of potatoes. When the labor details returned in late afternoon, she and Wilner donned Magen David armbands and slipped into the long formations. "The guards at the gates were checking everyone carefully," Lubetkin recalled. "They had dumped out the potatoes of the man in front of Frumka, and they were rolling around on the road." Frumka kept her cool. She was exceedingly pretty, a prerequisite for the job, and said something flirtatious to the Polish and Ukrainian guards, who waved her through with a cursory pat-down.

"I'll never forget the drinks in honor of that event," Isaac Zuckerman said of the celebration that evening at Valiant Street. "We were thrilled. There was genuine joy."

Alas, it proved short-lived. On September 3, 1942, the Gestapo arrested ZOB co-founder Joseph Kaplan. A few hours later, they shot his colleague Samuel Braslaw. The two Young Guard leaders had formed half of the ZOB's command staff. Isaac had no time to mourn. As soon as he heard that Kaplan was in the hands of SS interrogators, his thoughts raced to the ZOB's weapons cache. The arms had been stored at a Young Guard safe house on Cordials Street. "I gave orders to bring the weapons to us," Zuckerman recalled. While a courier was transporting the grenades and guns, she stumbled across a German patrol. "This, then, was the sum of our day," Isaac recalled glumly. "Kaplan arrested, Braslaw killed, and our weapons captured."

CHAPTER 24

LITTLE ANGEL

Simha Ratheiser forced himself to smile and shifted in the late summer sun, which still blazed brightly in September 1942. He tried his best to feign amusement, since his life depended on it. The Germans were watching him, expecting him to share in their mirth. They were clearly enjoying themselves, these tall and dashing cavalrymen, with their polished boots and riding crops, as a trembling, elderly Jewish man urinated in his pants. The cavalrymen pointed at the dark stain spreading down the terrified man's trousers, and made jovial remarks that Simha was meant to appreciate as well. He willed himself to smile and thrust his hands in his pockets, partly to conceal their trembling and largely because he feared he, too, would "wet myself, I was so frightened."

Operation Reinhart, the SS code name for the liquidation of Polish Jewry, had reached Klvov. In the waning days of August 1942, the hamlet's twenty Jewish families were herded into a makeshift ghetto of roped-off walls and were told they could not cross the staked-out lines on pain of death. A group of Waffen-SS cavalry officers rode into town a few days later, intent on using the captive Jewish villagers for sport.

"Come here," they had ordered the elderly man. When he did as he was told, crossing the putative ghetto boundary in the process, they screamed, "You are outside the area!" in feigned outrage. The startled old man was accused of committing a capital crime and was tossed against a barn wall. "I was standing ten feet away," Simha recalled. "The Germans had no idea I was Jewish too." They were busy conducting a mock trial, doubled over with laughter, debating with exaggerated gravity whether to execute their victim. Ratheiser couldn't bring himself to look into the old man's pleading eyes. He knew the man vaguely. He was one of his relatives' neighbors, and he, in turn, knew Simha's true identity.

Since Simha had never worn the yellow star and had chosen to work for Gentiles, the Germans presumed he was a simple farmhand, an eager spectator to their sport. Perhaps his strong Aryan features led the cavalrymen to assume that he appreciated the service the SS was rendering Klvov by ridding it of Jews.

Ratheiser nodded with all the enthusiasm his pounding heart could muster and the soldiers roared in approval. Simha felt shame for playing their cruel game. But his urge to live outweighed his instinct to flee, or to shout indignantly that he, too, was Jewish and that the cavalrymen were murderous scum. So he remained rooted to the spot, praying that the old man would not address him in Yiddish.

Just then, to Simha's astonishment, the leader of Klvov's minuscule Jewish community stepped in front of the firing squad to plead the condemned man's case. At first the Germans were amused. But when the Judenrat chairman gently tried to push one of the rifle muzzles down, the cavalrymen were nonplussed by his defiance. Their grins faded, and their faces took on a uniformly hard look. In unison, they raised their rifles and shot the chairman at point-blank range. "I remember the blood pooling on the ground near my feet," Ratheiser recalled. "I was so frightened I wanted to run. But I couldn't move. I couldn't show any emotion. The Germans were watching my reaction."

For Simha, the execution "was the first time that I really understood what was happening to my people." He realized that while he could continue to hide among the Gentiles, the notion of passively observing genocide filled him with a deep sense of shame. Then and there, Ratheiser decided to return to Warsaw to rescue his family before it was too late.

In the Polish capital, a collective guilt also gripped the Jewish community as shell-shocked survivors of the *Gross Aktion* struggled to come to terms with the full enormity of the deportations. "So many of our comrades were gone, and we were too ashamed to look one another in the eye," Zivia Lubetkin recalled.

The "resettlement" program was officially over. The last transport to Treblinka had departed on September 21, 1942—Yom Kippur—carrying two thousand Jewish policemen. Their services were no longer needed, now that the seven-week extermination campaign had reduced Warsaw's Jewish population by over three hundred thousand.

The Ghetto itself had become a ghost town. On street after street, block after block, buildings stood hauntingly empty. Other than the still-functioning Peacock Prison, the central core of the district was completely deserted. Every tenement south of Forestry Boulevard was vacant. All the residents along the Cool Street corridor were dead, as was every inhabitant south of Mushroom Street.

Throughout the abandoned areas, doors to thousands of apartments were left eerily ajar. Inside, the moldy remnants of interrupted meals and half-smoked cigarettes stood testament to the savage urgency of the final phase of the *Gross Aktion,* when entire blocks had been emptied in the space of a few hours. The looting that followed had transformed these deserted sections into postapocalyptic landscapes where nothing stirred save for the strips of torn clothing that flapped from bits of broken furniture.

At street level, the billboards advertising chewing gum, shampoo, and travel agencies still beckoned, but all the storefronts had been shattered, the shelves stripped of anything of value, the lighting and toilet fixtures carted off by bands of scavengers. In ransacked apartments, prewar electricity and phone bills, family letters and postcards lay scattered on bare floors, the desks and bureaus that had contained them having been chopped up for firewood or hauled off for resale. Mice and rats scoured the debris for leftover crumbs.

It was only at dusk that the depopulated parts of the Ghetto began to show faint signs of life: a moving shadow here and there; a bent figure scurrying from a courtyard; the crunch of glass underfoot; the echo of a can being kicked inadvertently in the dark. Occasionally, the red ember of a cigarette might glow in the distance, or a whispered greeting might be heard. But otherwise, blackness and silence stretched in every direction—until an abrupt explosion of life and light: the shops.

The shops housed the 34,969 Jewish slave laborers who had been spared deportation so they could toil in German-owned factories that supplied the Wehrmacht with everything from winter coats to camouflage netting. Clustered in four separate enclaves, each barricaded with barbed wire and wooden fencing, the shops comprised some four hundred converted apartment buildings and were now the only places in Warsaw where Jews had a right to live. Anyone outside the four cordoned industrial sectors was considered an "illegal," subject to summary execution, and had to hide in the "wild," in the vast depopulated dead zones that now comprised most of the empty Ghetto.

In one such wild area, in a dark and damp cellar near the Wilfried Hoffman Works, where twelve hundred Jewish tailors sewed SS uniforms, Zivia Lubetkin and Isaac Zuckerman tried to regroup the remnants of the decimated Jewish Fighting Organization. A single candle lit the room, and several dozen ZOB members sat around a sparse meal prepared from canned goods scoured from neighboring tenements. Food was no longer an issue now that the Ghetto was mostly empty and the "legals" were fed by their Nazi employers. Almost anything could be foraged at night from the tens of thousands of vacant apartments and later traded on the Aryan side for fresh produce. Still, Zivia and Isaac ate without appetite. "We were consumed with shame," she recalled. "How could we live when we had watched hundreds of thousands of Jews taken to slaughter?"

The question tormented the young Zionists, now that the immediate danger of death was over. During the deportations, no one had had the time or the luxury to reflect. Escaping the daily roundups had been all-consuming. Now there was no escaping from the full horror of the calamity. The toll was staggering in every demographic. Of 51,458 Jewish children under the age of ten in Warsaw, for instance, only 498 remained alive. Ninety-eight percent of all teenage girls had been sent to Treblinka, as had an only slightly less devastating 89.5 percent of males in their twenties. The genocide spanned all age brackets, occupations, and political orientations. Statistically, only the various underground organizations had fared better than the general population, losing around half to two-thirds of their members, thanks to their clandestine experience.

Ironically, this heightened survival rate now filled many with guilt. "We hid like mice in holes," Isaac Zuckerman lamented. "That was our shame and our disgrace." As he looked around the cellar at the hunched figures of newly orphaned teenagers, of fellow Resistance members whose brothers and sisters were dead, the same thought ran through everyone's mind: Why hadn't they risen up? Why hadn't they picked up a stick, a knife, a stone, and flung themselves on the Germans, as Joseph Kaplan had valiantly done? Kaplan and Samuel Braslaw had died heroically. In the furtive glances directed at Ari Wilner, the blond and blue-eyed courier who was now the ranking Young Guardsman in the ZOB, the unspoken question appeared to be whether they should do the same.

"What now?" someone broke the gloomy silence. "I don't remember who spoke first, Zivia or Ari," Zuckerman said. "The words were bitter, heavy, determined: There would be no Jewish resistance. We were too late. The people were destroyed."

It was pointless to continue, the speaker said. "When there were hundreds of thousands of Jews in Warsaw we couldn't organize a Jewish fighting force. How will we succeed now, when only tens of thousands are left? We didn't win the trust of the masses. We have no weapons and we almost certainly won't have any. There's no strength to start all over again. Honor is trampled."

Murmurs of assent and looks of shame followed the statement. It was true, someone declared. They had failed. The situation seemed utterly hopeless until one of the younger ZOB members spoke up. They should go out in a blaze of redemptive glory, he suggested, using the one weapon they still had: hundreds of gallons of gasoline stored in canisters throughout the basements of abandoned buildings. "Come on," exhorted the youth. "Let's go out in the streets tomorrow, burn down the Ghetto and attack the Germans. We'll be liquidated. We are sentenced to be liquidated anyway. But honor will be saved."

That suicidal outburst changed the tone of the conversation. Zuckerman would later call it one of the ZOB's seminal moments.

The proposal unleashed a torrent of pent-up anger. In one instant, the gloom lifted. Everyone started talking at once. Plans for kamikaze-style attacks were presented and shot down. Fierce arguments broke out over how best to die.

In the end, with great effort, Isaac managed to quash the notion of a collective suicide mission. Instead, he argued, they needed to rebuild the organization, find more guns, and replenish their decimated ranks. "Ari must go back to the Aryan side. We must look for new contacts," Isaac declared. "We shall raise money in the Ghetto and buy weapons from private dealers." They would build bunkers and shelters and rent safe houses on the Aryan side. And they would wage war on informants, Gestapo agents, and the remnants of the Jewish Police, all but four hundred of whom had been deported. "We started organizing again," Zuckerman recalled of the turning point. "Forty-eight hours later, Mordechai Anielewicz entered the Ghetto."

If there was ever a time when young Jews in Warsaw needed a bold and decisive leader, it was in the sorrowful, soul-searching days after the *Gross Aktion.*

For all his charisma, his legendary sense of humor and politician's gift for speech making, Isaac Zuckerman was not necessarily that leader. Isaac lacked the all-consuming fire, the inner drive and self-discipline, the unwavering self-confidence necessary to inspire blind obedience. Zivia Lubetkin did possess that single-minded focus and intensity, but she was not an extrovert; she was too distant and emotionally detached, and she shied away from the spotlight. Her romance with Isaac—the two had now been open about their affair for some time—also decreased her ability to lead, particularly in the eyes of the Young Guardsmen, who may not have been aware of her lengthy independent history as a professional Dror activist.

What really killed Isaac and Zivia's leadership chances, however, was their presence and relative passivity during the deportations. Mordechai Anielewicz, on the other hand, was not tainted by this stigma. He had left Warsaw in disgust earlier that year, because no one would heed his calls for an immediate revolt. The twenty-three-year-old Young Guard leader had been dismissed, even within his own relatively militant organization, as a dangerous hothead. Party elders had cringed when he arrived from Vilna in late 1941 waving a gun around, warning anyone who would listen that they would all die unless they rose up. At the time, such talk was viewed as dangerous fearmongering and Anielewicz was written off as a hysterical troublemaker. The teenagers—the seventeen- and eighteen-year-olds who made up the bulk of the Young Guard—loved him. But his superiors in the Po'alei Zion Left saw him more as a powder keg: unstable, and above all hard to handle. When Anielewicz furiously stormed out of the Ghetto swearing to search for less docile Jews elsewhere in Poland, relief had swept over some who worried that his actions would only serve to attract the Gestapo's wrath.

Effectively, Mordechai had been sent packing, a loose cannon who no one was ready to believe. Now, returning from Silesian exile, untainted by the expulsions that discredited his critics, he was welcomed back as a prescient sage, a warrior in waiting, and one that young Zionists were desperate to follow.

For Anielewicz, the vindication was also a homecoming. He was a Varsovian, born and raised in the shantytown section of Riverside, which had been known before the war as one of the roughest slums in the Polish capital, if not in all of Poland. Riverside clung to the muddy western banks of the flood-prone Vistula; most of its flimsy wooden structures felt temporary, since the low-lying area regularly washed out. Warsaw, unlike Prague or Budapest, which hugged its riverbanks, had shunned its temperamental waterway, opting to build at a safe distance on elevated ground. Riverside had been sacrificed to the elements and left to smugglers, gangsters, and illicit distillers—a shady place where mud, squalor, and filthy outhouses were the norm. "Jews considered it the underworld suburb," Simha Ratheiser recalled. His grandmother had owned a tavern there. "Drunkards haggling and quarreling were an everyday sight," he remembered. "The ambulance visited the tavern frequently. So did the police."

It was in Riverside, among almshouses, homeless shelters, and convents catering to unwed mothers, that Mordechai Anielewicz acquired his Marxist yearnings for social justice. He initially was drawn to Betar's brand of muscular Judaism, its paramilitary camps, discipline, and combative atmosphere. But Betar proved too bourgeois. Mordechai crossed over from the far Zionist right to the far left while in his midteens, perhaps because his humble roots did not mesh with the more prosperous backgrounds of many conservative Zionists.

The Anielewicz family lived on Solec Street, where some of the buildings were derelict grain silos and salt depots converted into crowded dwellings. Mostly Gentiles resided in the rickety structures, though property registers indicated that the Rozenwein and Bromberg families had small shops down the street, near the massive concrete footings of the Poniatowski Bridge, under which an unlicensed open-air market operated.

Anielewicz's father, Abraham, owned a small convenience store, and like every other business owner in Riverside, he had to pay tribute to racketeers. Mordechai's mother had a stall that sold fish, and she could not always afford to buy ice to keep the fish from spoiling in the summer heat. The Anielewiczes were poor, but not penniless. Mordechai and his younger brother Pinchas, a brawny wrestling champion, mostly ate potatoes and cabbage, but they had meat at least once a week—and there was always fish. Their clothes were threadbare and unfashionable but clean and neatly pressed. Despite their difficult financial situation, the family managed to send Mordechai to Laor, one of the best private Jewish schools in Warsaw. Laor was on Cordials Street in the Jewish district, which required Mordechai to take the P or Z bus lines, and he often fought off local Gentile bullies—*sheygetzes*—who tried to steal his thirty-groszy, or nickel, fare. He graduated at the top of his class, mastering Hebrew in the process, and he picked up his future nom de guerre, Aniolek, or Little Angel in Polish, while still in high school. It was a play off his surname and deceptively angelic face—for Anielewicz was as boyishly handsome as Simha Ratheiser, with delicate features and searching green eyes that masked an explosive temper. His Christian neighbors gave him another nickname, which paid tribute to that temper and his quick fists: Mordek, roughly translated as Little Thugface, a diminutive of Mordechai that by Riverside's rough-and-tumble standards was actually a term of endearment.

Shortly after Anielewicz's return, the ZOB received another piece of welcome news. The Bund wanted to talk. It had little choice by this point. Within its discontented lower ranks a mutiny was brewing. The generational divide that had been building for over a year between impatient younger members and their more risk-averse superiors finally erupted into full-blown revolt after the deportations, as many junior Bundists blamed their bosses for idly standing by while the Nazis emptied the Ghetto.

That the Bund, like the Zionists, had saved a disproportionate number of its own operatives from the gas chambers only heightened the group's collective sense of anger and guilt. "That didn't fill me with pride," Boruch Spiegel said of being among the living. "I didn't think I deserved to live." Not when his father had starved to death in front of his eyes. Not when he had watched his mother and sisters dragged down Zamenhof to the Umschlagplatz, where they were crammed into cattle cars so overcrowded that people regularly suffocated before the trains even left Warsaw. Not when Berl, his idol and inspiration, had disappeared without a trace. Boruch couldn't bring himself to imagine what had happened to them once they reached Treblinka: the final humiliation of forced nudity, the sinking horror of the concrete showers, the hiss of searing gas, the scrape of the bulldozers plowing pale limbs into the black earth.

So when the Bund arranged for him to be given a job at a German plant, he wasn't grateful. He was ashamed. He didn't care that people were paying the equivalent of thousands of dollars in bribes to buy the precious work permits, or that those with means went to astonishing lengths to secure spots at the miserable factories for their loved ones. "It wasn't important to me that I was alive." In Boruch's shop, many others felt similarly unworthy. "Father, mother, sister all burned, my Zille in Majdanek, my only child in a Catholic convent," cried Zalman Friedrich, the blond Bund courier who been sent to uncover the truth about Treblinka. "All I want now is to be consumed in the battle for revenge."

The self-loathing rage that welled from survivor's guilt quickly morphed into resentment toward Bund leaders like Maurice Orzech. Orzech had downplayed the threat of extermination. He had refused to join the Jewish Fighting Organization. He and other leaders like Bernard Goldstein, had advocated calm and caution when urgent action was needed. "They had misjudged the situation very badly," Spiegel reflected.

The criticism was not unfounded, but also not entirely fair. Bund bosses had worked tirelessly to prevent their ranks from being thinned by the deportations. They had successfully used their trade union connections to shelter hundreds of Bundists in the burgeoning slave labor mills. As a result, new industrial enclaves like the Brushmakers District, which flanked Krasinski Park in the easternmost quadrant of the Ghetto, had become Bund strongholds. The factory where Boruch Spiegel worked, in the main shops district on the western end of the Ghetto, also had a large contingent of Bundists. The plant belonged to a Nazi entrepreneur named Kurt Roerich, who made leather accessories for the Wehrmacht: belts, holsters, stirrups. With only five hundred employees it was one of the smaller shops, tiny compared to the sprawling operations of the Schultz brothers next door or the two giant Toebbens factories, which had a combined twelve thousand workers and supplied 60 percent of the winter clothing worn by German soldiers on the Eastern Front.

Boruch's girlfriend, Chaika Belchatowska, was also at Roerich, and the pair had grown even closer since the deportations. "She was all I had left," he felt. Chaika worked on the line while Spiegel was a janitor, charged with sweeping the factory floor. Their shifts were twelve hours, seven days a week, and they lived together in a neighboring tenement designated for Roerich employees. Every morning between six and seven o'clock they joined the throngs of other slave laborers making their way to the shops. This, and the six-to-seven-o'clock return trip each evening, were the new Ghetto rush hours, the only times Jews were allowed on the streets of the cordoned-off industrial enclaves. Anyone moving about during off-hours was shot.

Despite the best efforts of Bund bosses, dissent and dissatisfaction spread in the crowded shops. To young Bundists like Boruch and Chaika, the ideological gulf that divided the Bund and the Zionists seemed like a wasteful distraction. Rightly or wrongly, the collective anger focused on Orzech. He was effectively deposed by being quietly exiled to a safe house on the Aryan side, where he would be out of harm's way and no longer able to issue orders. The old guard no longer commanded the respect of the rank and file. Even the grizzled special ops chief Bernard Goldstein, the Bund's resident warrior and its biggest hero before the war, was being pensioned off. "Bernard didn't grasp the reality of the conditions in the Ghetto," Mark Edelman noted regretfully.

Edelman—now twenty-two, but aged beyond his years by his experience at the Umschlagplatz—was one of the leaders of the palace coup against party elders. "As usual Mark was carelessly dressed," Goldstein bitterly recalled of the day in early October 1942 when Edelman, his former errand boy, escorted him out of the Ghetto and into forced retirement in a safe house. "Neatness never seemed important to him. Life had made him outwardly unsentimental and hard, but behind that close-mouthed grimness were keen intelligence and warm generosity. And he was utterly without fear. He led me by the arm. A year or two before, this same Mark had escorted me through the Ghetto to many illegal meetings. He would walk behind at a distance of ten or fifteen paces without taking his eyes from me for a moment. Then he would stand patiently in the street outside the building, guarding the meeting place. Today he led me by the arm. We were so much closer now than we had been then, but how far, far apart we would soon be. My feet protested every step."

When the baton passed to the young, the old ideological barriers to unification were quickly thrown aside. Within a week of Goldstein's forced retirement, the final hurdle to the creation of a unified Jewish front fell. On October 15, the Bund formally joined the Jewish Fighting Organization. It had taken three years and the death of nearly four hundred thousand people, but the Jewish Resistance finally was largely unified. Mark Edelman and Boruch Spiegel, Isaac Zuckerman and Zivia Lubetkin were now on the same team, fighting for the same cause in the same ranks. Organizationally, it was a seminal moment. Edelman, befitting his heightened status, was delegated to the organization's new five-man command staff, to serve alongside Isaac and Mordechai Anielewicz. He did not know Isaac well, and he knew next to nothing about Anielewicz. But he took an immediate shine to Zuckerman, who was a few years older and a full head taller. "We saw eye to eye," Mark recalled wryly of the man who would become his closest friend. Isaac reciprocated the warm sentiments. The thin, mustachioed Bundist possessed a no-nonsense dignity, a serene "nobility," that appealed to Zuckerman.

The Jewish Fighting Organization had taken its first step toward becoming the supreme authority in the Warsaw Ghetto. In short order, its ranks were expanded to include the parent groups of Dror and the Young Guard, Po'alei Zion and Po'alei Zion Left, Communists from the Polish Workers Party, and the Gordinia and Akiva youth arms of the centrist General Zionists. Only the religious Agudas Israel party refused to join, its Orthodox leaders preferring to trust their fate to God, while the Revisionist Zionists, who had their own well-established paramilitary arm in the Jewish Military Union, were never asked. "They were subordinate to fringe [Polish] ultranationalists that we could never trust," Edelman said of the JMU's Gentile patrons. The ideological gulf had narrowed enough for the left and center to unite, but the leap to the far right was still too daunting.

Even within the ZOB, trust between new and old members was a major issue. "Stupidities and petty arguments" plagued early meetings, according to Edelman and Zuckerman. Mutual suspicion ran sufficiently high that the Polish Workers Party felt compelled to cable their handlers in Moscow to complain that the Bund "sharply opposed us and was especially virulent against the Soviet Union."

The flood of new names and faces and divergent political orientations within the ZOB violated one of the cardinal rules of clandestine activity. In any underground organization, Edelman explained, "you didn't bring anyone in unless you knew them from childhood and could personally vouch for them." Yet he was now sitting next to complete strangers on the organization's five-man command council. The only thing Edelman knew about most of his fellow commanders— Anielewicz, Hersh Berlinski from Po'alei Zion Left, and the Polish Workers Party delegate Michael Roisenfeld—was that they were all Marxists. And that did not fill him with confidence.

The ZOB needed a leader who would bring the disparate forces together. Isaac Zuckerman was a natural choice, since the Jewish Fighting Organization had been his brainchild. Mordechai Anielewicz, however, coveted the post. It was not clear how Zuckerman felt about a relative outsider parachuting in at the last minute to steal center stage in the organization he had founded. Isaac was not without ego, and he was almost certainly not pleased by this unexpected development. Publicly he would only say: "Mordechai Anielewicz wanted to be commander of the Organization and was fit for it in every respect. He believed in his own strength and he was ambitious. He proposed himself for the job and I gladly accepted it even though there had been talk about me being commander."

Not everyone agreed that the brash newcomer had the right temperament for the post. "What is there to say?" Edelman later chose his words carefully. "Anielewicz really wanted to be leader. It was very important to him and not so important to us. So he became leader."

CHAPTER 25

SIMHA RETURNS AND JOANNA FLEES

By the fall of '42, Simha Ratheiser had returned to the outskirts of Warsaw. His trip from Klvov was uneventful. He traveled on false documents bought from a Gentile. They identified him as a Catholic farmhand, and since he looked the part after eight months in the country sun, no one bothered him.

Simha still had no idea when he arrived in the Polish capital that 90 percent of Warsaw's Jews had been exterminated. At this stage in the war, most Poles outside Warsaw were either unaware of the Holocaust or, in some cases, indifferent to it. The Polish Underground press was only belatedly waking up to the tragedy, and the horrifying stories it printed were initially dismissed by many as wild exaggerations. The Jews may have been deported, but it was inconceivable they had all been killed.

Simha's ignorance spared him the agony of presuming his parents and sisters were dead. "I had a lot of confidence in my mother. I knew she could take care of herself. It was my father I worried about." Ratheiser remembered that his mother, Miriam, had planned to get the rest of the family out of the Ghetto. He also knew that she had stayed in regular contact with their former Gentile neighbors, who had provided her with food on many occasions, and who might now know of her whereabouts. So he headed to his old neighborhood, Czerniakow, on Warsaw's leafy southern flank, hoping to track down his family.

He did not have to look far, as it turned out. Miraculously, Miriam and his father, Zvi, were alive and well, living on a huge suburban estate on the eastern banks of the Vistula. The rambling property was similar to the Polish Underground base that had sheltered Joanna, Hanna, and Janine Mortkowicz until recently. It spanned several hundred acres, contained dozens of outbuildings, had orchards and its own artificial lake, and belonged to a sympathetic aristocrat who turned a blind eye to the clandestine activities conducted on his premises. The principal difference was that the Zatwarnicki estate in Czerniakow was run by the ZOB rather than the Polish Resistance.

Isaac Zuckerman had found the place in 1940, when he and Zivia Lubetkin were looking for land to farm on the outskirts of Warsaw. Despite growing hunger in the city, the estate's fields had been left fallow as a result of labor shortages caused by the mass deportations of Polish workers to the Reich. With some trepidation, Isaac approached Zatwarnicki about setting up a kibbutz on his property. It would help feed Dror members in Warsaw and provide the aristocrat with an income. Zuckerman wasn't sure what to expect. Many Polish nobles resented Jews for surpassing them in wealth and influence following the Industrial Revolution, when Poland's nobility had stubbornly and disastrously chosen to remain agriculturally based. When power predictably shifted from the land to factories and urban financial centers, many aristocrats were left behind, angry, impoverished, and looking for scapegoats for their own mistakes. But not Zatwarnicki. "He wasn't an anti-Semite, quite the opposite," Zuckerman found.

The two struck a deal, and Zatwarnicki proved to be a very obliging landlord over the years. Food grown at the estate was continuously smuggled into the Ghetto. Couriers came at night and left at dawn. Underground pamphlets were stored in the barns for distribution to other cities. During the deportations, the Czerniakow farm became a refuge for hundreds of Zionists, ZOB members, and even some nonaffiliated Jews. "We wanted to save the people," Zuckerman explained. "But we didn't know what to do with them in Warsaw. We sent them to Czerniakow."

Somehow, Simha's mother, Miriam, had talked her way into this group of refugees, and Ratheiser found his family living at the far end of the fields in a tent near the banks of the Vistula. (The farm's outbuildings were so overcrowded that people slept in bunks stacked three high.)

The estate, by November 1942, had morphed from a Dror outpost into the ZOB's first base of operations. The organization's archives were kept there, along with a small weapons cache consisting of several rifles and a crate of grenades. ZOB deputy commanders Mordechai (Mort) Tennenbaum and Tuvia Borzykowski used the premises to train defense units in combat tactics.

Simha's parents, as nonaffiliated outsiders, were not privy to the estate's secrets. He himself had to keep a low profile because he had sneaked onto the farm unannounced and was sleeping surreptitiously in the guard hut where his father worked as a night watchman. Unless someone in the ZOB vouched for him, his presence would be viewed with suspicion by the farm's underground leaders.

It was a few weeks before he recognized a familiar face: Rivka Pasmanik. She was twenty-two and a member of Akiva, the centrist Zionist youth group Ratheiser had flirted with joining before the war. Akiva was now part of the ZOB and Pasmanik was involved in running couriers for the organization. She took one look at Simha—at his sunburned Aryan features and innocently boyish expression that had already fooled countless policemen, anti-Semites, and German gendarmes—took in his accent-free Polish and carefree demeanor, and knew exactly how to use him. "Would you go on a mission to the Ghetto?" she asked.

Six months had passed since Joanna Mortkowicz-Olczak left her doll, along with her childhood, in the muddy fields of the Zbikow estate. By October 1942, her life had changed so drastically that she was literally a different person. She had a new identity and a new family tree, with every Jewish limb carefully pruned. She was on her own now, living apart from her doting mother and strict grandmother for the first time in her life. And although she was only eight, she had already learned that the slightest indiscretion on her part could result in many deaths.

Joanna's leap into adulthood started a few days after the Gestapo raid on Zbikow. No longer under the protection of their Resistance hosts, Hanna had begun the arduous process of finding a new place to stay. Returning to Warsaw was ruled out. The Mortkowiczes were well-known in the Polish capital, so the risk of running into an indiscreet acquaintance, or an informant, blackmailer, or anti-Semite, was too high. They were safer in the exurbs, where there was less of a police presence, and fewer permanently posted Germans, and where the Polish Resistance operated more openly.

The closest town to Zbikow was called Piastow. It was nine miles west of Warsaw, and heavily industrial. The smokestacks of Poland's largest tire factory, the Piastow Rubber Works, which had 1,070 employees, dominated the skyline. The nation's second-largest battery maker, Tudor Accumulator Systems, stood next door, spilling out 450 workers after each shift. Both plants had been expropriated from their Jewish founders: Tudor now produced batteries for the U-boats wreaking havoc on American convoys in the Atlantic, while the rubber works made most of the tires on which the Wehrmacht was rolling across the Eastern Front.

Hanna knew the grimy town reasonably well. Her old country house had been in the same region, and she used to go to Piastow occasionally for groceries and garden supplies before the war. Now she began wandering its familiar streets looking for rooms to let, an inherently risky proposition. A random patrol and routine document check could mean disaster, since Hanna, despite her impeccable Polish, did not "look good." Her dark features were not typically Slavic, and she did not have false papers to rely on in case her appearance aroused suspicion. What's more, it was not just the Germans she had to worry about. Professional blackmailers—derisively known as *szmaltzowniki,* or greasers, because they fed off human fat—were a growing phenomenon in Poland. Their numbers had exploded as the systematic liquidation of ghettos across the country created ever more lucrative extortion opportunities. Tens of thousands of Jews had gone into hiding rather than face deportation, and every one was a potential mark. Some of Hanna's cousins had already had an expensive run-in with shakedown artists in Warsaw, and she was anxious to avoid the same fate.

Though Hanna may have had misgivings about asking strangers for help, she hid her apprehensions as best she could. Fear betrayed people. It was noticeable. It attracted attention, and often the wrong sort of attention. But she had little choice in the matter at this point: They needed to live somewhere, and soon. At one shop, when she casually inquired about lodgings in the vicinity, Hanna was told that a woman named Grabowska had a big home nearby and sometimes took in boarders. This was not unusual. Many Poles let out rooms during the war, both to offset the housing shortage and to cushion the blow of spiraling food prices.

Grabowska's building was on Rej Street in the very center of town, a few blocks from the busy train station. It was indeed quite large, rising above the neighboring stores and gabled townhouses. Hanna mustered her courage and rang the doorbell. Her first impression was that Mrs. Grabowska seemed cultured and kind. Hanna also must have passed muster. She was, after all, a ranking member of the prewar cultural elite—one of central Europe's biggest publishers, a Ph.D., and someone accustomed to moving in notoriously snobby literary circles. In a blue-collar town like Piastow, her mannerisms would have been instantly identifiable as educated and upper-crust. As for her Semitic appearance, Mrs. Grabowska showed no hint of either recognition or concern. "We moved in at dusk," Joanna recalled.

Within a few weeks, it became apparent that Mrs. Grabowska was aware of the provenance of her new tenants. Their status as outlaws under the Nazis may even have played a role in her decision to take them into her home—and into her confidence. Mrs. Grabowska, like the Mortkowiczes, had secrets that needed keeping, and the benefit of Jewish boarders was that they could never go to the authorities.

"At first we found the heavy traffic that passed through the house on Rej Street worrying," Joanna remembered. "There was a never-ending stream of young people dropping in and out, bringing in and taking out all sorts of packages, and sometimes staying overnight." Mrs. Grabowska's daughter Irene appeared to be directing this nocturnal traffic. She often disappeared for days at a time, only to return "bringing strange, quite evidently frightened people to stay the night. It was not hard to guess that they were wanted by the Gestapo."

The Mortkowiczes had stumbled upon yet another conspiratorial cell. "Miss Irene was in the A.K.," Joanna later explained. A.K. was the Polish acronym for the Home Army, the new name of the unified Polish Resistance, which, like the ZOB, had finally succumbed to intense pressure to unite under one umbrella organization. Much of that pressure had come from British Intelligence, which helped fund the A.K. and was growing tired of the incessant bickering and maneuvering between competing Polish Underground factions and their representatives abroad. So much backstabbing plagued Poland's government in exile that frustrated British officials thought the Poles seemed more intent on fighting one another than the Germans. The creation of the Home Army was meant to redress this shortcoming. Under the new arrangement, sworn enemies such as Socialists and Nationalists would work together under a single commander in chief and subordinate themselves to a central military hierarchy. Virtually every splinter group in the political spectrum was being incorporated into the amalgamated Home Army, which eventually grew into the largest resistance movement in Europe and launched the biggest and bloodiest uprising of the Second World War. The one notable exception to the Home Army's inclusive policy was the Communist Workers' Party. The ZOB ally was rejected as a Stalinist puppet and forced to form its own small militia, the Popular Army, or A.L. in Polish.

Irene's duties in the Home Army were not immediately clear to the Mortkowiczes, but she seemed to play a role similar to that of the mysterious Monika Zeromska. That both young women were exceedingly attractive was not a coincidence. Much like the Jewish couriers selected by Zivia, they were chosen at least in part for their looks.

Hanna quickly developed a deep respect for their landlady's courageous daughter. "If Irene sped off somewhere with a bag, she was sure to be taking supplies or clothes to someone in desperate need. If she was running off to the train station at an odd hour, her eyes red with tears, she was sure to be hurrying to save someone in trouble or to assist the family of someone arrested." Irene, Hanna later wrote, "was like a breath of life, like a wave of hope, fragrant, dashing, and fair."

It was the bold and beautiful Irene who took Joanna away from her mother and grandmother in the fall of 1942 and brought her to live under an assumed identity in a convent in Warsaw. The family did not have much choice. The approaching school year had created a potentially serious security problem. Since the Germans allowed elementary schools up to the sixth grade to operate legally in Poland (no further education was deemed necessary to train future generations of slave laborers), keeping Joanna home from school would have aroused suspicion. Sending her to school, on the other hand, posed a different set of risks. The environment at public school was difficult to control. There were hundreds of students from different backgrounds. All it took was for one of them to come from an anti-Semitic home, and Joanna could be denounced as a Jew. Anti-Semitism was sufficiently widespread that it was almost a statistical certainty that someone would eventually tip off the Germans. The Gestapo would then take Joanna away and execute everyone at Irene Grabowska's house.

The solution to Joanna's pedagogic dilemma came from a seemingly unlikely savior: the Sisters of the Order of the Immaculate Conception of the Blessed Virgin Mary. This was the same order of Dominican nuns that had sheltered the Mortkowiczes at the Zbikow estate and helped ZOB courier Ari Wilner in Vilna. The sisters had a boarding school for girls in Warsaw that was ideally suited to Joanna's particular needs. It was within the confines of a walled convent, away from prying eyes and in an environment strictly controlled by the local Mother Superior. Joanna would be welcomed there and protected from both Germans and blackmailing greasers. The school was already providing sanctuary to a dozen other Jewish girls, her mother and grandmother were informed by Irene.

The offer was not easily spurned. Nor was it widely extended by the combative Roman Catholic Church in Poland. After centuries of relatively peaceful cohabitation, the Church had recently become increasingly hostile toward Judaism. The belligerence was partly the result of the same late-nineteenth-century socioeconomic forces that had embittered the rural aristocrats left behind by the Industrial Revolution. In rapidly growing cities, as once modest synagogues morphed into soaring edifices that rivaled cathedrals, the Church, like the agri-culturally based nobility, suddenly felt threatened. It fought back by aligning itself with the nationalist forces that spearheaded the wave of political anti-Semitism that swept Poland after independence. During the Depression, Catholic publications had been among the loudest critics of perceived Jewish economic dominance. During the Holo-caust, the Church distinguished itself largely by its silence.

Fortunately for Joanna, individual members of the Polish clergy were willing to buck papal indifference and risk their lives to save Jews. Nuns in particular were free to act on their own conscience be-cause each convent operated independently from the hierarchy during the Nazi occupation. The temporary autonomy afforded to the Naza-rene, Ursuline, Albertine, Franciscan, and Carmelite orders would re-sult in the rescue of at least twelve hundred Jewish children.

At the convent where Joanna was to live, the Mother Superior had taken the unusually democratic step of putting her admission to a vote. "Sister Wanda called us together," a young nun, Maria Ena, re-called. "She began by reading the Gospel of St. John 15:13–17," in which it is written that there is no greater love than laying down one's life for another. "She explained that she did not wish to jeopardize the house, the sisters, the community. She knew what could be awaiting us." Two nuns from their order had just been executed in the town of Slonim for hiding Jews. "Was it prudent to risk it for a few Jewesses?" Sister Wanda asked. "It was our decision."

Heightening the risk was the fact—which Joanna's mother did not know—that an entire SS battalion was garrisoned in a fortified com-plex directly across the street from the convent. The barbed wire bar-ricades, guardhouses, and snarling German shepherds were a frightful sight for new pupils. Once inside, however, an entirely different atmo-sphere reigned. "I clearly remember my first encounter with that place," Joanna later wrote. "I am standing on the threshold of a huge gymnasium, holding Irene's hand tightly. The shining floor smells of fresh polish. By the wall a large group of girls are sitting cross-legged, all staring curiously at the new girl. I am dying of embarrassment and fear. For the first time in my life I must remain alone in a new place, with strange people. I want to tear away from Irene and run home cry-ing, but I know it is not possible. There is no home and if I 'make a

scene'—my grandmother's most abusive definition of hysterical behavior—I shall compromise myself in the eyes of these girls forever,
and that will not help me at all. So I make the first conscious decision
of my entire life; I let go of Irene's hand, and, on that shining floor, in
defiance of fate, I do a somersault, then a second, and third, and keep
rolling until I end up at the other end of the room. The girls clap and
the nuns laugh. I know I have won their hearts; I feel accepted and thus
safe."

Joanna's days soon became a blur of regimented discipline. At
seven she rose, washed, tidied her bed, and did gymnastics. Breakfast
and prayers followed punctually at eight. Between nine o'clock and
noon, classes were held. After lunch, one hour of organized games
was followed by another hour of manual labor. At three thirty everyone did homework and chores until the dinner bell summoned them to
the cafeteria at five thirty. After supper, the girls had half an hour of
free time followed by evening prayers at seven. A half hour later the
lights were turned off.

Only then, when the girls were alone in their bunks in the dark,
would they let their guard down and whimper. During the day, every
child hid her true emotions behind a "jester's mask" of cheerful jovial-
ity, Joanna recalled. "This was the special skill of many occupation-
era children. None of the dozen or so Jewish girls hidden at the
convent, some of whom already had terrible experiences behind them,
ever showed their sadness or fear about the fate of their loved ones.
The crying was done at night."

Though boarders were not supposed to discuss their personal
lives, talk about their backgrounds, or use their real names, almost
everyone soon knew which children were Jewish and which girls were
the daughters of Home Army officers on the run. Even if the Jewish
boarders looked and sounded "good," the smallest slips, sometimes
even a single word, could give them away. One blond girl was presumed to be Gentile until she referred to her torn undershirt as a *lejblik,* something Christians never did. Another also fooled everyone
until she cried out in Yiddish in her sleep one night.

Joanna was luckier than most of the other girls in that she was
able to see her mother and grandmother every second week, when
Irene would come get her and take her to Piastow for the weekend.

Most of the other children received occasional care packages and letters from relatives. Parental visits, however, were extremely rare. Many of the Catholic boarders were war orphans. The parents of most of the Jewish girls were also either dead or trapped in the Ghetto, while the daughters of senior Home Army officers could not see their families because of security risks. The Germans would not hesitate to use them to catch their "terrorist" fathers if their true identity was revealed.

The threat of the Gestapo loomed large over the Sisters of the Immaculate Conception, and not solely because the dreaded SS were their neighbors. The cassock or nun's habit offered little protection from the Nazis. One in five Polish priests died at the hands of the Germans during the war. Nuns and monks fared slightly better, but nearly a thousand were shot for various offenses. The Germans knew well that the Polish Church had a long history of fighting foreign oppressors, whether czarist, fascist, or communist, and targeted it accordingly. In Sister Wanda's case, the suspicion was warranted. In addition to harboring Jews and the children of Resistance leaders, the Mother Superior also allowed illegal high school and university-level courses to be conducted on convent grounds, held training seminars for Home Army chaplains, and opened her doors to Underground operatives in need.

Because of the looming threat, Joanna and the girls practiced for Gestapo raids in the way most schoolchildren participate in fire drills. "When an internal bell rang during lessons, we gathered the prewar books for Polish and history [both banned subjects] from our desks double-quick and shoved them into a special storage space," Joanna recalled. "Sometimes the alarm was real—then the nuns hid the endangered children in the infirmary, behind the altar in the chapel, or in the enclosure." Joanna had to stay in the altar for several hours during one such search. "By then I was already thoroughly versed in conspiracy. I knew by heart all the new facts of my [forged] identity card. My mother was called Maria Olczak, née Maliszewska, and my grandmother had become her own daughter's mother-in-law, borrowing the name Julia Olczak, née Wagner, from my father's late mother. My grandmother's sister Flora, alias Emily Babicka, née Plonska, daughter of a carpenter born in Luninsk in Byelorussia, was no longer her sister, just a chance acquaintance. Flora's husband Samuel was now Stanislav. Luckily, he was still her husband, which made his life much easier, because his daughters, Caroline and Stefanie, who had two different surnames and were not apparently related to each other or to their parents, were always making blunders and were incapable of hiding their family connections. It was all very complicated."

CHAPTER 26

BORUCH AND ROBERT LEARN DIFFERENT LESSONS

Joanna's cousin Robert was also posing as a Christian student in the fall semester of 1942. Only the Jesuit school Osnos attended taught in English rather than Polish and was located three thousand miles away, in Bombay.

Robert was twelve, in the first awkward stage of adolescence, and the war was so far removed from his daily life that it soon became nothing more than a distant memory. Of his days in Warsaw during the 1939 siege, all that eventually remained was a vague recollection of burying himself in Jules Verne and Mark Twain, his "escape." Of his flight to Berlin with his mother, Martha, there was only the faintly bitter aftertaste of his great-uncle's inhospitality. All he would remember of the flight from earthquake-ravaged Romania to Turkey was the lingering terror of a few hours when he got separated from his parents and found himself lost and alone in Istanbul. The stopover in Iraq was more memorable, but fleeting, since his parents kept moving farther east. As for the journey from Iraq to India, just one acronym stayed lodged in his mind: POSH—Port Out, Starboard Home. "Because of the sun, the elegant people were housed on the shady, port side of the ship on the way out and on the starboard side on the way in." Robert, Joseph, and Martha Osnos were in steerage. Broke, they cobbled together funds for the trip through the sale of some jewelry, then gambled on an immigration loophole. "In Baghdad, my father had heard that if you had a transit visa, the British just let you stay in India," Robert recalled. Joseph Osnos had obtained such a visa back in Bucharest, to the Dutch East Indies. He had thought it useless at the time. Now, armed with this facilitating document, the Osnoses booked passage to the port of Karachi, where the colonial authorities were desperate for skilled Europeans to buttress the war economy.

It was so hot in the hold of the ship that the Osnoses often slept on deck. Robert imagined himself as Sinbad the Sailor, while his parents marveled at the ocean glowing "phosphorescent like green gold fire and stars like we'd never seen them before." Their liner languidly traversed the parched coastline, calling on Gulf ports in Persia, Oman, and Bahrain, where Robert was captivated by Arab dhows and sword-bearing local officials in ornate turbans and flowing black robes.

"We had this wonderful feeling of a suspension of time and problems," Martha reflected on the idle weeks the family spent at sea. She did not know what awaited them in India, how they would earn a living, or whether any country would ultimately take them in. But they were together, safe, and overwhelmed by the generosity of their Arab shipmates, who gave them dates and pomegranates, offerings so exotic to Martha that she "didn't even know what they were or how to eat them."

When at last they docked in Karachi, Robert was mesmerized by the sights: the heaving mass of barefoot coolies that descended on the vessel; the sacred cows that sauntered unobstructed around the harbor, trailing garlands of flowers; the beggars, lepers, and legless invalids; the blind children, all with supplicating outstretched palms.

Amid the unofficial welcoming committee that greeted the Osnoses was a young Pole who met every boat, hoping for news from his ravaged Carpathian hometown. He was destitute, stateless, and stranded. But he knew his way around Karachi and was eager to help Polish travelers. The Osnoses had encountered helpful fellow countrymen on virtually every leg of their journey. In Baghdad, it had been a Polish linguist—whom Martha dubbed "John the Savior"—who took the family under his wing and counseled them on the India visa loophole. Their new patron in Karachi welcomed them into his home, a cheap one-room rental that he provided with a flourish of Slavic hospitality, and advised Joseph on the lay of the land. The jobs, he said, were in Bombay. With Joseph's manufacturing background, he should have little difficulty finding work.

Joseph's business acumen had already served the Osnoses well. It had funded Martha and Robert's escape from Poland and permitted the family to live during the prolonged flight. Joseph always managed to make the best of an opportunity. And whether it was a testament to his charisma and salesmenship, or a reflection of dire labor shortages, he landed a job in Bombay almost immediately. On the strength of his experience as a former owner of a small appliance factory in Warsaw, he was hired to manage a furniture plant that was being retooled to build life rafts for the British navy.

The position came with a huge, well-appointed apartment and five domestic servants. Martha's fluency in six languages was also quickly put to use by the colonial administration. She started working for the Bureau of Censors, reading refugee mail.

Overnight, Martha, Robert, and Joseph's lives became normal, almost to the point of banality. It was an astonishing transformation. One week they were itinerant refugees, virtually penniless, without a fixed address, destination, or means of support. Suddenly they had a cook, a maid, a driver, a laundress, and a nanny. They lived in a compound reserved for the elite and held respectable positions in society. Blessed with dual incomes—"Money was never a problem in India," according to Robert—they could entertain, travel, and resume the upper-middle-class lifestyle they had enjoyed in Warsaw before the war.

"My parents were very active socially in Bombay. Mom was always going to parties and Dad played bridge all the time." Their circles, however, were restricted to other émigrés. "My parents didn't mix with the English. They spent all their time with fellow Poles."

Bombay's Polish community was tight-knit. Shunned by the class-conscious British, the Poles were uncharacteristically inclusive among themselves. In India, Polish Jews and Gentiles socialized together. Ironically, only exile brought Poles to accept American-style views on citizenship. Abroad, one's passport, rather than ethnicity or religion, was the sole determinant of nationality. This far from home, all Poles were expatriates, equally foreign in the eyes of the law.

While his parents spent time with their new friends, Robert was free to do as he pleased. "My parents were borderline negligent in leaving me to my own devices," he later laughed. He wasn't complaining, though. "It was wonderful. For me, India was paradise." He could ride the trams, exploring different neighborhoods. He lounged by the pool, went to cricket games, and became a fixture at the local movie theater. "I must have seen every film ever made," he recalled: *Gone with the Wind, The Thief of Bagdad,* anything with Paul Muni, Leslie Howard, or his favorite Indian matinee idol, Sabu, who also starred in Hollywood productions such as *Jungle Boy.*

Like his parents, Robert mostly played with other Polish children. Only one of his close friends was not part of the émigré community, a half-Indian boy whose mother was English and whose father was an Indian army officer. "He couldn't go swimming with us because the pool was for whites only." The schools were also segregated, and to attend the academy run by Welsh monks where his father had enrolled him, Robert had to pose as a Christian. "Of course you're a Jew," his classmates taunted him. "This was the only real dark cloud for me during our stay in India," he said of the charade. "I resented it bitterly. Not the fact that I was Jewish. But that I had to pretend that I wasn't."

The upside of a Jesuit education was that Robert, by the fall of 1942, spoke fluent English, albeit with a Welsh accent. The downside was that girls were emerging as a major frustration. "Because I went to an all-boys school, I had no exposure to them. They were like creatures from another planet to me."

Osnos had the luxury of worrying about such typical adolescent preoccupations because the war no longer intruded on his world. "There were no tangible signs of war whatsoever in Bombay. There was no military presence or rationing," he later reflected. "What strikes me most in retrospect was how completely normal my life had become once we reached India. I remember that I worshipped Churchill and Roosevelt, like all the other kids, and played field hockey and soccer at school."

Robert had no idea that back in Warsaw almost every Jewish child had been exterminated, or that Cousin Joanna was practicing Gestapo raid drills in a convent. Nor did his parents have any knowledge of the developing tragedy, because the Holocaust was still virtually unpublicized outside Poland. Thus far, the sole reference to the wholesale slaughter of European Jewry in *The New York Times,* for instance, was a two-inch-long notice buried at the back of the paper's June 27, 1942, edition. "700,000 Jews were reported slain in Poland," it read, stressing that the figures were unconfirmed.

The story dominating British and American newspapers in the fall of 1942 was the siege of Stalingrad. Hitler's bid to take the city before winter was faltering. His 6th Army Group had pinned the Soviets to a tiny sliver of land on the banks of the Volga, but though they controlled 90 percent of the city, they could not dislodge the stubborn defenders. In November, the Red Army regrouped and launched a massive two-pronged counteroffensive that cut off the Germans' supply lines. Now the vaunted Wehrmacht was pinned down and surrounded. And winter was fast approaching.

The astonishing reversal grabbed headlines worldwide and relegated the *Times's* scanty coverage of the Holocaust that fall to another news brief. "Two million Jews have been killed and five million more face extermination," it announced on page 20. The story, only the second reference to the Holocaust in America's paper of record, appeared in mid-December 1942, just as Joanna Mortkowicz-Olczak began to panic because Irene had failed, for the second time in a row, to pick her up from the convent for her scheduled visit with her family. Joanna knew something was wrong. What she didn't know was that Hanna and Janine had been caught by greasers.

While Joanna and Robert studied catechism at Catholic schools, back inside the Ghetto, Boruch Spiegel was attending a different type of class. Spiegel accepted his instructor's pistol warily, cradling it in both hands like a newborn baby. It felt hard and out of place in his small palms, making him shudder involuntarily. He turned the weapon over, weighing its heft and possibilities. He had never touched a firearm before, and the sensation was both frightening and empowering. Though guns were as much a part of the natural landscape in wartime Warsaw as snow in December, for a Jew to wield one, to feel its lethal power and liberating potential, was such an alien and intoxicating concept that Boruch's hands trembled.

"I was afraid it would go off accidentally," he remembered. He carefully handed the VIS pistol back to his ZOB instructor, watching with a mix of relief and regret as the next eager pupil accepted the gleaming black object. The oily revolver was passed around the room so that all the young trainees could feel its cold steel and grasp its import—the taking of fate into one's own hands. Every individual who touched the pistol likely felt the same excitement, the same trepidations, the same fearful longing to fire as Boruch. Was it the weapon that had been used to kill the new Jewish police chief, Jacob Lejkin? Spiegel wondered. Or the Judenrat scoundrel Israel First? Those assassinations, the first of many carried out by the ZOB, had warned what was left of the Ghetto that a new force was emerging in the Jewish district—the unchecked reign of Gestapo stooges was over. With just one gun they had accomplished this astonishing turnaround. Imagine, Boruch and the others were told, what could be done now that the first real shipment of arms had been delivered, in the second week of December 1942, by the Home Army.

Spiegel was inflamed by the possibilities. He visualized himself shooting at Germans, and he contemplated joining one of the hit squads being formed to eliminate traitors. "It filled me with purpose and hope," he said of that first contact with a pistol. He didn't realize that the old revolver might not have even worked. Nearly half the guns in the long-awaited shipment were not operational. But persuading the Home Army to part with even these surplus weapons had proven so drawn-out and deflating a process that frustrated ZOB leaders like Isaac Zuckerman doubted whether the Jewish Fighting Organization would ever arm itself.

The protracted process had begun nearly three months earlier, when Zuckerman dispatched courier Ari Wilner to the Aryan side of Warsaw to establish contact with the Polish Underground. First a meeting was arranged with an intermediary named Hubert, who was actually Alexander Kaminski, a thirty-nine-year-old scoutmaster. In addition to serving on the command staff of the Gray Ranks, he was also editor in chief of Poland's largest Underground newspaper, the *Information Bulletin,* with a circulation of forty thousand.

Kaminski listened politely to the blond and blue-eyed ZOB emissary, twirling his dark mustache with the detached interest of a hard-boiled newsman. At last he rose and said that someone might be in touch with Wilner in the near future. A few weeks later, Wilner received a message requesting another meeting, this time with an actual representative of the Home Army.

The representative sent by Kaminski introduced himself as Vaclav. He was in fact Captain Henry Wolinski, a forty-year-old attorney who headed the newly created Jewish Affairs department in the Home Army's Bureau of Information and Propaganda. His job was to keep the government in exile in London apprised of "the Jewish situation" in Poland, and he had been chosen for this grim task partly because his wife was Jewish.

Wolinski didn't know anything about Wilner or the ZOB, other than the fact that Kaminski vouched for them. But a few days earlier, he had been contacted by the Bund's envoy on the Aryan side, Leon Feiner. Feiner, who was known from prewar days, had asked for the Home Army's help in preparing a detailed firsthand report on the extermination of Polish Jews, which was still being viewed with extreme skepticism by the Allies. "Naïvely, we thought that if the world knew what was happening to us, they would do something," Zivia Lubetkin recalled.

Wolinski arranged to send one of the Home Army's top international couriers to the Ghetto and to a death camp to corroborate the accounts of genocide. The courier was a towering twenty-eight-year-old economist by the name of Jan Karski. He was blessed with a photographic memory, spoke fluent German and English, and later personally briefed President Roosevelt and British leaders on the situation in Poland, entering history as the man who told the world about the Holocaust. Mark Edelman served as one of his Ghetto guides.

"This way," said Edelman, when they met for the first time at the Ghetto wall. Karski pulled a cap down over his eyes, and adjusted his torn parka. The six-foot-four-inch future Georgetown University professor was accustomed to wearing disguises. Sometimes he dressed as a German oil executive and took the train through France to meet the fishing boats in Normandy that regularly ferried him across the Channel. Other times he wore the double runes of an Estonian SS man and made his way through Scandinavia. But nothing in his travels as an international courier prepared him for what he saw in the Ghetto.

"As we walked, everything became increasingly unreal," he later noted in his report. Children appeared "with skins so taut that every bone in their skeleton showed through." Men stared out of eyes "glazed and blank." Corpses lay in every second doorway. "Why are they naked?" asked Karski.

"When a Jew dies," Edelman answered matter-of-factly, "his family removes his clothing and throws his body in the street. If not, they have to pay the Germans to have the body buried."

Karski turned pale. "I was shocked," he recalled. Whenever he was anxious, Karski would reflexively run his tongue against the hollowed-out dentures that lined the left side of his jaw. The Gestapo had knocked out half his teeth during an interrogation in Slovakia several years earlier, unwittingly creating the perfect place to carry microfilm.

"Hurry, hurry, now you'll see something," said Edelman, pulling Karski up a flight of stairs to a second-story window. They watched as a car stopped in the middle of the street. Two blond boys in Hitler Youth uniforms emerged from the vehicle. "With their round rosy-cheeked faces, and their blue eyes, they were like images of health and life," Karski recalled. "They chattered, laughed, pushed each other in spasms of merriment. At that moment, the younger one pulled a gun out of his hip pocket and then I realized what I was witnessing. He was looking for a target with the casual, gay absorption of a boy at a carnival."

Karski was already on his way to London by the time Ari Wilner finally met a senior officer of the Home Army, in mid-November 1942. The delay had been caused by the Home Army's reluctance to recognize the ZOB. "They pretty much said you don't represent the Jews since you're nothing but members of a youth movement, and [we] do not talk with youth movements," Zuckerman recalled. "So we told Ari Wilner to tell them he represented two institutions: the political institution, the Jewish National Committee, which united all forces in the Ghetto, and the Jewish Fighting Organization, the military arm."

There was no such thing as a Jewish National Committee, but it sounded good and lent the youthful ZOB the illusion of having gray-haired supervision. The bureaucratic Home Army bought the hierarchical charade, and Zuckerman had to scramble to create the heretofore fictitious body. Unfortunately, the Bund refused to join any national committee that included Communists. So Zuckerman invented a second putative civilian body, a Communist-free Coordinating Committee under the National Committee that oversaw the activities of the ZOB. The Bund accepted the convoluted compromise, and it was on this somewhat confusing basis that the Home Army was hoodwinked into formally recognizing the ZOB on November 11, 1942.

The following day, Captain Wolinski took Wilner to see his superior, a man who was introduced as Surgeon. "What do you need—money?" Surgeon asked. His real name was Major Stanislaw Weber. "No," Wilner replied. "We can get money by squeezing the rich in the Ghetto. We need arms and ammunition, grenades, explosives, combat training, and specialists to build bunkers."

His request was passed up the chain of command until it reached General Stephen Rowecki. As the Home Army's leader, Rowecki was the most wanted man in Nazi-occupied Poland. He went by the code name Grot, and his mustachioed photo hung in every Gestapo office along with the caption "Enemy Number One of the Third Reich." Like many career army officers in prewar Poland, Rowecki held deeply conservative views that did not make him a natural ally of Jews. Left to his own devices, he might simply have ignored Wilner's request. But his commander in chief, General Wladislaw Sikorski—the head of the London government in exile—was cut from different cloth. Sikorski's prewar criticisms of the fascist-sympathizing Sanation regime had been so vocal that he was forced into exile in the late 1930s, and he taught at a war college in Paris before moving to London. He was very close to Winston Churchill, who endearingly referred to him as his "First Ally." Sikorski was demanding better treatment of Jews in the name of democracy—and political expediency. "We must remember," he cabled Grot in September 1942, "that the position of the Anglo-Saxon world concerning anti-Semitism is unequivocal. The best means of assuring full support for our interests is by showing and granting equal rights." "I therefore plead with you," Sikorski added in another cable on October 19, 1942, condemning anti-Semitism, "that in Poland the principles of democracy come broadly to the fore. We must remember that the war is carried on precisely for these ideals."

General Rowecki was thus under pressure from his superiors in London to give the Jewish resistance a fair hearing. Nonetheless, he was deeply skeptical of both the ZOB's fighting abilities and the organization's loyalty to Poland because of the Marxist leanings of some of its member groups. As a precondition for providing any help, he demanded written assurances that the Jews would commit themselves to fighting the Soviet Union if and when the time came to take up arms against the Red Army. Zuckerman and Edelman had no problems with issuing such a blanket declaration, but Mordechai Anielewicz and some of the others did. In the end, the ZOB penned a vague, watered-down compromise letter. "Since we are citizens of Poland," it reassured General Rowecki, "the decisions of the Polish government are binding on us."

Rowecki was not entirely convinced. He declared the ZOB a "partly Polish" resistance group, an equally vague classification which meant that it was not automatically entitled to aid. "Jews from all sorts of communist groups," he cabled London to cover his tracks, "are asking us for guns. As an experiment I gave them some pistols . . . but this could be a Soviet provocation."

When the shipment finally arrived in mid-December, Isaac Zuckerman flew into a rage. All that trouble, those months of negotiations, of jumping through committee hoops—for ten measly handguns. Four of them were not even in proper working order. To Isaac, this was not about trust, or loyalty. It was pure and simple anti-Semitism: "Instead of saying 'I hate you' it was easier for them to say 'I don't believe in you.'"

The hell with the Poles, Zuckerman decided. If they wouldn't help, he would procure weapons another way. He would steal them from the Germans.

CHAPTER 27

ISAAC'S NOT-SO-MERRY CHRISTMAS

The gun heist Isaac planned was to take place in December 1942 in Krakow, the beautiful medieval city that had been turned into the administrative center of the General Government. The Germans were less guarded in the turreted shadow of Wawel Castle, from which Hans Frank ruled occupied Poland like a personal fief. His grip on the walled town was so firm, his bureaucrats so numerous and comfortably ensconced in the luxurious apartments and villas seized from Jews and wealthy political prisoners, that few took the extreme security precautions used by their counterparts in the "terrorist" swamp that Nazi officials labeled Warsaw. "Nothing but trouble ever comes from that forsaken city," Frank famously quipped.

The ZOB planned to take advantage of the relative complacency in Krakow. Shortly before Christmas, when German officials were busy feting the holidays, Zuckerman boarded a train bound for the ancient capital, seat of King Kazimierz the Great, the fourteenth-century monarch who first invited Jews to settle in Poland in 1334.

Isaac traveled with a new courier, Havka Folman. She had been promoted when Lonka Kozibrodzka was caught and killed by the Gestapo while on a mission to Bialystok in April. "We were traveling openly. I looked like a rural Polish nobleman," Isaac recalled of his journey with Havka. "I wore a three-quarter-length coat, a hat, jodhpurs stuffed into boots, a mustache. Havka also looked Aryan. My looks and my clothing, which was like a uniform, were those of a person in a specific military formation in the internal government in Krakow."

Disguised as Germans, members of the Jewish Fighting Organization's Krakow branch were told to launch diversionary attacks on drinking establishments frequented by off-duty German officials: the Esplanade, the Bohemian Café (a favored haunt of the businessman Oskar Schindler), and several other locales. The idea was to seize as many weapons as possible and then raid an armory in the ensuing chaos.

The attack was coordinated by local ZOB leader Abraham Leibowicz, a General Zionist from the youth group Akiva. In Zionist circles Leibowicz was already a legend. "He could keep his cool in any situation," Zivia recalled. "He used to walk around [the Aryan side of] Krakow dressed as a Polish policeman. He then promoted himself to a German army officer and went around town loaded down with guns." Despite the fact that Leibowicz, or Laban, as he was more commonly known, looked nothing like a Gentile, he managed to pull off the charade for months through sheer chutzpah.

At the appointed hour, when Christmas parties were in full swing, Laban's partisans struck. They lobbed grenades into the bars and restaurants and stormed in, firing pistols. Isaac was part of the team that hit the upscale Bohemian Café, where several Mausers were pried from the hands of a tableful of dead Gestapo agents.

The Germans were so stunned by the brazen assault—the first major rebellion in their otherwise tranquil stronghold—that all the assailants got away safely. "That night we got together to toast the success of the operation," Zuckerman jubilantly recalled. The weapons haul was smaller than anticipated, but that didn't dampen their spirits. Thirteen Germans were dead and a dozen more were in the hospital. It was revenge, pure and simple, and unburdened by moral dilemmas. There were no innocent bystanders in a place like the Bohemian Café—from the waiters to the women of loose virtue who trolled for German clients, everyone there was complicit in the Occupation in one way or another.

To throw the vengeful Gestapo off track in the aftermath, the ZOB raiders left behind leaflets implicating the Home Army. This, they hoped, would prevent reprisals by the angry SS on innocent Jewish residents of the Krakow ghetto. The shirking of responsibility was a risky gambit that could have provoked the wrath of the Polish Resistance had the Germans retaliated against the Gentile population instead. The Nazis, however, knew full well who was behind the "terrorist" actions because they had two informants in the Krakow branch of the ZOB. The collaborators tipped off the Gestapo to the location of a deserted hospital where Zuckerman was supposed to rendezvous with Leibowicz the following day. The SS was waiting for him when he arrived. *"Halt, Hande Rauf,"* he heard someone bark, followed by shots. Isaac bolted. "After five steps, I began to feel warmth and a sharp pain in my leg." He was hit. Havka Folman and Abraham Leibowicz had been caught. Their capture allowed Isaac to slip away, but he was now bleeding profusely with nowhere to run. His only option was to hide in plain sight. "I took out a cigar, lit it, and very slowly walked." His long coat masked his wound, and the blood pooled in his boot without leaving a trail. He willed himself not to limp and frantically searched for the closest refuge. The city was being locked down, and with loudspeakers announcing that curfew had been moved up, he could no longer wander the cobblestoned streets without attracting attention. Zuckerman ducked into a church, but the frightened priest insisted he leave. Back in the open, with only minutes to curfew, Isaac saw a doctor's office.

The sign outside the office was exclusively in Polish, which Zuckerman took as a good omen: In Germanized Krakow, where signage was bilingual, it heralded the physician's patriotism. The doctor, alas, was not in. Isaac was going into shock. He felt cold and dizzy, shivering and sweating wildly. He crumpled to the floor in the waiting room and lost consciousness. He wouldn't remember how long he was out, but perhaps he had mumbled in Yiddish in his sleep, because two young men shook him awake and offered to take him in a cab to the ghetto. "I said they could take me to the Gestapo in a cab, but I wasn't moving." The men conferred, left, and returned a few minutes later with some bandages to crudely dress Isaac's throbbing bullet wound. They moved him out of the doctor's office into the staircase hall. "Let him stay till morning," Isaac overheard one of them say. "He's lost a lot of blood and isn't getting medical aid. He'll die anyway."

In the morning Zuckerman was still alive. The steps on which he'd slept were covered with blood, Christmas cookies, and all sorts of holiday treats left during the night by children who lived in the building. The sight of the stricken Jew abandoned by adults and left to the care of those still too young to discriminate shamed the building's elderly doorwoman. "Hard times!" she burst into tears. "We are turning into wolves." The old woman brought Isaac into her tiny apartment and fed him something hot. She tried to dress his wound, but his leg had swollen so much that she could not remove his boot. The effort was so excruciating that Isaac passed out from the pain. When he awoke, it was evening and the old lady tearfully apologized that he had to leave. Her son was due any moment and he would make a scene. Apparently, he would not approve of harboring a Jew.

Zuckerman somehow mustered the strength to drag himself back into the snowy streets. It was already dark, and the cold winter air helped clear his thoughts. Instinctively, Isaac grasped that his only real option was to return to Warsaw. If he didn't get medical attention soon, the wound would start festering and gangrene would set in. Sooner or later, someone would catch him if he kept stumbling blindly around Krakow. He could not risk going to a local ZOB safe house since the entire network in the city was blown; in addition to the informants, Leibowicz and Havka would almost certainly talk under Gestapo interrogation. In the end, everyone did. His only chance, Isaac decided, was to go straight to the railway station with his last reserves of strength and board the next train to Warsaw.

Fortunately, it was Christmas Eve, when Poles and many German Catholics held their celebratory feasts and opened gifts. There would be fewer passengers on the train, Isaac reasoned, and a smaller chance of running into a patrol. He was wrong on both counts. "The station was full of Germans. I sat down right across from a cripple with crutches, and dreamed of pulling the crutches away from him. As I sat meditating, Germans appeared and began snatching people for work. They snatched me too."

In the ensuing tumult, as all the able-bodied men were herded onto a different train bound for the slave labor mills in the Reich, Isaac managed to escape. His heavy limp saved him. "Since I didn't have the strength to walk, I lagged behind." Zuckerman continued falling back until he reached a point where the Nazi press-gang no longer noticed him. He then reboarded the train to Warsaw. "Fortunately it was dark and empty," since most of its intended passengers were now on their way to Germany.

On Christmas morning, Zuckerman, pale as snow, his pants leg red as a Santa suit, stumbled into ZOB headquarters in the Warsaw Ghetto. "Until the moment I entered the building I held up," he recalled. "As soon as I saw Zivia, I managed only to say 'It's all lost' and fainted."

Zuckerman was still laid up in bed recuperating on January 18, 1943, when the SS launched the second wave of mass expulsions to "resettle" the remaining fifty-odd thousand Jews in Warsaw.

This constituted the first major assault on the Ghetto since the summer *Gross Aktion*. Throughout the fall, the Germans conducted only occasional minor raids, grabbing a few hundred people every few weeks in order to sow terror and keep the population compliant. The factory where Boruch Spiegel worked had been targeted during one of these sporadic dragnets, and his girlfriend, Chaika Belchatowska, was caught hiding on one of the plant's upper floors. "They found us," she recalled. "An SS man, he had a whip, a leather whip. And he hit us over the head. And he hit and hit and hit. Then he took us out in a corridor, which was maybe one meter wide. And there was a window, on the fourth floor. And he opened the window and he said, 'You see, I'm going to throw you out.'"

Instead, Chaika and sixty other slave laborers from the Rorich shop were marched to the Umschlagplatz and forced into a crammed cattle car. None of them had any illusions about its destination. As soon as the train started moving, "this boy, he pushed towards the window." Each freight car was fitted with a narrow grate for air circulation. "In his shoe, in the sole of his shoe, he had a little saw. And we picked him up, and he sawed this grate off. Next to me stood a man who owned a drugstore across the road from my house. He said 'What are you doing? You are going to get us killed.' "

Chaika ignored her former neighbor. She and seven others jumped. By luck, the train had been lumbering over a sandy embankment that cushioned the landing. Chaika rolled to a stop in a ditch and began searching for her friends. The Germans, luckily, had not posted rooftop sentries to shoot at escapees. There had been virtually no breakout attempts before.

"We started marching," Belchatowska recalled. "We didn't know where we were." The train, they guessed, had traveled about thirty miles by the time they jumped. So they were not far from the city. More important, they had money. "There was one girl with us whose parents were quite well off. She had sewn in her coat American dollars. So she ripped this out and gave us each a banknote. One got a twenty-dollar bill, another got ten dollars, whatever she had."

Chaika and the escapees headed for the nearest village. With their highly prized foreign currency, which was valued next to gold, they might be able to buy shelter and transport back to Warsaw. Or they might be robbed, raped, killed, or sold to the Germans. There were plenty of terrifying tales of Polish peasants preying on lonely Jews in forests, attacking them and turning them over to the Nazis for an easy profit. Chaika and her friends had all removed their armbands. Nonetheless, it was with some trepidation that they approached two men and offered to pay to be smuggled to Warsaw. The men agreed. "They recognized that we were Jews," she recalled. "They were nice enough that they didn't take us to the Gestapo."

When Belchatowska returned to the Ghetto several days later, Boruch thought he was seeing a ghost. He had given her up for dead. "She had been taken on her birthday," November 11, the same day the Home Army recognized the ZOB. "But in reality she was born again that day. Her birthday present was the gift of life."

Boruch, like most Warsaw Jews, had come to accept the small raids as a fact of life in the Ghetto. But the scale and timing of the next major *Aktion,* which took place on January 18, caught everyone by surprise. "We felt certain the Germans were too busy with their roundups on the Aryan side to bother with us," Zivia Lubetkin recalled. Just prior to the *Aktion,* twelve thousand Varsovian Gentiles were arrested in one of the single largest crackdowns on the Polish capital up to that point. Peacock Prison alone now held seven thousand detainees, and to make room for more, eleven hundred inmates were sent to the Majdanek death camp near Lublin. The Gestapo wave of terror was partly a response to the increased activities of the Home Army. Emboldened by the Wehrmacht's astonishing setbacks in Stalingrad, Boy Scouts had erased virtually every German street name in Midtown during the night of January 14 and papered walls with forty thousand insurgent leaflets. At daybreak, the Home Army staged a series of spectacular bank robberies and conducted several high-profile assassinations while bombs rocked German-only hangouts such as Helgoland, Mitropa, and the Apollo Theater.

The SS reaction was so swift and brutal that Lubetkin recalled her couriers from the Aryan side, reasoning that they would be safer in the Ghetto until the storm passed. "Even some Poles from the underground sought refuge in the abandoned sections of the Ghetto," she said. Zivia didn't think the Germans had the manpower to go after both Jews and Gentiles simultaneously. But that was precisely what they did.

It was still dark and minus twenty degrees Celsius at 6 A.M. on January 18 when trucks carrying two hundred SS troops and eight hundred Ukrainian and Latvian auxiliaries roared into the Central Ghetto. This was the largest of the Ghetto's remaining four sections, spanning Goose Street and the Umschlagplatz rail terminal and housing the majority of the Ghetto's surviving thirty-five thousand slave laborers—those classified as "productive" with valid work permits or so-called life tickets.

Six A.M. was rush hour in the Central Ghetto, when the day shift at a dozen factories started, and the SS timed its assault in order to corral the maximum number of people out on the streets. Life tickets no longer afforded Jews protection. The identity cards that had provided so much comfort, that cost thousands of dollars to obtain, were simply torn up or ignored by enraged Ukrainians and Latvians, who began firing indiscriminately at the crowds.

Zivia and Zuckerman were awakened by the shots and screams that inaugurated the second *Gross Aktion*. They were at their new fourth-floor safe house on the corner of Zamenhof and Low Streets, fifty yards from the dreaded Umschlagplatz, and they had an unimpeded view of the carnage below. They had chosen the location precisely because of this strategic vantage point, which they thought would provide ample warning of any German movements. Isaac was still laid up with his bullet wound. Nonetheless, he was furious that the Jewish Fighting Organization had been caught completely off guard. He had no idea where Anielewicz was. He didn't know if Mark Edelman and the rest of the Bundists in the Brushmakers District were also being rounded up. How was the ZOB going to launch any kind of coordinated defense when it could not even maintain basic lines of communication?

Runners were frantically dispatched, and one of the breathless messengers was Simha Ratheiser. Ratheiser had been in the Jewish Fighting Organization for several months. Initially he had joined an Akiva unit, but as the lines between the disparate groups within the ZOB slowly began to blur, he was exposed to leaders outside his immediate circle. "I don't think Isaac, at this stage, even knew who I was," Simha recalled. "Naturally, I knew who he was."

Simha was assigned to lookout duty, while Zuckerman and some of the other more senior ZOB members broke out their weapons stash. "We had three pistols and three grenades," Tuvia Borzykowski recalled. "Those who had no weapons armed themselves with lengths of iron pipe, sticks, bottles, whatever could serve to attack the enemy." This time there would be no hiding. This time they would not let themselves be taken. This time they would fight with their bare hands if necessary.

Already, hundreds of Jews were being herded to the train depot in a repeat of the *Gross Aktion*. The same guttural shouts and screams and slurred Ukrainian and German invectives reverberated up and down Zamenhof. "My God, that's Angel." Simha beckoned Zivia to the window as the procession passed beneath them on the way to the Umschlagplatz. "We've got to help him," cried Zivia, spotting the boyishly handsome ZOB commander. "We must do something," she repeated moments later, mostly out of frustration as she realized that they were essentially helpless.

Mordechai Anielewicz—Angel—had almost all their guns in his possession. He had needed them for his hit squads. And now he and a dozen Young Guardsmen were caught in the middle of a rapidly grow-ing throng of horrified Jews being frog-marched down Low Street. But what was he doing? Zivia and Simha could see Anielewicz's team dis-persing in the mob, positioning themselves near the Ukrainian and German guards. Angel was right behind one now. He was reaching into his pocket.

All at once shots rang out, and complete pandemonium erupted on Low Street.

CHAPTER 28

THE ORGANIZATION

When Mordechai Anielewicz launched what would become known as the January Rising, Isaac, Zivia, and Simha barely had time to cheer. Just as Anielewicz's dozen fighters opened fire on the stunned German guards, another unit of SS troops stormed the building on Zamenhof Street where Zuckerman and forty ZOB members were holed up.

"The doors suddenly burst open and in flew a band of Germans," Lubetkin recalled. But this time the ZOB was prepared. Two young Zionists from Lodz were posted in the foyer of the apartment at the time. They pretended to be deeply immersed in reading and did not react to the violent intrusion. The Nazis ignored them and pressed forward with their search. As soon as their backs were turned, one of the Zionists pulled out a revolver and shot two of the intruders from behind. Shocked, the Germans retreated down the staircase, tripping over themselves to get away. Several other ZOB members pursued the fleeing Germans and managed to wound another intruder before the rest of the shocked SS men fell back.

Although only a few hundred rounds were exchanged on January 18, 1943, the shots reverberated throughout Warsaw. At Gestapo headquarters on Szuch Avenue, there was consternation. Faced with their first encounter of armed resistance, the Germans were forced to halt their *Aktion* after liquidating a mere five thousand Jews—a fraction of the intended haul. This was the first major failure of any *Aktion* anywhere in the General Government since the campaign to liquidate Polish Jewry began. Even more worrisome from the Gestapo's point of view were the mini-rebellion's ramifications outside the Ghetto. With resistance activity—"terrorist acts"—already on the rise in Warsaw, German counterintelligence now feared that the example set by the Jews could incite a citywide revolt by the Home Army, the prospect that most alarmed Occupation authorities. The Home Army counted 380,000 registered members across Poland. Though lightly armed and mostly civilians, their sheer numbers—greater than the French Resistance or any other insurgent group in Europe—made them a potentially formidable guerrilla force.

And there was little doubt that the Home Army was impressed by the actions in the Ghetto. Virtually every Underground publication lauded the January Rising with superlatives not often associated with Jews in the traditionally anti-Semitic Polish press. The *Information Bulletin* praised Jewish "bravery" and "sense of honor," in a front-page dispatch headlined HOW THE WARSAW GHETTO IS DEFENDING ITSELF. "The street was in the hands of Jewish fighters for fifteen to twenty minutes," the *Bulletin* reported. "Only large reinforcements enabled Germans to gain control of the situation. . . . The organized points of resistance defended themselves on Monday and Tuesday. They only retreated when faced by two SS squadrons that had been brought into the Ghetto on Wednesday in full combat readiness with machine guns, mortars and ambulances. A bloodbath ensued among the population, which, incited by the events of the previous days, offered active resistance with the aid of the most primitive of means such as iron rods, bars and stones. The German losses were ten dead police and SS troops."

As for the Home Army high command, General Rowecki was forced to reverse his position that firearms would be wasted on traditionally pacifist Jews. "I doubt they will use them," he had cabled London only days before the January Rising. Now he had his answer. Not only were Jews capable of using weapons, but they proved they could put them to good use against insurmountable odds. Rowecki no longer had an excuse to avoid supplying the ZOB with more guns.

The January 18 mini-rebellion, however, made its greatest impact within the Ghetto. "It changed everything," Boruch Spiegel recalled. Overnight, Mordechai Anielewicz became a household name. Outside ZOB circles, he had been relatively unknown before the Rising. Now his name fell from the lips of virtually every Jew in Warsaw. That he was the sole survivor of the heroic firefight on Low Street only increased his near-mythical status among Ghetto residents.

The ZOB as an organization won instant recognition as the dominant political and policing force within the Jewish district. "We are no longer in charge. A new authority now rules the Ghetto," conceded the chairman of the previously all-powerful Judenrat. "The Jewish Fighting Organization." Ghetto elders and skeptical residents could no longer claim that armed resistance was irresponsible and would result in wholesale slaughter. The revolt demonstrated that tens of thousands of lives could be saved by opposing the Germans—at least temporarily, for no one doubted that the SS would eventually be back to finish the aborted *Aktion*. But at least the ZOB had bought itself some time to prepare, and, just as important, it had won the support of the remaining Jewish masses, who began referring to the group with awe simply as the *Organizacja*—or the Organization.

Simha Ratheiser was by this time a full-fledged member of the Organization, rapidly rising through its youthful ranks. He had distinguished himself shortly after the January Rising by taking part in a brazen attack on the Jewish prison to free several jailed ZOB operatives. "My assignment was to distract the [Jewish Police] guards by pretending to deliver a package to a prisoner. My colleagues would then rush in with guns." The plan was inspired by a similar operation carried out on the Aryan side by the Gray Ranks, the Home Army's Boy Scout unit. Since one hundred and forty Gentiles had been executed by the SS in reprisal for that successful jailbreak, the ZOB hoped to divert Nazi retaliation by using Simha's Slavic features. His would be the only face unmasked. The ruse worked. Shocked Jewish policemen mistook him for a Gentile and "word spread like wildfire that the operation had been commanded by a fighter from the Polish Underground."

Ratheiser's superiors were so impressed by his cool demeanor during the breakout—"When others became nervous or agitated I got calmer. Everything slowed down for me in such situations," he explained about his sangfroid—that they promoted him to an elite unit led by twenty-two-year-old Hanoch Gutman. Gutman was one of the heroes of the January Rising, and his team did some of the ZOB's dirtiest work: so-called "Exes," which included both execution of traitors and expropriation of funds to finance weapons purchases. The unit was part hit squad, part extortion ring—but its targets hardly qualified as innocent victims. The notorious Gestapo agent Alfred Nossig, who claimed to be related to Zionist founder Theodor Herzl, was the first to be shot. He was followed by Mieczyslaw Brzezinski, the head of the Jewish Police's hated Umschlagplatz unit. "Isaac [Zuckerman] would tell Hanoch who had been sentenced to death," Simha recalled, "and he would carry it out."

The responsibility for issuing the death warrants weighed heavily on Zuckerman. "I wanted to drink, and I drank too much," he confessed. "It couldn't get rid of the gnawing worm. It was the sense of responsibility for a human life."

Boruch Spiegel, who reportedly joined an Exes group in the main shops district, refused to discuss the killing and extortion of fellow Jews. "I'm sorry, I won't talk about that," he demurred. Mark Edelman was more forthcoming about the sort of victim the ZOB shook down and the mafia-style tactics employed. "A Jewish policeman, a real son of a bitch, wouldn't give us money," he recalled. "We said, 'You don't want to pay? Fine,' and shot him."

The activities of the ZOB during this brief but controversial period of its evolution were in fact very similar to those of the American mob. Every underground baker in the Ghetto was forced to pay tribute to the ZOB by delivering free daily bread. Those who balked had their shops wrecked. Since the Organization needed to raise the equivalent of millions of dollars to buy arms for its members, it targeted the rich with a special "tax." A disproportionate percentage of surviving residents were wealthy, because money, gold, and diamonds was what kept people alive in the diabolically corrupt Nazi system. There was also no shortage of smugglers or collaborators to squeeze. "We would kidnap their children and ransom them," Simha explained of one tactic to secure contributions for the ZOB's weapons fund.

It was during one of these Exes that Ratheiser acquired the pseudonym that followed him for the rest of his life—the nickname by which his Israeli grandchildren would address him, the nom de guerre on his email address seventy years later. A rich Jew had refused to pay the ZOB "tax." "I put the barrel of my revolver near him," Simha recalled. "Then Hanoch [Gutman] ordered 'Kazik, kill him!' Why did he call me Kazik?"—a Polish diminutive for Casimir. "When [the rich Jew] heard 'Kazik,' he understood he was dealing with a Gentile, and you didn't get smart with Gentiles, especially not in those days. He broke down and gave us his contribution."

So much money was being raised through extortion that a violent turf war nearly erupted. The rival Jewish Military Union had its own Exes program, and competition between the two groups over territory and marks eventually led to a confrontation. Zuckerman, Edelman, and Anielewicz went to meet with unnamed leaders of the JMU to try to resolve the dispute. "They drew their guns, we also brought guns," was all Edelman would say. "I won't discuss it any further than that."

Whatever the origin of the conflict, it seemed that the ideological differences between the Jewish left and the Revisionist right remained irreconcilable in the winter of 1943, precluding any military cooperation. Though Edelman would not name the individuals with whom he had clashed in the armed standoff, one was likely Paul Frenkel, the young Betarist challenging David Apfelbaum for leadership of the JMU. Frenkel, at the time, was making large weapons purchases and needed to raise significant sums. Since Apfelbaum jealously guarded his contacts in the right-wing Home Army splinter group that had provided the JMU with weapons in the past, Frenkel needed to establish his own independent supply line. He had recently done so through a libertarian Home Army faction known by the Polish acronym PLAN. One of PLAN's Gentile underground leaders, John Ketling, recalled meeting Frenkel a few months earlier at a safe house in an industrial suburb of Warsaw: "In a low dark room where large amounts of ammunition, hand grenades, and pistols had been stored on planks, I found some young Jews dressed in civilian clothes. Only the pistols and hand grenades stuck in their leather belts gave away their identity as members of a military organization," he wrote in a postwar deposition. "The purpose of the meeting was explained to me by Paul [Frenkel], the head of their delegation. I learned that they considered themselves adherents of Jabotinsky and claimed that the pre-September 1939 Polish government had come to their assistance several times." Frenkel now wanted to extend that prewar cooperation to jointly combat the Nazis. "I liked the attitude of the Jewish fighters, their fanatical will to fight, their willingness to take a high risk for the cause . . . the lightheartedness and familiarity with which these young boys treated the danger that awaited them made a very strong impression on me."

In January 1943, Ketling was invited to visit JMU headquarters on Muranow Square, on the northern edge of the Central Ghetto enclave. He entered through a tunnel, one of several dug by the JMU's Engineering Department in the summer and fall of 1942. "It began in the cellar of number 7 Muranow and ended across the street in number 6." On the odd-numbered side, just next to the sidewalk, "a high wall made of red bricks and covered on top with broken glass and barbed wire" separated the Ghetto from the Aryan side. The tunnel, whose opening "was only a meter in diameter," ran under the barrier. "After lifting the cover of the entrance"—it was camouflaged with earth to mask its whereabouts, Ketling reported—"you would enter the tunnel on all fours. It was lit with electrical light and padded with blankets."

The fortified bunker into which the tunnel led was later described by the Ghetto chronicler Emmanuel Ringelblum, one of the few left-wing Zionists who managed to maintain cordial relations with the Revisionists: "In the command room was a first-class radio that received news from all over the world, and next to it stood a typewriter. I talked to people in command for several hours. They were armed, with revolvers stuck in their belts. Different kinds of weapons were hung in the large rooms: light machine guns, rifles, revolvers of various kinds, hand grenades, bags of ammunition, German uniforms etc. . . . There was great activity in the command room, as in any army headquarters. Fighters received their orders for the barrack-points where future combatants were being brought together and instructed. Reports arrived of expropriations of wealthy people carried out by individual groups for the purpose of arming the JMU. While I was there a purchase of arms was made from a former Polish Army officer amounting to a quarter of a million zlotys. Two machine guns were bought at 40,000 zlotys each, as well as a large number of hand grenades and bombs."

The ZOB, though far better known than its smaller and more secretive right-wing rival, had nothing to match that arsenal. And it did not have much time to play catch-up before the SS struck again.

In February 1943, the Home Army "saluted" the Organization's courage during the January Rising by delivering fifty pistols and grenades. The shipment was only a fraction of what Zuckerman and Edelman were expecting, because General Rowecki remained skeptical of the ZOB's political leanings and loyalties. But at least he no longer complained that weapons were wasted on Jews.

In a cable to London, the Home Army detailed how the arms were distributed among the different ZOB units being formed in the Ghetto's three enclaves: "Nine squadrons were concentrated in the center of the ghetto, eight in the area of the Tobbens and Schultz workshops, five in the Brushmakers District." The deployment incorporated a tactical lesson learned during the January Rising. Because the Ghetto was divided into noncontiguous zones separated by depopulated dead zones, it had been impossible to coordinate any cohesive battle plan from one unified headquarters. Consequently, the ZOB decided to split itself into three regiments, each acting independently under its own commander. Anielewicz assumed control of the largest force in the Central Ghetto. Zuckerman was in charge of the main shops area between Forestry and New Linden Streets. And Edelman headed the smaller Brushmakers District, on the westernmost edge of the Ghetto, near New Town.

Between the three of them they had as many as five hundred fighters, all of whom were now required to leave their families and live together in platoons so as to maintain constant battle readiness. "We did not want to be taken by surprise again," explained Ratheiser, whose group was barracked on Franciscan Street in the Brushmakers District. The platoons were structured along party lines—Bundists were garrisoned with Bundists, Young Guardsmen with Young Guardsman, members of Isaac's Socialist Zionist Dror with Dror—but all were of mixed gender. Inevitably, the cramped coed living arrangements led to many pairings: Simha fell hard for a girl named Dvora, and they became an item. His team leader, Hanoch Gutman, also shared his bunk with a girlfriend, as did Anielewicz and Boruch Spiegel. And of course Isaac and Zivia were still together.

During the day, most of the would-be warriors went to work at the various German shops. At night they trained for battle by pretending to shoot at targets. "We would aim and shout Bang, Bang," Spiegel recalled. Bullets were far too precious to waste on practice, since the revolvers from the Home Army had arrived with inexplicably empty chambers. "Allocating weapons without ammunition impresses us as being a bit of a mockery of our fate and confirms the assumption that the venom of anti-Semitism continues to permeate the ruling circles of Poland," Mordechai Anielewicz angrily declared. That the unloaded pistols were all of different vintages, makes, and calibers further aggravated the ZOB's dire munitions problems.

General Rowecki's token "goodwill gesture" had armed barely one in ten combatants. A few additional Mausers had been liberated from dead Germans during the rising, and some rifles were bought at the illicit arms market on Jerusalem Boulevard near Central Station. The black market was proving a disappointment as a source of weapons. It was rife with rip-off artists and Gestapo informants. The ZOB could purchase only one or two guns at a time since large orders would arouse suspicion, and what it had managed to buy was "a pittance," in Zuckerman's frustrated words. So he sent courier Ari Wilner back to the Aryan side to press the Home Army for more guns. Though it was not widely known, Wilner had fired the first shot of the January Rising. His role was less heralded than Mordechai Anielewicz's because it had taken place behind closed doors rather than in full view of the public. Nonetheless, having a German kill under his belt lent Wilner tremendous credibility with the Polish Underground. Even if some of the more conservative Polish army officers had misgivings about Jews, they respected Wilner personally. One of his greatest admirers was Captain Henry Wolinski, the Home Army's Jewish Affairs liaison officer.

Wolinski had a Jewish wife hidden at home, and he was sympathetic to the ZOB. He secured a promise for a further shipment of arms: "a machine gun, a tommy gun, twenty pistols with magazines and ammunition, 100 hand grenades, and diversion materials such as time bombs and delayed action fuses." Wilner and Wolinski also arranged for the ZOB to receive training at the Home Army's underground explosives laboratory, so engineer and Bundist Michael Klepfish was sent for an intensive course on bomb making.

Klepfish returned three weeks later with dynamite, two thousand liters of kerosene, and a slew of volatile recipes to set up his own laboratory. Simha Ratheiser and Boruch Spiegel both recall scouring the Ghetto for empty bottles and burned-out lightbulbs for Klepfish's bomb factories. The bulbs were injected with sulfuric acid, while the bottles—very hard to come by—were filled with a mixture of kerosene, gasoline, sugar, and potassium cyanide to create incendiary devices whose burn rates could be controlled by altering the ingredients. The assembly of these bottle bombs had to be concealed in well-ventilated attics because "the odor of the chemicals was overwhelming." One such lab was on St. George's Street in Edelman's Brushmakers District, across from Krasinski Park in the building next to one in which the Ratheisers had lived when Simha first moved to the Ghetto. The lethal cocktails were mixed in large barrels and carefully funneled into vodka bottles that often had to be smuggled in from the Aryan side.

Since drainpipes were plentiful and could be fashioned into grenades, hundreds of bathrooms throughout the Ghetto were dismantled for their cast iron fixtures. "We would remove the pipes with a larger than normal diameter, saw out a piece of about 30 to 40 centimeters, solder one side, and make threads for a screw on the other side. Inside the hard metal pipe, we would put a thinner tin pipe and load it with explosives. We would fill the space in between the two pipes with pieces of metal, nails and such. The effect of the explosion was not only from the pipe but also from the scraps of metal and nails. We would carve slits in the pipe, which scattered the slivers. In the screwed-on top, we would make a crack to put the wick."

The work was dangerous and not without mishaps. "One morning the entire ghetto shook to a mighty explosion, which threw everyone into a panic," senior ZOB operative Tuvia Borzykowski recounted. "Only a few knew that the bomb was our own."

Slowly but surely, the Organization's weapons and munitions caches grew. Every day, a few revolvers trickled in from the black markets on the Aryan side. With each passing week, the stores of homemade grenades increased. With each shift, the rows of bottled Molotov cocktails lengthened.

During the feverish preparations, the question arose of whether to follow the JMU's lead and build fortified bunkers and tunnels. Underground hideouts were being frantically excavated in basements and cellars throughout the Ghetto in February and March 1943, in anticipation of the next *Aktion*. The vast majority were dug by ordinary residents and never intended as entrenched fighting positions. Their purpose was purely concealment. Many of these hideouts were engineering marvels, with lighting and electricity, running water, and complex ventilation systems. A thriving cottage industry of skilled contractors had sprung up to design and build shelters for those who could afford them. Others dug their own, crude crawl spaces shored up by planks ripped from the floors of abandoned apartments. Some of the more sophisticated designs could house hundreds of refugees, with stores of food and drink for several weeks. These were so well camouflaged, with false walls and entrances through the coal furnaces in boiler rooms, that even the residents of the buildings above could not find them.

Zuckerman advocated mimicking the JMU's bunker strategy. The January Rising proved that it was impossible to fight the Germans in the open from exposed positions. And now the element of surprise was gone. The SS would be better prepared next time, expecting resistance. The ZOB, he argued, needed escape routes and fallback positions where it could regroup and hunker down.

Mordechai Anielewicz had a different view. The point of any future battle, he argued, was not survival. There would be no survivors; the only hope was to inflict the maximum possible casualties on the enemy before the inevitable demise. To accomplish this would require holding the high ground: the rooftops and attics that provided the optimum lines of sight.

Zuckerman thought "this was a mistake." Edelman grumbled that "not all of us were in such a hurry to die." But Anielewicz's reasoning prevailed. He was, after all, the great hero, the living symbol of resistance who had already attained cult status within the ZOB's largely teenage rank and file. If he wanted to reenact a modern Masada, they would follow him to their martyr's graves.

Zuckerman and Edelman viewed their co-commander in a less hallowed light. Isaac and Mark had become close. During Zuckerman's convalescence from his leg wound, the two spent a lot of time together. They struck up a genuine friendship that transcended their ideological differences. Not so with Anielewicz. "I had not gotten to know him well because I didn't mix with Communists," Edelman explained frankly. "Isaac and Zivia lived with him for a while. They used to read his journal entries in Hebrew and laugh. He'd never seen the Umschlagplatz and yet was so desperate to lead. Seeing 400,000 people go to their death changes you—you can break down. That's certainly why the [April] uprising turned out much harder on him."

Zuckerman, Lubetkin, and Edelman resented the implications of Anielewicz's private diaries: that had he been in Warsaw during the *Gross Aktion,* he might somehow have single-handedly saved the Ghetto. They felt better prepared for the coming conflict precisely because they had already witnessed death on an unimaginable scale. In their view, Anielewicz had not yet paid his psychological dues.

Edelman's few interactions with his commander served only to reinforce his reservations that Anielewicz was "very emotional and sometimes acted rashly." This spontaneity caused significant friction between the ZOB leaders when Anielewicz, in late March 1943, shot two Latvian SS auxiliaries on Pleasant Street in the Central Ghetto. Edelman and Zuckerman were furious. While the ZOB had openly assassinated Jewish collaborators—at least sixty traitors, possibly more, were killed in all—it had never targeted Germans because of the risk of retaliation. The Gestapo did not care if a Jew was murdered in the Ghetto, but an SS auxiliary was a different matter. Within hours of the hit on the Latvians, more than two hundred Jews were rounded up on Pleasant Street, lined up against walls, and machine-gunned. Many ZOB leaders held Anielewicz responsible for the deaths of those innocent people. "After this incident the Coordinating Committee of the ZOB wanted to remove him from his post," Edelman recalled.

Anielewicz's good standing with the ZOB's impatient teenage rank and file was unaffected by his actions, and because of his popularity he survived the no-confidence vote. The ZOB suffered another, potentially more serious blow when envoy Ari Wilner fell into German hands. His arrest prompted the Home Army to immediately suspend all contact with the ZOB. Wilner had been betrayed by a Polish informant during an arms pickup. Taken to Gestapo headquarters, he was tortured, suspended upside down, the soles of his feet burned with branding irons. The Germans had no idea he was a Jew and their interrogations focused entirely on the Home Army. He endured the questioning for several weeks before finally breaking down and confessing that he was a Jew. When the Gestapo confirmed this, they lost interest in him. They were only after information on the Home Army, so Wilner was sent to Peacock Prison in the Ghetto.

The Home Army, in the meantime, completely disappeared from the ZOB's radar. Every effort to reach Captain Wolinski failed; every channel of communication suddenly went silent. As the weeks passed and March faded into April, the frustrated ZOB leaders became convinced that General Rowecki was using Wilner's arrest as an excuse to suspend further aid. At the time, Mark Edelman felt the same way. Only later did he learn that "the Home Army had an iron-clad rule that if someone was burnt, all contact was ruptured for six weeks." The underground term for this was quarantining an "infected" agent. (The security precautions were standard procedure, though hardly foolproof. In June 1943, General Rowecki himself was betrayed by an infected member. Sent to Berlin, he was subjected to months of interrogation before being shot at Sachsenhausen.)

Almost six weeks to the day after Wilner's arrest, Captain Henry Wolinski reestablished contact. The call came on April 12, 1943, with a cryptic message stating "if you don't want the salt to spoil the meal, you should come immediately to pick it up." Presumably this meant the Home Army had a weapons shipment ready. But whom would the ZOB send to retrieve it? A replacement had to be found for Wilner, someone with sufficient gravitas to act as the Organization's new ambassador on the Aryan side.

Once more the choice came down to Mordechai Anielewicz or Isaac Zuckerman. Anielewicz's advantage was that he was a native

Varsovian. "He talked and looked like a typical Warsaw Pole. He didn't speak like the Jewish intellectuals, who, because of their fluency and literary speech, would fail and be exposed. . . . My disadvantage," Zuckerman went on, "was that I came from eastern Poland, from Vilna. In normal times, Warsaw Poles mocked the Polish of Vilna, which had many Russianisms."

Anielewicz also had the considerable advantage of having led the January Rising. The Poles would respect that. Unfortunately, though, he had no intention of playing diplomat; Mordechai wanted to stay and fight. So in the end it was Isaac who represented the Organization on the Aryan side. He packed his belongings and left the Ghetto on April 17, 1943. Little did he know that he would never again set foot in the Jewish district.

CHAPTER 29

ZIVIA LETS LOOSE

It was 2 A.M. on April 19, 1943, less than forty-eight hours after Isaac Zuckerman's departure to the Aryan side as the ZOB's new liaison officer with the Home Army, when a courier burst into Zivia Lubetkin's quarters.

From the boy's grave expression, Zivia immediately sensed something was wrong. For an agonizing instant, she thought Isaac might be in trouble: betrayed by an informant or apprehended by the Gestapo. These things usually happened quickly, at the outset of a mission, when inexperienced operatives blundered into traps. Zivia's heart skipped a beat. Much as she tried to conceal her emotions behind the hard mask she wore in public, Lubetkin constantly worried about her lover. She couldn't forget that the last time Zuckerman had left the Ghetto, he'd barely made it back, with a bullet lodged in his leg. And she was only too keenly aware that the man he was now replacing as ZOB envoy, Ari Wilner, had been betrayed to the Gestapo and tortured.

The runner, however, wasn't bearing news of Isaac's capture. The Germans, he stammered, were massing troops throughout Warsaw.

Word from the Home Army was that special SS units would storm the Ghetto at first light.

Relief swept over Lubetkin. Not only was Isaac safe, but the hour she had long awaited was finally at hand. This was what the Jewish Fighting Organization had been preparing for since its inception. This was what all the sacrifice was about: the weapons training, the Exes, the bomb making, the rip-offs and endless haggling with the uncooperative Polish Underground and unscrupulous arms dealers. Zivia had been anticipating this moment for weeks now; the entire Jewish community had been preparing for it for months. The civilians had feverishly dug their bunkers and camouflaged their hiding places; the combatants—from both the ZOB and its rival, the Jewish Military Union—had fortified their defenses and honed their strategies.

Everything that could be done had been done. The guns had been distributed. (Boruch Spiegel, who had been afraid of accidentally shooting himself when he first held a revolver, now couldn't sleep unless he had his trusted pistol under his pillow.) Sandbags had been filled and food supplies laid in. Mines and improvised explosive devices had been buried beneath the entry gates to the Ghetto's three remaining sections. Molotov cocktails had been strategically stored in upper-floor windows overlooking every major artery that the Germans would have to traverse. Holes had been cut in attic fire walls so that fighters could slip unseen from building to building and track their prey from above. The ZOB's twenty-two fighting units had all been mobilized and deployed. Nine were in the Central Ghetto, eight in the main shops district, and the five battle groups under Mark Edelman's command were positioned in the Brushmakers Area.

By 4 A.M. the Ghetto was on high alert, a hive of activity as fifty thousand residents scrambled into basements, disappearing behind false walls and trapdoors that opened onto preprovisioned hideouts. "In the bunkers, people push and shove and lie down on planks," Zivia noted. "Suddenly a child begins wailing. It has gotten separated from its parents. Immediately, from all sides, people rush to calm the frightened child, whose cries can alert the Germans and doom them all."

The apartments were almost empty now. The last stragglers were burrowing underground, and silence once again returned, as if, thought Zivia, "all life was erased from the face of the earth."

The only Jews the Germans would encounter now—Zivia smiled at the thought—were armed Jews. There were roughly 750 of them dispersed throughout the Jewish district's three remaining sections: five hundred from the ZOB and the balance from the JMU, whose forces were concentrated in the northernmost part of the Central Ghetto near Muranow Square. The two groups would fight separately, despite a last-ditch attempt to overcome their differences. But Zivia wasn't thinking about that. It was too late for recriminations. Her only regret now was that the ZOB didn't have more guns. If not for the weapons shortage, "we would have a thousand warriors rather than five hundred," she sighed.

Lubetkin holstered her pistol and took up her preassigned position in the predawn gloom. She was calm and completely unafraid, almost giddy with anticipation. "At last," she thought. "The day of revenge is upon us."

Had Zivia seen what Simha Ratheiser was witnessing at that very moment from his forward position on the easternmost edge of the Brushmakers District, she might have felt decidedly less confident. For only the second time in his life, Ratheiser was truly scared. The scene unfolding before his eyes was terrifying. As the sun rose pink over the horizon, wave after wave of German troops were crossing Cordials Street on their way to the Central Ghetto. Ratheiser watched them in the weak morning light, dense helmeted blocs moving in robotic unison just outside the wall. They formed "an endless procession," he recalled. "Behind them were tanks, armored vehicles, light cannons and hundreds of Waffen-SS units on motorcycles." Further still were the ambulances, field kitchens, and communications trucks. The rumble of the approaching armada grew steadily louder, more ominous. Windowpanes began rattling from the reverberations of track treads on cobblestone. Diesel fumes permeated the still-frigid air. The bark of marching orders grew louder.

It seemed to Simha as if the entire German army stood at the Ghetto's gates. He tried to gauge the enemy's strength but quickly lost count. There were too many regiments, platoons, and companies to keep track of. It looked like thousands of soldiers, maybe many thousands. At least one thing was clear. This was not like previous *Aktions*. Those, in comparison, had been mere police exercises. This was a full-fledged military operation; even the Latvian and Ukrainian units were sober and clean-shaven. The SS had apparently drawn its own lessons from the January revolt. This time it had come prepared for resistance.

Simha swallowed hard and glanced at the teenage fighter crouched next to him. He was thin, ragged, and nervously clutching a cumbersome homemade grenade. The next combatant down the line was a girl barely out of high school holding a bottle filled with gasoline. Simha and his fellow fighters all looked like this: desperate undernourished kids, untrained and ill equipped. The vast majority of them had never even fired a gun. Ratheiser turned his attention to the sprawling gray-green military machine moving in lockstep formation toward the Central Ghetto. The contrast was so stark that he could draw only one conclusion: "We don't stand a chance," he suddenly realized. "We are going to get slaughtered."

The Germans struck at precisely 6:00 A.M., hitting the large Central Ghetto simultaneously from the north and south. Zivia Lubetkin was at her post at the intersection of Goose and Cordials Streets, near one of the main entrance gates through which the enemy needed to pass. These gates were artificial choke points that favored the defenders, since SS planners, in their zeal to seal off the Jewish community behind stout walls, had inadvertently limited their own assault options to a few predictable entry points. It had never occurred to the Nazis that they might actually have to fight their way *into* the Ghetto, but Mordechai Anielewicz immediately recognized this inherent weakness and threw his meager resources into blockading critical gaps. Strategically, it was the urban equivalent of an army having to funnel through a narrow ravine to reach the open battlefield. Jewish partisans, perched on the rooftops and upper floors of the buildings that mimicked canyon walls, could then rain fury on the exposed invaders.

The SS approached the Ghetto in parade formation, marching six abreast and singing the Horst Wessel song, the Nazi anthem. They did not attempt to hide, cover their positions, or secure their perimeters. The assault was more theatrical than tactical: a display of force and confidence intended to dissuade potential resistance and send the message that opposition was pointless. To some extent the intimidation tactic worked, since it successfully magnified the Germans' true strength. Contrary to what observers like Ratheiser believed, there were not thousands of soldiers descending on them. There were only 850 Waffen-SS troops, drawn more or less equally from the SS Panzer Grenadier Reserve Battalion and the SS Cavalry Reserve Division, and they were supported by 150 Ukrainian and Latvian auxiliaries—also known derisively as Askars, or Deutsch-Negers, after the African units that fought alongside whites in the Boer wars.

The illusion of superior numbers, however, did little to stanch the determination of the defenders. If anything, it brought a knowing and expectant smile to the faces of the many young Jews lurking behind window sashes and sills, ready to pounce. The arrogant Germans were walking straight into a trap, a minefield strewn with improvised explosive devices.

"Let them come," said Zivia, ordering her impatient young troops to hold their fire. Fingers tightened around triggers. Everyone took a deep breath and took aim. But discipline held. No one shot early. And the Germans drew closer. Still singing as if they were on a leisurely stroll, the unsuspecting invaders were now treading on IEDs, connected with buried wires to detonators.

"Now!" someone screamed, and in an instant, multiple explosions rocked Cordials Street. Cobblestones flew in every direction and fountains of dirt went crashing against the bordering buildings, shattering the windows of the old Bon Appétit restaurant. Debris landed as far away as the defunct Lunch Café, with German helmets smashing against walls, rifles being flung three stories high, and body parts everywhere. "I could see torn limbs flying through the air with my own eyes." Lubetkin remembered cheering wildly.

The singing abruptly stopped, replaced by the agonized screams of wounded soldiers, the confused and contradictory orders of stunned officers, and the clatter of jackboots on cobblestones as the proud SS ran frantically for cover. One private, whose helmet was grotesquely ablaze, kept yelling *"Juden haben Waffen! Juden haben Waffen!"*—The Jews have weapons! The Jews have weapons!—as if he were witnessing a military miracle. No one had anticipated that the

defenders would be armed with explosives. The Nazis expected to encounter revolvers, perhaps the occasional rifle. But it had apparently
not dawned on them that Jewish insurgents could manufacture incendiary bombs and grenades in vast quantities. Those crude homemade
weapons didn't require expertise to throw or drop from above. They
did not need to be well aimed or carefully placed to have devastating
effects, since the target areas—streets bordered by plate-glass
windows—were so narrow. And the walls of the buildings served to
magnify the lethal ricochet effect. For the exposed Germans there was
only one real option: to turn and flee. But they had nowhere to run,
because ZOB rebels had shrewdly positioned themselves on all four
sides of the Cordials and Goose Street intersection, creating a deadly
cross fire that cut off their retreat and gripped the Nazis in a vise of
bullets.

From the north end of Cordials, five or six hundred yards away,
soon came the chaotic sounds of an almost identical battle, the faint
pop and crackle of gunfire, the low concussive blasts of grenades. The
Germans were trying to breach the Wall on Muranow Street near the
Jewish Military Union's heavily fortified base. At the same time, a few
blocks west of there, closer to the Umschlagplatz exit, other SS units
were trying to secure Zamenhof Street, the corridor of death that led
to the rail terminal. They would need to clear that passage to liquidate
the Ghetto's remaining fifty thousand residents, a fact that Mordechai
Anielewicz had counted on. He had deployed four fighting units along
the route.

The thirty fighters in Zivia's group—led by twenty-year-old Zacharia Artstein, a hero of the January Rising—now unleashed their own
hail of grenades and Molotov cocktails. Cordials Street burst into an
impassable inferno as bottles filled with fuel crashed onto the road
and sidewalks, erupting with a *whoosh* of sucked oxygen that sent
black fumes streaking across the marquee of the Astor Dance Club.

Pinned down and panicked, the Germans could barely return fire.
Many pressed themselves flat against the indentations of doorways.
Some tried to force their way into blocked courtyards. Others sought
refuge in abandoned storefronts. All the while, their Jewish tormentors showered them with abuse, hurling every German curse word
they could think of and plenty more in Yiddish. "We couldn't help

ourselves," Lubetkin laughed. Revenge was sweeter than any of them could imagine. The elation of turning the tables on the murderous SS was so intoxicating that even the most restrained combatants found themselves screaming *"Fuck you, Nazi bastards!"*

The reinforcements called in by shocked SS platoon leaders collided with reality the moment they crossed the Ghetto threshold. They ran straight into a wall of flame and fire. With more German units piling into the cauldron, forced forward by furious officers at the rear, Artstein's brigade opened fire with their pistols and their few precious rifles. For the Nazis, the bottleneck was proving a death trap. They couldn't advance, but their officers would not let them retreat. Zivia and the others, meanwhile, tried to pick off the cowering soldiers, using windowsills to steady their aim. Most of the shots missed their mark—the young Jews were hardly marksmen—but several more Germans fell, writhing in agony, clutching their bloodied abdomens. Every hit brought a roar from the upper floors and balconies; and the news that Anielewicz's groups had knocked out a tank on Zamenhof Street brought the loudest cheer of all.

From his guard post in the nearby Brushmakers District, Simha could not see the fighting in the Central Ghetto. But he could hear the shooting and shouting, could distinguish the wild staccato bursts of German submachine guns from the steady crackling of the ZOB's revolvers. After a few hours, he began to realize that he was not listening to a massacre, but that his fellow fighters, against all odds, were holding their ground. He, too, began to cheer, especially when Germans reappeared in his sightlines, retreating toward the safety of the Aryan side. Simha couldn't believe it. In this opening battle, at least, David had defeated Goliath.

"We can't get into the Ghetto," Col. Ferdinand von Sammern-Frankenegg conceded shortly before 8 A.M. He was half a mile from the scene of the aborted *Aktion,* on the top floor of the elegant Bristol Hotel in a luxurious suite reserved for Jürgen Stroop, one of the SS's top counterinsurgency experts.

General Stroop had made a name for himself on the Eastern Front, initially in the wild Caucasus mountains, hunting Soviet commando units, and then in the killing fields of Ukraine, rooting out and dispatching partisan groups with such brutal efficiency that Himmler had summoned him to Warsaw to watch over the inexperienced Von Sammern-Frankenegg, in case the Jews proved difficult to handle.

"We are not in the Ghetto," Von Sammern repeated, shaking in disbelief. "We can't get in."

Stroop smoked impassively as the agitated colonel tallied the morning's losses. Twelve men were dead or wounded, a tank was wrecked, and two armored personnel carriers were burned beyond recognition. Stroop betrayed no emotion. He knew all this. He had been working the phones to Berlin and Krakow, poisoning the bureaucratic well for the incompetent colonel. "That idiot, Von Sammern-Frankenegg, drove a tank into those narrow streets," he complained to General Wilhelm Kruger, the ranking SS officer in occupied Poland. "It's a disgrace," Kruger agreed. "That Tyrolean fool, that cow, has brought dishonor to the good name of the SS and should be immediately arrested."

At this, Stroop allowed himself a small, self-satisfied smile. He had been rooting for Von Sammern to fail ever since he got the call from Himmler. It wasn't solely because he was fiercely ambitious. Stroop's ruthlessness had already won him rapid promotion. In Ukraine, where he had picked out a four-hundred-acre parcel near Lvov on which to build his estate after the war, his counterinsurgency tactics exceeded even the SS's most brutal standards. Any village suspected of harboring "terrorists" wasn't merely targeted for reprisal. It was entirely wiped out; every inhabitant was killed, every building was burned, all the livestock was slaughtered. This hard-line approach to quashing resistance was exactly why Himmler had tapped Stroop. For Stroop, success in Warsaw could lead to a string of high-profile assignments: in Yugoslavia and Greece, where Communist partisans were becoming a nuisance; in France and Holland, where the British were stirring up local resistance movements.

There was another, more personal and vindictive reason Stroop wanted Von Sammern to fail. He hated his type. The man was "soft," an effete intellectual, an aristocrat from a prominent Austrian family who owed his cushy position to influence rather than hard work. In Stroop's view, there was no place in the meritocratic SS for well-

connected "dandies" who were afraid of getting blood on their manicured fingers. They should stay in the class-conscious Wehrmacht
with the rest of the old Junker nobility.

Stroop's background was markedly different. His father had been
a humble policeman in a tiny town. While Von Sammern had the luxury of completing a doctorate in philosophy in Vienna, Stroop's formal education ended after elementary school, and he toiled as an
apprentice surveyor until the Nazi Party offered him a chance to prove
himself. He didn't have Von Sammern's polished manners or his elaborate vocabulary, but that didn't matter in the SS, because results
counted more than lineage. Nor did Stroop share Von Sammern's taste
for "alcohol, parties, and loose women." He had once pulled Von
Sammern's Gestapo file, which detailed the colonel's frequent outings
to the notorious Adria, one of Warsaw's most degenerate "German-
only" nightclubs. Worse still was the company Von Sammern kept
there: Wehrmacht officers, arrogant Prussians who considered themselves superior to the brutish SS but didn't have the stomach to do
what was needed to ensure the Reich prevailed over its enemies. In the
Third Reich, the SS was the new aristocracy, and it had no room for
dilettante throwbacks like Col. Ferdinand von Sammern-Frankenegg.

Stroop couldn't bear to listen to Von Sammern's hysterical report
any longer. Stubbing out his cigarette (the Simon, billed as the "finest
Egyptian tobacco in the world," was a privilege of rank, along with
his new BMW and the estate he would soon build in Ukraine), the
general rose from his gilded chair, waving for the china and silverware
to be removed from his breakfast table. He was an imposing man, six
feet tall, slim and strong with a long stern face, and his slick black hair
was meticulously parted down the center, showing no signs of gray
despite his nearly fifty years.

"I'm assuming command," he said, striding over to the suite's
panoramic window, which looked down on the cream-colored façade
of the European Hotel across the street, another German-only establishment. The renamed Hitler Platz could be seen directly behind it,
then the budding treetops of Saxon Gardens, and finally Cordials
Street, the symbol of Jewish Warsaw, the city's prewar commercial
hub, and now the humiliating site of SS disgrace. The time for half
measures was over, Stroop declared. "Mobilize all forces," he ordered.

CHAPTER 30

JOANNA PRAYS

The sprawling SS garrison next to the convent where Joanna Mortkowicz-Olczak was hiding had been on high alert since early that morning, April 19. Now an endless stream of trucks and motorcycles with sidecars emerged from its black steel gates as General Stroop called up more reserves to quash the Jewish revolt. Joanna, like any nine-year-old, only vaguely comprehended the significance of the stepped-up activity. "I don't really remember much beyond the fact that someone said there was shooting somewhere in the city," she later recalled. Sister Wanda, however, immediately grasped that the Ghetto was under siege. She knew the Jews had been planning an armed revolt because she had briefly sheltered the ZOB envoy Ari Wilner.

Sister Wanda's main concern was for her Jewish charges. Some of the girls still had families in the Ghetto, and she wanted to shield them from unnecessary trauma. There was nothing they could do other than cry and despair, and that might betray them to nosy outside observers. So the boarders were kept in the dark about the Uprising, and she busied them with intensified preparations for their First Communion. This would not only take their minds off the fighting raging a few miles north, but, more important, it would buttress their Catholic credentials should the Gestapo later come searching for Jews who managed to escape from the Ghetto siege.

The Germans had already come looking for Joanna once, shortly after her mother, Hanna, and her grandmother, Janine, were shaken down by the dreaded greaser blackmailers, who had extracted a princely sum to let them go and probably still tipped off the Gestapo to Joanna's whereabouts. That had been in December 1942, the beginning of what proved to be a very difficult winter for the Mortkowicz clan. First Joanna's mother and grandmother disappeared, leaving the anxious child alone and frightened for weeks as they tried to give the greasers the slip. How they finally managed to evade their blackmailers, Joanna did not know, but it almost certainly involved large payments and the promise of more. Then, just as her family reestablished contact in January 1943, an unimaginable relief for the grief-stricken Joanna, tragedy struck. Grandma Janine's older brother, Ludwik Horwitz, a scientist, was arrested by the Gestapo. He had been hiding "on the surface," that is openly, under his own name, conducting a major research project for the State Geological Institute of Warsaw. Astonishingly, no one had bothered him before now. Within days of his submitting the research paper he had been working on throughout the occupation, the Gestapo picked him up. He was shot a few weeks later, in February 1943.

Around this time, Sister Wanda informed Joanna that it was no longer safe for her to stay at the convent. The Germans had searched the place, asking for her by name, a sure sign that the Gestapo had been tipped off to her presence. "They demanded an inspection of all the children, and had come with precise instructions to hand over the little Olczak girl, whose mother was a Jew," one of the other boarders, a Christian, later recounted. "The three Germans started to go up the stairs. We remained on the first floor. I can still hear their heavy footsteps—I can remember that appalling fear—we knew all too well what would happen to her" if the Germans discovered Joanna hiding behind the chapel enclosure on the second floor. "Some Sisters were praying in the chapel as the footsteps approached the door of the enclosure. Then there was a moment of silence and we heard Sister Wanda calmly say: 'I shall once again remind you that this is the enclosure.' And again there was a silence, in which it felt as if everything around us and inside us had and gone still. And then the footsteps coming down the steps and they were gone."

But who had sent them? Who had denounced Joanna? Could it have been the spiteful greasers, angry at having lost their lucrative prey? Or poor Uncle Ludwik, under torture? Or perhaps there was an informant in Monika Zeromska's Home Army cell? Not knowing was the most frightening part. It meant betrayal could come at any moment from any quarter. This constant state of anxiety plagued a large segment of the city's population—Home Army officers, Underground activists, Jews passing themselves off as Gentiles—resulting in inordinately high numbers of nervous breakdowns in wartime Warsaw. Children proved among the most psychologically resilient to prolonged stress. "I don't remember being especially frightened," Joanna recalled. "There were moments of terror, sure. But it was not the norm." Joanna would credit the nuns for their calming influence, for trying to keep the children in a protective bubble, isolated from the evils of the outside world.

Alas, she had to leave that bubble; the comforting "smell of ersatz coffee and slightly burned porridge" in the refectory, the familiar sound of fellow boarders chasing one another down long corridors, giggling maniacally. Her one consolation was that she would rejoin her mother, Hanna, in yet another distant suburb, a miserable town called Pruszkow that was perhaps best known as Poland's hotbed of organized crime. The family's plight was still precarious. Hanna and Janine had been forced to split up to avoid suspicion, and they had changed safe houses three times in as many months. It took Joanna only a few days to realize that their new hideout, at the back of a grimy grocery store, was far from safe. Every few days mysterious sacks arrived at the storage room, and the deliveries were followed by frantic floor cleaning around the secret trapdoor under which the large bags disappeared. The potato sacks left a telltale silvery dust that had to be scrubbed clean in case the Germans inspected the premises. The dust was actually tiny bullet slivers, the fallout from tens of thousands of rounds of ammunition rubbing against one another.

Joanna stayed at the clandestine munitions depot for only a few months before Sister Wanda sent for her again, but she would forever be curious as to how her family ended up in all these conspiratorial locales. "Was it through mutual friends?" she would later ask one of her wartime hosts. "No, no one ever exchanged names in those days," came the answer. "No questions were asked, and the reasons why people were in hiding were never revealed. They reached us through Home Army contacts. That was enough of a recommendation."

Isaac Zuckerman was finding the Home Army far less cooperative. Throughout the morning of April 19, 1943, he tried desperately to arrange an emergency meeting with ranking Home Army representatives. But his every attempt was rebuffed. The HA high command had made its position clear and saw no reason to revisit its decision now that the actual fighting had begun. Captain Henry Wolinski, its "Jewish Affairs" officer, was apologetic and sympathetic. But while he declared his admiration for the valor being displayed in the Ghetto, there was nothing he could do. His superior officer, Major Stan Weber, had sent a terse message refusing to see Isaac.

The only assistance Wolinski was authorized to offer was to reiterate an earlier proposal from the Home Army to evacuate ZOB members from the Ghetto and redeploy them as partisans in the forests around the capital. There would be no other help because the Home Army had warned the ZOB not to revolt. The danger that the uprising would spread into the rest of the city was deemed too great. That same fear, in fact, was foremost on General Kruger's mind when he spoke to Stroop earlier that morning and ordered that all Wehrmacht and Luftwaffe battalions stationed in Warsaw also be put on high alert and a state of emergency be declared over the entire Polish capital. Himmler had been equally concerned, expanding the order to include all armed forces in the entire General Government. "Don't provoke the Poles," the Reichsführer warned Stroop. "Appease them if necessary."

For Himmler, the prospect of subduing the 380,000-strong Home Army was far more daunting than resistance from a few hundred rebellious Jewish teenagers. Little did the SS leader know that the Home Army had issued strict orders of its own: All units were to stand down. The Poles had absolutely no intention of launching a citywide rising.

It was far too early for that, Captain Wolinski regretfully informed Zuckerman. "Poland has to wait and gather its strength," allowing the Soviets and the Nazis to "bleed one another until they are exhausted." Only then would the Home Army strike and liberate Warsaw from its Nazi captors. The time, however, was not yet ripe. The Soviets had just started turning the tide on the Eastern Front. In Stalingrad, the Wehrmacht had been decimated and hundreds of thousands of German soldiers taken as prisoners of war. The Red Army had retaken Rostov and Kharkov and most of Crimea. But the Russians were still thousands of miles from Warsaw. If the Home Army joined the Jewish revolt now, it would be slaughtered. Hitler would take revenge on the whole city. "A million people would die."

The message could not have been clearer, or more dispiriting. The Home Army was not about to risk Warsaw for the sake of the Jews. The Jews were on their own.

Unaware that they had been abandoned by the outside world, Zivia Lubetkin and the fighters on Cordials Street were still celebrating their unexpected victory later that morning. The jubilant combatants danced, played Schubert, and clapped one another on the shoulder as they surveyed the devastation around them. Cordials Street was strewn with rubble and pockmarked like a lunar landscape. It was smeared with charcoal and reeked of kerosene and cordite, utterly unrecognizable, leached of all its vibrant prewar color, of the billboards and store names that had plastered its crowded façades, of the stalls and street vendors that had spilled out onto its congested sidewalks, of the brightly painted banners proclaiming *Sprzedaz* (Sale) that used to lure shoppers from all over town.

Little remained of the avenue's glorious past. Number 33 Cordials, the bullet-scarred edifice in which Zivia currently stood, had once housed, among its many commercial tenants, the E. Gitlin bookstore, which offered "a wide assortment of Hebrew dictionaries, textbooks, and self-teaching guides." The famous Moskowicz Cheese Shop had been next door, along with Goldstein's Laundry, on the floor above it, and the Magazinik Gramophone and Record Shop, known to music lovers from all parts of the city. Directly across the street, Sheinblum Paints and the Fenomen Kitchen Stoves outlet were no more, and nothing but a smoke-streaked mask was left of Zonenstein Sporting Goods or its much larger neighbor, the old Rozenthal Department Store.

Zivia and her fellow insurgents did not mourn the devastation of once proud Cordials Street. At that moment, most were still flushed with the adrenaline high of the morning's skirmish, and since the destruction had been wrought by their own hands in defense of Jewish honor, it was well worth the price. In human costs, it was a bargain. Zivia's group had not taken a single casualty, while inflicting half a dozen on the enemy. As a bonus, they had also increased their weapons arsenal in the exchange. Lutek Rotblatt, one of the unit's deputy commanders, proudly distributed the haul of Mausers that had been abandoned by fleeing Germans. The ZOB could now turn the Nazis' own guns against them.

The rejoicing was abruptly cut short when a courier came running up to Zivia and Zacharia Artstein shortly after noon. German troops, the boy said, were massing once more. Hundreds of soldiers were arriving at the main southern gate, at the intersection of Zamenhof and Goose Streets, three or four hundred yards away. The SS was preparing to come at them again, this time from the west rather than the east.

The change in direction prevented Simha Ratheiser from catching an early glimpse of the approaching forces. He was still at his post on the balcony of a nearby tenement on Embankment Street, with his finger on the trigger of an improvised detonator attached through a long cable to a large mine that lay just beneath the main gate to the Brushmakers District. His enclave had thus far been spared, as had the main shops district where Boruch Spiegel's unit was deployed, because both were part of what was known as the Productive Ghetto, where the German-owned factories were most heavily concentrated. The biggest industrialists, moreover—war millionaires like the Shultz brothers, or Walter Casper Tobbens, the richest and most influential of them all—also had their factories in the main shops district and the Brushmakers District. They had gone to considerable lengths to persuade their Wehrmacht clients to pressure the SS to stay away from those highly profitable enclaves, and their bribes had won Simha,

Boruch, Mark Edelman, and thousands of other Jews a brief reprieve from the onslaught on the Central Ghetto.

There was no singing or marching in parade formation as the Germans entered the Ghetto this time. Stroop, borrowing from the bitter experiences of the Wehrmacht in Stalingrad, had strung out his men in long, scattered files better suited to urban fighting. They hugged the wall on Goose Street commando-style, scurrying from doorway to doorway, seeking shelter under balconies or behind any protrusions, securing their perimeters as they advanced. There would be no simultaneous attacks on multiple fronts, either. Stroop was going to hit one position at a time, take it out, and clear a path to the next resistance hub. He intended to repeat this methodical procedure until all the rebel strongpoints were flattened. And he was starting with Zivia's group.

Team leader Zacharia Artstein gathered Zivia and his other deputies and hurriedly issued instructions to prepare for battle. In case they were overrun, he ordered everyone to regroup at a specific fallback point, the nearby Ghetto hospital just down the block on Goose Street. "No sooner had he finished speaking than the house shook to heavy fire coming from all sides," recalled Tuvia Borzykowski, whom Isaac had asked to watch out for Zivia in his absence. The firing that Borzykowski referred to was likely shelling from light artillery or from a tank that Stroop kept at safe distance from ambush. As in Stalingrad, the purpose of the cannonade was to distract the defenders long enough for advance SS platoons to safely reach their forward positions.

Once that was done, they set up a makeshift barricade on the corner of Goose and Cordials. The fortification was not particularly sturdy, however, consisting of hundreds of mattresses hastily grabbed from a nearby warehouse and piled in the middle of the intersection. The stacked mattresses afforded the Germans limited protection. "Afraid to stick their heads out, they fired blind, wasting enormous amounts of ammunition," Tuvia recalled. The Jewish defenders returned fire, but their pistols were of limited range and accuracy. Grenades and Molotov cocktails proved far more effective, especially the kerosene-filled bottles that ZOB members heaved at the barricade. Mattresses burn, as the cowering SS men quickly discovered. They began to flee, and one fell, hit by a lucky shot. Once again cheers erupted from the rooftops and upper windows of 33 Cordials Street. Once more it looked as though the Jews would prevail.

Then came the terrifying shouts of ZOB fighters on the lower floors. The building was on fire. Smoke was rapidly rising. The flames were gaining momentum. Artstein ordered an evacuation. Everyone rushed into the attic, where a prearranged escape route had been hacked through the walls of neighboring structures. The buildings were all more or less the same height, four or five stories, creating a concealed road network for the ZOB. The fighters had just started squeezing through the narrow exit passage when they encountered a breathless scout coming from the opposite direction. The enemy had occupied the rendezvous point at the Goose Street hospital. Vengeful SS men were taking out their frustrations on the patients, going from bed to bed and shooting immobilized victims.

Zivia and Zacharia Artstein stared at each other in disbelief. At twenty, Artstein was nine years younger than Lubetkin, and very much her junior in the Socialist Zionist party hierarchy. That he outranked her in the ZOB chain of command was more a function of prevailing chauvinistic norms than of any superior military or tactical experience. Zivia's notoriously frosty demeanor, however, lent itself well to crisis. She kept her cool and dispatched scouts to look for other ways out. For the time being, the combatants were stuck. Going forward into the arms of the waiting Germans was out of the question. Staying put too long also meant certain death.

The minutes passed agonizingly slowly and the attic began to fill with smoke. People started coughing and covering their mouths with torn bits of clothing. The temperature steadily rose; everyone was soon sweating. "We were beginning to feel the fire," Tuvia Borzykowski recalled. "The smoke was so thick we could hardly see each other. We were starting to choke, our eyes were full of tears, pieces of burning wood were falling from the roof, the floors were beginning to give way, and tongues of flames were already licking our clothes."

This was it. They had run out of time. In another minute they would all be dead. The mood in the burning attic abruptly changed. The shouting and panicked running from corner to corner ceased. Everyone became still, as if they were all making peace with their maker.

All of a sudden, one of the scouts burst into the flaming room. He had found a way out. "It was a way so difficult, leading through such narrow tiny passages, that it seemed unbelievable that a human body could pass," Borzykowski remembered. "But we were desperate. And in such a state the impossible becomes possible."

BOOK FOUR

Be well, my friend. Perhaps we shall meet again.
The main thing is the dream of my life has come true.
I lived to see a Jewish defense in the Ghetto
in all its greatness and glory.

—Last message from
Mordechai Anielewicz to
Isaac Zuckerman

CHAPTER 31

GHETTOGRAD

The Ghetto was ablaze by the fifth day of the Uprising. Fires raged uncontrollably in every enclave, sending plumes of ash over the entire city of Warsaw.

With each passing hour the inferno intensified, fed by the flame-throwers that squirted lethal streams of liquid hell. The jets of pressurized kerosene could reach second- and third-story windows, penetrate crevices, and breach the narrowest openings. They had become Jürgen Stroop's most effective weapon, the fiery pillar of his new strategy to smoke out the stubborn "Jewish bandits" who, contrary to all expectations, were still holed up in pockets of determined resistance.

The Uprising should have been over by now—Stroop had assured his superiors as much: Kruger, in the daily teletype reports he sent to Krakow, and, more important, Himmler in Berlin, during a series of jarring late night phone calls. The Reichsführer was a notorious night owl and had an unsettling habit of ringing his underlings at all hours. Unaware of the SS leader's insomnia, Stroop had exploded with indignant fury the first time his phone jingled at three in the morning.

"Damn you," he had roared into the receiver before realizing the identity of his caller. "How dare you wake me? Are you stupid?" The Reichsführer had only laughed. "Don't be angry with me, my dear Stroop," he apologized in his famously soft cadences, at once maternal and menacing.

Stroop savored every word of that glorious conversation. Himmler had called him Maestro—music to the general's ears—and compared his tactical rout of Zivia's group to a "Wagnerian overture": masterful, with the promise of heightened crescendos. "Continue to play thus, Maestro, and our Führer and I shall never forget it," Himmler had promised his eager conductor.

The nocturnal calls had continued, but the pitch and tenor of Himmler's voice progressively changed. The Reichsführer remained punctiliously polite. That was his manner. But he was growing impatient. So was Kruger, to the point that the Higher SS and Police Leader East was making a special trip up from Krakow to personally review Stroop's progress. His concern was motivated by office politics in Wawel Castle, where Hans Frank, the Governor General and Himmler's hated rival, had seized on the Ghetto revolt to make trouble for the SS. Frank had Hitler's ear because of his long service as the Führer's personal attorney. And he was sending increasingly alarmist dispatches to Berlin that Warsaw was out of control, that the SS was unable to subdue a handful of Jews. The Wehrmacht was also beginning to snicker. Jokes were starting to circulate throughout the army about how the vaunted SS, unaccustomed to frontline action, was facing a Jewish Stalingrad, its very own Ghettograd.

In truth, Stroop was taken aback by the determination of the Jews. After his forces had overrun Zivia's position on Cordials Street that first day of fighting, he had met very stiff resistance from his next target: the JMU stronghold off Muranow Square, on the Ghetto's northeastern edge. Though Stroop had no idea he was battling a separate rebel group, the right-wing Zionists led by Paul Frenkel and David Apfelbaum proved far more difficult to dislodge than the ZOB. For one thing, they were much more entrenched: Muranow was the Jewish Military Union's headquarters, complete with a tunnel to the Aryan side, reinforced underground bunkers, relatively sophisticated communications gear, and makeshift pillboxes. A pair of flags defiantly flew over the converted tenement/fortress, as if to attest to its permanence: the blue-on-white JMU banner and the red and white national colors of its Polish Underground partners. The combatants at the Muranow bastion were also far better armed, thanks to the four submachine guns delivered by Security Corps, the conservative, arch-Catholic Home Army splinter group that had been supplying the JMU since 1939. (It had always operated quasi-independently of Home Army command and had apparently decided to ignore the "stand down" directive.)

Stroop, in his report to Kruger, referred to the Muranow fort "as the main Jewish fighting unit" of the Ghetto, noting that it was reinforced "by a considerable number of Polish bandits." This was an exaggeration—there were only five confirmed Gentiles in the JMU fortress at the time. But the specter of Polish partisans helped justify Stroop's heavy losses—officially fifty-two wounded soldiers and one dead officer, in reality many more—and the embarrassing fact that the two rebel flags, though riddled with bullets, continued to stubbornly flutter for all of Warsaw to see. "Get those flags down, Stroop," Himmler had hissed, his voice a menacing whisper. "Whatever the cost."

Despite the Reichsführer's chilling exhortations, Stroop fared no better when he regrouped and tried to take the Brushmakers District next. Inside the tiny eastern enclave, the smallest of the three remaining in the Ghetto, Simha Ratheiser waited impatiently. The nineteen-year-old was no longer scared or intimidated. Now that it was at hand, the moment he had daydreamed of a thousand times seemed anticlimactic. He was itching for the Germans to strike, his finger on the trigger of an IED, yet somehow he was not elated at the prospect of killing. Revenge didn't taste as sweet as he had thought. Though he was intent on wiping out as many Germans as possible, he drew surprisingly little pleasure from the prospect.

As Stroop's assault squad crept cautiously toward them, Simha's commander, Hanoch Gutman, snatched the detonator from his hand and exploded the huge mine that had been buried under the enclave's main gate. It was the biggest bomb yet made by the ZOB, and its concussive wave was so powerful that it pinned Ratheiser to a wall, knocking the air out of his lungs. By the time he regained his senses, his fellow fighters were pummeling the disoriented invaders. Many of the hundred German and Ukrainian soldiers in the assault party had been flung so high by the explosives that body parts and cobblestones had soared over upper-story balconies before falling back into the giant crater carved out of Embankment Street. At the center of this grisly shower of rubble and human entrails, a geyser of water shot straight upward: a city water main had been ruptured by the blast.

The crater and the street soon flooded in a murky, impassable mess, forcing the invaders back and preventing their ambulances from collecting the dead and wounded. The assault had failed. Once again the Ghetto resounded with the sound of Jewish cheers and German moans. Once more a visibly rattled Stroop shook his head in disbelief. Simha also couldn't believe his eyes when a few minutes later he saw a pair of SS officers waving white flags. The Nazis wanted a truce so they could evacuate their wounded and offer a final chance for civilians to flee the combat zone. This uncharacteristic concern stemmed from the fact that most of the four thousand slave laborers hiding in cellars in the Brushmakers District belonged to the industrialist Walther Casper Tobbens. He planned on relocating many of them to his new factories near Lublin, and he desperately wanted to protect his assets. Stroop was under strict orders not to damage the goods.

Mark Edelman responded to the flag bearers in typically brusque fashion. "Shoot them," he ordered casually. Edelman famously suffered no fools. And the SS officers were obviously taking him for one if they thought he was going to negotiate. Despite his youth and lack of military experience, he had already earned a solid reputation for his hard and unflappable demeanor as area commander. He could nap between skirmishes, astounding everyone around him, and bark out orders with the ferocity of a drill sergeant within seconds of waking. With his mustache, red angora sweater ("taken from a very rich Jew"), twin ammunition belts crisscrossed over his chest, and two holstered pistols, he was the perfect picture of a revolutionary. "Use the machine gun," he added, for enhanced effect. It was the ZOB's only automatic weapon in the Brushmakers District, and Edelman wanted to make a lasting impression on the Nazi commander.

The fusillade sent the SS officers scurrying back to Stroop, who was seated at a folding table a few blocks away, poring over Ghetto maps and feigning calm. It took him several more hours, long after it became obvious that no civilians were answering the evacuation call, to work up the nerve to attack again. The result was much the same. The Jewish defenders, now five fighting units strong because Edelman had redeployed all his resources to the point of attack, peppered the assault force with fragment grenades and drenched them in burning oil. "Hans, look, a woman!" Simha overheard a shocked German say, as one ZOB member hurled a Molotov cocktail at a fallen SS man. Four of the ten fighters in Simha's group were women, and they were rapidly proving themselves to be some of the ZOB's fiercest combatants. "These females fired pistols from both hands," Stroop later remarked with evident awe.

The general had had enough. This was turning into a miniature Stalingrad. He would not fall for the same "rat trap" that had decimated the 6th Army Group. The ruse, also known as the "hugging" strategy, had been shrewdly used by the Soviets to deprive the Germans of their vast technological, tactical, and training advantage by luring them deep into the city of Stalingrad and forcing them into house-to-house combat that favored dug-in defenders. Denying a superior adversary room to maneuver was the military equivalent of immobilizing a karate expert in a bear hug; as long as he was trapped in close quarters, all his moves, speed, and agility would be rendered useless. Only brute force and fierce determination would matter.

Stroop ordered his men back and the artillery forward. To hell with Tobbens and the other greedy Wehrmacht contractors; they were costing SS lives. He was going to flatten the entire Brushmakers District, regardless of collateral damage.

Within minutes, the whistle of mortar, antiaircraft, and howitzer shells filled the air. The buildings around the ZOB positions began to shake and shudder, releasing large dust clouds with every impact. For Simha, the most frustrating aspect of the barrage was not the clumps of plaster falling on his head, or the brick fragments flying across rooms with decapitating speed. It was the maddening fact that he had no one to shoot back at. The Germans had withdrawn behind the wall into Count Krasinski Park, safely out of pistol range behind the elliptical gravel paths and swing sets where Jewish children had once played.

Soon Ratheiser, Edelman, and their fellow fighters could see holes the size of automobiles perforating the roofs of neighboring buildings. Balconies and façades fell away like concrete icebergs calving into an asphalt ocean. Glass flew in every direction, slicing through anything in its murderous path. It was violence on a scale that Simha had not experienced since the September 1939 siege that had killed his brother and left him with a gaping neck wound. Still, he and the other defenders refused to budge. Then, just as it had with Zivia's group, fire broke out.

Later that evening, in the regal splendor of his new lodgings near the Royal Gardens, in the most exclusive German-only district, Stroop surveyed the dense black clouds drifting over the fifteenth floor of the Prudential Life Insurance Building and smiled. Fire! Fire was the solution. It was his salvation: the answer to his two biggest problems. In one incendiary swoop, it would deprive the rebels of their high ground and at the same time smoke out the rest of the Ghetto's seemingly vanished inhabitants.

This latter dilemma had initially stumped Stroop. Where were all the damned Jews? He had expected to round up thousands each day. He had trains waiting to deport them to Treblinka II. But the transports had been sitting mostly empty. Only now did Stroop finally solve the mystery of the missing Jews. "During the night the fires we had started earlier forced the Jews to appear," he cabled Kruger. They had been hiding in cellars and attics. "Masses of burning Jews—entire families—jumped from windows or tried to lower themselves using tied-together bed sheets." Stroop's men had dubbed the jumpers "parachutists," and the leaping women and children were a tremendous boost for SS morale. They provided great sport for target practice, and an easy way to avenge fallen brothers. Thousands more were crawling out of basements, coughing uncontrollably, and Stroop could choose to shoot them at will or finally start to fill his lagging deportation quotas.

Fire was also the only way to flush out the insurgents. "I have therefore decided," Stroop cabled Kruger, requesting permission to switch tactics, "to embark on the total destruction of the Jewish quarter by burning down every residential block, including the housing blocks belonging to the armament enterprises."

Under this new plan, he was no longer going to fight the Jews. He was not going to get sucked into Russian-style wrestling matches. He was going to incinerate them and reduce the entire Ghetto to cinders, leaving the insurgents with nowhere to hide.

Boruch Spiegel stared at the open sewer grate with dread. "I'm not going in there," one of his fellow fighters, a tall and improbably thin young man, kept repeating. "I'm not going down there." They stood in an alley off Forestry Boulevard at the southern edge of the flaming Main Shops District, just three blocks from the Dragon Street Gate, where the Waffen-SS had spearheaded its attack on the Productive Ghetto a week earlier. The Germans had struck from the north, from the large depopulated dead zone that separated the Main Shops District from the Central Ghetto and the smoldering ruins of the Brushmakers District. As many as eighty ZOB members had participated in the opening battle for the Main Shops District. Less than half were still alive in the waning days of April 1943, crowded around the opening to the sewage canal, overwhelmed by the putrid odor of human waste and weighing whether to enter the bowels of the earth or to stay aboveground and perish in the creeping inferno.

Boruch glanced at his girlfriend, Chaika. She was filthy, her hair matted with mud and blood, her faced bruised and streaked with charcoal. Her clothes were torn at the knees and elbows from crawling on all fours under the dense canopy of smoke that enveloped the Main Shops District. To Boruch, she had never looked more radiant— perhaps only when he had caught sight of her in the heat of battle hurling a homemade sulfuric acid grenade at a German. Boruch often relived that glorious moment in his mind, played it over and over again. What a sensation: to shoot at the Nazis! Every time he had pulled the trigger, he thought of his brother Berl, of his father, his mother, his sisters, his friends; of everyone the bastards had killed. That satisfaction was quickly replaced with concern, however, as Boruch and his fellow combatants quickly realized that their rebellion was unsustainable. "We had run out of everything," he recalled. "We had no ammunition, grenades, or Molotov cocktails. I didn't have a single bullet left. We were out of food and there was hardly any water. We had never planned on fighting for more than a few days. And I don't know if anyone," he added, referring to the ZOB leadership, "had made any real escape plans."

The very strength of Anielewicz's strategy—what had determined its early success—had become the ZOB's greatest weakness after Stroop had changed tactics. Once all the buildings had been set on fire, the vast network of attic passages that the Jews had used so effectively to strike their enemy from above had become death traps. They had also been rendered militarily useless. And there was no contingency or fallback plan of the sort that Isaac Zuckerman had advocated when he argued that the ZOB should build underground bunkers. Anielewicz had prepared for one glorious, honor-redeeming battle. Alas, he had not envisioned, nor made any provisions for, survivors of that epic struggle. "We are going to die," Mark Edelman heard him say repeatedly. "There's no way out, we'll die for honor, for history."

The ZOB's lack of a coordinated exit strategy first became obvious in the Brushmakers District, the earliest enclave put to fire. "One after another we staggered through the conflagration," Edelman bitterly recalled. "The sea of flames flooded houses and courtyards. There was no air, only black, choking smoke, and heavy burning heat radiating from the red-hot walls, from the glowing stone stairs." At every turn, Edelman, Simha Ratheiser, and the other ZOB fighters encountered an unbroken wall of fire. "The stench of burning bodies was everywhere. Charred corpses lay around on balconies, in window recesses, on unburned steps." The pavement under their feet melted from the heat. Glass liquefied in window frames and dripped like white-hot rain. At night, the flames were so bright that there was no cover of darkness. In the end, all they could do was crawl away from the scorching blaze and try to seek refuge in the still largely intact Central Ghetto.

It took longer for the fires to reach Spiegel's position in the Main Shops District, the last sector to be attacked. Eventually his unit faced the same dilemma Edelman's had earlier. They had run out of ammunition and were running out of places to hide. They considered making one last heroic stand and attacking the Germans with rocks, clubs, and knives. But this was rejected as certain death. "We didn't think of committing suicide," said Boruch.

Then someone suggested the sewers. What other option did they have? Even the dead zones were being dynamited and set ablaze by Stroop's relentless sappers and engineers. In the Central Ghetto, Edelman dispatched Simha Ratheiser and Zalman Friedrich to make contact with Isaac Zuckerman on the Aryan side so he could organize a rescue mission. They had located a promising tributary to a sewer trunk line next to the wall, and this was where Boruch now stood. He looked at Chaika, then looked down at the rusted ladder leading into the slimy canal. It ran across Forestry Boulevard, boring under the broad granite stairs of the old Municipal Courts building with its soaring six-story columns, and emerged on Garden Street on the Aryan side. This location had once been part of the notorious Cool Street corridor, the deep territorial incision that had cut into the Ghetto before the *Gross Aktion*. The entire area, everything south of Forestry in fact, had since been incorporated into Aryan territory to relieve Warsaw's dire housing shortage. Tens of thousands of Gentiles lived there now, in former Jewish homes. This meant that Stroop's inferno ended at Forestry Boulevard. Beyond that was off-limits for his flamethrowers. But the SS general had thought of the sewers, and he had ordered all the sluices in the main channels leading out of the Ghetto to be mechanically shut. This cunning precaution created subterranean dams that backed up the sludge and submerged large sections of the system, though smaller-diameter tributaries such as the one on Forestry Boulevard remained open.

It was a 450-foot crawl to safety if the passage was clear, if you didn't drown in feces or take a wrong turn and get lost in the maze of claustrophobic tunnels and reemerge under a collapsing building in the middle of the Ghetto—worse off than when you started. And then there were the toxic fumes. Stroop was said to be pumping poison gas into the sewer network. His troops were dropping concussion grenades and specially designed "smoke candles" under every manhole cover. The sewers, in many respects, could be more lethal than the surface. But at least they offered hope, a dwindling commodity in the scorched Ghetto.

All these unappealing prospects raced through the fugitives' minds as they stared into the putrid abyss. Rising from the dark hole, mingling with the bacterial stench of excrement, was the faint sweet odor of chemicals. "I won't go," the tall, malnourished youth next to Boruch kept mumbling. "I'm not going in there."

———

The Jewish Military Union did have a viable escape tunnel. It was un-damaged and undetected. But David Apfelbaum and Paul Frenkel, by the end of the second week of the Uprising, were reportedly refusing to use it. They were determined to fight on, to continue staging ambushes from concealed bunkers around Muranow Square. Their problem was ammunition. The JMU had nearly exhausted its stockpile by the ninth day of fighting. Apfelbaum was also wounded, as were a number of other senior leaders, including Leon Rodal and Kalmen Mendelson. They needed help and sent an urgent message to their Gentile allies requesting more bullets and grenades and medical supplies.

The call was answered by Major Henry Iwanski, the controversial Security Corps officer who had fought alongside Apfelbaum in the September 1939 siege. An unlikely hero, Iwanski, like many rabid nationalists, was not a natural admirer of minorities, least of all Jews. Nonetheless, he claimed to have been deeply impressed by the Uprising, as was almost all of Warsaw—with the notable exception of far-right groups like ONR and Falanga. These cryptofascists and other anti-Semites were openly cheering for Stroop, bringing their children to watch his artillerymen level the Ghetto and applauding each salvo with the glee of vacationers watching fireworks. Despite such callous displays, the vast majority of Varsovians were captivated by the courage on display in the Ghetto. Even the moderate right was moved. "It is impossible not to sympathize with and admire the Jewish population, who have set aside their passivity in order to carry out their heroic struggle which has no chance of succeeding against Nazi hangmen whose forces are a hundredfold stronger," one conservative gazette opined. "The smoke clouds over Warsaw cannot disappear without a trace," another, more liberal underground publication declared, "for all that was considered courageous would also disappear and the horrors which cry out for vengeance would also vanish."

To the Gestapo, such outpourings of support for the Jewish rising were worrisome. Fearful that enthusiasm for the rebellion could spark a citywide revolt, the Germans responded to the surge in philo-Semitic sentiments with a media barrage of their own. They blanketed newsreels and newspapers with coverage of a grisly discovery made by German troops on the Eastern Front. Deep in the Russian forest of Katyn, the Wehrmacht had uncovered the mass grave of nearly twenty thousand murdered Polish army officers (including Joseph Osnos's brother Zano, who been a physician in the Polish medical corps). HORRIBLE CRIME COMMITTED BY JEWS FROM THE NKVD, the *New Warsaw Courier* cried in banner headlines.

The propaganda was a bold-faced lie that fed upon the deeply entrenched myth in Poland that Jews harbored Communist sympathies. The campaign was surprisingly successful, particularly in the "patriotic" segments of Polish society that were only too eager to believe in stereotypes. "The Jews' struggle has nothing to do with Poland, with Poland's problems," pronounced an outraged right-wing daily, promptly washing its hands of the Ghetto Uprising. Iwanski, however, was not swayed. He had grown fond of Apfelbaum over the years: so much so that in pushing for Apfelbaum's recent promotion from lieutenant to captain, Iwanski had been willing to overlook the inconvenient fact that his friend had been supplanted by Paul Frenkel as JMU commander. (Frankel's role would not be contested by historians, who over time would grow increasingly skeptical of Iwanski's claims.)

When Iwanski heard that his old trenchmate was hurt, he decided to personally mount a rescue mission. Eighteen members of a Security Corps extraction squad were mobilized, including Iwanski's two brothers and his sixteen-year-old son. The heavily armed group entered the Ghetto on the morning of April 27, sneaking in through the Muranow Street tunnel, according to the U.S. historian Dan Kurzman. "With Iwanski leading the way, the men plodded along in single file, shielding their Sten guns and grenades from the sand that sifted down constantly from the ceiling and walls of the narrow rubble-strewn passage." Each man dragged a burlap sack filled with extra ammunition and a quart of vodka for the wounded, as they emerged, one by one, inside the Ghetto and tried to get their bearings. Muranow was unrecognizable. The prewar landmarks were all gone. The street had been one of the wealthiest in the poorer northern part of the Jewish district. But there was nothing left of the Gdansk Café, Nathan Gershwin Pharmaceuticals, the Style hairdressing salon, or any of the other businesses that had occupied the buildings where the tunnel emerged, because the buildings themselves were gone, scattered in tangled heaps of twisted rebar and charred rafters.

"Thank God you've come," Apfelbaum reportedly said, embracing Iwanski, once the Gentiles had been led safely through the labyrinth of rubble. His arm was in a sling and his head was bandaged. He was limping badly, leaning on the shoulder of another JMU fighter, dressed in a stolen SS tunic. As grave as his injuries appeared, Apfelbaum would not countenance any talk of evacuation. Rescue some of the younger fighters and as many civilians as you can, he told Iwanski, but he was staying. Iwanski was taken aback, according to the Israeli historian Chaim Lazar. He had only planned on dropping off the ammunition sacks and taking Apfelbaum out. But his friend's courage must have moved him, because the major later testified that he decided to stay and fight as well.

That same day, Jürgen Stroop launched one of the largest "mop-up" operations in the Ghetto to date. He dispatched "a special battle unit"—three hundred and twenty German and Latvian SS troops, supported by armored personnel carriers and two Panzer tanks—to clean out the pockets of resistance in the vicinity of Muranow Square. The sector was proving frustratingly difficult to subdue. Despite being flattened beyond recognition by artillery and arson, stubborn Jewish rebels—"subhuman criminals," in Stroop's words—were still hiding beneath the rubble, using the mangled remnants of tenements to stage hit-and-run guerrilla raids on his patrols. The attackers, moreover, often wore SS uniforms to sneak up on their German victims. While the ambushes were not inflicting significant losses, they were bad for morale. His men constantly had to look over their shoulders and could not concentrate on unearthing bunkers where thousands of noncombatants were still holed up, often clustered around tiny air holes or telltale ventilation shafts. Stroop, therefore, decided to depart temporarily from his firebombing policy and sweep the troublesome area for insurgents.

What happened next would become a matter of heated historical debate. According to some accounts, popularized by conservative circles in Israel and based largely on the uncorroborated testimony of Gentile participants, Iwanski's team fought side by side with the JMU.

Together the two groups reportedly managed to destroy a tank and to hold out until nightfall, when the SS withdrew. Skeptical Polish and Israeli historians, however, would later cast doubt on many of these claims, accusing Iwanski of self-aggrandizement and overinflating both Security Corps' and the JMU's role in the Uprising. The truth has been difficult to determine because there were virtually no Jewish survivors of the events of April 27, 1943. The one outside observer with no horse in the race, Jürgen Stroop, would shed only partial light on the dispute. In his official report that day, he made no mention of "Poles"—Gentiles, in official German parlance—participating in the skirmishes inside the Ghetto. He would, however, recommend that an SS officer be awarded the "Iron Cross 1st Class" for attacking a building "adjoining but outside the northeastern part of the Jewish Quarter"—presumably the tenement that housed the exit of the Muranow tunnel to which Iwanski and the JMU reportedly withdrew at dusk. "The assault party discovered a gang of 120 men, heavily armed with pistols, rifles, hand grenades and light machine guns, who offered resistance." The fighting was particularly fierce, Stroop elaborated, and many of the insurgents wore German uniforms. But the SS officer in charge, First Lieutenant Diehl, "pushed ahead with great energy" and managed to overrun the rebel position. "Polish terrorists were identified with certainty among the bandits who were apprehended or killed. We even succeeded in apprehending and liquidating one of the founder-leaders of the Jewish-Polish defense formation."

The true sequence of events will probably forever be lost to the fog of war. The only indisputable facts are that Iwanski's brother Edward died on April 27, 1943, and his sixteen-year-old son, Roman, was fatally wounded and died the following day. David Apfelbaum, according to some accounts, also succumbed to his injuries on April 28, 1943. Iwanski promoted him posthumously to major.

CHAPTER 32

FALLEN ANGEL

By early May 1943, Stroop could see light at the end of his tunnel. The fighting in the Ghetto had ebbed. He was now suffering one or two casualties a day rather than several dozen, and the sporadic skirmishing tended to take place after dusk, when his patrols were withdrawing and the cowardly "terrorists" took potshots at them. During daylight hours he owned the Ghetto. In the morning when the sun rose over the smoldering ruins it was almost peaceful; only the squawks of the crows that swarmed the charred corpses pierced the silence, or the occasional screams of families being dragged from some rabbit hole. His daily haul of civilians had also vastly increased now that his men had experience uncovering hideouts. They used dogs, seismic echolocation devices, and, most effectively, informants, who in exchange for promises of clemency led Stroop's sappers and engineers to some of the most cleverly camouflaged hideouts. Slowly but surely Stroop was filling his deportation quota. "The total number of Jews apprehended has risen to 40,237," he reported to Kruger on May 2, noting that the remaining few thousand holdouts, deprived of food, water, and fresh air, would not be able to stay underground much longer. "Setting fires still remains the best and only method for destroying the Jews."

What still eluded Stroop, however, was the location of the rebel command bunker. His men had combed the entire Ghetto and could not find the vipers' nest. He was certain the nocturnal raids were being directed from some central resistance hub, and he knew he could not declare victory until it had been destroyed. As a professional soldier, Stroop could not wrap his military mind around the notion that the ZOB would not have dug a massive command post. Ironically, that amateurish omission had left the Jewish insurgents scattered and largely incommunicado once the fires started raging—and thus much harder for Stroop to corral. In their scramble to find sanctuary, ZOB units had pounded on countless bunkers, only to be turned away by the noncombatants who had built them. "You couldn't blame them," Edelman said of the rejections. "We brought certain death to their door." When rebel units did stumble upon civilians willing to take them in, they often lost touch with their fellow fighters, sometimes for days. In one of those instances, for example, Mark Edelman and Zivia Lubetkin managed to reconnect only by chance. Both of their groups had sent out reconnaissance teams dressed as Germans one night. They started shooting at one another before someone cursed in Yiddish and they realized their mistake.

The bunker where Zivia initially holed up had been dug by wealthy members of the Judenrat to accommodate one hundred people in a stooped position. Despite its low ceiling and earthen floor, it had electricity, ventilation, a kitchen where her hosts roasted a chicken in Zivia's honor, a radio that captured the Polish prime minister in exile's BBC broadcast devoted to the Ghetto Uprising, and an operating room where some of her injured comrades had been patched up by a resident surgeon. "Anyone walking on top of the rubble would never have believed that only a few meters beneath the wreckage people are sitting—or rather lying—hundreds of people, living, breathing, talking, eating, dreaming."

The hideout where Edelman had taken refuge was just as big, an entire floor excavated under the cellar of a large apartment building on Franciscan Street. It was two hundred yards from the site of the first battle of the Rising, near the devastated intersection of Cordials and Goose Streets and bordering the no-man's-land between the Central Ghetto and the ravaged Brushmakers District. Since he'd arrived there on April 22, Edelman had fallen into a routine of sleeping during the day and going out on missions after dusk. This was not unusual. Jews had become nocturnal creatures, only venturing out after dark. It had been days since Zivia had seen a ray of sunshine, and Edelman, in a macabre attempt at humor, joked that he felt like a vampire.

On the afternoon of May 2, Edelman was awakened by a frantic aide. German engineers were digging in the rubble overhead. They had found one of the hidden entrances to the bunker. Panic erupted among the shelter's terrified occupants, as stooped figures crawled in every direction through the low crowded corridors, crashing into one another, whispering of certain death. Mark tried to think of a way out. Every hideout had at least two escape routes. Some had three or four secret exits, designed for this type of eventuality. "Everyone out," he ordered. "Prepare to attack." Edelman's calm had a startling effect on the frightened civilians. Though he was only a guest in the bunker, they all looked to him for leadership, even Ghetto elders like Abrasha Blum. The Bund's ranking statesman only a few years ago viewed Edelman as a child, a shy orphan who used to fetch cigarettes for him. "Mark was very cold, but he was also very brave," one of his bunker-mates would later recall. "He was ruthless, but you felt safe around him," another member of his brigade would say.

Now Blum watched with wonder as his former errand boy outlined their escape strategy with the poise of a five-star general. The Germans and Ukrainians, Edelman knew, would be too afraid to enter the bunker. They would toss smoke bombs inside and stand around the entry hole waiting for Jews to stagger out, gasping, coughing, blinded by the sudden daylight. Then they could shoot them, one by one, or round everyone up and march them to the Umschlagplatz to join the rest of the day's haul. Mark's plan was to send them a distraction, a pretty young ZOB member. The Ukrainian or Latvian auxiliaries would never shoot her. They would want to save such a catch for their evening entertainment. Edelman and the rest of the ZOB fighters, meanwhile, would sneak out the rear exit and attack the SS men from behind.

The battle that ensued proved one of the longest sustained fire-fights of the Warsaw Ghetto Uprising. It lasted, with brief pauses, nearly seventy-two hours, and when it was over, Stroop's daily casualty rate had spiked to seven, due to precisely the sort of hand-to-hand combat that he had sought to avoid. Mark lost half his company in the three-day engagement with the two SS platoons, but not a single Jewish combatant had been taken alive, to be led in ignoble humiliation to the waiting trains.

It wasn't until May 6, when the enemy finally withdrew, that Edelman could search for another bunker. He found one just up the block on Franciscan Street, a cramped and foul-smelling dugout that had been excavated by Ghetto garbage collectors. The sanctuary was secure: It lay beneath a putrid heap of decaying refuse that the germ-averse Nazis were not likely to disturb. But it was small, unbearably hot, and overcrowded. Edelman had no choice but to evacuate many of his exhausted survivors to the massive shelter on Pleasant Street where Mordechai Anielewicz and a large number of fighters were holed up.

This was the elusive "vipers' nest" that was driving Jürgen Stroop mad. Though it had not been built by the ZOB, the sprawling bunker was now effectively serving as the Jewish Fighting Organization's default headquarters. Zivia had fled there earlier in the week, after the Germans uncovered the Judenrat bunker she had been using. Several ZOB members had been killed fighting their way out that day, and those who managed to escape had regrouped on Pleasant Street. Pleasant Street's subterranean population had swollen in recent days. By May 7, with the influx of Edelman's team, it was over three hundred. At least a third of the occupants were armed members of the ZOB.

The huge shelter had been designed for comfort, and no expense had been spared in its nearly yearlong construction. Like many bunkers, it was wired for electricity and had its own dedicated well for fresh water. But it also boasted unheard-of amenities, such as private quarters with beds, a grand reception area, separate reading and recreation rooms, and a dining hall with a fully stocked liquor cabinet. The luxuries had been fitted out by the bunker's underworld proprietors, a smuggling and prostitution ring led by Samuel Asher, a career criminal of prewar repute. "He behaves here in the bowels of the earth like king of the roost," Zivia recalled of her hulking and tattooed host. "He runs everything in this place: our nourishment, sleeping arrangements, and decides when it possible to go out on sorties and obtain necessities."

Despite his fearsome appearance and reputation, Asher had opened his doors to Anielewicz after many eminently more respectable members of the Jewish community had turned the ZOB away. The honorable mob boss ordered his henchmen to give up their private rooms and to share all their food stores. "He and his pals treated the Fighting Organization with great respect," Lubetkin recalled. "Everything we have is yours, he said, and we are at your disposal. We are strong, we're skilled at undoing locks, we can move around at night, climb over fences and walls, and we know by heart every lane and crevice in the ruins of the Ghetto."

Navigating the rubble was critical for staging nighttime ambushes and planting IEDs for the Germans to trip during the day. In the dark, amid the mountains of broken brick that had replaced once familiar landmarks, it was easy to get lost. Most of the streets didn't exist anymore. Entire blocks were engulfed by fallen debris and ash, and the raging fires had erased all signage, making the entire neighborhood uniformly black. The footing was treacherous and one could crash through some crevice in the rubble. Or, everyone's worst nightmare, one could be groping in the dark and suddenly feel the crisply soft tissue of a burned body. "We feared meeting the dead more than living Germans," Zivia recalled. Asher's agile crew were expert at avoiding such pitfalls, and they proved instrumental in guiding ZOB patrols. On the evening of May 7, one of his cutthroats, "a notorious thief," led Zivia, Anielewicz, and Anielewicz's girlfriend, Mira Fuchter, to Edelman's new hideout.

Anielewicz and Edelman had always had a slightly strained relationship. Whether their differences were ideological or personal was difficult to tell, but Mark had consistently been one of the few people to criticize Mordechai. That evening, however, Edelman was anxious to lift his commander's flagging spirits. Anielewicz had not been himself the past few days. He had grown lethargic. Zivia had noticed it as well. "His face sagged with worry," she later explained. "It was as though he'd achieved his goal, an armed Jewish revolt, and didn't know what to do next."

Anielewicz had ample reason for concern. He no longer had the resources to launch major assaults, and in the battle of attrition the Jews were losing badly. With each passing day, there were fewer and fewer of them. The one glimmer of hope was that he'd received a message from Isaac Zuckerman saying Simha Ratheiser had gotten through to the Aryan side. He had stumbled across the JMU's tunnel, and after spending the night in the same tenement where Iwanski said he had lost his brother and son battling the SS, Simha had reached Isaac. They were working on a plan to get everyone out. It was that faint hope that brought Anielewicz to the trash collectors' bunker that Edelman now shared. One of the garbagemen there apparently knew his way around the sewers and was offering to guide the ZOB out of the Ghetto.

It was well after midnight by the time the discussions ended and Anielewicz and his girlfriend returned to Pleasant Street to inform the others of the escape plan they had hatched. Zivia stayed at Franciscan Street, at Edelman's urging. Mark wanted to spend time catching up with his friend while they waited for Anielewicz to send word the next day about his final decision on the evacuation. When the day passed and no messenger arrived from Pleasant Street, Zivia and Mark grew worried. Mordechai was probably waiting for the cover of darkness to send out his courier, they reasoned. But by nine o'clock there was still no word and Edelman's patience had worn thin. "We have to go to Pleasant Street," he said, grabbing a candle to light the way. Zivia protested. Using any sort of light was strictly against the partisan code because it could attract the Germans, but Edelman didn't care. "Mark was always full of bravado, flouting safety regulations." Besides, Stroop, through bitter experience, had learned to keep his men in barracks after dusk. He may have owned the Ghetto during the day, but at night it still belonged to the Jews.

Edelman, Lubetkin, and another ZOB fighter gingerly picked their way through the jagged ruins, clambering over upturned slabs and wall fragments. At one point the wind blew out the candle, and when Mark relit it, Zivia was gone. She had fallen through a crevice, losing her pistol in the inky blackness. Bruised, bleeding, and with her pride damaged, she managed to limp the rest of the way. By the time they neared Pleasant Street, her spirits had been restored. "We started thinking about what practical jokes we could pull." But when they reached the bunker's hidden entrance, Lubetkin noticed that something was off. The carefully placed debris camouflaging the door was scattered, as if it had been cleared. With a sinking feeling, Edelman called out the password: "John." The response, "Warsaw," never came. Zivia, her voice rising with urgency, repeated the prearranged code word, and again there was silence. She realized that everyone inside was dead.

Mark Edelman stood in the darkness outside the demolished Pleasant Street bunker and silently cursed Mordechai Anielewicz. How could Mordechai have allowed this to happen? Eighty ZOB members were dead, and when Mark discovered how they died, he could barely contain his anger. "First Anielewicz shot Mira," his girlfriend, "then himself." The mass suicide had occurred in the afternoon of May 8, when a large detachment of German troops had surrounded the area around one of the hideout's hidden entrances. The huge bunker, according to Zivia, had six different escape tunnels. Historians would cite five. Surely Anielewicz could have counterattacked through one of these secondary exits, Edelman complained, as he himself had done when the SS uncovered his Franciscan Street shelter. "A leader has no right to commit suicide," Mark growled. "He must fight to the end, especially as there was a chance of escaping from the Ghetto." Edelman had fought his way out of a similar jam, and he held Anielewicz to the same high standard. "He took the easy way out."

There were a handful of survivors, as Mark and Zivia discovered. Three of them were prostitutes who had managed to crawl out through one of the bunker's secret passageways. They were now pleading with Edelman to take them with him. He refused. It was not a moral judgment. Prostitutes had shared bagels and other food with him in the past. In fact they had been kinder to him than most of the wealthy, morally upright wives of Jewish Council members. His refusal was based solely on a cold numerical calculation. He was going to attempt a mass escape through the sewers, and there were only so many people he could take with him. Non-ZOB members would have to fend for themselves. He couldn't afford civilian stragglers.

CHAPTER 33

SIMHA THE SAVIOR

A few miles south of Pleasant Street, Simha Ratheiser was staring at Isaac Zuckerman in disbelief. They were in a safe house outside the Ghetto, and Simha was still adjusting to his new surroundings: the frilled curtains and cushions on the sofa, the carpets and paintings on the wall, the potted plants and bookshelves filled with actual books—all the trappings of ordinary life that had long disappeared from Jewish reality.

The apartment belonged to the Sawicki sisters, Anna and Marisa, who were Underground activists from the Socialist Party, the Bund's traditional allies. They were Home Army but acting independently, outside the chain of command, much as Iwanski had been doing. "The welcome of the two women whom I'd just met dazzled me," Simha recalled. "But I didn't forget why I'd come."

Simha's nerves had been so raw when he crossed over to the Aryan side at the end of April that the mere act of bathing—his first attempt at hygiene in nearly two weeks—had proven traumatic. How could he luxuriate in scented water, with fresh soap and clean towels, when his colleagues were trapped in rat-filled cellars gasping for air? The food and vodka the Sawicki sisters had generously laid out for him and Zalman Freidrich had prompted a similarly guilty reaction. He and Friedrich had no right to lounge around. They had to get back to the Ghetto, to get their friends out. They didn't have a moment to lose. And yet they would lose an entire week sitting idle.

This was why Ratheiser was so furious with Zuckerman. In Simha's teenage eyes, the twenty-eight-year-old ZOB deputy commander had been a legend, a leader to be looked up to with awe. Yet now, in this tiny apartment, at the hour of need, Zuckerman seemed lost and completely out of his element. He had made no plan, no preparations to engineer a mass escape, and the prolonged frustration of waiting helplessly while his colleagues were massacred had taken a visible psychological toll on him. "I initially thought my job was to tell Isaac that the others were ready [to be evacuated] and that he would arrange the rest," Simha recalled. "But it really hit me hard that no one was ready to help. Nothing had been done" to lay the groundwork for an organized escape.

Three excruciatingly long days had passed since he'd delivered his message. Simha had eaten his fill, slept on a soft bed, and watched with mounting anger as smoke from the Ghetto blanched Warsaw's hazy skyline. All the while, Isaac had paced the small apartment like a caged tiger. He was evidently troubled, exasperated to the point of a breakdown. It wasn't his fault that he had been thrust into the role of ZOB liaison on the eve of the Uprising and that he hadn't had time to nurture the contacts and personal relationships critical to his mission. He wasn't to blame for the Home Army—the ZOB's best hope—effectively turning its back on the Jews. He had pleaded with, cajoled, and finally cursed Captain Wolinski, his sympathetic but ultimately powerless Home Army counterpart.

In desperation, and against his better judgment, Isaac had even turned to the ideologically suspect Communists, the People's Army. The Moscow-backed group had been far more cooperative, partly because it was in the Soviet Union's interest to stir up as much trouble as possible in Warsaw, the main transport hub for the Eastern Front. Every day, 180 trains loaded with soldiers, replacement tanks, artillery, and munitions left Warsaw for the east. Stalin wanted a citywide rising in the Polish capital because it would disrupt the flow of men and materiel to the battlefields in Russia. The People's Army, however, could not accomplish that on its own. Its network in Poland was minuscule compared to the huge, London-backed Home Army. Nor did it enjoy popular support among the staunchly anti-Bolshevik general population. In Warsaw alone, the Home Army had 72,000 operatives. The People's Army had barely 5,000 members across the entire country. A few Communist units had already tried to attack the artillery batteries Stroop had deployed just outside the Ghetto. The attempt neither slowed Stroop, who moved his howitzers into a crowded square nearby to deter future rebel strikes, nor incited a citywide insurrection. Despite the setback, the People's Army had supplied Isaac with several crates of Red Army–issue rifles. The guns were a godsend, immeasurably more effective than revolvers. Unfortunately Isaac had no way of getting them into the hands of his fighters since their lines of communication had been disrupted. All in all, the past two weeks had been among the most difficult in Isaac's life. Never before had he felt so helpless, so raging with impotence. He couldn't do anything for his comrades, for his people, for his wife. (Zivia and Isaac had married, though the discreet ceremony would not enter the historical record.) He should be by Zivia's side instead of being stuck on the Aryan side. Simha had reassured him that she was healthy and in good spirits the last time he'd seen her. But that was days ago. Was she still safe? Had she been captured? Had she been wounded? Was she on a train to Treblinka? Was she already dead? Isaac had no answers to the wrenching questions that mercilessly pounded his brain. He could only numb their anxious refrain with vodka.

Finally, after a few more days of inaction—probably around May 3 or 4, while Edelman's company was deep into its firefight with the two SS platoons—Simha erupted. "If you don't go, I'm going to go back in myself!" he shouted at Zuckerman. "We need to do something!"

"Fine!" Isaac yelled back, losing his temper. They would take the Russian rifles into the Ghetto through the sewers and attack the Germans, he proposed. "That's suicide," Simha snapped. "If you are going in to fight to the death, that's okay," he argued. It was Zuckerman's business how he chose to die. But the only reason Simha would ever set foot in the Ghetto again would be to rescue his friends. "If you are going in to save them," Ratheiser pressed his point, "we need a plan."

It took a few more frustrating days for the plan to be put into action, but on the night of May 8, 1943, Simha Ratheiser pushed open a manhole cover, gingerly poked his head out, and immediately ducked as the blinding beam of a searchlight swept past him. It took him a fraction of a second to get his bearings, but the towering Umschlagplatz gates were unmistakable. He was in the Ghetto, though just barely. His bungling guides had misjudged their position and led him to an opening right under the Germans' noses. In fact, they had almost overshot the Ghetto, traversing its entire length underground. The fools were sanitation workers from the city's sewer maintenance department. They had been approached by contacts from the People's Army, and Simha had paid them handsomely to steer him and another ZOB member through the subterranean labyrinth. Unfortunately the terrified Gentiles had fortified themselves heavily with alcohol, and then lost their nerve shortly after descending into the canals on the Aryan side. Simha had been forced to pull a gun on them and snarl: "You can keep leading us, or you can die right here." He kept the gun's short muzzle pressed into the small of a worker's back as they all staggered through the waist-deep muck.

Now the guides would not go any farther. Richard Mozelman, the other ZOB member, would have to stay in the sewer and guard the inebriated Gentiles, or they would surely bolt. Simha would go looking for survivors. Richie had been a last-minute addition to the rescue party, replacing the Bundist Zalman Friedrich, who had pleaded not to go. He had a daughter who was being sheltered by nuns in Warsaw (at a different convent than Joanna Mortkowicz-Olczak) and had begged for permission to see her. Mozelman, a member of one of the ZOB's five Communist units, had been a logical replacement because he had participated in a similar rescue operation a week earlier. Boruch Spiegel and his girlfriend, Chaika Belchatowska, had been part of the group of forty ZOB fighters spirited out of Warsaw by Mozelman, Tuvia Sheingut of the Marxist Young Guard, and Wladislaw Gaik, a lieutenant in the People's Army. "It took a few tries but we managed to get out of the Ghetto," Spiegel remembered. "It was terrible down there." They had crawled out of the sewers on Garden Street just south of the Main Shops District and stayed hidden in the nearby attic of a Communist operative while the People's Army arranged transport. Finally, after a forty-eight-hour wait, a furniture moving truck delivered the exhausted refugees to a forest five miles north of Warsaw, where escaped Soviet POWs were forming partisan cells. Boruch's evacuation now served as the blueprint for the larger rescue mission Simha was mounting.

Right away, though, there was a complication. When Simha made his way through the dark ruins to Edelman's Franciscan Street shelter, no one was there. In the week that had passed since he'd gone over to the Aryan side, Edelman must have moved, Simha reasoned. He doubled back and tried Anielewicz's command bunker, assuming Anielewicz would know where to find Mark. But on Pleasant Street, when he whispered the password, John, there was again no answer. Simha grew worried. "I spent three hours looking for my friends." He tried every hideout he could remember. He scoured the debris for any secret entrances he might have missed—all in pitch blackness, with only the sound of his breath and the soft scrape of his footsteps to intrude on the postapocalyptic silence. "I looked around the rubble," he recalled, finally giving up hope and his search, "and I felt as though I was the last Jew on earth."

In the garbagemen's bunker, meanwhile, only fifty yards from where Simha was searching, Zivia and Mark were debating what to do. The atmosphere in the crowded shelter was despondent. No one slept. No one ate the meager meal that had been prepared for the half dozen survivors of Pleasant Street. Some of them were injured, and moaned quietly. Others were crying. Everyone was deflated. The shocking discovery of the mass suicide at the command bunker had sapped them all of energy, of the will to fight on. Edelman and Lubetkin knew that it was now only a matter of time before the Germans uncovered this hideout as well. They had to start the evacuation immediately, Zivia decided. Her husband's old friend Tuvia Borzykowski would lead the first group.

Tuvia had fought alongside Zivia in the opening battle of the Uprising, and he had already tried twice to find a way out of the Ghetto through the canals. "I will never forget what I saw when I first descended into the sewer," he recalled of his initial attempt. "Masses of refugees were huddling in the filth and stink in pipes so low and narrow that only one person could pass at a time." Rats scurried over the semisubmerged bodies, jumping on people's heads, scratching their scalps and necks. "Some of the elderly people and children had fainted, with no one paying attention. The stream of sewage washed away their bodies." A bullet had grazed Tuvia's cheek on the second try; the three other ZOB members with him that day had been caught or shot by the Germans when they reached the Aryan side. The SS had been waiting for them next to the manhole cover. He was thus not anxious to repeat the experiment and pleaded with Zivia to let him rest through the night. But she pulled rank. The Germans would probably be here in the morning, she said. He had to leave immediately. He brought eight lead scouts to start their desperate journey. "It was midnight," Tuvia recalled. "When we lowered ourselves into the sewer and hit the cold water, the shock was so powerful that we all lost consciousness for a moment. . . . We felt the slime sticking to our bodies. We kept coming upon pieces of clothing, remnants of human beings who had tried, as we were now, to save themselves."

They moved forward, dislodging the bloated corpses that blocked many of the narrower passages. After an hour of wandering, it became apparent that they were completely lost. At forks in the channels, they had turned blindly, letting fate steer them. Now the numbing cold and the configuration of the pipes began to wear them down. The network was too low to stand in and too deep to sit and rest. They had to remain stooped, up to their necks in the freezing sludge. Eventually, hypothermia would set in, when they could faint and be swept under by the surprisingly strong current. Tuvia had already begun feeling drowsy. Then he saw something that stopped him in his tracks. "We had been walking for several hours when we received a jolt. A bright light, as if from a powerful electric torch, appeared in the distance. The only explanation could be that the Germans had entered the sewer to look for refugees. We had heard before that they were doing that, pumping in gas and throwing grenades. Instinctively we started to withdraw, but then we realized that there was no way back."

The light grew bigger and brighter. Tuvia began saying his fare-wells. He was now certain he would die in this dark, wet tomb. Strangely, the prospect did not bother him. He had accepted his fate. He was in a state of total resignation when from behind the approaching glare came a magical word: "John?"

Simha and Tuvia ran into each other's arms with unbridled joy. They hugged and even kissed each other like long-lost relatives, and Ratheiser had jubilant sensation of unexpectantly seeing loved ones return from the dead. He distributed the hard candy and lemons he had brought in his rucksack and watched his vitamin-deprived colleagues devour the fruit, peels and all. After they had all calmed down and exchanged stories of the battle on Franciscan Street and of the tragedy at the command bunker, Simha outlined his plan. Richie Mozelman, through his contacts in the Communist underground, had arranged for trucks to be waiting for them on the Aryan side. The rendezvous was on the corner of Straight and Hard Streets, in what had once been the southernmost part of the original 1940 Ghetto. It was now deep in Aryan territory, more than a mile away, and necessitated a grueling hike through the freezing sewage system. But the distance had its advantages: the Germans would not be guarding manholes as closely so far from the besieged enclaves. As an additional precaution, Simha had paid off a local mob boss to ensure that the greaser blackmailers that prowled the Ghetto's perimeter would not bother them. Once in the trucks, it would be a short ride to the forest.

The ten of them had to set out immediately, Simha insisted, because it was already 3 A.M., and the escape needed to take place under the cover of darkness. He instructed Tuvia to send two messengers to fetch Zivia, Mark, Hersh Berlinski, Zacharia Artstein, Israel Kanal, and the remaining forty fighters from the trash collectors' bunker. The runners would lead the larger group out of the Ghetto by following the arrow signs Simha would chalk on the canal walls, and they would all meet up under the manhole on Straight Street.

Tuvia listened to the daring plan with mounting apprehension. Simha seemed "too optimistic" for Borzykowski's liking. "We were not accustomed to good news"; too many things could go wrong. "It all sounds too good to be true," he thought to himself.

———

It was not until 11 A.M. that Zivia's main group from the trash collectors' bunker reached Straight Street. By that time, Tuvia Borzykowski's advance party had been waiting beneath the manhole for six hours. From above, they could hear horns blaring, pedestrians crossing the road, snippets of conversations. Sunlight slanted through the perforated manhole, inviting them upward. But they couldn't move. They had missed their window of opportunity because Zivia and Mark had taken so long. Lubetkin had not wanted to leave the bunker, had delayed the departure for as long as possible to give Zacharia Artstein's unit time to return from their night patrol. Everyone would leave together or no one would leave at all, she had insisted. It had taken all of Edelman's powers of persuasion to overrule her, to explain that they would all die unless they followed Simha's precise instructions and set out immediately. Many of the civilians in the bunker had wanted to go with them, but Edelman had taken a firm stand with his hosts as well. There were only two trucks waiting on the Aryan side, with barely enough room for the fifty-odd ZOB members. No one else could come.

Many of the fighters were injured, unable to walk on their own. "We drag[ged] them over the putrid water," Zivia recalled, "pulling them by their arms and legs." The journey had taken four excruciating hours, "crawling in single file in the dark, not seeing one another's faces." Some of the fighters contemplated suicide. Others fainted from the cold and had to be revived. When at last they reached the rendezvous, the worst part began: the waiting. "We lay in the sewage, body pressed to body, and counted the passing minutes," Tuvia Borzykowski recalled. "Occasionally a passerby would step on the perforated cover and cut off the bit of light penetrating the sewer. Each footfall served us as a warning that we had to keep absolute silence so as to remain undetected."

The hours passed, with the rays slanting through the manhole acting as an inverted sundial. Soon they were gone, and the manhole well was plunged into darkness. Where the hell was Simha? Where were the trucks? Didn't he realize that they were dying down there? "Our despair grew from moment to moment," Tuvia remembered. Just then, a note came down through the manhole. No rescue could be attempted that evening, it said; too many German patrols. "We were crushed. It meant waiting another twenty-four hours. Such a long time in the sewer meant slow and certain death to all of us."

That night proved to be one of the longest any of them had ever endured: the cold, the hunger, the swarms of rats that mercilessly assaulted their heads and necks. Their thirst grew so severe that Zivia saw the fighter next to her drink sewer water, the brownish slime dripping from his parched lips. By dawn, they had reached the limits of their considerable endurance. Edelman and Lubetkin pushed their way to the front of the long queue under the manhole well and conferred with Borzykowski. They would not last much longer. Even if it meant a street fight with the Germans, they had to attempt a breakout this very morning. A note was scribbled to that effect and slid through the sewer grille. *It's now or never*, it said.

Simha read the soggy plea and very nearly panicked. He had spent the night at the local mob boss's hangout with Lieutenant Gaik, the People's Army operative, better known by his code name, Shrub, and Tuvia Sheingut, the blond, blue-eyed professional actor who served as one of the ZOB's most convincing couriers. Their paid-off gangster host, who called himself the King, had been told that he was facilitating a Home Army operation. But he was beginning to suspect that Jews might be involved. If this was the case, he intimated, all bets were off. His boys made a good living extorting money from Jews. This could be a bonanza for them. Simha, Sheingut, and Gaik, who was in fact a Gentile, had done everything they could to throw the King off the scent. But they were running out of time. The trucks Gaik had organized would not come until nightfall because his superiors were refusing to sanction a risky daylight rescue. By then, the King's men, the greasers, might be on them. It was true that they could not afford to wait any longer. But what to do?

In the end, it was Sheingut who came up with a plan. Why not order the trucks from a private moving company? Tell the movers there is a load of furniture to be picked up and then hijack the vehicles. Amazed by the simplicity of the solution, Sheingut and Gaik rushed off to find a telephone directory.

At around 10 A.M. a large tarpaulin-covered lorry with the logo of a freight forwarder painted across its worn canvas rack rumbled onto Straight Street. Lieutenant Gaik calmly walked over to the idling vehicle, jumped into the cab, and put a gun to the driver's head. "Drink this." He thrust a flask of vodka at the trembling mover.

Stunned pedestrians on Straight Street then witnessed the sight of a truck parked in the middle of the road, its opened flaps straddling a manhole from which a stream of filthy figures were emerging. Inside the sewer, Zivia and Edelman were directing traffic. "Move, move," they exhorted their colleagues, who slowly, painfully slowly, tried to pull themselves up the ladder in the manhole well. Many were too weak from their ordeal to muster the strength to pull themselves up. Pushed from below and tugged from above, their limp bodies were forced through the opening and heaved into the waiting truck. The second truck had failed to arrive. Simha realized there would not be room for everyone. "Hurry, hurry," he beckoned.

Already a crowd had gathered, gaping at the astounding spectacle. Five, ten, then fifteen minutes elapsed, and still the sewer disgorged its human cargo. To Simha, the operation seemed to be moving in slow motion. At the rate they were going, a German patrol was sure to detect them. Another five horrifyingly long minutes passed. Then Simha spotted a Blue Policeman. The Pole had noticed them and Simha raced over to cut him off. "I told him this was a Home Army mission, and made sure he saw the bulge of my pistol." The cop nodded and turned away. But Simha knew they had pushed their luck long enough. "We have to go," he said, pulling Zivia out. "There are a lot of people down there," she protested, pointing at the manhole. Nearly twenty ZOB fighters were still in the sewer. "We can't leave them."

"We'll come back for them," Simha promised. Lubetkin wasn't having it. "*No!*" she yelled, shoving Ratheiser and insisting they had to wait for everyone. They were not budging unless every one of their comrades was on board. "The truck is full," Simha finally snapped. "I'm in charge, and we are leaving now."

"Stop! Stop!" Zivia screamed as the lorry pulled away.

By the time Boruch Spiegel spotted the approaching truck, he, Chaika Belchatowska, and the forty other ZOB survivors from the Main Shops District had been in the Lomianki forest for over a week. They had set up a makeshift camp with the People's Army in the dense woods, chopping down a few of the towering pines, with their peeling rust-colored trunks, to erect primitive lean-tos in the sandy, moss-covered soil.

Though Lomianki was close to the city, it was part of the Kampinow National Forest Preserve and teemed with wildlife. Boars rooted for mushrooms. Deer grazed on the low ferns, and badgers and foxes and other small predators roamed about. Germans, however, rarely ventured into the woods. It was too dangerous. The Nazis had effectively ceded the massive tracts of wooded land that surrounded the Polish capital to the Home Army and other partisan groups while retaining control of the city. The trade-off, for the General Government, was that the Gestapo could focus on keeping the urban population docile, while the partisans were freed to be a nuisance in the countryside: to launch occasional diversionary attacks on rail lines or to engage in other acts of minor sabotage. Hundreds of rebel camps ringed Warsaw: some with only a few dozen guerrillas, others large and sophisticated operations with underground communications bunkers equipped with long-range radios supplied by British Intelligence. The Resistance cells came from dozens of semi-independent organizations that fought under the broad Home Army umbrella. Unfortunately for the ZOB, they included the virulently anti-Semitic National Armed Forces. The group was rabidly anticommunist and comprised of large numbers of prewar fascists who were as likely to attack People's Army outposts and Jewish refugees as German garrisons.

The woods, luckily, were big enough that renegade groups rarely met. For Boruch, the virgin forest, so verdant with vegetation, exploding with the green hues of the spring bloom, had come as a shock after years in the monochromatic Ghetto, where not a single blade of grass grew. He and Chaika had walked in the woods, gaping at the wildflowers that poked through the moss, very nearly stupefied by the sensory overload. It was a sight neither had thought they would ever see again, and the contrast for them was as surreal as the gleaming white tiles of the bathroom where Simha had showered after tunneling his way to the Sawicki sisters' safe house.

Psychologically, the departure from the Ghetto had touched almost all the ZOB fighters, though in different ways. Mark Edelman seemed most affected. When the truck bearing him and the rest of the evacuees from Straight Street arrived in Lomianki, he did not participate in the joyful reunion, or the meal that was hastily cooked over an open fire to feed the exhausted new arrivals. Even on the way to the forest, in the truck, Edelman had started acting strangely. It was the sight of the city, he later explained, that set him off: of children, neatly dressed, playing in playgrounds; of stores with goods in their windows catering to shoppers; of crowds walking openly in the streets, of cars and traffic lights. "I could not believe that only a few hundred yards from the Ghetto ordinary life went on."

Something inside him snapped. Edelman began moaning and tugging at his nose, at his "Jewish nose," as if he wanted to rip off his Semitic features. In the Ghetto he had been unflappable, fearless and cold-blooded to the point of ruthlessness. Now the prospect of survival on the Aryan side seemed to fill him with paralyzing dread. "Mark has had a breakdown," some of the other fighters whispered. (More likely, he was exhibiting symptoms of what psychiatrists would later label post-traumatic stress disorder.)

Zivia Lubetkin also did not celebrate their escape from the Ghetto. As soon as the truck had slowed to a stop in Lomianki, she leaped off, unholstered her pistol, and made straight for Simha Ratheiser, shouting that she would kill him for abandoning their comrades. Simha pulled out his own revolver and leveled it at Zivia's head. "Go ahead," he said, "pull the trigger, and we both die." The standoff lasted for a few tense seconds before Zivia lowered her gun and burst into tears. Simha tried to console her. He had had no choice, he explained. Staying any longer would have meant sacrificing the entire group. Edelman, who had made many similarly difficult decisions, would later support Simha. Zivia, however, would never entirely forgive him, even though Simha turned the truck around, as he had promised he would, and sent Richie Mozelman and a few other ZOB fighters to collect the remaining evacuees from Straight Street. None of them ever returned, a fact that would weigh heavily on Simha's conscience for the rest of his life: "Those people died because of me," he would say, unprompted, after a few vodkas nearly seven decades later. "But we would have all died had I acted differently."

They were alive. They were safe. And they were together. But for the eighty survivors of the Jewish Fighting Organization's original five hundred members, a burning question presented itself: What would they do now?

CHAPTER 34

HOTEL POLAND

By August 1943, the surviving members of the Jewish Fighting Organization had split into two groups. The more senior combatants, including Zivia Lubetkin and Mark Edelman, returned to Warsaw, while the bulk of the force went deeper into the woods.

Boruch Spiegel and Chaika Belchatowska reluctantly remained with the rank and file. Since both occupied lower rungs in the ZOB hierarchy, they had little choice but to obey Isaac Zuckerman's order to relocate farther east, to a remote forest near the Bug River on the old Soviet-Nazi demarcation line. The People's Army was forming a partisan cell there, composed largely of escaped Soviet POWs, and Zuckerman, not knowing where else to stash his fighters, had arranged for Spiegel's group to join them.

It was far from an ideal arrangement. Not only did Bundists like Boruch bristle at the notion of teaming up with Communists, but virtually all the Jews, as urbanites, had no idea how to live off the land. That the rules of survival were vastly different from those in the city quickly became apparent, as ZOB fighters started dying within days of arriving in the new staging area. The region was boggy and mosquito-infested, and it boasted more wolves and wild boars than human inhabitants. It was also completely lawless, a dumping ground for brigands and renegade Resistance brigades. Marauding bands robbed, raped, and murdered at will. Women who strayed from camp were particularly vulnerable in the harsh anarchic landscape, and it was not unheard-of for rival gangs to raid one another's encampments, especially when food was in short supply.

"Life in the world of partisans in eastern Poland was extremely cruel, perhaps the worst of any place in Europe," the historian Richard C. Lukas later remarked. "Human life had no value and incidents of barbarity and betrayal were commonplace."

The camps themselves were not permanent settlements with fixed wooden structures, but rather a collection of camouflaged dugouts with low earthen ceilings reinforced by tree limbs and covered in transplanted shrubs. Inside the muddy trench residences "it was dark and damp, like lying in a grave," according to one partisan. Larger dugouts had planks on the floor and little tin stoves for heat, but the poorly ventilated smoke left their occupants with a hacking cough. Water was carried in buckets from a stream. The lack of latrines turned the nearby field into a minefield of human excrement.

About a hundred and fifty partisans formed the People's Army cells in the forest of Wyszkow. Their numbers were roughly divided between the ZOB contingent, Gentile Communists who were mostly Belorussians, and crude Soviet soldiers, who eyed the dozen or so Jewish women in the camp with undisguised longing. Uncouth and undisciplined as the Russian soldiers may have been, they were fierce fighters, brave and bold and capable of enduring great hardship. With the Russians at the helm, the cells sabotaged rail lines and cut telegraph wires. They attacked convoys and police stations in the closest towns and harassed Wehrmacht units whenever the opportunity arose. Boruch carried a rifle on these missions, a weapon he sorely wished he'd possessed during the Uprising. The gun had been part of the arms shipment Zuckerman received earlier from the People's Army. Twenty-eight of the Soviet-made rifles had been distributed to the Jewish partisans, a significant increase in firepower over the revolvers they had used in the Ghetto.

Over the summer, the cells wreaked enough havoc to attract the attention of the local Gestapo, which began sending heavily armed patrols into the woods to search for the disruptive guerrillas. The ZOB soon began to suffer serious losses from the patrols. "From fifty people in our original group [from the Main Shops District], we were down to around fifteen," Boruch recalled. Tragically, a significant portion of the casualties had not come at the hands of the Nazis. The group had also been set upon by rogue units of the National Armed Forces, the ultraviolent resistance movement whose ranks included many former Falangists and ONR fascists—the same thugs who had preyed on Jewish students before the war and had spearheaded the failed Easter pogrom in 1940. This rabidly right-wing organization was not subordinated to the Home Army or to the London government in exile in 1943. It operated outside established Underground laws, and its members followed their own code of conduct, which equated Jews and Communists with enemies of Poland. Already they had wiped out several ZOB and JMU partisan units in other parts of Poland, and in Wyszkow, they had been responsible for the death of at least ten of Boruch's brothers and sisters in arms.

Spiegel himself had narrowly avoided a similar fate, thanks to the intervention of Simha Ratheiser. Simha frequently visited the Wyszkow forest in his capacity as Isaac Zuckerman's new lead courier. Usually he carried instructions and medications, small arms and ammunition. At times he was called upon to solve minor emergencies, such as arranging for a doctor to perform an abortion by candlelight on one of the girls in the camp. But mostly he brought his isolated colleagues news from the outside world. It was through Simha, for instance, that Boruch and his fellow Bundists learned that their representative in the Polish government in exile, Arthur Ziegelbaum, had committed suicide in London to protest the intransigence of the British, Polish, and American authorities. Spiegel was shattered by Zeigelbaum's death, which came on the heels of a conference in Bermuda devoted to aiding European Jews. The United States and Great Britain had jointly announced after the bilateral talks that nothing could be done because "the problem is too great for solution by the two governments here represented."

In late summer, Simha traveled to Wyszkow to defuse a mutiny by some of the Bundists who wanted to return to Warsaw. While there, he was also supposed to meet a local forest ranger who had proven himself useful to the ZOB. The ranger lived in another part of the forest, deep in the woods. It was pouring rain by the time Simha and six other ZOB members reached his hut. They were warming themselves by the fire when shots suddenly rang out, seemingly from all directions. Everyone hit the dirt, assuming the Germans had spotted them. Peering out from one of the log cabin's rustic windows, Simha could see that partisans had surrounded the hut. He had no idea who they were or what faction they belonged to. The forest ranger's elderly wife soon grasped what was happening. Someone had spotted strangers roaming their neck of the woods and called in reinforcements to defend their territory. Braving the volleys of bullets that peppered the cabin's log walls, the old woman flung open the door and started shouting "Stop it, they're our people!" The firing abruptly ceased and their attackers melted away into the dripping underbrush like a flash storm.

Though the immediate danger had passed, Simha knew that the peace wouldn't last. If the trigger-happy partisans were in fact from one of the anti-Semitic or fascist factions, they would eventually realize their error and return in full force. And even if they were ideologically more benign, they still posed a serious threat, since they clearly had a policy of shooting first and asking questions later. Simha decided he had to find out who this other partisan band was and try to broker a modus vivendi. He returned to Warsaw and asked Isaac Zuckerman to make inquiries with his Home Army contacts. The group, Zuckerman reported a few days later, was undisciplined, violent, and prone to banditry. But it was not part of the murderous National Armed Forces. Relieved, Simha went back to Wyszkow and prevailed on the forest ranger to arrange a meeting. "I pretended I was a big shot in the Underground."

The partisans of Wyszkow apparently did not receive many high-ranking envoys from Home Army headquarters, for when Simha arrived, the rugged woodsmen had dressed in their Sunday best in his honor. "Miraculously, one of them had even gotten hold of a starched collar, cuffs, and tie. He looked elegant and formal, even though he didn't have a shirt on his back."

Their leader treated Simha with deference, offering him home-distilled vodka and ceremonial toasts. He intimated, after a few courteous rounds of moonshine, that he had been planning to attack the

Jewish camp. But before he acted he wanted to make sure they were not affiliated with any of his sister organizations. If they were, they would be left in peace. If they were just random Jews, on the other hand, they would be destroyed. Simha nodded knowingly, pretending to see the soundness of such logic. Unfortunately, Simha sighed, his superiors felt differently in this particular case. "I told him that the ZOB had to be left alone," Ratheiser recalled. "That it was orders from Warsaw."

The grizzled partisan leader would almost certainly have shot Simha had he realized that he was being duped by a blond Jew half his age. But Simha was convincing. Spiegel and the others would be spared. Boruch, however, had had enough. That close call was the last straw for him. He was not cut out for partisan life, he decided. What's more, fall would soon be upon them, and living in the cold, and eventually in the snow, would become immeasurably harder. Some of the ZOB fighters were electing to stay. But he and Chaika would return to the city and take their chances in Warsaw.

By the time the first frosts glazed the Polish capital in early October 1943, Zivia Lubetkin and Mark Edelman had changed safe houses four times. Their hiding places, homes of sympathetic Gentiles, kept getting "burned" (exposed) with maddening regularity.

Although Warsaw had been declared *Judenrein*—Clean of Jews—by a triumphant Jürgen Stroop when he completed the Ghetto liquidation on May 16 by symbolically blowing up the Great Synagogue near Banker's Square, there were still an estimated twenty-eight thousand Jews hiding in and around the city. Many, like Joanna, Hanna, and Janine Mortkowicz, had been on the Aryan side all along, having never set foot in the Ghetto. Some, like Simha's parents, Miriam and Zvi, had escaped before the 1942 *Gross Aktion,* when the Ghetto's walls had been more porous. Others still had made it out after the January rising and during the twenty-eight days of the main Uprising, through the sewers or the JMU's two tunnels. Keeping these people alive and out of the clutches of the Gestapo and their greaser accomplices had become the primary function of the Jewish Fighting Organization.

It was a daunting task. Already, in the few short months since the final liquidation of the Ghetto, the Gestapo had snared thirty-five hundred Jews with a single fiendishly clever trap. The affair was known as the Hotel Polski, and it had claimed two deputy commanders of the ZOB, Israel Kanal and Eliezer Geller, who had been in charge of all forces in the Main Shops District. It had very nearly claimed Zivia as well. The sting was orchestrated by Warsaw Gestapo chief Ludwig Hahn, who spotted an opportunity to lure Jews out of hiding by promoting a little-known international exchange program that traded Jewish refugees for German POWS. For years, the World Jewish Congress in Switzerland had been securing visas and passports for Jews to Latin American countries by arranging diplomatic *promessas* of the sort that Martha and Robert Osnos had used to leave Poland. To receive the *promessas,* the World Jewish Congress bought small parcels of land in South America in the name of the refugees, which entitled the owners to citizenship. The Nazis had largely ignored the *promessa* requests, and thousands of the unused Latin American visas had accumulated while their intended recipients had been exterminated. Colonel Hahn, in the summer of 1943, let it be known that these precious documents could now be bought, and that the identity of the purchasers was of no interest to him because Berlin intended to swap refugees for German soldiers imprisoned by the Allies.

The initial response was muted. Jews were understandably leery of German largesse. So Hahn arranged for a group of Jewish prisoners to be released from Peacock Prison—the only institution still operating in the former Ghetto. The inmates were transferred to Warsaw's Hotel Royal, fed, clothed, and eventually sent to the spa town of Vittel in France to await the ship that would take them to South America. Postcards from picturesque Vittel soon flooded Warsaw, igniting a stampede for *promessas.*

The astronomical sums the Germans charged for the travel documents lent the scheme an air of corrupt credibility. In time, so many Jews were buying the visas that the operation was moved to the much larger Hotel Polski on Long Street, a few blocks south of the defunct Brushmakers District. When prominent figures in the Jewish community signed up for the plan, including the poet Yitzhak Katznelson and David Guzik, the widely respected head of the American Joint Distribution Committee in Warsaw, Isaac Zuckerman started thinking about sending Zivia.

Lubetkin was bitterly unhappy. Unlike her husband, she could not live "on the surface" in Warsaw because her Semitic features and poor Polish would instantly betray her as Jewish. Zivia had to remain indoors cooped up in a tiny apartment. She could not go to the store or down to her courtyard to smoke a cigarette. She could not lean out the window to catch a fleeting glimpse of the sun. She could not even raise her voice or walk too loudly, for fear of alerting the neighbors. Lubetkin was going stir-crazy. She was now useless to her husband and the ZOB, entirely reliant on others for everything from food to reading material, which she needed to ward off the debilitating boredom. And the boredom promised to be endless. Her confinement would not be a matter of weeks or months. It would be a permanent condition until the war was over. If the Nazis won, it could be indefinite. Isaac didn't think Zivia would make it. Her depression and drinking were only getting worse. Sooner or later, he worried, the inaction would break her.

Yet Zuckerman also had serious misgivings about the visa scheme. It seemed too good to be true. When he decided to visit the Hotel Polski to see for himself, he couldn't believe his eyes. The lobby was teeming. A beautiful flower arrangement sprouted at the center of the gleaming marble floor. Porters carried suitcases, and the concierge behind the mahogany reception desk handed out keys to the Jewish guests. A pair of smiling Germans stood by the main door, opening it with polite expressions of *"Bitte.* Welcome." Isaac watched in amazement. The Gestapo was warmly greeting Jews, courteously helping them with the paperwork for their South American visas. It all looked aboveboard, and Zuckerman started to waver. Maybe it was for real. After all, several thousand Varsovian Jews had already taken advantage of the program. They had departed for France in fancy Pullman railcars. Perhaps the Nazis were coming to their senses. The war had been going badly for Hitler lately. His ally, Mussolini, was finished. The Americans had taken Sicily and were climbing up the boot of Italy. In the Atlantic, his vaunted U-boats were being decimated thanks to improved antisubmarine tactics. The North African campaign was lost, and the victorious British had landed in Greece. Worst of all, his tanks had just been defeated in the Battle of Kursk on the Eastern Front, the biggest armored clash in the history of warfare. And the triumphant Soviets were marching westward and had reached the outskirts of Kiev. So perhaps the Germans were getting nervous and hedging their bets, Isaac mused.

Still, something did not feel right. The sight of so many well-dressed Jews lounging in the hotel bar, ordering cocktails and acting as if there was no war—smiling, laughing, excitedly making plans for a new life—struck Isaac as dangerously surreal. His every instinct told him to flee. "It was hard to rationalize that while some Jews were getting caught in the street, others were sitting comfortably in the Hotel Polski," he reasoned. To him, there was only one explanation for this: "It was a trap."

Indeed, of the thirty-five hundred visa applicants who registered to stay in the luxurious hotel during the three-month sting operation, not one survived. From Vittel, France, the refugees were shipped to Bergen-Belsen instead of Brazil and gassed to death. Trains bearing the final group of would-be emigrants dispensed with the French charade altogether and were routed directly to Auschwitz.

Isaac's suspicions intensified the moment he left the Hotel Polski. Crossing Long Street, he noticed a group of unsavory characters following him. He jumped on a passing tram, but his pursuers were nimble and quickly boarded as well. Usually, Zuckerman avoided trams at all costs, since the risk of getting caught in a forced labor roundup was too high. But this time he had little choice. The men who had followed him were greasers, and they were on his trail. "I rode inside the tram and they stood on the platform constantly chanting 'Jew, Jew, Jew!' They stuck to me only because I came out of the Hotel Polski."

Unlike Simha, who was always armed, Isaac preferred not to carry a weapon. The likelihood of a random search was too high. So instead of confronting his current pursuers, he tried to shake them. Changing trams, he rode all the way across the river to Praga, the blue-collar neighborhood on the eastern banks of the Vistula. And still he could not escape the whispering taunts of "Jew, Jew."

The greasers—*smaltzowniki,* as they were derisively known in both Polish and Yiddish—were now arguably the single greatest threat to Jewish survival in Nazi-occupied Poland. The Gestapo had only a few dozen officers hunting Jews on a full-time basis in Warsaw. They relied heavily on local collaborators to do their dirty work for them, to be their eyes and ears on the street, to ferret out which apartment buildings had received mysterious new tenants, to uncover which landlord was buying inordinate amounts of food or why certain tenants never received mail or visitors—to look, in other words, for any of the telltale signs that someone was "keeping cats," the popular euphemism for harboring Jews. Greasers provided the Gestapo with an invaluable for-profit intelligence network. But who were these traitors? Precious little is known about the composition of this underworld group of violent shakedown artists. While reams of books would be written in Poland about so-called Righteous Gentiles who risked their lives to help Jews, virtually nothing would appear in print detailing the evildoings of the greasers—as if the subject was best swept under the historical carpet. In one of the very few frank examinations of their shameful activities ever to be published in Poland, the Polish-Canadian historian Jan Grabowski later estimated the total number of greasers in wartime Warsaw to be between five and ten thousand—a staggering number that by the fall of 1943 translated into at least one greaser for every four Jews. "The extent of their criminal behavior is difficult to measure," Grabowski would write, "but the scale was wide-ranging; from blackmail and denunciation to robbery, rape, and murder."

For every individual they turned in, greasers received a bounty from the Gestapo, typically 20 percent of the assets seized from the victim. Most greasers, however, were not content with such a small slice and took it upon themselves to steal or extort everything their prey possessed. Only then would they sell their catch to the Nazis—or occasionally, out of pure malice, slit their victims' throats. The most damning aspect of the greaser phenomenon was that the extortionists plied their brutal trade more or less openly. This was possible, according to Grabowski, because society at large viewed their crimes merely with "disapproving indifference rather than widespread condemnation."

Tolerance of the greasers cut to the heart of prewar Jewish-Gentile relations, exposing the core belief in Poland that Jews, as non-Christians, were outside society's moral and legal sphere of obligations. Technically, greasers who targeted Jews were not even committing a crime under the Code of Conduct, the body of Underground laws that governed the rights and behavior of citizens during Nazi occupation. "The problem was that the authors of the document had defined nationality on the basis of ethnicity rather than citizenship," Grabowski explained. Since the first point of the first section of the Code stipulated that "Polish is your mother tongue," 95 percent of Warsaw Jews, who were native Yiddish—or in a few cases Hebrew—speakers, were effectively disenfranchised and afforded no protections under the Code. The wording gave greasers license to prey on Jews and to commit acts that would have earned them a death sentence from Underground courts if the victims had been Gentiles.

Isaac Zuckerman complained bitterly about this travesty of justice to his Home Army liaison, Captain Henry Wolinski, who had served as a state prosecutor before the war. Isaac also penned a scathing letter to Wolinski's superiors detailing the wanton murder of Jews in the forests as well as the city. His letter was so harsh and incriminating that Wolinski advised him to keep a low profile for a few weeks after sending it, for his own safety. Apparently, powerful people had been offended, and there were rumblings in Home Army headquarters that Zuckerman needed to be taught a lesson in civility.

Isaac's angry pleas, however, did not fall entirely on deaf ears. Shortly after Isaac sent his reproachful letter, in September 1943, the Home Army executed its first greaser. His name was Jan Pilnik, and he appeared eighth on a list of ten individuals sentenced to death by Underground courts. Their various crimes were enumerated in leaflets pasted around the city to serve as an example to other would-be traitors. Over the course of the next year, a dozen of the two hundred executions carried out by the Resistance in Warsaw would be for blackmailing Jews. As far as Zuckerman was concerned, it was too little, too late. By the time the Home Army started cracking down on the greasers, the extortionists had already done most of their damage.

The men tailing him now certainly had not been discouraged by the Home Army executions. Isaac had purposefully led his pursuers to Praga, which was less crowded than Midtown and had a smaller police presence. "When I got off the tram, they surrounded me," he recalled. "What do you want?" Isaac asked.

"Why did you run from us?" one of the greasers demanded.

"What do you want?" Zuckerman repeated.

"What you've got," the thug leaned forward menacingly.

Just then a voice startled the blackmailers. "Gentlemen!"

Simha Ratheiser stood a few paces behind the group of assailants. He routinely shadowed Zuckerman, acting as his discreet bodyguard. And like some gunslinger in an American Western, he was now brandishing a pair of pistols, one in each hand.

It was not only greasers that the ZOB had to worry about in the fall of 1943. That October, the Gestapo launched a terror campaign in Poland that was almost certainly tied to the Reich's reversals of fortunes on distant battlefields. The repression was particularly brutal in Warsaw, the center of perceived or potential resistance.

On October 13, massive street raids began in the city center. Thousands of people were arrested, and 1,400 men and 487 women, all Gentiles, were sent to Auschwitz on the first day alone. The roundups were accompanied by a new sight in the Polish capital: The Germans inaugurated the practice of street executions. In the past, the Gestapo had conducted their killings in the Palmiry forest north of Warsaw. Now, in order to spread maximum fear, public firing squads were convened daily in different locations throughout the city. On October 16, for instance, twenty people were shot on Independence Street in the upscale neighborhood of Mokotow. The next day another twenty were lined up against the wall of the main telephone switching station in working-class Wola, while sixty more were murdered the day after that near Woodrow Wilson Square in Jolie Bord. On October 21, another sixty were shot in Praga, almost exactly where Zuckerman had led his greaser pursuers. The mobile killing squads then moved on to Jerusalem Boulevard and New World Street, in the heart of the Midtown shopping and restaurant district. Then they moved north again, lining up victims outside the Gdansk train station, the Grand Theater, Krasinski Square. This went on for six straight weeks until thousands had been murdered in plain sight. Megaphones announced every execution, warning, "You've brought this on yourselves. Why do you provoke us?"

As Varsovians became inured to the daily street shootings, the Gestapo upped the psychological ante in November 1943 by switching to
public hangings. This method of killing was deemed more effective
because the hanging corpses left a lasting impression. They dangled
from ornate Art Deco lampposts, left to slowly decompose instead of
being removed and buried like the firing squad victims. Some swung
suspended by the neck from the wrought iron balconies of residential
buildings, so pedestrians were forced to walk beneath their urine-
soaked trousers.

In addition to the public executions, the SS redoubled its efforts to
penetrate the various resistance movements, which were growing
bolder with every Allied victory. This was most effectively accomplished by using families as hostages to turn agents. The Home Army
was badly hit by the wave of informants: General Rowecki, the Warsaw commander who had issued the order not to participate in the
Ghetto Uprising, was dead, as were several other senior leaders who
had been betrayed, arrested, tortured, and eventually killed.

Isaac's frequent dealings with the People's Army and the fractious
Home Army left him exposed to the treachery of Gestapo agents who
infiltrated virtually every Gentile insurgent group. Already he had
begun to suspect Shrub, the code name for Lieutenant Gaik, the People's Army officer who arranged transport for the sewer escapees to
Lomianki. Shrub's bona fides were rock solid: he had saved eighty
ZOB members, and he had been the driving force behind the establishment of the partisan cell in Wyszkow. But he had recently begun to
behave strangely. Visiting Wyszkow, he insisted on leading a mission to
attack a police station that ended disastrously. Virtually everyone except for Shrub died in the botched assault. German troops had been
waiting for the partisans, as if they had been expecting them. This of
course could have been just bad luck. But it made Isaac think about
how the second half of the May 10 sewer rescue mission had also
ended in a similar slaughter. The moving truck that Simha sent back to
collect the remaining ZOB fighters from the sewers had been ambushed on the way to the city. Richie Mozelman and several other ZOB
members died before ever reaching their colleagues, as if the Germans
had been expecting them, too. This could also have been a coincidence.
But then a third incident convinced Zuckerman otherwise.

Late in the summer of 1943, Gaik helped transfer another group of Jews to the partisan cell in Wyszkow. They had been carrying a large sum of money, hundreds of thousands of zlotys and thousands of dollars. Gaik inexplicably ordered the funds to be turned over to him. Furious at the robbery, Isaac went to Shrub's commander and ordered an inquiry, which resulted in the People's Army issuing a death warrant against Gaik for theft. Gaik disappeared. A year later he was shot by the Germans while trying to rescue two Jews. Had Shrub been a collaborator, or merely a thief? Had he played double agent? Or had the People's Army tried to take the money for its own uses, with Shrub just a victim of the paranoia that pervaded the Underground?

Another lethal incident involving the People's Army left no such doubt. It led to the death of one of the ZOB's top couriers, Tuvia Sheingut, and it very nearly cost Simha Ratheiser his life. Both Ratheiser and Sheingut had risen very rapidly in the ZOB's thinning ranks, thanks in part to their role in the sewer rescue. More important, both possessed the qualities that ZOB operatives needed most at this point in the war: the ability to move freely among the general population. Simha, in particular, had benefited from his ease at playing a Gentile. Because of this ability, he had replaced Tuvia Borzykowski as Isaac's "right-hand man." Tuvia had been Zuckerman's closest friend and confidant in the Ghetto. It was to Tuvia that Isaac had entrusted the care of his wife during the Uprising—though Zivia Lubetkin would doubtless have protested the idea that she needed anyone to look after her. But now Tuvia was as handicapped as Zivia, and Mark Edelman, who was also forced to stay indoors because of his Semitic looks. Tuvia's appearance wasn't an issue for him. He was a big strapping lad with fair Slavic features. His disqualifying barrier was linguistic. "Tuvia's Polish wasn't Polish," Zuckerman noted regretfully.

Ratheiser and Sheingut had been running guns to a ZOB cell in southern Poland for the past few months. One of Simha's contacts, a trusted Gentile by the name of Stephen Pokropck, had a line on some weapons for sale. A friend of a friend had access to a cache and was interested in joining the Communist partisans. If Simha put the friend's friend in touch with the right people in the Communist group, he would sell the arms to the ZOB at a discount. Ratheiser relayed the proposition to Zuckerman, who passed it along to the People's Army.

Isaac ordered Simha to meet with the man in question, who introduced himself only as Czarny—Black in Polish. It was risky, but the ZOB was desperate for guns. The People's Army, meanwhile, ran a background check on Black. Word filtered back that he appeared legitimate. The Communists then tested Black with a small mission. He passed. Simha was instructed to set up the buy. The exchange was to take place at Pokropek's Praga apartment, which Simha was using to store weapons. He already had a batch of disassembled revolvers there that he and Sheingut were in the process of stripping and cleaning. Black showed up at the appointed hour and asked if Simha and Sheingut had brought the money. They had. He would be back in an hour, he said, with the revolvers and bullets.

"I told [Sheingut] there was no point in both of us hanging around and that he should go," Simha recalled. Sheingut, however, was in no rush to leave. And just then a hammering at the door startled them both. "Gestapo. Open up!" Simha reacted instinctively. He leaped out the window and ran as fast as he could. "Bullets whizzed by my ear." Sheingut and Stephen Pokropek were not as agile. Both died on the spot.

Simha rushed back to the western side of Warsaw and reported the raid to Zuckerman. At the time they didn't know if Sheingut and Pokropek were dead or in German custody. They also had no way of knowing whether the whole thing had been a setup or pure chance. "We were tormented by suspicion, and, naturally, it fell on Black."

Black disappeared, just like Lieutenant Gaik, leaving the ZOB to wonder whom they could trust. Simha's lingering doubts were dispelled a few weeks later. "I'm walking down the street and I see this big convertible. It's full of Gestapo agents and there's Black sitting in the backseat. He spots me and starts shouting 'Stop him, stop him.'"

Ratheiser gave the Gestapo the slip. He could not, however, rid himself of a persistent fear: How many more Shrubs and Blacks were out there, just waiting to trip them up?

CHAPTER 35

ROBERT'S AMERICAN PLEDGE

On December 15, 1943, as a blizzard lashed Warsaw and Allied bombs fell on Berlin, Joseph, Martha, and young Robert Osnos found themselves with only forty-eight hours in which to pack their belongings and leave Bombay. They were not being expelled from India, where they had comfortably settled after their harrowing flight from Poland. Their American visas, after three years of bureaucratic delays, had finally come through.

The short notice was a security precaution, in the event that the Japanese had spies in India ports ready to tip off enemy submarines about the departure of U.S.-flagged ships. "Out of the blue my dad got a call that our papers were ready and that a troop transport was leaving for California," Robert, who was thirteen at the time, recalled. The vessel was the USS *Hermitage,* a scized Italian passenger liner, and for the astounded Osnoses the question at the time had been whether to board the ship at all. *Why go?* Martha and many of the Osnoses' Polish friends had argued. India had been good to European exiles. They had all found work in the booming war economy. Most had servants and spacious homes with lovely gardens and swimming pools. Joseph and Martha played bridge every weekend and Robert attended private school, where he was well on his way to becoming a proper young Englishman, albeit with a Welsh accent. Most important, he was safe. In India, there was no threat of invading forces or aerial attack. There wasn't even rationing.

It was easy to see why so many of the Polish émigrés, both Jewish and Gentile, felt fortunate to have landed in India. Their British hosts may not have invited them to join the top clubs, but their services were valued and they were treated fairly. Joseph had done extremely well running the small plant that made life rafts for the British navy. In fact, Martha had felt secure enough to have a second child. Robert now had a few-months-old little brother named Peter.

India had offered its refugees a lifeline, a rare chance at stability and prosperity at a time when neither was available in Europe. It was not surprising that many thought they had a future there. Joseph Osnos was of a different mind. Just as he had instantly grasped that Poland was finished in September 1939, and that the only recourse then was flight, he now foresaw that the privileged position of Europeans in India would eventually come to an end. "I don't know how, but my father guessed that there would be a backlash against colonialism after the war," Robert recalled. "Somehow he knew that India would seek independence and that being white would no longer be an advantage. So he insisted that we go to America now, even though my mother had just had a baby."

The USS *Hermitage* had once been an elegant passenger liner plying the Mediterranean for its Italian proprietors. Stripped down to the bare essentials, it now ferried wounded GIs to the United States on the far more dangerous passage across the still contested Pacific. On this voyage, in addition to injured soldiers, it carried 120 civilian passengers, mostly Persian oil workers and Chinese missionaries. In the lower holds, in cargo compartments that had been converted into a large brig, there was also a group of Italian POWs. To Robert, the smiling Italian officers he occasionally saw smoking and laughing on deck seemed nothing like the icy SS men who had barged into his mother's apartment in Warsaw, looking for antiques to requisition, in 1939. Seventy years later, that chilling experience in Warsaw would remain his most vivid memory of the war, more deeply ingrained than the bombings of September 1939, his sojourn through Berlin the following year, the earthquake in Bucharest, the deserts of Iraq, or his first brush with the great naval campaigns that raged in the Pacific theater.

He had followed the American victories and setbacks on the Movietone newsreels that preceded the films he watched in Bombay, and knew that the Pacific was still far from safe for any U.S. ship. The *Hermitage* had no escort. Nor was it part of a convoy. During the day, the solitary vessel meandered unpredictably, threading an invisible slalom course to throw off the aim of any pursuing submarine. At night, it traveled under a strict lights-out policy, with the portholes blacked out and smoking forbidden on deck. One of the Osnoses' fellow passengers was nearly clamped in irons for violating the no-smoking rule; the suspicion that he was a spy trying to betray the *Hermitage*'s position followed him all the way to port.

Thinking about Japanese destroyers and aircraft carriers bearing down on their defenseless vessel, Robert enacted their tactics on the board game he had brought for the voyage. For hours each day he played Battleship Down while Joseph played bridge and poker with the other passengers and Martha dutifully mixed the Pablum baby formula she had brought for tiny Peter. Once, in the middle of the night, when the vessel was sailing without lights, she dispatched her sleepy husband to fetch water for the powdered formula. In the dark, he groggily stumbled into the ladies' bathroom by mistake. A scandal ensued and Joseph was hauled in front of the captain to explain himself. "He was accused of being a Peeping Tom," Robert recalled. "We were really worried that the U.S. authorities would deny us entry because of the incident."

On New Year's Eve the ship docked in Melbourne, Australia. A few weeks later, it refueled in Bora Bora, and on February 2, 1944, after almost six weeks at sea, it arrived in San Diego, California. To everyone's relief, the customs and immigration officials knew nothing about the bathroom incident. But they were deeply troubled by Robert's battleship game. "They thought it was some sort of codes. They made us wait for two hours while they examined it."

For Joseph Osnos, a journey that had begun on September 7, 1939, was now almost over. It had taken nearly four and a half years to escape from the Nazis and to find a place to start all over. By now, 95 percent of Warsaw Jews were dead. If not for Joseph's split-second decision to run for the Romanian border on the day Stalin joined Hitler's dismemberment of Poland, the Osnoses would have likely become part of that tragic statistic.

Robert Osnos made two pledges to himself upon setting foot on American soil. The first was to get rid of his shorts, which had been popular in India. American boys were pointing at him and laughing, saying, "Hey buddy, you lose your pants or something?" The second was to jettison another vestige of India. "The only thing that really bothered me about our stay in Bombay is that I had to pretend I was Christian in school. I promised myself that in America I would never again lie about my religion."

Joanna Mortkowicz-Olczak had no idea that her cousin was in California. Robert had gradually ebbed from Joanna's thoughts. Like many nine- or ten-year-olds, she tended to forget those she had not seen in years, and her long-departed relatives had been replaced by a new group of wartime intimates: nuns, Home Army heroines like Monika Zeromska or Irene Grabowski, and the silent but strong Jewish girls who only cried in their bunks at night in the convent on Casimir Street. The other two people missing from her mental menagerie were Hanna and Janine Mortkowicz. She had not seen either of them for eight months, not since July 1943, shortly after finally making her first communion. Of the seven girls in the ceremony, five had been Jewish. "We were petrified that the Host would stick in our throats," Joanna later wrote.

After the rite, on Whit Sunday, Joanna had gone to see her mother and grandmother, who were hiding in the suburbs at the time. As usual, Irene Grabowska came to pick her up for the periodic visit. "On the commuter train a guy latched on to us, trying to make jokes and conversation. Irene was accustomed to men accosting her, and sent him packing with a few sharp remarks. But I was taken in by his cajoling. 'Joanna,' he said to me. 'Why don't you want to talk to me? I know your mama very well and your grandma. Her name's Janine Mortkowicz, right? And now she's living with your mama. And you're going to see them, aren't you?" Joanna was puzzled by the stranger's familiarity. Had he been a prewar acquaintance? A family friend? Irene Grabowska suspected otherwise. She shooed Joanna away from the interloper and they disembarked at the next stop, already well out of the city. "When we got off, he waved to us and disappeared." As usual, doubts crept in. Maybe the encounter had been an innocent coincidence after all. Perhaps Irene had been unnecessarily rude and paranoid. War could bring out the worst in people.

"We went on our way," Joanna recalled. "I had only just thrown my arms around my mother's neck when he appeared in the doorway. He had followed us along the country paths. We had led him directly to his prey."

By the despicable standards of greasers, the man who had latched on to the Mortkowiczes was only moderately evil. Joanna did not know what payment he extracted from her mother—it would almost certainly have been in the thousands of dollars in contemporary figures. But the blackmailer thankfully did not go to the Gestapo after collecting his blood money. It still meant that her mother and grandmother's hideout was "burned," and Joanna felt horribly guilty for having brought a predator to their door. She was terrified they would ingest the poison many Varsovians carried with them in case of capture, and she tearfully agreed to return to the nuns only if they promised not to commit suicide. "Then I went back to the convent like a good girl, to my French and grammar lessons," she later wrote. She did not know where her mother and grandmother moved next because it was deemed too risky for her to continue visiting them. Joanna's sole link to her family was permanently severed when the Gestapo arrested Irene Grabowska. She was taken to Peacock Prison, tortured, and eventually executed in March 1944.

By March, Boruch Spiegel had been back in Warsaw for six long, cold months. The Polish capital was snowed under. Burst pipes in poorly heated buildings formed crystal waterfalls on countless façades. Corpses still dangled from balconies, their anguished death masks now frozen solid. The alternating power blackouts on opposite sides of the street continued as the Germans desperately diverted more and more energy to their sputtering war machine. And the price of coal on the black market had shot so high that some residents were burning old phone books and furniture to stay warm. Despite the inclement conditions, Boruch did not own a coat, a hat, a pair of gloves or boots. He didn't need them. During the entire winter, he and Chaika Belchatowska never left the apartment they were hiding in. Under ZOB regulations, they were not allowed to set foot outdoors. "You needed official permission to go out from your *melina*," Boruch recalled, using the slang for safe house.

Like Zivia Lubetkin and Mark Edelman, Spiegel could not live "on the surface." Greasers would have spotted him immediately. The Slavic-style mustache he had grown did little to disguise his Semitic features. "Even my eyes were Yiddish," he lamented. "And it wasn't just how you looked. Your accent, your mannerisms, everything was a minus."

Boruch and Chaika were billeted with the family of a Home Army officer by the name of Joseph Pera, "a fantastic man," Boruch later said, "kind, brave, and generous." Pera was the manager of the Hotel Metropole, a German-only establishment, and had polished his impeccable manners during eight years in France. He and his family lived on the corner of Iron and Mushroom Streets, in a large sixth-floor apartment that had been inside the Ghetto until 1942. After the *Gross Aktion*, when the southernmost part of the Jewish district had been turned over to Gentiles, Pera, his son Mietek, and his brother-in-law had begun sheltering Jews. Boruch and Chaika lived in the attic above their flat, in a room camouflaged by a bookcase.

Zuckerman came by every few weeks, bringing money for food. "He did everything to boost our morale. He always had a ready joke or a funny story to tell." Isaac also brought pens and large supplies of paper. "Write down everything you know, he said." Spiegel had little enthusiasm for this assignment. Writing had never been his strong suit. But Zuckerman was insistent. He wanted a complete record of Jewish suffering to survive, even if none of its authors did.

What Spiegel remembered most about this period of the war was the excruciating boredom. People did what they could to pass the time. Books were devoured, regardless of the subject. Every form of card game was played. Joanna's mother, who was hiding in an apartment near the campus of the shuttered Warsaw Polytechnic about ten blocks from Boruch, wrote a novel. Her grandmother translated *Dr. Dolittle's Return* into Polish. The two women practiced languages to keep themselves from going stir-crazy. "One day they would speak only in French," Joanna recalled, "the next day in Russian, then English, or French." Hanna and Janine, like thousands of other hidden Jews, would do anything to keep their minds sharp and to distract themselves from the fact that they were living in a tiny storeroom whose door was hidden behind heavy bookcases from which they were not to emerge for fourteen very long months. Some likened hiding in secret rooms or behind false walls to solitary confinement. "We had the feeling of being prisoners sentenced to an indefinite term," Tuvia Borzykowski recalled. "Had we at least known the waiting would end some day, the waiting would have been easier." Many couldn't take it. A few were driven insane. These unfortunates were popularly known as "crazy cats."

The ZOB had entered a new phase in its evolution. The procurement of weapons and armed resistance were no longer its raison d'être. The fighting, for the foreseeable future, was over. The Organization's goal was now survival, not only that of its own dwindling membership, but of any and all Jews still alive in Warsaw. Fewer than twenty thousand remained in the Polish capital by March 1944, and with each passing month, greasers steadily eroded their numbers. Even the Gestapo were impressed by the blackmailers' diligence. "You Poles are strange people," one SS officer remarked. "Nowhere in the world is there another nation which has so many heroes and so many denouncers."

Isaac Zuckerman echoed that perplexing dichotomy. "Remember," he often reminded Simha Ratheiser, "it only takes one Pole to betray a hundred Jews, but it takes ten Poles to save one Jew." The math was exaggerated, but his point was clear. Between forty thousand and sixty thousand Varsovians were actively involved in sheltering Jews, according to the Ghetto chronicler Emmanuel Ringelblum, who himself was being hidden at this time in a specially constructed bunker under a greenhouse in midtown Warsaw. Some Western historians put the number as high as ninety thousand, when so-called secondary helpers were factored in. "These noble individuals face not only German terror but also the hostility of Polish fascists," Ringelblum noted in the report he penned while living under the greenhouse. "It is, however, the anti-Semites as a whole, infected with racialism and Nazism, who created conditions so unfavorable that it has been possible to save only a small percentage of the Polish Jews from the Teuton butchers."

Boruch Spiegel was more forgiving of the limited assistance from fellow countrymen. "What a lot of people don't realize is that the Poles had it pretty bad too. Most of them were too busy trying to survive. They had their own problems." Ultimately, it would be the deeds of those who harmed rather than those who helped that would resonate loudest in the historical record. Yet to Simha, there was a karmic balance between betrayal and assistance. Greasers and anti-Semites were offset by people like the Sawicki sisters. "Once I was on the run and went to Marisa [Sawicka's] apartment. The Gestapo had just been there." They had come to arrest her nephew, Stephen, who was later executed for helping the ZOB. "She was scared and I would have understood had she turned me away. But she still let me in. I'll never forget that."

The principal difference between good and evil at this point was that acting decently was punishable by death, while heinous acts carried virtually no consequences.

Not all of those rendering assistance to Jews were motivated by pure altruism, however. "Keeping cats" was a for-profit enterprise for many Varsovian landlords, the only way for cash-strapped families to make ends meet. The hyperinflation, high unemployment, and economic devastation wrought by Nazi occupation had reduced standards of living in Warsaw to levels far below the worst of the Great Depression. Food was prohibitively expensive, accounting for the bulk of most family budgets. As they had in the Ghetto, smuggling and the black market filled the cruel caloric gap left by starvation-level German rations. For homeowners with no alternative sources of income, taking in boarders became a necessity.

Warsaw also had more room at this stage of the war. The capital's non-Jewish population had shrunk by more than a fifth since 1939. With nearly a quarter of a million residents dead or in labor, concentration, or POW camps, the city's perennial housing shortage had been temporarily alleviated, leaving vacancies that were eagerly filled by refugees from the Ghetto. The monthly rents that illegal Jewish tenants paid were astronomical, often ten to twenty times the rate charged for Gentiles. The daily rate for boarding a Jewish child, for instance, was 100 zlotys, more than Mark Edelman earned in an entire month as a hospital orderly in 1940. The premium factored in the risks for landlords, whose entire families could be shot for harboring Jews. Still, thousands engaged in this dangerous game of real estate roulette, because the Nazis had assigned the death penalty to so many mundane activities by then that the sentence had lost its meaning. "Death threatened for bacon and gold, for weapons and false papers, for evading registration, for a radio and for Jews," noted one Varsovian writer. "The wits said that they were afraid only of sentences higher than death; to them the death penalty was like a prewar jaywalking ticket. Over the city there hung a deadly absurdity."

In this treacherous environment, Jews sometimes became pawns in intra-Gentile disputes. Vindictive neighbors denounced landlords for "keeping cats" for reasons that often had nothing to do with anti-Semitism. A lovers' quarrel, a divorce, an unpaid debt, or an old score to settle could result in an anonymous letter to the Gestapo. It was in this fashion that Emmanuel Ringelblum and forty other Jews hiding under the care of a sympathetic Socialist Party activist by the name of Mieczyslaw Wolski were caught and killed by the Germans in March 1944. Wolski's ex-girlfriend tipped off the authorities after a particularly contentious breakup.

The capture of Ringelblum hit the Zionist community hard. He had been one of its most prominent and respected members in the Ghetto, and Isaac Zuckerman was especially dispirited by the senseless loss. During the day, when he made his rounds visiting the various ZOB *melinas,* Isaac put on a brave face, dispensing his usual quips and anecdotes. At night, when he was alone with Zivia and Mark Edelman, the mask of good humor faded and his despondency showed through. Attrition was decimating the remnants of Polish Jewry. If the war dragged on for a few more years, none of them would be left. Isaac consoled himself with vodka. He had started drinking in 1941 to numb the guilt he felt when he found out that his entire family had been murdered in Vilna, to ease the nagging remorse that he should have been with them. Now his alcohol consumption became a regular coping mechanism. It did not, however, appear to interfere with his work.

Part of the ZOB's newly expanded brief was to act as a de facto underground welfare agency, to arrange false documents and *melina* safe houses, to help defray the high cost of rents and to distribute money collected abroad to Jews in hiding. For this, Zuckerman turned to the Jewish National Committee, the Ghetto-era civilian body that he had created to help get the ZOB formally recognized by the Home Army. The Jewish National Committee had already been working with a Home Army civilian agency known as the Council to Aid Jews. This underground organization, founded in late 1942, was loosely connected to the Home Army and funded by the government in exile. To its paymasters in London, it was partly an instrument to expiate guilt, and partly a cynical exercise in political correctness to appease Poland's British and American allies, who themselves had done little to ease the plight of European Jews. In Warsaw, on the other hand, the Council was staffed by a small group of idealists and romantics, many of whom paid dearly for their humanitarian efforts. Most hailed from intellectual liberal backgrounds, the traditional provenance of Poland's small philo-Semitic community. But not all. Ironically, one of the Council's co-founders, Sofia Kossak, had been a rabid nationalist and prewar anti-Semite. A successful historical novelist—a translation of her book about Saint Francis of Assisi, *Blessed Are the Meek*, was a bestseller in the United States in 1944—she had published tract after tract demanding that Jews emigrate from Poland before 1939. But after being shocked by the Holocaust, she turned full circle in 1942, devoting herself to the preservation of Polish Jewry. Kossak was in Auschwitz in the winter of 1944, while her book was climbing *The New York Times* bestseller list, but the Council by then had a staff of several hundred dedicated clandestine workers. Among them were individuals like Wladislaw Bartoszewski, a twenty-year-old Auschwitz survivor who became Poland's foreign minister in 2001, and Irene Sendler, who rescued three thousand Jewish children during the Ghetto liquidation and whose 2008 funeral in Warsaw was attended by Israeli heads of state.

Two Jewish representatives sat on the Council's executive committee, the Bundist attorney Leon Feiner and Adolf Berman, a psychiatrist who headed the Warsaw branch of Po'alei Zion Left. It was through them that Isaac Zuckerman tapped into this small but invaluable network of future Righteous Gentiles committed to saving Jews. Their organization worked on multiple levels. For Jewish refugees who looked and sounded "good," they facilitated the procurement of false identities through the Home Army's forgery department so that escapees from the Ghetto could "live on the surface," which was far cheaper and in some ways safer than hiding. Simha Ratheiser was one of the earliest ZOB beneficiaries of such manufactured identities. His papers—an *Arbeitskarte* work card and the all-important *Kennkarte* identity card, with his photo, fingerprint, and serial number—were virtually foolproof because they were genuine, issued by the General Government itself. Simha had applied for them in person, armed with the birth certificate of a recently deceased aristocrat. The Germans had no idea that the real nobleman had passed away because deaths were rarely reported to the authorities in wartime Warsaw. Instead, the Underground resurrected their identities. Recipients of such recycled documents were ghoulishly known as the living dead, and there were tens of thousands of them roaming the Polish capital.

Simha had additional papers that said he worked for a German organization that sent Polish slave laborers to the Reich. This extra identification allowed him to travel all over occupied Poland, and he had once used the fake ID to go to the Plaszow concentration camp outside Krakow to try to foment rebellion there. The SS had stopped him. "I was so sure of myself, and the guard looks at my pass and says 'Where did you buy it?'"

Ratheiser hadn't panicked. "I was always calmest whenever I was in the most danger. I looked the guard in the eye and smiled." The SS hauled Ratheiser over to a General Government registry office in Krakow to see if his papers were genuine. While there, Simha shamelessly flirted with the pretty young German secretaries on duty. It did not hurt that he was rather handsome himself. "When the guards had gone into one of the back rooms where they kept the files, one of the secretaries winked at me to escape."

In addition to forged documents, the Council also provided Polish lessons and religious instruction to those who looked Slavic but had linguistic or cultural limitations. One such school in Warsaw operated out of a beauty parlor. "It was filled with women wearing all kinds of creams, curlers, sitting under heating lamps and dryers," according to one participant. While the students received manicures they were given instruction in the Catholic faith, knowledge of which was often used by greasers, the Gestapo, and the Blue Police to test suspected Jews. Not knowing one's Name Day, for instance, was the equivalent of a death sentence because Christians in Poland celebrated the birthday of their patron saint instead of their own birthday. Similarly, a policeman might ask a suspect to recite a certain prayer, or to name their parish priest. Something as simple as tram schedules could trip someone up. The public transport system had changed routes and lines since the inception of the Ghetto. Not knowing which tram number ran on which street was a dead giveaway that someone had been out of circulation for a long time.

The Council's greatest contribution was financial. At its peak in 1944, its budget exceeded two million zlotys a month. Funds from the government in exile were parachuted into Poland by RAF airdrops. The Home Army and the British air force had a long-standing association. It was through Home Army spies, for instance, that the British eventually located and destroyed the Baltic coast rocketry installation at Peenemunde that produced the V-1 Flying Bombs that terrorized London. The Home Army scored an even greater intelligence coup by stealing an entire V-2 rocket, the far more powerful successor to the Flying Bomb, when one of the missiles misfired and landed more or less intact in a bog. Polish agents disassembled it and transported the pieces to a secret landing strip where British engineers retrieved it for analysis in English laboratories.

The money flown in from the Polish government in exile was arguably the most important lifeline for the few remaining Warsaw Jews at this stage of the war. By 1944, after nearly five years without income, most had depleted their resources. Without external support, they could not afford the skyrocketing costs of staying hidden on the Aryan side. The five-hundred-zloty monthly subsidy from the Council prevented eviction for many of the twelve thousand recipients of the Council's stipends. Isaac Zuckerman and the ZOB became key cogs in the underground distribution machine. Master lists were kept with names, addresses, and tallies of recipients. These documents, some of which still survive, were among the best-guarded secrets in Warsaw. Had they fallen into German hands, the Gestapo would have had a blueprint, literally a road map, to annihilation. "I had a list of three thousand names," Zuckerman recalled. Unlike the Council, he did not include the addresses of those in his care. Isaac demanded that they be committed to memory by his couriers. "I contrived a system for myself for finding streets and people, and to this day I can't get away from it," Simha Ratheiser recalled.

Simha's parents were not on any of the lists. He had lost touch with them, and while he suspected that Miriam, his blond, Polish-speaking mother, had managed to fend for herself, he was sure his father, Zvi, was doomed. "I was certain he had no chance." As a Yiddish-speaking Orthodox Jew, Zvi had no hope of living on the surface. Yet in reality that was precisely what he was doing. Simha underestimated his father's resilience and resourcefulness. Zvi Ratheiser proved far tougher than his son had imagined. He had selflessly separated from his wife, knowing that Miriam was better off on her own, and he took a job as a stable hand for the Germans. "He bandaged his face and pretended to be mute," Simha later remarked with evident pride. The turnover of Germans was sufficiently high that no one noticed that Zvi's facial wounds never seemed to heal. As for the stuttering grunts he uttered, these, too, seemed to render him invisible to the arrogant occupiers: just another example of a subhuman Slav.

Simha knew none of this. At the time, he was focused on helping strangers by delivering money on his rounds through the city. Zuckerman was in charge of collecting the funds from Home Army intermediaries who retrieved the parachuted cash drops. Some came from Jewish sources in Switzerland and America and were in foreign currency—dollars, pounds, and Swiss francs—which led to disputes with the Home Army over exchange rates. Isaac bitterly complained to Captain Wolinski that he was being shortchanged in many of the transactions. Wolinski himself was above reproach: He personally headed a cell that was sheltering 280 Jews. But Home Army couriers did appear to be taking a very large cut for smuggling the cash into Poland, and the currency was often delivered late. Simha was not privy to these heated negotiations. "I can testify only that a lot of money did arrive," he noted.

Carrying such vast sums posed problems of its own. The Blue Police were notoriously corrupt. The currency traders who hung around Saxon Gardens or across from Central Station were often on Gestapo payrolls. Greasers and common thieves killed for far less than Zuckerman regularly had strapped to his chest. This was why Ratheiser, armed with two pistols and a grenade, shadowed him wherever he went. "I was a bodyguard. And a couple of times it was a good thing [for Zuckerman] that I was there."

Zivia Lubetkin, who did much of the accounting—the only way she could be helpful to the ZOB while in enforced seclusion—was scrupulous about not wasting the precious funds. The equivalent of millions of dollars passed through Isaac's hands during the course of the war. In just one October 1943 cable to London, he acknowledges receipt of $10,000 and £10,000, complaining that he was still awaiting the promised delivery of another $15,000 and £9,000. Isaac and Zivia were keenly aware that the money was not intended for their personal consumption. Some of it had to be spent on clothes for couriers like Simha. But this was a necessity to ensure their cover. For themselves, they kept only a minimal allowance for food. "The only luxury on the menu was a glass of vodka," Simha recalled. "And we insisted firmly on that."

CHAPTER 36

ZIVIA GETS HER GUN

On April 19, 1944, Isaac, Simha, Zivia, Mark Edelman, Tuvia Borzykowski, and other ZOB leaders gathered at an apartment on Forestry Boulevard. The second-floor safe house had been rented by Marisa Sawicka, their Gentile patron saint. It had a false wall built of brick and plaster and stood next to a Protestant church one block east of the old Main Shops District, where not a single building remained standing.

In the year since the Ghetto Uprising, the Germans had made no effort to clean up the demolished Jewish district. It had been left a heap of rubble stretching as far as the eye could see, a permanent reminder to Varsovians of the price of resistance. Here and there a church steeple rose from the ruins, undamaged, like a solitary monument to Nazi religious restraint.

In the rest of the city, church bells pealed in anticipation of the Easter holiday. The weather had warmed after the brutal winter, and buds were forming on the chestnut trees in the Saxon Gardens and Count Krasinski Park, the former playgrounds of generations of Jewish children. Seeds from the parks were carried by birds and winds into the nearby Ghetto, where Nature had begun her own reclamation project. Weeds were sprouting in the rubble of the Brushmakers District, while farther west, at the far end of the former Ghetto, saplings were already poking through the untended graves of the abandoned Jewish cemetery. These would eventually grow into a dense, dark forest.

The ZOB's remaining leaders, on that first anniversary of the Rising, gathered to pay tribute to the dead and raise a toast to Mordechai Anielewicz and all their other fallen comrades. How many had died no one knew for sure. Of the original five hundred ZOB members, probably no more than thirty were left in Warsaw. A few were still fighting in the Wyszkow forest near the Bug River. Several had left to lead cells in other towns. What was certain was that the ZOB's ranks had been severely thinned. Mere survival, a tightrope balance of treachery and trust, had preoccupied ZOB commanders for much of the past year. But in the spring and early summer of 1944, their thoughts turned once more to armed rebellion.

The war was now going very badly for the Germans, so badly that, for the first time since September 1939, Boruch Spiegel became convinced that Hitler was going to lose. Spiegel devoured news reports from distant fronts. He eagerly snatched every issue of the *Information Bulletin,* the Home Army's press organ, that his host, Joseph Pera, brought home. The paper was distributed almost openly in May 1944. Its illicit print run had reached an astounding forty-seven thousand copies a day, a circulation that exceeded that of some legitimate publications, signaling that the Gestapo was losing its iron hold on the Polish capital.

There were other, even more telling signs. In mid-May, German bureaucrats were issued handguns after a wave of assassination attempts. At airfields around the capital, Junker bombers began to explode mysteriously. In the city center, several police stations were attacked in broad daylight. Desertions began to plague the Polish Blue Police. After the Red Army pushed the Wehrmacht to the fringes of eastern Poland, nervous cops started turning in their uniforms or offering to betray their German masters. The hated Volksdeutsche also underwent a dramatic transformation. Their haughty demeanor began to change perceptibly in late May 1944, when, after six months and nearly a hundred thousand Allied casualties, Polish troops under General Anders finally took the Italian redoubt of Monte Cassino, paving the way for U.S. forces to conquer Rome.

By June, the occupiers themselves were beginning to show signs of fear. After the Allies landed in Normandy, German patrols no longer ventured into Old Town, the historic warren of narrow, winding streets perfectly suited to ambushes. Two weeks later, following the Soviet rout of several Wehrmacht armored divisions in Belarus, Warsaw's black market was flooded with military goods. Demoralized German soldiers were selling guns, grenades, truckloads of brand-new parachutes and blankets, and, in some cases, the trucks themselves. "In the street markets," a Home Army officer cabled London, "German military nurses are selling openly watches and cigarette cases that they purloined from wounded soldiers in field hospitals."

Amid all these developments, Simha raced from Home Army safe house to People's Army hideout to catch the latest reports from the BBC and Radio Moscow. The ZOB had no radio, so Mark Edelman kept dispatching Simha on news-gathering errands. After being cooped up indoors for over a year, Mark wanted to know everything: the mood on the streets, the attitude of the Underground, the price of goods, the sight of retreating troops, the sense of impending doom sweeping the German-only parts of town, where civilian officials scurried to their cars, looking over their shoulders for the Home Army hit squads that had begun to assassinate Nazi functionaries.

By July, the Soviets were in Vilna and Lvov, and moving vans had become a regular sight outside the luxurious apartment buildings flanking the Royal Gardens in the German-only district. Nazi officials began selling gold, jewels, diamonds, and looted art at steeply discounted prices. Stories circulated about the Gestapo executing German deserters, and of drunken SS officers going on shooting sprees, indiscriminately firing on crowds or tramcars full of passengers to vent their sodden frustration. German morale sank further when headlines in the July 21, 1944, edition of the *New Warsaw Courier,* the General Government's propaganda sheet, carried the shocking news of an UNSUCCESSFUL ATTEMPT ON ADOLF HITLER'S LIFE. Wehrmacht officers had tried to kill the Führer!

By then, the Red Army had crossed the Bug River and was less than thirty miles from Warsaw. The advancing Soviets established a political bridgehead in the castle town of Lublin, the former Hasidic stronghold where Joe Osnos had spent the night during his September 1939 flight. A Polish Committee for National Liberation had been formed there, a Soviet puppet government in waiting, staffed with the few Polish Communists the NKVD could find in Moscow. They were so few because Stalin had killed them all during one of his periodic purges, the murderous secret police campaigns that murdered millions, including Janine Mortkowicz's cousin Max Horowitz, who had co-founded the Polish Worker's Party. "He played the great socialist with our bourgeois money," Janine used to complain.

In radio broadcasts, the Polish Committee for National Liberation already was calling the London government in exile a "usurper" and appealing for a popular revolt against both German and Polish fascists. "People of the Capital! To Arms!" it exhorted. "Assist the Red Army in their crossing of the Vistula. Send them information. Show them the way."

In Warsaw, meanwhile, the situation deteriorated daily. Column after column of dirty, bedraggled Wehrmacht units were shuffling across the bridges over the Vistula, retreating from the east. They looked nothing like the indestructible warriors who had paraded through the city five years earlier with their gleaming helmets and bayonets and expressions of vicious arrogance. They were almost a pathetic sight now, bandaged and limping, covered in dust and mud, supporting one another, their heads hanging. Seeing them fill the length of Jerusalem Boulevard, a once mighty army pitifully reduced, sent the terrified Volksdeutsche panicking and packing. The General Government had the same reaction. Colonial administrators started evacuating nonessential personnel and the families of all officials. Trucks and big black BMW sedans roared through the streets, all heading westward.

Twenty thousand troops still remained in Warsaw, however, fortified by tanks and heavy-machine-gun posts hastily positioned at critical intersections. The soldiers were frightened and trigger-happy. Their nerves were so frayed that patrols on Marshall Street shot at the slightest provocation: A car backfiring could result in an entire square being riddled with bullets. It was usually the elderly, since they were not spry enough to leap for cover, who fell victim to these panicked outbursts. Even so, people began staying indoors, preparing shelters in their basements.

At Boruch Spiegel's apartment, Sergeant Joseph Pera and his twenty-year-old son, Mietek, who was also in the Home Army, disappeared for lengthy periods of time, returning well after curfew, and sometimes staying out all night. Mietek Pera, code name Frenchy, was in fact ferrying Sten guns from Home Army arms caches across the Vistula in a small rowboat under the cover of darkness. Though Boruch was not aware of the details, it was obvious that his hosts were plotting something. An atmosphere of pent-up anticipation gripped the Polish capital. Something big was about to happen. Everyone, including the Germans, could sense it.

On the muggy afternoon of August 1, 1944, the city of Warsaw erupted. At precisely 5 P.M., the height of the evening rush hour, sirens and church bells rang throughout the capital, followed moments later by the sound of a thousand guns. From windows and doorways and alleys and cellars, partisans suddenly starting shooting at anything in a German uniform. Bullets riddled Nazi administrative offices and police stations. Checkpoints and guard huts were struck. Vehicles carrying officers careened wildly and smashed into lampposts or crashed through storefronts. "In the twinkling of an eye, the remaining civilians disappeared from the street," one witness recalled. "All traffic ceased. From the entrances of houses, our partisans streamed out and rushed to the attack. In fifteen minutes an entire city of a million inhabitants was engulfed in the fight."

Nearly forty thousand Home Army combatants had risen up, striking simultaneously in virtually every Warsaw neighborhood. Hundreds of Jews, including Boruch, took part in the fighting. But Isaac, Zivia, Simha, and Mark did not. The ZOB leadership had been completely surprised by the Warsaw Uprising. Zuckerman was furious and his pride was seriously wounded. Thousands of people must have known about the rebellion. The logistics alone would have required weeks of intense preparation: unearthing weapons and surreptitiously transporting tons of ammunition from caches, coordinating tactics and identifying points of assault, arranging and provisioning medical teams, storing food and water, securing channels of communication—everything that the ZOB itself had done a year earlier, but this time on a scale a hundred times greater. And still, despite the colossal size of the undertaking, Isaac had not gotten wind of Operation Tempest, the code name for the revolt. Captain Wolinski, whom he trusted, whom he considered his friend, had not taken him into his confidence. That stung Isaac worse than a betrayal. Once more, in his mind, the Home Army had let him down.

Zuckerman's contacts in the People's Army had not breathed a word about the rising either, because the Communists had also not known about Operation Tempest. The Home Army intentionally kept its rival in the dark. "Most Poles saw the [People's Army] as phraseologists or as aliens," Isaac later commented, or worse, as "Moscow's lackeys." Their exclusion was intentional. "It was obvious to us that the insurrection had twin goals," Zivia Lubetkin elaborated. "Militarily it was against the Germans. Politically it was against the Soviet Union." Varsovians had no intention of swapping occupiers. They wanted to ensure that before the Red Army crossed the Vistula, the Polish capital had already liberated itself; that it had its own armed militia in place and a functioning government—all the trappings of de facto sovereignty.

These political machinations concerned Isaac and Zivia less than the immediate dilemma now facing the ZOB. There was no question that the Jews would fight. They had weapons and experience in guerrilla warfare. For Isaac personally, it was imperative that he take up arms. Fate had precluded his participation in the Ghetto Uprising, a fact that haunted him even as he assumed leadership of the ZOB following Anielewicz's death. Though he never said so publicly, he may have felt that being sidelined during the revolt diminished him in the eyes of his colleagues. So he was doubly anxious to prove himself. The issue facing him now was whether to join the ranks of the Home Army or the People's Army.

It was not an easy decision. Nor did Isaac have a lot of time to make it. Warsaw, by the second day of fighting, was devolving into a patchwork of German and rebel-held territory. Some parts of the city had quickly fallen into Home Army hands. Within a few hours, most streets had been sealed off: Trams had been toppled and roads ripped up to form makeshift barricades, along which motley rebel crews—some wearing World War I uniforms, others in civilian garb—peppered German positions with an equally unorthodox assortment of weapons: Sten guns, Mausers, Enfield rifles, Soviet surplus pistols, and crudely welded homemade machine guns. The insurgents knocked out fifty tanks, seizing a huge munitions warehouse, the main power station, and the financial district. The Polish flag once again flew atop the Prudential Life Insurance Building, Warsaw's tallest tower. But the price of these victories was high: In the first twenty-four hours of combat, the Home Army lost two thousand men, while the Wehrmacht's losses were estimated at five hundred soldiers. The Germans were holding key sectors firmly, particularly in the western parts of the city, where they fought fiercely to control the critical highways that they would need either to escape or to get reinforcements into the capital.

Up to this point, Isaac had not needed to choose between the rival Polish Undergrounds. He played a delicate and discreet double game, working with both. "The People's Army knew of our contacts with the Home Army," Simha Ratheiser recalled, "whereas the Home Army was not supposed to know that we also dealt with the People's Army." Now Zuckerman was forced to take sides, because his ZOB unit was too small to fight on its own. It would have to merge into an existing formation, formally entering a hierarchical military structure.

Numerically, the Home Army had an incomparable advantage. Its forces outnumbered the People's Army by a factor of fifty to one. The ZOB's few dozen remaining fighters thus hardly tipped the scales, which was perhaps why no one bothered to inform Isaac of the uprising in advance. There was also the matter of Zuckerman's bruised ego. His feelings were plainly hurt by the conspiratorial snub. What's more, the Home Army had never offered him a commission, unlike the People's Army, which had bestowed on him the rank of major. Isaac, like many handsome and charismatic leaders, was not above vanity. He had a surprisingly thin skin and easily took umbrage at perceived slights. Nonetheless, he swallowed his pride because joining the much bigger and better organized Home Army made the most sense from a military point of view. Isaac called Simha Ratheiser, and the two rushed over to Old Town on August 2 in the torrential rain to offer the Home Army the ZOB's services. "They put me off with hemming and hawing."

For Isaac, it was the last straw. He and Simha marched straight to the People's Army's makeshift headquarters. It was easy to find, Ratheiser recalled, because of the big red flag. It fluttered over an ancient mustard-colored edifice, just outside the medieval brick battlements of the famous Barbakan tower gate. Today, a brass plaque on the building informs visitors that double Nobel laureate Marie Curie had once lived there. Zuckerman saluted the guard, went inside, and repeated his offer. To his shock, the Communists also declined. "It would be too great a historical responsibility to send the few survivors of the Ghetto Uprising back to war," Zuckerman was informed. "We have to keep them in a museum to protect them." At this Isaac burst out laughing. Try telling that to his wife or to Mark Edelman, he quipped. Both, after their yearlong seclusion, had had enough of being locked up like museum pieces.

Indeed, Edelman had rushed outside almost as soon as he heard the first shots of the uprising. He felt euphoric, as if he had just been released from jail, and he ran straight over to Iron Street to visit his fellow Bundist prisoners Boruch Spiegel and Chaika Belchatowska. They had not seen one another since the May 1943 sewer rescue. Even though their safe houses were only ten minutes apart, they had not been permitted to interact while in hiding. They stayed up all night talking, catching up, trying to decide what to do next. Boruch wanted to join Sergeant Pera's Home Army platoon. Edelman wanted the ZOB to form its own unit. Chaika just wanted to be a master of her own destiny after being locked away for so long, utterly reliant on others. "Finally we can start living again," she sighed in relief.

The heady sensation proved fleeting. The next morning, as explosions reverberated throughout Warsaw, Mark set out for Forestry Boulevard, four blocks north. He got within a few hundred yards of his safe house before he was pinned down by fire. Ukrainian SS auxiliaries from nearby Peacock Prison had cut off his path. "I hid in a store that was burning. Its ceiling looked like it was going to collapse." Edelman waited for ten excruciating minutes inside the flaming shop before leaping back out into the street. Shots ricocheted around his feet as he dived through a courtyard gate. Cutting through back alleys, where he knew the Ukrainians were unlikely to follow, Mark ran headlong into a Home Army patrol. His relief turned into horror when he saw that they, too, had their guns trained on him. They surrounded him, yelling, "Jew, you set the building on fire. You're a German spy." Edelman was stunned at the absurdity of their accusation. While they debated whether to execute him on the spot, Mark wrestled himself free and bolted. His captors gave chase. Edelman and his pursuers ran into another Home Army unit, this one with officers. There was a long discussion among the officers and they eventually let Mark go.

Shaken, he returned to Marisa Sawicki's safe house just as Isaac Zuckerman and Simha Ratheiser were coming back from their frustrating negotiations in Old Town. A representative of the Council to Aid Jews was also there, delivering $40,000 in U.S. currency and a warning for the ZOB. His name was Alexander Kaminski, and he was the editor in chief of the Home Army's *Information Bulletin*. Kaminski was sympathetic to the Jewish Underground, stemming from his prewar association with the Bund. Under his editorship, the *Information Bulletin* had never printed a single anti-Semitic statement, and the paper had often encouraged its readers to assist Jewish refugees. The ZOB, Kaminski now warned, should not join the Home Army. Jews would not be safe in its newly expanded ranks.

The reason had to do with rebel realpolitik. In anticipation of the uprising, the Home Army had struck a deal with the National Armed Forces, the far-right anti-Semitic organization that until then had been ostracized by the mainstream Polish Resistance. The two factions agreed to fight under the same banner on the condition that the National Armed Forces renounce its quasi-fascist leanings. Only part of the right-wing group's members had accepted the terms. Yet to liberal Home Army officers like Kaminski (a future Righteous Gentile), the merger represented a pact with the devil, a desperate gambit to help even out the overwhelming odds against dislodging the Wehrmacht and then fending off the Red Army. The trade-off boiled down to legitimacy in exchange for firepower. The pariah National Armed Forces, with 72,439 members nationwide, had significant stores of weapons, which the Home Army desperately needed. Only one in ten Home Army soldiers was properly armed. Worse still, the Gestapo had seized a stockpile of 78,000 grenades during a raid on an underground explosives plant just three weeks earlier. One hundred and seventy flamethrowers had also been lost in that July raid. The far right's arsenal could potentially tip the scales toward the rebel cause. The ZOB's contribution of twenty fighters, on the other hand, would make no difference whatsoever, other than possibly disrupting the fragile new alliance. In the cold calculus of war, the welfare of Warsaw's few remaining Jews had not even entered the equation.

Already, Kaminski said, some Jews had been killed by joint National Armed Forces–Home Army units under the dubious pretext that the Jewish victims were Volksdeutsche. The only choice for the ZOB, Kaminski advised, was to join the People's Army.

Under different circumstances, Edelman, as an anticommunist Bundist, would have recoiled at the thought. But now he didn't hesitate. "I wasn't going to fight with people trying to kill me."

On August 3, 1944, the ZOB formally became the third platoon of the People's Army Second Brigade. The People's Army took them in largely out of numerical necessity. The tiny Communist faction could not afford to reject volunteers. Isaac, Zivia, Mark, Simha, Tuvia Borzykowski, and a dozen other veterans of the Ghetto Uprising were assigned to man barricades on Bridge Street. This was one of the most strategically important arteries in Old Town, a position heavily defended by both rebel forces and the Wehrmacht. Bridge Street sloped down the escarpment along Old Town's crenellated battlements toward the Vistula, where it connected to the river-spanning viaduct from which it took its name. For the Germans, this was a vital crossing that needed to be held at all costs to prevent Soviet tanks from entering Warsaw. The street itself was unusually wide by the standards of the cramped historic district. It was cobblestoned and lined with three- and four-story Gothic townhouses, each intricately decorated with pastel murals and glass mosaics depicting folk tales. A creamy baroque cathedral crowned the hill where Bridge Street merged into ancient Freta Street at the foot of the Barbakan tower, linking the walled quarter with New Town, its seventeenth-century suburb.

Bridge Street was one of those natural urban choke points that leave no room for maneuvering and give adversaries no alternative but to ram straight through one another. At its foot, where it abutted the Vistula, the Germans had dug in Tiger II tanks, 68-ton behemoths that were almost twice the size of American Shermans, with nearly twice the armor and twice the firepower. The demarcation line was the forward German position, a stately burgundy edifice that became known as the Red House. It was about a hundred yards from the rebel line, a whitewashed theater dubbed the White House. A barricade was excavated there, a deep incision that acted as an antitank trench. Different units took turns manning it, exchanging fire with German machine gun nests. Isaac's group was on duty for twenty hours at a time before returning to Old Town to rest for a day. As shifts changed, the weapons stayed on the barricade. Mark Edelman remembered how Zivia Lubetkin struggled with the oversized rifle she was lent—"It was twice her size." But she refused to relinquish it. The shortage of rifles was so acute that two or three combatants had to share each gun. The Home Army had only one thousand rifles in all of Warsaw, and Isaac suddenly understood why the Polish Resistance leaders had been so stingy about arming the ZOB in 1943. At the time, he had ascribed the parsimony to anti-Semitism. Now he recognized that the poverty Captain Wolinski had pleaded was very real.

While clashes flared across the rest of the city, with buildings, blocks, and entire districts changing hands daily, a deadlock evolved on Bridge Street. The two sides hurled insults at each other more often than grenades, and neither appeared anxious to leave their defensive fortifications. Ironically, it was safer on the ZOB front line than in the rear, because the barricade was too close to the Tiger tanks for German artillery to shell. Farther up the hill, Old Town was mercilessly pounded by canons and strafed by Messerschmitt fighter planes. This was where most people died, crushed by collapsing medieval buildings or buried alive in cellars. The ZOB unit had enough experience with German tactics to know it should stay away from old stone structures. Fighting alongside the Home Army proved less hazardous than Zuckerman had feared. "As we went from the barricade to the rear and back, all the Gentiles knew that this was a Jewish unit," he later recalled. "We didn't feel a trace of anti-Semitism."

On the Bridge Street barricade, the fighting differed from the bat tles the ZOB had experienced in the Ghetto. It was more akin to the trench warfare of World War I. The Wehrmacht garrison made no attempt to attack, because its primary focus was defending the bridge to Praga. The Germans kept the insurgents at bay with snipers, machine gun bursts, and the occasional mortars while keeping a lookout for the Soviet T-34 tanks that were expected to storm Praga from the east. The Red Army, however, was nowhere to be seen. After racing through Ukraine and much of Poland, the Soviet offensive mysteriously ground to a halt only miles outside the Polish capital. Marshal Konstantin Rokossovsky said his eight hundred thousand troops were exhausted. Supply lines had been stretched too thin by the rapid advance. His armored divisions, which enjoyed a seven-to-one numerical advantage over the retreating Germans, needed a breather.

Historians debate whether the ill-timed pause was intentional. Some say Stalin decided to let Hitler do his dirty work by giving the Germans time to wipe out the Home Army. And even if the Soviets did not intentionally double-cross the Poles by inciting them to revolt and then sitting on the sidelines as the Germans killed them off, the suspended Soviet campaign had dramatic consequences for the Uprising. The revolt was supposed to last a few days before the Red Army rolled in. The planners of Operation Tempest, General Bor and Colonel Monter, both career military men, had budgeted ammunition and supplies for a brief battle. They expected the Germans to retreat, ceding the Polish capital in order to concentrate their defenses around Berlin. But Bor and Monter had not counted on Stalin's sudden reluctance to push forward, or on Hilter's resolve with regard to Warsaw.

They should have known better. The Führer had always hated Warsaw. He made no secret of his contempt for the Polish capital, its Russified architecture, its slovenly Jews, its unruly horde of Slavic inhabitants. His rage was only magnified by the recent attempt on his life by his own officers. In Berlin, Jürgen Stroop was stringing up hundreds of Wehrmacht officers with piano wire to uncover the depth of German army disloyalty while his boss, Heinrich Himmler, was demanding that Warsaw be erased from European maps. "Mein Führer," the SS chief pleaded, "the action of the Poles is a blessing. We shall finish them off. Warsaw will be liquidated and this city . . . that has blocked our path to the east for seven hundred years, ever since the first battle of Tannenberg, will have ceased to exist." The Reichsführer was not speaking figuratively. "No prisoners to be taken," he subsequently instructed his generals. "Every inhabitant to be killed, every single house to be blown up and burned." Warsaw dared to defy his beloved Führer; for that Himmler intended to wipe if off the face of the earth.

BOOK FIVE

*Our policy in the East is bankrupt, and we are erecting
a final memorial to it with the destruction of Warsaw.*

—CAPTAIN WILM HOSENFELD,
the German officer who saved
Jewish musician Wladyslaw Szpilman,
portrayed by Adrian Brody in
the Oscar-winning film *The Pianist*

CHAPTER 37

SIMHA'S SECOND
SEWER RESCUE

On August 5, 1944, a Saturday, fifty thousand German troops poured into Warsaw. They were spearheaded by the dregs of the SS, the most brutal and least disciplined of the auxiliary forces that Himmler managed to recruit during the Wehrmacht's conquest of the Soviet Union: the infamous RONA Brigade from the renegade Russian National Liberation Army. The reinforcements also included two Cossack battalions; an Azerbaijani regiment of irregulars; the Oriental Muslim Regiment, comprised of Kazaks and recruits from the Caucasus; the dreaded Vlassov Division of Russians and Ukrainians, many of whom had served in the notorious *Einsatzgruppen* Holocaust killing squads; and, perhaps worst of all, the Dirlewanger Commando Battalion, a penal unit composed of convicted murderers and rapists who had been released from German jails.

These special counterinsurgency units were supported by the regular Waffen-SS, a Wehrmacht Panzer division, Luftwaffe guard regiments (both in the air and on the ground), and an artillery brigade redeployed from Russian lines "thanks to the improved situation" caused by Marshal Rokossovsky's unexpected pause. They struck, as in 1939, from the west, sweeping into the industrial neighborhoods of Ochota and Wola, on the other side of Warsaw from the ZOB's relatively tranquil position near the banks of the Vistula. It was a campaign rarely seen in the annals of modern warfare. The SS all but ignored the Home Army defenders and made straight for the civilian population of the two unfortunate districts. That Saturday they murdered twenty thousand residents in Wola alone. Over the next few days, they slaughtered at least thirty-five thousand and perhaps as many as fifty thousand people in an orgy of bloodletting so violent that Zuckerman remarked "If I changed the Polish names, it would sound like a Jewish story."

At 10 A.M. on August 5, 1944, one witness later testified to a Polish war crimes tribunal, a detachment of SS men and Ukrainian irregulars entered his building. "They drove us from the cellars and brought us near the Sowinski Park. They shot at us when we passed. My wife was killed on the spot; our child was wounded and cried for his mother. Soon a Ukrainian approached and killed my two-year-old child like a dog; then he approached me together with some Germans and stood on my chest to see whether I was alive or not. I lay thus from 10 A.M. until 9 P.M. pretending to be dead. During that time I saw further groups being driven out and shot near the place where I lay. The huge heap of corpses grew still bigger. Those who gave any sign of life were shot. I was buried under other corpses and nearly suffocated. The executions lasted until 5 P.M."

Similar massacres were carried out in virtually every block. "Between 11 and 12 noon," another woman later testified, "the Germans ordered all of us to get out, and marched us to Wolska Street. This march was carried out in dreadful haste and panic. My husband was absent, taking an active part in the Rising, and I was alone with my three children, aged 4, 6, and 12, and in the last month of pregnancy. I delayed my departure, hoping they would allow me to remain, and left the cellar at the very last moment. All the inhabitants of our house had already been escorted to the 'Ursus' [tractor factory] works in Wolska Street. I went alone, accompanied only by my three children. It was difficult to pass, the road being full of wire, cable, remains of barricades, corpses, and rubble. Houses were burning on both sides of the street; I reached the 'Ursus' works with great difficulty. Shots, cries, supplications and groans could be heard from the factory yard. The people who stood at the entrance were led, no, pushed in, not all at once but in groups of 20. A boy of twelve, seeing the bodies of his parents and of his little brother through the half-open entrance door, fell in a fit and began to shriek. The Germans and Vlassov's [Ukrainian] men beat him and pushed him back, while he was endeavouring to get inside. He called for his father and his mother. We all knew what awaited us here. I came last and kept in the background, continuing to let the others pass, in the hope that they would not kill a pregnant woman, but I was driven in with the last lot. In the yard I saw heaps of corpses 3 feet high, in several places. The whole right and left side of the big yard was strewn with bodies. We were led through the second yard. There were about 20 people in our group, mostly children of 10 to 12. There were children without parents, and also a paralyzed old woman whose son-in-law had been carrying her all the time on his back. At her side was her daughter with two children of 4 and 7. They were all killed. The old woman was literally killed on her son-in-law's back, and he along with her. We were called out in groups of four and led to the end of the second yard to a pile of bodies. When the four reached this point, the Germans shot them through the backs of their heads with revolvers. The victims fell on the heap, and others came. Seeing what was to be their fate, some attempted to escape; they cried, begged, and prayed for mercy. I was in the last group of four. I begged the Vlassov's men around me to save me and the children, and they asked if I had anything with which to buy my life. I had a large amount of gold with me and gave it them. They took it all and wanted to lead me away, but the German supervising the execution would not allow them to do so, and when I begged him to let me go he pushed me off, shouting 'Quicker!' I fell when he pushed me. He also hit and pushed my elder boy, shouting 'Hurry up, you Polish bandit.' Thus I came to the place of execution, in the last group of four, with my three children. I held my two younger children by one hand, and my elder boy by the other. The children were crying and praying. My elder son, seeing the mass of bodies, cried out: 'They are going to kill us' and called for his father. The first shot hit him, the second me; the next two killed my two younger children. I fell on my right side. The shot was not fatal. The bullet penetrated the back of my head from the right side and went out through my cheek. I spat out several teeth; I felt the left side of my body growing numb, but I was still conscious and saw everything that was going on around me."

Boruch Spiegel experienced the full fury of the SS as the Nazis pushed eastward from Wola into the city center. He had gotten separated from the ZOB and had joined Sergeant Pera's unit, which was supposed to be fighting in the 6th District, third region, as platoon number 693. That was in Praga. But amid the chaos and confusion, the platoon ended up on Sienna Street, in what had once been the most elegant avenue in the southern, most prosperous part of the former Ghetto. The entire area was now unrecognizable, a sea of flames and rubble, after intensive German shelling. As for Pera's unit, it, too, had been transformed. It had become a disorganized jumble of Jews, Gentiles, Home Army, and People's Army combatants and fighters from the quasi-fascist National Armed Forces. They were pitted against the RONA Brigade, the rogue Russian SS division commanded by Miechislav Kaminski, whose brutality had already become legendary. Even hardened Gestapo officers were repulsed by the excesses of his troops, half of whom had deserted to form their own criminal bands, intent on rape and pillage. Pera was fatally wounded in the battle with the Russian SS, but the Poles held their ground because Boruch and the other defenders were not merely fighting for their lives. They knew that defeat meant death for their wives and children, their parents and neighbors. By then it was evident that the Warsaw Uprising could end only in victory or complete destruction. That was a powerful motivator.

The savage German counteroffensive finally reached the ZOB barricade in Old Town on August 19, 1944. The huge Tiger tanks that had been pointing their turrets across the river at the phantom Soviet menace swiveled around to face the insurgents. The smell of diesel filled the air as their engines roared to life, and with a shudder that scattered clouds of accumulated dust, they lurched forward. Bridge Street trembled with the clatter of steel on cobblestone as the 68-ton monsters bore down on the Jewish and Gentile defenders. "To the credit of the Poles," Zuckerman recalled, "they were brave people who stuck to their guns. I didn't see any panic or running away."

Only one boy, Mark Edelman remembered, a twelve-year-old courier, succumbed to fear and bolted. He was shot by a People's Army officer. But no one had time to be stunned or outraged. The Tigers were too close. They opened fire with their heavy machine guns, their massive treads now only yards away from Isaac, Zivia, Simha, and Mark. "I have been scared many times in my life," Isaac later wrote. "But those moments on the barricade were beyond fear."

By the end of August 1944, the Uprising death toll exceeded one hundred thousand. With each passing day, the Home Army's *Information Bulletin* was receiving over one thousand new missing persons reports, and the Germans were stepping up their artillery barrages. To punish the Polish capital, Himmler ordered the deployment of one of the biggest howitzers ever built, a locomotive-drawn mammoth whose seven-foot-long shells could take out an entire city block.

The Home Army had long run out of bullets by then, and it was only thanks to two million rounds of ammunition airlifted to Warsaw by converted RAF bombers that pockets of resistance were managing to hold out. Most of the city—or what was left of it—was back in German hands, a lunar landscape of craters and mangled rubble, the Warsaw Ghetto writ large. Fires raged uncontrollably, and the heat they generated created microclimates of howling winds and flaming dust devils that could set a person ablaze. "Cinders were flying everywhere. You couldn't see the sun for all the ashes," one witness recalled. "I had to urinate on my handkerchief and cover [my wife's] head with it to keep her hair from burning."

The ZOB's $40,000 had gone up in flames in the conflagration, which spread unchecked because all the capital's water mains burst during the daily German bombardments. The Luftwaffe flew sorties every half hour, pinning hundreds of thousands of civilians down in shelters. Joanna Mortkowicz-Olczak's convent was flattened, as were a number of houses of worship, including the Holy Sacrament Monastery in New Town, where a thousand people who had taken shelter all perished. Fortunately, Joanna and the other girls in her convent had been safely evacuated to the countryside a few days prior to the Rising by Sister Wanda, their well-connected Mother Superior. Joanna's mother and grandmother, however, were trapped in a cellar on Mokotow Street, in the middle of the target zone, where they would remain with virtually no food or water for six weeks.

While Stuka dive-bombers pummeled the city during the day, British B-24 Liberators flew their vital supply missions at night, aiming their precious loads of Sten guns and grenades, Spam and Philip Morris cigarettes at the dwindling dark spots that indicated rebel territory in the sea of flames drowning Eastern Europe's biggest metropolis. The largest of these drop zones were the Jewish cemetery and the area around the landmark Prudential Life Insurance skyscraper in Napoleon Square. Unfortunately, more than half of the green six-foot-long supply canisters dropped by the RAF fell into German-controlled sectors. Some of the parachutes got tangled on church spires and had to be cut down. Others touched down in so-called Swiss zones, no-man's-lands where Germans would also try to retrieve them, anxious to get at the cigarettes and Hershey bars. The Wehrmacht, meanwhile, lit up the sky with powerful spotlights and peppered the low-flying B-24s with AA antiaircraft batteries. One stricken plane came screaming down over Zivia and Isaac's heads near Bridge Street, erupting in a fireball on the banks of the Vistula.

Zuckerman and Lubetkin were still alive, and Old Town, after nearly a month of shelling, still held. But gunboats, two armored trains, 75 mm field guns, a tank battalion, and several howitzer batteries were raining hell on the one-square-mile district. Ten SS infantry battalions were closing in from the west, while the Tiger tanks had sealed off the Vistula corridor. Gradually the two German forces were closing in on the five thousand defenders caught in the middle. As the gap narrowed, the fighting became increasingly ferocious, more and more reminiscent of the street battles of Stalingrad. "A single house could change hands several times a day," Mark Edelman recalled, and sometimes territory was contested floor by floor, room by room in hand-to-hand combat. German losses during the latest push exceeded

1,570 men, but the tide was slowly and inexorably turning against the rebels. The historic district was now completely surrounded by enemy forces, cut off from food and water. Its 130,000 trapped residents, most of whom were civilians, were starving. People traded jewelry and fur coats for loaves of bread, and a kilo of butter soared in cost to a staggering 2,400 zlotys, equivalent to several years of the average pre-war salary.

The lack of medical supplies was also becoming dire, condemning the estimated 7,500 seriously wounded combatants and civilians in the besieged Old Quarter to a slow and painful death. In makeshift hospital wards in dark brick cellars built during the late Middle Ages, the stench of gangrene was overwhelming. Outside, scattered amid the ruins of Gothic arches and baroque altars, innumerable corpses were putrefying in the summer heat. The dead included the People's Army's entire command staff, leaving Isaac Zuckerman as a ranking officer of the four-hundred-strong organization. Isaac had narrowly escaped the showdown with the Tiger tanks, retreating to higher ground after his position on the barricade had been overrun. It was now up to him to coordinate an emergency evacuation plan with the Home Army. The rival rebel groups had buried the hatchet during the Rising. The People's Army had agreed to subordinate itself to the larger London-backed force, and the feared anti-Semitic attacks had not materialized. In fact, "the opposite was true," Zuckerman found. "The Home Army showed us camaraderie." Zivia Lubetkin was also pleasantly surprised. "I have to say that everyone, including the civilians, treated us cordially."

Nonetheless, it was evident to all that the ancient quarter could not hold out much longer. The insurgents were losing ground and up to three hundred fighters a day. The few mechanized vehicles they possessed—so-called Bear Cubs, Chevrolet Suburbans retrofitted with camouflage-painted steel plates to form homemade armored personnel carriers—had proven ineffective in the narrow maze of winding streets. All were destroyed. The Germans had also adapted their war machines to fit Old Town's cramped fighting conditions, but with far greater success than the rebels. To penetrate trenches, the Germans started using Goliaths—miniature remote-controlled tanks that maneuvered 500-kilogram explosive charges into tight corners and defensive ditches. To reach insurgents hiding on the top floors and rooftops of townhouses, they deployed specially constructed mine throwers that became known as "Bellowing Cows" for the panic-inducing sound of the phosphorus bomblets they flung through windows and onto balconies. "The carved oak beams in houses burned like matchsticks," one witness recalled. "The old buildings collapsed like houses of cards, burying those who had sought shelter in their cellars. They soon became the communal graves of thousands of people who were buried alive."

By the last week of August, Old Town was burning without pause. The area under rebel control was reduced to the size of about five football fields. The only food left was tinned tongue and wine. Fighters were down to their last rounds. "It became clear that no one was going to survive much longer," Simha Ratheiser recalled. The defenders had to find a way to rejoin Home Army formations in other parts of the city. Fighting their way out was impossible. German forces were too strong. Sewers offered the only viable escape route.

Since the ZOB had gained invaluable experience navigating subterranean passages during the Ghetto revolt, Simha was tapped to help chart a course through the sewage canals. "I was placed in charge of a unit of mainly sergeants and officers who had served in the Polish Army, all of them much older than me," he recalled. Simha's team plotted a route north to Jolie Bord, which was still a Home Army stronghold. This meant traversing more than a mile of booby-trapped sewer pipes, all under German-held territory, with trip wires, dams, and SS troops perched over manholes, ready to drop concussion grenades. Such an arduous trek was possible for only the fittest combatants. The wounded, the civilians, and the bulk of the Old Town rebel forces would go through a shorter set of canals, heading southeast to Midtown, near the former Ghetto, which was much closer but under heavier German assault. Working feverishly, Simha's team fixed guide ropes and disabled booby traps, clearing blockages along the labyrinth of tunnels, some of which were wide enough to drive a horse cart through, others so narrow that Simha had to crawl on his hands and knees, immersed to his neck in human excrement. He used chalk arrows to mark the way, as he had done in May 1943.

The mass escape started at midnight on September 1, 1944. For

ZOB members, descending into the sewers was a familiar sensation. "My nostrils were assailed by a well-remembered repulsive odor," Tuvia Borzykowski recalled. "We were climbing down so close to one another that my feet practically touched the head of the man below me while just above my head were the feet of the man following me. Each time I heard a splash, I knew that someone had already reached the bottom, his body waist deep in the filth."

Zuckerman, Lubetkin, and Edelman were just ahead of Borzykowski, part of an unbroken human chain that "stretched for kilometers." Every few hundred feet, the body of someone who had drowned floated in the filth. The currents were much stronger in this part of the sewer system than they had been in the Ghetto because of its proximity to the Vistula, into which the city's entire canal network drained. The lower elevation and increased pressure created waterfalls and treacherous whirlpools at junctures where channels merged. Simha had charted a course to avoid the most dangerous of these crosscurrents. But it required lengthy detours, adding to the exhausting journey. Already it had taken six hours to reach the halfway point, and the evacuees' strength was visibly beginning to ebb.

Suddenly, at around 6 A.M., an explosion rocked the canal. A trip wire had been snagged, and the Germans, alerted by the detonation, were throwing hand grenades down manholes, blocking the passage. Everyone froze, panicked. Going forward meant death, but going back meant returning to Old Town, which was tantamount to the same thing. There was only one alternative route. They would have to go through the waterfalls and whirlpools, against the raging currents.

Zivia was the first to fall. Tuvia grabbed her and pulled her by the hair, but he also lost his balance and fell. Just as he was beginning to get up, a surge knocked him down again. Mark Edelman grabbed Tuvia, but he, too, was sucked into the vortex, and as he spun helplessly with his head submerged, Zuckerman dived in after him. While they struggled to free themselves from the grip of the swirling waters, Tuvia felt something tugging at his leg. Another person was down there, frantically trying to pull himself up. Tuvia could feel himself "being torn in two. The man below me managed to raise himself and grab hold of the strap of my rucksack. The strap broke. The man fell back and drowned."

Zivia, meanwhile, had fainted, and Isaac carried her on his shoulders. "The water came up to my neck. I walked first and she floated as she slept. We stepped on bodies under the water."

At noon, twelve hours after they had entered the sewers, the group emerged in Woodrow Wilson Square in Jolie Bord. In all, some 5,200 people managed to escape Old Town through underground canals. When the Germans took the historic district and neighboring Riverside on the following day, the dreaded Dirlewanger Commando Battalion, the psychopathic SS penal unit, killed all the wounded left behind. In hospitals, "drunken soldiers practiced Caesarean sections with bayonets," one shocked witness reported. Thousands of civilians were rounded up, shot, burned alive, or tied to the front of tanks to act as human shields. The Russian RONA Brigade gang-raped hundreds of women literally to death.

CHAPTER 38

FOOLISH ERRANDS

By the sixth week of the insurgency, as Robert Osnos was enrolling in middle school in New York, the death toll in the Warsaw Uprising was approaching 150,000, bringing the total number of deaths in the Polish capital to well over 700,000 since the start of the war. More Varsovians, both Jewish and Gentile, had died at the hands of the Nazis than American combatants had perished during the Civil War. Two-thirds of the city lay in ruins. And the Russians had still not crossed the Vistula. Marshal Rokossovsky's 3,360 tanks were now in Praga, just across the river, within sight through the Home Army's binoculars. But they might as well have been in Moscow for all the good they would do the insurgents, as the Kremlin had made clear. The Rising, a spokesman for Stalin informed U.S. diplomats, was "a purely adventuristic affair to which the Soviet government could not lend a hand." The revolt, Foreign Minister Vyacheslav Molotov added in a letter to Winston Churchill, was a "provocation" launched "without the prior knowledge of Soviet military command, undermining its operational plans."

Neither the Americans nor the British needed to remind the Russians that Radio Moscow had repeatedly called on Varsovians to rise up. Yet amid frantic Allied efforts to get more aid to the beleaguered Poles, it was now obvious to all parties that the revolt had been doomed from the start. While Paris had been liberated a few weeks earlier in a seamless transition, with virtually no bloodshed or destruction of property, Warsaw was being cruelly sacrificed, caught between the competing furies and territorial aspirations of Stalin and Hitler.

Home Army leaders knew by mid-September 1944 that they had no chance. By then, most Varsovians were simply praying for survival. Many, in fact, now blamed the Underground for the mass rapes, murders, and horrific destruction visited upon the population by the Nazis. The only reason they did not push for unconditional surrender was that the SS policy of massacring prisoners and civilians precluded any sort of capitulation.

Ironically, in his lust for vengeance, Himmler had unleashed a monster even he could not control. The Russian, Kazakh, Ukrainian, and Azeri auxiliaries recruited by the SS to do its dirty work had run completely amok, deserting, disregarding orders, flouting military discipline, and committing such atrocities that even the most hardened Nazis were disgusted. "They're pigs, not soldiers," General Ernst Rode, Himmler's chief of staff, said of the Dirlewanger penal battalion. The Wehrmacht, which always held its SS rival in contempt, very nearly mutinied after witnessing the barbarities of the SS's eastern hordes. Some soldiers, racked by guilt, were said to have committed suicide. "I've got used to the sight of male corpses," one distraught private wrote his fiancée in Germany. "They are part of everyday life; but not to the remains of women's bodies, where a life of love and innocence once grew, or when I see the bodies of children, all of whom I consider innocent whatever their mother tongue, and all of whom I love in these horrendous times. I know you will say I must not write about it."

Anger and alcoholism were rampant in the discontented Wehrmacht ranks, while officers sometimes crossed SS cordons to rescue women and children from Ukrainian killing squads. "He took me and my mother by the hand," one woman remembered of her German savior. "And he walked us past the machine gunners. The SS men yelled in protest, but the Wehrmacht officer ignored them. Thanks to him, we lived. All our neighbors were shot."

Some Wehrmacht officers apparently were so repulsed by the behavior of the Russian RONA Brigade that they plotted the assassination of its leader, General Kaminski. According to one version of events, his motorcade was ambushed by a Wehrmacht commando unit. Historians suggest instead that the Gestapo itself secretly executed him for dishonoring the SS. Whichever the case, the consensus among scholars is that Kaminski was killed by Germans rather than by Polish partisans, as the Nazis claimed.

Himmler's plan to annihilate the entire population was proving untenable. In Warsaw, there were too many witnesses. The Polish capital was not a remote ravine in Western Ukraine, where a hundred thousand bodies could be disposed of discreetly. Nor was the city a closed concentration camp with no bystanders. And, perhaps equally important, there was a difference—in the eyes of Germany's regular army—between Christians and Jews. Though Slavs were also categorized as subhumans, the Wehrmacht would not stand for the slaughter of defenseless Polish women and children. It ran counter to the Prussian military code of conduct. In the end, Himmler had to scuttle his plan to kill every resident. Only men would be executed. The city of Warsaw itself, however, would still be erased from the map.

A nearly mile-long trench separated the rebel and German positions in the northern suburb of Jolie Bord. Compared to the inner city, the upper-middle-class neighborhood was thinly populated, with tree-lined streets and single-family homes.

After the twin hells of the Ghetto and Old Town, Jolie Bord seemed like a bucolic paradise to Isaac Zuckerman. The place was relatively unscathed by war. There were gardens and flowers and picket fences. Kids rode bicycles on sidewalks even as the Russians were shelling parts of the district close to the river. To Jolie Bord's residents, the hundreds of dark, ragged figures emerging unsteadily from the sewers presented an equally astonishing sight, "all black and splattered with mud, reeking and covered in feces, swaying on their feet, their knees bloodied and torn." They were also ridden with lice, and Mark Edelman remembered how a kind woman brought the combatants buckets of scalding hot water. "She ordered us to dunk our heads into it. When I immersed my hair, the entire surface of the water crawled with pests."

The ZOB was assigned to a barricade facing the Gdansk train station, Warsaw's northernmost rail hub, where the Wehrmacht had parked the massive 1,400-ton howitzer whose shells could pulverize an entire block. The Jewish group was mostly intact. Only Simha and Boruch Spiegel were still in the city center. Spiegel had long been separated from the others, fighting in a notoriously violent mixed unit alongside fascist ONRites in what had been the southeastern quadrant of the Ghetto. This was perhaps the most lawless and anarchic sector of Warsaw, a ten-square-block area where half of the thirty documented murders of Jews by Gentile insurgents were committed during the Rising. Former greasers were part of fascist National Armed Forces Home Army units deployed in the sector, and they took to killing and robbing any Jews they came across. To cover their tracks, at one point they tried to frame Boruch Spiegel's friend and patron Mietek "Frenchy" Pera. On September 21, according to official Home Army reports, Frenchy was arrested for looting. "Part of the evidence was that Frenchy was frequently seen in the company of a Jew." That Jew was Spiegel, and the charges, in the opinion of Polish historians, were "concocted" by an anti-Semitic officer to "muddy the waters" and protect the real culprits. In effect, Boruch was fighting not only Germans, but also murderers within his own camp.

Simha, meanwhile, had been sent by Zuckerman on what turned out to be a fool's errand. Not realizing that their safe house on Forestry Boulevard was now in enemy territory, Isaac had dispatched Ratheiser to retrieve the ZOB's documents and archive. Simha thought the exercise pointless and told Isaac so. "Why endanger ourselves for papers?" he asked. "For history," Isaac replied. The two fought bitterly, though in the end Simha reluctantly followed orders. All contact with him had since been lost.

Barricade duty afforded the ZOB a chance to recuperate from the trauma of Old Town. Much like the initial trench warfare on Bridge Street, there was a deceptive calm as each side took occasional potshots at the other but launched no real offensives. The Germans were busy mopping up Old Town and Riverside and driving a wedge into Midtown, closing the pockets of resistance in the city center. Jolie Bord was not as strategically important, and the Nazis had garrisons in Marymont, just to the north, which meant that the suburb was effectively surrounded from three sides and hemmed in by the Vistula. The SS could deal with it at its leisure.

Several thousand Jewish refugees found their way into the enclave after the apartments they had been hiding in were destroyed or overrun by the Germans. There was no way of knowing, at this stage, how many of Warsaw's Jews were still alive. Many had perished in the air raids, shelling, and fires—historians estimate as many as 4,500—and some had doubtlessly been caught up in the mass executions of Gentiles. The survivors needed to be housed and fed, and Zuckerman bitterly regretted the loss of the $40,000 the ZOB had received from the Council to Aid Jews. Since there was a lull in the fighting, Isaac got in touch with Dr. Adolf Berman, his old contact from the Council. The psychiatrist and Marxist Zionist leader was in Jolie Bord, a guest of the Home Army, and was trying to billet homeless Jews. "He immediately brought out a large sum and gave it to us," Zuckerman recalled. "Then we started gathering Jews."

Isaac divided his time between his military obligations and organizing an impromptu welfare net for his destitute co-religionists. Money was not the issue. Berman appeared to have ample funds and was scrupulously honest about sharing them. The problem was that no amount of money could buy food that did not exist. The dire shortages that had plagued the inner city also reached the suburbs, where the population had swollen overnight. Civilians were worse off than combatants, since the Home Army controlled the only meager stores—grains seized from the Haberbusch and Schiele breweries and canned goods from several Wehrmacht warehouses. Isaac managed to persuade a local commander to part with some of his reserves so that no one would starve.

The supply situation improved when an unexpected bonanza rained down from the skies on September 18, 1944. The U.S. Army Air Corps, after protracted negotiations with the Kremlin, had finally been given permission to use Soviet airspace to fly a daring daytime mission over Warsaw. Unbeknownst to most insurgents, who felt as abandoned by the outside world as their Jewish counterparts had during the Ghetto Uprising, the Home Army had a champion in Moscow: U.S. Ambassador Averell Harriman. The heir to one of America's biggest fortunes had been tirelessly pressing Stalin to lift his de facto embargo on the Poles. Harriman had long-standing ties to the country. He had co-owned Poland's largest zinc producer, the Silesian-American Mining Co., until the Nazis seized it in 1939. Along with his partner Prescott Bush, father of the future U.S. president, Harriman had promoted Polish government bonds, and his investment bank, Brown Brothers Harriman, had offices in Warsaw before the war.

Harriman grasped that the future of Poland was at stake in the Rising. He also saw that the geopolitical forces that would govern postwar Eastern Europe were being shaped with little American input. His frustration was visibly mounting, and Stalin, who was receiving tens of billions of dollars of U.S. military aid under the Lend-Lease program, threw him a bone by allowing a supply flight to take off from the sprawling Poltava airfield in central Ukraine. Some one hundred and ten B-17 Flying Fortresses, escorted by 72 Mustangs, made the four-hour journey and appeared over the burning city at 1 P.M., shocking the Germans. Amazingly, only one of the giant bombers was shot down, while the agile Mustangs knocked ten Luftwaffe fighters out of the sky. Hundreds of tons of supplies filled the sky with white-and-beige-striped parachutes. Unfortunately, most of the supply pods landed in German territory. But Tuvia and Isaac managed to retrieve one, gaining Smith & Wesson revolvers as well as cigarettes, a first aid kit, and, most important, antitank guns. The American mission proved to be one of the last efforts by Poland's Western allies to save the Home Army. Soon afterward, the British were forced to suspend their airlift because they were losing too many planes. When RAF pilots complained that much of the shooting was coming from the Russian-held bank of the Vistula, Red Army officials conceded that planes had been downed "accidentally," adding that the Soviet Union could no longer guarantee the safety of Allied airmen who ventured over Warsaw. Henceforth, only Moscow would supply the insurgents, Stalin decreed.

Still, stuck in Midtown, Simha Ratheiser found himself trapped in a surreal situation. Flames licked the sides of the building he was hiding in while a German military band performed in the courtyard. Simha couldn't pry his eyes off the strange sight. He was on Forestry Boulevard in the charred ruins of the ZOB safe house, staring at trumpeters and trombonists while a flamethrower doused his hideout with jets of burning fuel. It was, he would later say, one of the weirdest experiences of the war. "Everything around going up in flames, walls caving in—and that music. Through the window I saw players blowing into their instruments and I stood still, hypnotized. Walls were collapsing, people were being killed, and there they stood and played."

Ratheiser was so mesmerized by the band in full military regalia that he momentarily forgot how furious he was with Zuckerman for sending him into a death trap. The building was surrounded. The entire street was filled with Germans and Ukrainians, who had launched an offensive into Midtown, pushing the Home Army farther back and stranding Simha and a few other unfortunate holdouts.

This was not the first time Ratheiser had been separated from fellow Jewish fighters or stuck in enemy territory. During the initial Old Town siege he spent a week with a Home Army unit stationed in the old Municipal Courthouse building. His temporary defection from the People's Army had not been political. Simha had simply been restless and bored with trench duty. He could never sit still, Edelman laughed of his irrepressible younger colleague. "This river rat was always squirming his way everywhere, finding out everything." Indeed, Simha's clothes were so filthy from his constant forays across German positions that his Home Army unit had nicknamed him Mud.

But this time the situation was different. There was nowhere to run, no tiny crevice to squeeze through, no breach in Nazi defenses through which to escape. The entire block was sealed and he, his girlfriend, Irene, and Marisa Sawicka were stuck. They had jumped out a second-story window only to find themselves pinned down by enemy fire, and had retreated back into the same burning edifice from which they had fled. Only its latrine was not on fire, a communal bathroom on the ground floor. It contained a large water cistern whose contents had long since been drained by parched residents. They climbed inside, momentarily safe. But after a few hours, Simha felt a stinging sensation in his eyes. The pain soon grew excruciating—it felt as if his retinas had completely dried out. His vision grew blurry and then he lost sight entirely. Exposure to smoke or noxious gasses that accumulated in the cistern was blinding Ratheiser. When it became too painful to blink, Marisa and Irene, who apparently were not affected by the fumes, took turns spitting on his eyes and licking them. All the while, the jarring thuds and reverberating clangs of objects crashing on the cistern's steel cover kept Simha from passing out. But the structure around them was slowly collapsing.

After twenty-four hours Ratheiser could no longer bear being trapped in the metallic tomb. His vision was gradually returning and he was desperate to get out of the water tank before it became completely buried by rubble, imprisoning them inside. It was dusk when they emerged. In the fading light, Simha could see that the streets were still swarming with Germans and their Ukrainian henchmen. They had set up a sector headquarters in an undamaged church next door, surrounding it with sandbags and machine gun nests while snipers and lookouts were posted in the belfry. Making a run for it was suicide. Simha and his two female companions had no choice but to stay put and find a place to hide. The fires set the day before were still smoldering, but Ratheiser, from his Ghetto experience, knew that the cellars had probably survived intact. The Germans realized this as well, for trucks with mobile loudspeakers were slowly prowling the streets, calling for Poles to come out and surrender. Civilians would not be harmed, the megaphones promised. They would be taken to a large DP camp outside the city for future relocation. In reality, one hundred thousand people were already crammed behind the hastily strung barbed wire around the displaced persons camp, without food, water, or any sanitary facilities.

There were very few takers. Poles by now knew what "relocation" meant in Nazi-speak. Simha was also well aware of what would happen to Marisa and Irene if they fell into Ukrainian hands. Trying to escape with two young and attractive women in tow was out of the question. The three of them had to hide. Scouring the charred ruins, Simha found a small window to a basement filled with people. Simha was not surprised. He had witnessed similar scenes many times during the Ghetto Uprising. Inside the cellar, it was stifling hot. Row after row of terrified civilians and worn combatants lay side by side, pressing their faces to the cooler earthen floor. The building above them had burned to its rafters, and many people had wet rags spread over their backs to prevent falling cinders from searing their skin. Ratheiser recognized a few fellow Jews in the sea of pale, soot-streaked faces. He, Irene, and Marisa crawled into the crowded basement and glumly lay down next to the others.

For the first time since the war, for the only time he could ever remember, Simha was ready to quit. He was spent, mentally and physically, and he no longer had the strength or will to fight.

In the waning days of September 1944, as the British liberated Brussels and Antwerp and American troops reached the Siegfried Line on Germany's western frontier, the SS finally moved on the suburb of Jolie Bord.

Only a few pockets of resistance were left by then. The Home Army was still holding out in isolated parts of Midtown, but the large residential district of Mokotow had just fallen. In Mokotow the Nazis had changed tactics. To spur surrender negotiations, General Erich von dem Bach, the senior German commander, had permitted a two-hour cease-fire to evacuate nine thousand residents from the doomed neighborhood. The gesture was meant to reassure Home Army leaders that civilians would no longer be murdered if the rebels capitulated. After nearly two months of uninterrupted fighting and almost twenty-six thousand German casualties, including ten thousand dead, Von dem Bach was willing to make concessions to finally end the Rising.

The Panzer division that had subdued Mokotow, meanwhile, moved north to crush Jolie Bord, the last big enclave left standing. In anticipation of a final battle, the residents of the northern suburb delivered spare clothes and food to the remaining combatants on the front lines. Platoon commanders distributed the jealously hoarded supplies. "There were shiny new automatic weapons, tinned meat and milk," Tuvia Borzykowski recalled. "We treated each package as a dear friend."

At 6 A.M. on Friday, September 29, the Germans struck, unleashing an artillery barrage on a scale not yet seen in Warsaw. Virtually every field gun and howitzer piece in the city trained on the holdout suburb. Woodrow Wilson and Lelewel Squares were pulverized. "Every house in the quarter was hit several times by shells," Tuvia recalled. "We were deafened by the almost continuous explosions, blinded by the thick clouds of smoke and dust."

When at last the artillery fell silent and the dust began to settle, Tuvia and his comrades "saw all around us the long necks of tanks. They appeared suddenly out of the clouds of smoke, spitting fire. Behind them marched columns of infantry." Tuvia, Zivia, Isaac, and Mark were scattered at different points along the defensive barricades. Zuckerman had been put in charge of a front-line Home Army unit equipped with British PIAT antitank guns that had been airdropped by the Allies. None of his soldiers had experience with the heavy weapon, which weighed nearly forty pounds and had to be fired at very close range—less than fifty yards—to be effective. But they bravely ran out in front of the advancing Panzers and discharged their bulky weapons before diving for cover. Within a few hours, most of them were dead, and the few still alive could no longer hear anything because they had not been warned that earplugs needed to be worn when using the PIAT. "The echo of that shooting made me completely deaf," Isaac said, recalling the bizarre sensation of seeing buildings crumble, explosion flash, and bullets ricochet around him, all in total silence.

Zivia, meanwhile, was missing in action. She had been the only woman in a People's Army platoon in a forward base near the Gdansk train station. When the platoon's position was overrun, no one could find her. "The whole unit had come back, except for Zivia." Zuckerman was devastated. A search party was organized, and when it came back without her, his thoughts turned from German tanks and the war, from everything but his brave, foolhardy wife, who had insisted on fighting with the men, who had made such a fuss that they had relented and given her a rifle she could barely lift. Like Simha before him, Isaac had reached his breaking point. Paralyzed with grief, isolated in the ringing silence of his shattered eardrums, all he wanted was to curl up in a corner and seek solace in alcohol. "I asked one of the Gentiles to bring me some spirits to ease my worry," Isaac later wrote, confessing that he was spent. At long last, his will to fight was gone.

By Saturday, September 30, only Mark Edelman was still in the thick of it, defending a police station being stormed by a battalion of tanks. His group was taking heavy losses. An elderly man fighting alongside Mark was shooting at a Panzer from a window when the armored colossus suddenly fired back. The old man took the shell square in the chest. "Do you want to know what color a person who has taken a direct hit from a tank shell leaves on a wall?" Mark would later ask. "Lilac-pink."

Another fellow combatant, a young man named Carl, simply disappeared when Edelman turned around for an instant. There one moment, vanished the next. As he frantically searched the blood-spattered rooms of the police outpost, it suddenly dawned on Mark that of the twenty-one people in his unit, he was the only one alive.

CHAPTER 39

ZIVIA'S CUPBOARD

On October 2, 1944, Warsaw capitulated. After sixty-three days and nearly two hundred thousand fatalities, the longest, largest, and bloodiest uprising of the Second World War was over. The Home Army, following protracted negotiations, agreed to lay down its weapons on condition that the Wehrmacht, rather than the SS, administer the surrender. Under the terms of the armistice, civilians were not to be molested and combatants were to be treated as prisoners of war in accordance with the Geneva Conventions.

Nazi pledges of clemency, however, would not extend to Jews, as Simha, Isaac, Boruch, and Mark knew full well. Ratheiser was the first of the ZOB fighters to confront this reality. He had spent weeks in the cellar on Forestry Boulevard, subsisting initially on rainwater collected at night from buckets placed outside, and later from a shallow hand-dug well that provided a trickle of murky liquid. Food, ironically, was less of an issue. Residents of the building had hidden stores of tinned goods in the basement—just enough to prevent starvation.

While they were in the cellar there had been talk among the handful of Jews about what to do when the Germans finally uncovered the hideout. One older ZOB fighter, Joseph Sak, produced a vial of potassium cyanide. Snatching the poison, Simha shouted, "You can't do this!" The memory of Mordechai Anielewicz's mass suicide still stung. "You don't have the luxury" of taking the easy way out, Ratheiser admonished Sak.

In the end, it was a Ukrainian patrol that found them. "Don't shoot, there are women down here," Simha called out, in a calculated gambit, when the SS men stuck their rifles through the cave entrance. Ratheiser was hoping that the Ukrainian auxiliaries would not toss grenades into the basement if it held the promise of war booty and women. The SS had routinely wiped out shelters filled with civilians. One of their favorite methods of flushing out cellars, before the water mains were all destroyed, had been to run fire hoses through coal chutes to drown everyone inside. Parents would put children on their shoulders as the water level rose, and by the time it receded, the young were often the only ones alive.

In this case, Simha was proven correct. Greed and lechery trumped the murderous instincts of the SS auxiliaries. The thugs held their fire. In guttural, slurred shouts, they ordered everyone out. Their glassy gazes—some seemed drunk—immediately fell on Simha's girlfriend, Irene, another Jewish girl, Stasia, and Marisa, the ZOB's faithful Gentile advocate. Their jewelry was the first thing that caught the pillagers' eyes, and the three women were forced to relinquish bracelets and earrings.

The group was then led through the ruins of the city, squinting in the sun, which many had not seen in nearly a month. The devastation that had occurred during the time Simha had been hiding underground was staggering. The only standing structures seemed to be chimneys and the occasional church steeple. Everything else lay in mangled heaps. Some of the jagged mounds were several stories high. Bomb craters rendered streets impassable. It was hard to find one's bearings in the mess. "The ruins are exceptionally photogenic," a cameraman for the German news agency Transocean marveled. "A panoply of destruction, the signs of battle are omnipresent: spent cartridges and mortar shells split in half; enormous piles of twisted rebar; here, the burned-out shell of a tank; there, a torn parachute swaying in the wind from the top corner of a lone building."

Simha still had enough of a sense of direction to notice that the Ukrainians were not leading them toward one of the civilian collection centers that had been set up in Midtown. They were headed for the Ukrainian SS barracks in the former Ghetto, near Peacock Prison. Ratheiser shuddered, overcome by guilt and fear for his friends. "They were probably taking us there to rape the girls," he realized. It appeared that Marisa, Irene, and Stasia would pay the price for his gamble, which he now regretted. After they were done with the women, the Ukrainians might kill them all anyway, so as not to leave any witnesses to their private amusements.

Fate, providence, or simply dumb luck intervened. Along the way to the Ghetto, a Wehrmacht officer stopped the Ukrainians and asked where they were headed. Perhaps guessing what lay in store for Simha's group, the German officer ordered that the prisoners be turned over to the Wehrmacht and taken to a transit station. These collection centers were almost all in churches, the only structures still standing. Ratheiser and the others were marched to a big church in Wola, St. Adalbert's on Wolska Steet. Thousands had been murdered at St. Adalbert's during the first week of the Rising, and its cemetery had been transformed by the SS into a makeshift crematorium of huge fire pits. Refugees now crammed inside the soaring Gothic brick edifice. Wounded women rested on cots, and row after of row of baby carriages were parked beneath the stained glass windows in the nave. In packed pews, children sat on their mothers' laps. The elderly slumped shoulder to shoulder with teens. A low, steady murmur reverberated in the vaulted chamber as anxious families pondered their future. Warsaw was being depopulated. Its residents were being dispersed to labor, concentration, and refugee camps. The hushed conversations were punctuated by the echoing .click of the embedded steel in the jackboots of German guards walking up and down the marble aisles.

Relatively few men of fighting age were in the assembled crowd, which made Simha's group stand out. Ratheiser's fellow ZOB veteran, Joseph Sak, attracted particular attention. Sak had pronounced Semitic features, which was partly why he had favored suicide over surrender. An officer zeroed in on him and asked his name. Sak had been a professor of Polish literature before the war and rattled off the surname of a Slavic literary hero, prompting the amused German to inquire: "And how long have you had that name?"

To Simha's surprise, his friend was not taken away. The officer obviously suspected that Sak was Jewish, but for unknown reasons decided not to press further. Perhaps he was tired of the killing. Perhaps he was not an anti-Semite. Or maybe he was fed up with the war and no longer cared about Hitler's plans for the master race. In any event, Sak was allowed to join one of the long queues of refugees marching toward the bombed-out train station. These lines snaked throughout the demolished city, stretching for miles, an endless procession of bedraggled citizens carrying meager belongings wrapped in bedsheets. The SS were no longer shooting at civilians, and the columns moved slowly. The panicked flights of the past few months, with women clutching children, with the elderly stumbling and being riddled with bullets, with people being slaughtered by the hundreds on the streets, were mercifully over.

Trains between Warsaw and a huge new selection camp in Pruszkow, formally known as Durchgangslager 121, ran in a continuous loop. The facility was in the industrial exurb of Pruszkow, where Joanna, Hanna, and Janine Mortkowicz had lived during the early part of the war. It was about ten miles west of the capital, and had been chosen because of the extensive rail network that had fed its factories. Now the former industrial center processed people; an endless sea of them, packed tighter than sardines. Durchgangslager 121 had to be one of the most densely populated places on the planet. A whole city was crammed into an area not much bigger than an amusement park. A total of 650,000 people would eventually pass through its gates as Warsaw was systematically emptied.

The purpose of the new Pruszkow camp was to sort out which Poles were fit for slave labor in the Reich, which undesirables would be put on cattle cars bound for Auschwitz and other concentration camps, and which would be lucky enough to be released and relocated to undestroyed cities like Krakow. To accommodate the massive influx of refugees, the Germans hastily erected barracks within a barbed wire perimeter that spanned a dozen football fields. But these crude facilities were overwhelmed within a few days, creating a sanitary crisis that German propaganda films carefully omitted to mention. "Three hundred thousand people are now enjoying the fresh air," a Nazi newsreel declared on October 6, "after weeks spent in sewers and underground cellars."

Hanna and Janine Mortkowicz were among the huddled throng at Pruszkow's Durchgangslager 121, standing for hours to wait their turn for a cup of water from cisterns the Germans trucked in daily. Hanna, like countless other members of split-up families, had no idea where her daughter was. She had not seen Joanna in over a year and had no way of knowing if she was alive. In the Pruszkow camp, thousands of people were frantically looking for loved ones, putting up so many notices on Red Cross message boards that the paper pleas covered one another in layers. Simha, after a few days in Pruszkow, also searched for his parents. His mother, he felt certain, was still alive. He constantly scanned the crowds, hoping for a glimpse of her familiar blond mane.

Selection occurred several times a day at Durchgangslager 121. "Hundreds of human beings had to parade in front of German officers who decided whom to release and whom to send to labor camp," Ratheiser recalled. Since he was young and healthy, he was chosen for relocation to Germany to work as a slave laborer. So was his girlfriend, Irene, along with 150,000 other able-bodied Varsovians. Neither was suspected of being Jewish, or they would have been sent to Auschwitz instead. Simha, however, no longer cared. "A mood of apathy descended on me. I was fed up with the whole thing. I imagined that it would be better to be sent to Germany." Ratheiser's friends would not hear of it. Anything was better than a life of slavery, they argued. The war was almost over, they promised. The Germans would soon be driven out of Poland. Simha only had to hold out for a little longer. He had to find a way to escape.

On the night of Warsaw's surrender, Isaac Zuckerman and Tuvia Borzykowski spotted two figures in the dusk approaching their camp. They were dressed in German uniforms, walking unsteadily. At first Isaac thought they were drunken soldiers celebrating the cease-fire. But as they approached, he realized one was a woman. It was Zivia! She was limping, favoring one leg. And Mark Edelman was holding her up.

Against unimaginable odds, they had survived. "I suppose fate had dictated that we should live," Zivia sighed. The ZOB survivors had faced everything the Nazis could throw at them: Tiger tanks, treacherous sewer crossings, starvation, typhus, labor camps, Treblinka's gas chambers, the Gestapo and its greasers. And they had survived it all. But their ordeal was not yet over. Unlike combatants from the Home Army, Isaac's small group of Jewish fighters could not surrender.

The accord the Poles signed with the Germans did not cover the People's Army, of which the ZOB was formally a member. Communist partisans had been purposefully excluded from surrender negotiations and were not afforded any of the protections of the Geneva Convention. The Home Army felt betrayed by the Soviets and therefore punished their proxy group by leaving them out of the talks. The spiteful omission affected four hundred combatants in Jolie Bord. Despite having fought as bravely as any of the Poles, they were forsaken. The SS could shoot them on sight, torture them, or dispatch them to death camps. Although their predicament was unenviable, most veterans of the People's Army were still in a far better position than the ZOB members. As Gentiles, veterans of the People's Army could remove their insignias, don civilian clothing, and try to blend in with the hordes of refugees leaving the suburb. If they were lucky, and had good false documents that could withstand scrutiny, they might be able to slip through the selection process at the Pruszkow camp without being sent to Auschwitz. The ZOB had no such option. Zivia's and Mark's Semitic features precluded any attempt to blend in, and Tuvia's poor Polish was equally damning. "We didn't know what to do," Lubetkin recalled.

Isaac had already tried to lead a People's Army unit across the Vistula to reach Soviet positions on the eastern bank. Unfortunately, the river had been cordoned off by German forces. Many Communist rebels were shot while entering the water and their colleagues were forced to turn back. Now there was no choice but to remain in Jolie Bord and find somewhere to hide until the Germans finished emptying the district. One ZOB member, a courier and doctor, suggested going to the home of a Gentile family that had hidden her once before. The home had not been destroyed and the family had been evacuated to the Pruszkow camp. Only the paralyzed eighty-year-old grandmother remained, along with three emaciated Jewish women, who feared leaving their hideout.

The house was one block from the Vistula, perilously close to the

German fortifications that guarded against a Red Army crossing of the river. Its elderly occupants were less than pleased when heavily armed ZOB fighters started arriving late at night in pairs. "The women knew, and we knew, too, that our presence was not to their advantage," Tuvia Borzykowski understood. "Without us they could hope that even if the Germans discovered them they might not bother to do any harm to four old women, none of whom looked Jewish, and none of whom could be suspected of having taken part in the revolt. Our appearance robbed them of that precarious security."

"When we entered the basement," he went on, "we saw all four old women sitting or lying on beds, wrapped in featherbeds. A tiny candle flickered on the table, throwing gloomy shadows on the wall. The floor was strewn with pieces of broken furniture, shoes, kitchen utensils, linen, rags. Before we could ask where there would be room for us, one of them got up and pushed away a small cupboard, revealing the entrance to a tiny room."

The fifteen fighters squeezed into the minuscule compartment, securing the cupboard door from the inside by wrapping a wire around a nail. The space was so tight that Edelman could not turn around. Zivia was having difficulty breathing. One fighter had to perch on a shelf because there was not enough floor space. Isaac, still deaf from the blast of the antitank gun, talked far too loudly, and he had to be continually reminded to stay quiet. He soon grew "very mad at Zivia" because "it seemed she pinched me the hardest."

The first night passed slowly, in excruciating discomfort. The hideout was far too small. Fifteen people simply could not fit in such conditions. In the morning, talk of relocation was interrupted by the sound of jackboots on the floor above accompanied by the all-too-familiar German screams of *"Alle raus, alle raus!"*—everyone out! Only Zuckerman was unable to hear the imminent danger, but all at once he felt himself pinched from every direction while unseen hands clasped his mouth.

The old women, to their credit, kept their cool. One of them told the Germans that they had received permission from an officer to remain in their home because of their poor health. The patrolmen seemed skeptical but said they would check with their superiors. In the meantime they inquired, had the ladies seen any "armed bandits"?

The women said no. The patrolmen promised to return, adding that they doubted very much that the elderly occupants could stay much longer.

The reason for their certainty was an order issued by Heinrich Himmler shortly after the capitulation. Warsaw, the SS chief decreed, "must completely disappear from the surface of the earth and serve only as a transport station for the Wehrmacht. No stone can remain standing. Every building must be razed to its foundation."

The SS were taking their master's words literally, which was why the city was being evacuated. From a prewar population of 1.35 million, only an estimated five thousand remained hidden in the rubble by the end of October 1944. They were mostly Jews, who had nowhere to run, and the stranded unfortunates became known as Robinson Crusoes. Meanwhile, demolition experts, sappers, and engineers descended on the Polish capital from throughout the Reich to launch what would prove to be the most physically destructive campaign of the entire war. By the time they were done leveling the already ravaged capital, systematically dynamiting each and every structure as they moved methodically from house to house, street to street, and neighborhood to neighborhood, the physical destruction would surpass that in Hiroshima and Nagasaki combined.

CHAPTER 40

DESPICABLE YIDS

By November 1944's first snows, Warsaw echoed with the steady blast of explosions as plumes of dust rose and fell in gaseous clusters that resembled brown mushrooms. Seen from the air, the scale of destruction was so enormous that reconnaissance pilots in the Soviet air force took to calling the former Polish capital the "cemetery."

"Everything beneath us lies in ruin. There is not a living soul in sight. No one is shooting at us," one pilot reported. "The desolation is even more shocking than the hellish battles we saw the month before."

By this time, Simha Ratheiser was far away, as were Hanna and Janine Mortkowicz. All three were in the same refugee camp in a small village between Kielce and Krakow. Hanna and Janine's fake documents had passed a cursory inspection at Pruszkow, and since Janine was almost seventy, they had not been deemed a potential threat. As for Simha, once he had been persuaded not to give up the struggle, it had been shockingly easy for him to slip out of the long line of Varsovians destined for German labor camps. He and the other ZOB fighters had melted into a disorganized queue of elderly Poles, women, and children being relocated to the south of Poland. The women helped hide them as they boarded the train, and the guards were not nearly as vigilant as they had once been. Many seemed to be simply going through the motions, as if they, too, were giving up.

Flagging German morale was to be expected, given the bleak news from the various fronts. To the north, the Red Army had reached the banks of the Niemen in Prussia proper. To the south, Belgrade and Bucharest were in Soviet hands, and the Russians had entered Hungary. In the west, Belgium and almost all of France had been liberated. American forces had taken Aachen, the first major German city to fall into enemy hands.

In Warsaw, no German could forget that Rokossovsky's tank divisions still sat menacingly just across the river, biding their time. In anticipation of the eventual Soviet crossing, tens of thousands of mines were laid in the Polish capital. A specially trained Wehrmacht explosives unit, the 37th Sapper Battalion, arrived to plant booby traps throughout the ruins. Some were detonated by trip wires. Others exploded when someone turned a doorknob or a water tap. Knowing that Russian soldiers would scavenge for loot, they placed tiny charges in food cans or cigarette cases. Pens filled with a few grams of explosive, enough to remove a hand, were strategically left for the enemy to find. They were set to go off when picked up. In the end, the traps probably claimed more Jews—the "Robinson Crusoes" stranded in the ruins, scavenging at night for food—than Red Army soldiers.

On the train out of Warsaw, it was possible that Simha passed Hanna and Janine in one of the compartments without knowing them. They were likely on the same transport because they ended up at the same depot, an abysmally overcrowded makeshift refuge, rutted in frozen mud and reeking of human excrement. It was in a former shtetl called Suchedniow, chosen partly because its Jewish inhabitants had been sent to Birkenau a few months earlier after working as slave laborers in a nearby munitions plant. Homes in the town of five thousand inhabitants were mostly vacant, reducing the need to build flimsy barracks and pitch tent cities. The Mortkowiczes were mired there for months. Simha didn't stay more than a few days, just long enough to send a message to a contact in the area from the Council to Aid Jews, someone he knew from his travels in 1943 as a ZOB courier. He needed false documents, money, and a gun. And he needed to get to Krakow. Ratheiser was going back into the resistance business.

Four weeks had passed since Zivia, Isaac, Tuvia, and Mark descended into their infernally cramped hideout on Promyka Street in Jolie Bord. It was the longest, most trying month of their lives. The claustrophobia, boredom, unending darkness—candles only for emergency use—and prolonged periods of silence drove one member of the group to a nervous breakdown. He tried to kill himself at one point. His whimpering at times grew so loud and put them in such danger of discovery that there was talk of suffocating him.

They were all close to losing the psychological battle. One after another they succumbed to depression. To combat the crippling inertia, they devised activities to preoccupy themselves. They took turns giving lectures on a wide variety of topics: Zionism, fascism, American history. One ZOB member was a bacteriologist by profession, and they learned everything there was to know about germs. Every morning someone pretended to be a radio announcer, reenacting past news programs. Afternoons were for mind games: riddles and quizzes. Four o'clock was reserved for joke hour. The schedule was rigidly adhered to, thanks to the one working wristwatch among them. Isaac insisted on it to maintain morale. Mark and Zivia, who had spent a year cooped up between risings, were better prepared to endure the stifling boredom. But eventually even they showed signs of cracking.

Nights were their only solace, when the fifteen fighters could replenish their sanity with brief excursions outside the cupboard. Once darkness fell, teams took turns leaving the hideout to go on scavenging expeditions. They wrapped rags around their feet to muffle their footsteps and crept past the German patrols in their search for provisions. Water was the overriding priority. "We budgeted the precious liquid with mathematical precision," Tuvia recalled. "What we managed to collect during our nocturnal forays was dirty and had a bad odor." It had to be filtered and strained through linens, and was then shared by nineteen people, including the old women. It often amounted to as little as a cup a day per person. Since there was never enough for bathing, no one had washed since the surrender. They were all infested with lice, and the stench in the hideout grew so overwhelming that it threatened to give them away. Already the smell had attracted a cat that kept scratching at their cupboard's false door. Edelman had to strangle the creature lest it lead the Germans to them. The Wehrmacht patrolmen returned regularly to check on the four old women who were living in the house openly. The soldiers seemed to be decent and took to calling one of the elderly castaways "grandmother." They'd leave her a few cigarettes at each visit. Once, when Tuvia's girlfriend and another female ZOB member got caught late at night foraging for food and water in one of the neighboring houses, they told the patrolmen they were relatives of the old woman. The privates led them to a well and helped them carry pails of water back to their "grandmother." The next day the kind Germans even brought some food.

Toward the second week of November, the patrolmen announced that this was their last visit. Their unit was being rotated out of the sector, to be replaced by the Waffen-SS. The entire area, they also warned, was slated next for demolition. The four old women could not stay any longer. They were to be relocated the following day. A wagon was being arranged to pick them up.

Inside the cupboard there was panic. Isaac and Zivia stared at each other in horror. What would they do? Where could they go? How would they slip past the new SS detachment? One thing was clear. Their refuge had run its course. They had another two or three days at most before sappers reached their location. "Get us some help," Zivia pleaded before the women were carted away.

Krakow had not been destroyed, and its medieval streets teemed with refugees and Mercedes limousines speeding in and out of Wawel Castle, the enormous Gothic fortress that perched high atop the ancient city.

Simha Ratheiser did not know the city well and was nervous about his meeting. It had been arranged through the Council to Aid Jews, and he had followed all their instructions and given all the correct passwords. But something was amiss. His instinct told him so. Krakow was not Warsaw. The Germans had always held an iron grip over the ancient town, and not even Hitler could find fault with its architectural treasures. Legions of Nazi bureaucrats had made the old Austrian protectorate their home in Poland. The prevailing language heard around the fountains in the ornate squares was German. The signs in all the fully stocked stores and Viennese-style cafés were in German. And the Gestapo went to great lengths to protect the thousands of colonial administrators posted there, as Isaac Zuckerman had discovered in 1942 when the local ZOB cell had been infiltrated, nearly costing him his life.

The city filled Simha with unease. "I had a feeling that Gestapo agents were everywhere," he recalled. Already he had been stopped several times during random document checks, which seemed far more frequent than in Warsaw. His new false papers had passed muster, but he knew they were not of the highest quality. They were forgeries rather than the originals commonly used in Warsaw. Their serial numbers could be cross-checked against master lists, with disastrous consequences. Nor did Simha have a backstory to go with his new identity in case of interrogation. All this made him question the wisdom of getting involved with the Krakow resistance. Local underground activists did not inspire him with confidence. They acted like rank amateurs compared to the seasoned conspirators in Warsaw. To Simha, many of them seemed destined for Gestapo torture chambers. He started keeping his distance, and when one contact didn't show up for a meeting, Ratheiser concluded that he was in grave danger. After everything he had been through, it made little sense to fall prey to a Gestapo trap this late in the game. The wisest course would be to get out of town and to return to more familiar ground. "I was sure the SS would be looking for me sooner or later. I knew I had to run and go back to Warsaw."

Still trapped in the cupboard in Jolie Bord, the ZOB fighters were down to ten people. They had sent out two groups to try to organize a rescue mission. The first pair got caught, forcing Isaac to send another party. Days had passed, and there was no word from them.

Early one morning, the remaining fighters were startled from their sleep by the sound of heavy footsteps on the floorboards above them. "It seemed as if several platoons of soldiers had invaded the house," Tuvia Borzykowski recalled. "We lay motionless, tense with fear, afraid to make the slightest noise. The commotion above us was gaining in intensity. We could also hear them running around in nearby basements. At one point quick steps ran to our basement and approached the cupboard behind which we were hiding. I already saw in my imagination ten bodies lying in pools of blood."

The Germans came and went throughout the next two days, returning always in greater numbers, moving furniture, shifting gear, and delivering supplies. It dawned on Tuvia and Isaac that sappers were setting up their temporary headquarters in the house, a base from which to blow up the surrounding buildings. This kept everyone confined to the cupboard, and made venturing out for toilet breaks extremely risky. "We got to know the soldiers working around our house," Tuvia went on. "We could recognize each by his voice and even knew some of their names. The ones I remember best were Max and Willie, both experienced looters."

The scavenging sappers often prowled the basement, looking for keepsakes. "I remember one dramatic moment when Max and Willie came up to the cupboard, both holding flashlights. We saw the light through the cracks; it wandered from face to face, and though the two men could not see us, we felt as though they were probing our hideout. Then we heard them touching the cupboard, and we braced ourselves for the long-expected moment, but all we heard was Willie saying to Max 'There's some grain here.' We realized they had found a sack in the heap of rags lying around the cabinet. They took the grain and went away."

Meanwhile the detonations around them grew louder, closer, and more intense. Soon the sappers would be finished with their work, and they would then blow up the house in which they had set up their temporary headquarters. Isaac was growing frantic with despair. By his forty-second day in the hellish tomb, he could no longer sleep. "That night was a night of horrors. I had nightmares and then woke up to discover that it wasn't a dream at all: I dreamed that the Germans had burst in on us. We heard the banging of hammers on the wall I was lying next to. We prepared our weapons, our grenades, so that we wouldn't be taken alive," he recalled. Then everything went quiet. The sappers had gone on a break. "Suddenly we heard a knock at the door, and shouts of 'Celina, Celina.' "

Celina was Zivia's code name. It was the rescue party. Tuvia's girlfriend had managed to reach Home Army operatives at a hospital in one of the satellite camps that handled the overflow from Pruszkow. She told the doctors there that some Home Army officers were trapped in Jolie Bord. "She had to be careful since she didn't know whom she was telling it to," Zuckerman recalled. "But it turned out that the director of the hospital was one of the Righteous Gentiles. He and his comrades formed a delegation of six volunteers who had [fake] Red Cross passes."

The "Red Cross" delegation arrived at the perfect moment, just as the soldiers had gone to eat at a nearby mobile cantina. The rescue party was led by a young Jewish doctor, Ala Margolis, who was familiar to Edelman because she had previously worked with the Bund. Margolis stayed on the Aryan side during the Ghetto period, posing as a Gentile. She brought stretchers and white smocks with her now to give credence to the Red Cross cover story, and she ordered that Edelman and another ZOB fighter with pronounced Semitic features have their faces wrapped in gauze. These two were placed on the gurneys, while Isaac and some of the others played the role of orderlies and carried them.

"Passing Germans looked at us with curiosity," Tuvia recalled. "We were the only civilians around. Occasionally a German soldier would ask, pointing at the stretcher, 'Is he dead yet?'" Anna, a pretty blond nurse who spoke fluent German, flirted with the guards at each checkpoint, warning *"Achtung, Fleckfieber,"* which meant "Watch out, typhus," which produced the intended result: The party was waved on without inspection. She even persuaded one group of friendly patrolmen to supply her with a horse-drawn wagon so the orderlies would not have to carry their heavy loads all the way to the hospital. The wagon was driven by an old Wehrmacht veteran with an eye patch. When Anna asked where he had been wounded, the old veteran cursed that it had been during the Ghetto Uprising. "Despicable Yids," he growled. Anna shook her head sympathetically, while in the back of the wagon Isaac had to nudge Tuvia to keep him from bursting into laughter.

CHAPTER 41

MARK AND THE MOHICANS

On the night of January 16, 1945, as temperatures plunged far below freezing, the western outskirts of Warsaw groaned with the rumble of thousands of engines. Looking out the frosted window of their new hideout, a rented brick tenement in the exurban town of Grodzik, the startled members of the ZOB witnessed column after column of vehicles exiting the Polish capital. Tanks, trucks, half-tracks, Mercedes and BMWs, motorcycles, and horse-drawn wagons—all manner of conveyances clogged the roads heading toward the Reich. Mark, Isaac, and Zivia looked at one another, stunned. The Germans were pulling out.

Early the next morning, when the familiar charcoal gray of the Wehrmacht was replaced by olive-green Buicks and Fords bearing large MADE IN THE USA labels, there was momentary confusion. Only the crudely welded T-34 tanks, with their distinctively rounded turrets and ingeniously sloping deflective armor, were unmistakably Soviet. The Red Army, riding a fleet of Lend-Lease American vehicles, had rolled into Warsaw.

The jubilation was immediate. Lubetkin, Zuckerman, and Edelman threw on their threadbare boots and rushed out into Grodzik's market square to greet the liberators. Thousands of others had already done the same, tears freezing on their sunken cheeks as they jumped and shrieked and waved at the bewildered soldiers. It was less the sight of the fur-clad Russians that filled them with glee than the sudden exhilaration of being safe at last from imminent death. All at once the specter of the SS, of torture chambers and killing squads, of concentration camps and random cruelty, had been lifted. The sudden rush of freedom was overwhelming. Many broke down and sobbed with joy.

Mark Edelman was not among them. Scanning the exuberant revelers who were hugging, kissing, singing, and passing bottles of vodka around, he was suddenly overcome by sorrow. Of the thousands of flushed faces in the ecstatic crowd, he recognized none as Jewish. This square had been inhabited almost exclusively by Jews before the war. Now only the broad blond visages of elated Slavs stared back at him, chanting the Polish national anthem—"And Poland Has Not Yet Perished."

Mark had never felt as alone as he did at that moment, surrounded by thousands of cheering people. The enormity of what had been lost suddenly hit him. Now that he was no longer consumed with concern for his immediate survival, he realized for the first time that nothing would ever be the same. Grodzik's town center would never again reverberate with Yiddish. Its Market Square would never again scramble to shut down before the Sabbath. In Warsaw, Cordials Street was gone. So were the Jewish cabarets, the bagel bakeries, the synagogues, Gold's Pharmacy, the jazz bars, Haberdasher's Row, the row of shoe stores on Frog Street.

The list of missing landmarks was endless and heartbreaking. Half a millennium of Polish-Jewish culture had been wiped out and nothing could bring back the millions of dead. In Poland, Jews now had only a past. The future had been erased. "It was the saddest day of my life," Edelman would later say of January 17, 1945. After the liberation festivities, he crawled into bed, refused to eat, and did not reemerge for weeks.

———

Post-traumatic stress disorder can affect individuals in vastly different ways. Stoic Zivia, usually so self-possessed that many thought her cold, wept uncontrollably. Boruch Spiegel lost his memory. Seventy years later, he drew a blank when asked about the period preceding the Soviet entry into Warsaw and his first weeks of freedom from Nazi persecution. Tuvia Borzykowski lost the ability to feel free. He developed a claustrophobic fear of small rooms, and for months he could not enter one without feeling that he was trapped. As for Joanna Mortkowicz-Olczak, she lost the most precious commodity a child can possess: the ability to laugh, smile, and feel joy.

Simha Ratheiser was not even aware that he suffered from the stress. Only years later did he learn that every night, after he fell asleep, he cried, screamed, and thrashed in bed as though he were being tortured. In the mornings he awoke refreshed, unaware of the nightmares. Like countless other Varsovians, Ratheiser had returned to the capital as soon as the Soviets swept in. "I finally realized that it was over," he recalled of walking through the endless ocean of ruins, trying to find his bearings. Nearly 90 percent of the city had been destroyed by the time the Germans pulled out, leaving Simha with an overwhelming sense of emptiness.

"I had been too busy doing a million things before to think about anything," he recalled. Now he and Irene understood clearly that they were looking "at a different world" from the one they had grown up in. Ratheiser, however, had still not grasped the full magnitude of the seismic political shift that Poland was undergoing. Encountering a Soviet patrol, Simha mouthed off to the rude Russian soldiers. "Are you crazy?" Irene grabbed him by the arm. "Are you trying to get yourself killed?"

"I was naïve," Simha later acknowledged. "I thought the Soviets were our friends."

It did not take long for most Poles to comprehend that they had simply traded one occupier for another, and that the Red Army was not just passing through Poland on its way to Berlin. Within a few short weeks, the country's fate had effectively been sealed at Yalta in Crimea, where Stalin, Roosevelt, and Churchill gathered in February 1945 to decide Europe's postwar reorganization. That the meeting was held in Stalin's backyard, at his summer palace on the shores of the Black Sea, was a testament to the Soviet dictator's extraordinary negotiating position. He had forced the ailing and visibly frail American president to make the taxing Atlantic crossing and then fly over dangerous German-controlled airspace to come to him. Roosevelt had done so, in the words of one U.S. negotiator, because it had been his long-standing policy to accommodate the Soviets: "Give them everything they want, for after all, they are killing Germans, they are fighting our battles for us."

Statistics proved the statement true. Soviet losses were sixty-five times greater than America's in World War II, and eight out of ten Germans who died in the war had fallen on the Eastern Front. Three-quarters of Hitler's forces were engaged against the Red Army, leaving the United States, Britain, Canada, Australia, the Free French, Polish, Czech, and other Allied formations to face what were often second-rate or reserve Wehrmacht divisions. The battles raging in the Western European theater were undeniably important, but the war had been fought primarily in the Soviet Union—in the slaughterhouses of Ukraine and Belarus and on the ravaged Russian steppe. More than twenty million Soviet citizens had died fending off Hitler. And now that Stalin's T-34 tanks were within forty miles of Berlin, he was demanding a geopolitical return on his bloody investment. Although he wanted all of Eastern Europe, Poland represented the jewel in the wrested crown, the largest and most populous of the sought-after acquisitions.

It was also the biggest thorn in Soviet-U.S. relations. The "Polish question," as the fate of a free and democratic Poland was referred to in the flurry of diplomatic communications between Washington, London, and Moscow, had been the main sticking point in preparations for the Big Three talks at Yalta. In the run-up to the conference, Churchill had been vehemently opposed to acquiescing to Stalin's land grab, as had U.S. Ambassador Averell Harriman, who bombarded Roosevelt with increasingly desperate pleas to stem "the barbarian invasion."

Once in Yalta, the recalcitrant Churchill was largely shunned, treated as a third wheel in the negotiations. Stalin monopolized nearly all of Roosevelt's time, and the British prime minister barely had a moment alone with the exhausted American president. Harriman, who had forged a close personal bond with Churchill from his time in London as Roosevelt's point man on the Lend-Lease program, also found himself sidelined in Yalta. "Harriman was never included in the private talks on Poland," his biographer bitterly noted, "although he undoubtedly realized better than any other American present how seriously Poland threatened all of Roosevelt's postwar dreams."

Roosevelt would subsequently come under criticism from some historians for sacrificing Eastern Europe to keep Stalin happy and to secure his pledge to enter the war against Japan. In fairness, the FDR who posed feebly next to a beaming Stalin on the shores of the Black Sea was not the same leader who twelve years earlier had rallied Americans from the depths of the Great Depression. "He is a very sick man," Churchill's physician commented during the Yalta Conference. "He has all the symptoms of hardening of the arteries in the brain in an advanced stage, so that I give him only a few months to live." The diagnosis proved prophetic. Roosevelt died of a cerebral hemorrhage exactly two months later. On April 5, 1945, one week before the U.S. president passed away, the United States formally withdrew the accreditation of Poland's London government in exile and recognized the new Provisional Government of National Unity, the puppet pro-Communist regime installed in the eastern town of Lublin by the NKVD. In London a sorrowful Churchill informed shocked Polish officials that "his heart bled for them, but the brutal facts could not be overlooked." The Polish question had been relegated, he sighed, to "little more than a grievance and a vast echoing cry of pain."

Meanwhile in Warsaw, the population had rebounded to 162,000 by spring 1945, as people slowly began to return from labor and concentration camps. "I cannot believe how fortunate I am to be alive," Hanna Mortkowicz wrote a relative in her first postwar letter. "Five and a half years of torment—of having to hide, and drift like beggars from village to suburb, of being blackmailed, and running for dear life. Two years of not seeing my child . . . Warsaw no longer exists. Of our family on Mama's side only Lutek and Genia were murdered. On your side the toll is more tragic: Helen, Alex, and his wife were killed in the Lodz Ghetto; Kasia in Warsaw; Helka and Lola in the Eastern lands. I have yet to find out about Joseph and Martha's family in Warsaw, but there's little chance they survived."

Hanna still had no news of Joanna's whereabouts, though she was now frantically searching for any trace of her daughter. Simha was also still desperately looking for his parents. Last he had heard, they were hidden in a farming village outside the capital. He tracked down the peasant family that had initially sheltered his mother and father in 1943, but the family had since lost contact with them. The farmers did say they were almost certain Simha's father was still alive and that he had worked as a laborer for the Germans. Ratheiser thought this an utter fabrication. How could his father, a Yiddish-speaking Orthodox Jew, survive so long right under the Germans' noses? Maybe his mother, but never his dad. Simha reacted furiously to what he presumed to be a lie. The peasants, he was sure, were playing games with him. "I went crazy and almost killed them," he recalled. "I kept screaming, where are my parents? What did you do with my parents?" Simha still carried a gun, and he might have used it had Irene not calmed him down.

Only later did Simha learn that the peasants had actually been telling the truth. One of the first governmental agencies established in Warsaw was a bureau of missing persons, the Office for the Search for Relatives. The office eventually found both Zvi and Miriam, who had become separated, alive and well. Once reunited with his parents, Simha heard firsthand the astonishing story of how his dad had duped the Germans by bandaging his face and pretending to be mute and had worked as a groom in the Wehrmacht stables until the day the Russians rode in.

Simha was astounded. He had never really respected his fervently religious father. He had always found him hapless and mystical, strange in dress and manner, someone from another era. But after hearing of his surprising resourcefulness, Simha saw his dad in a different light, and he never again made the mistake of underestimating him.

By the time Hanna Mortkowicz-Olczak located her daughter, Hitler was dead and Nazi Germany had unconditionally surrendered. In the two years that had passed since they last saw each other, Hanna had aged tremendously. Though she was not yet forty, she looked ten years older. The poor diet, the accumulated stress, the lack of sunlight and fresh air had had a devastating effect. All this time, Hanna had wondered how Joanna had grown up: how her long dark hair would look, how her irrepressible personality and mischievous streak had evolved, whether her reading and writing had progressed, whether her smile was still as radiant as she remembered. "She thought a tearful little girl with long plaits would fall into her arms," Joanna said, describing the tense reunion. "Instead she found a short-cropped, self-possessed, resolute person" who stared at her suspiciously. Joanna failed to recognize her own mother. "To me, she looked like a stranger."

The Soviet takeover of Poland proved an unexpected boon for Zuckerman and the ZOB. Though Isaac was not a Communist, his decision during the first days of the Rising to join the People's Army now began to pay lasting dividends, not only for the ZOB but for tens of thousands of surviving Polish Jews.

Isaac's earliest indication that he would enjoy an elevated status in postwar Poland occurred on the first day that the Red Army entered Warsaw. A Soviet intelligence officer came to his door, saying that a brigadier general had requested an audience with him and Zivia. Baffled at the uncharacteristically polite invitation, Zuckerman was amazed to discover that the Soviet general had arranged a banquet in his honor. Apparently Jacob Berman, head of the new Moscow-backed Polish secret police that had replaced the Gestapo, told the Russian commander about the ZOB's exploits. Berman had spent the war in Moscow, being trained by the NKVD. But his brother Adolf had been Mordechai Anielewicz's party boss and worked closely with Isaac after the Ghetto Uprising providing aid and shelter to Jews. That family connection now gave the ZOB a direct pipeline to Poland's new rulers. The Russian general turned out to be Jewish. He showered Isaac and Zivia with praise, alcohol, food supplies, and, most important, special military passes that allowed them to go anywhere they wanted.

The tables had turned for Resistance groups in postwar Warsaw. The tiny People's Army was celebrated by the new regime, while the Home Army's leaders were hunted by the NKVD as reactionaries. Many doors were suddenly open to the ZOB, as Simha Ratheiser soon discovered. Simha was no more of a Communist than Isaac, but he was not above taking advantage of the cards that fate dealt him. When he needed a place to live where his parents could also stay, Ratheiser flashed his special Soviet-issue military pass at the housing authority. He had received the document so that he and Irene could carry messages from Isaac in Warsaw to Wladyslaw Gomulka, the newly appointed deputy prime minister of the Provisional Government in Lublin.

At the housing bureau, that government-issue pass translated into astonishingly courteous service. The agency was in Praga, across the Vistula, as were most of the makeshift government offices, because that neighborhood had been under Soviet control during most of the Rising and had suffered the least damage. In Warsaw proper, the only surviving structures were clustered in pockets of the former German-only sectors, and had been spared because Germans were living there at the time. The housing shortage was now so acute that many former Varsovians, including Hanna, Janine, and Joanna Mortkowicz, had to make new lives for themselves in places like Krakow, where many artists and writers migrated. In Warsaw it was virtually impossible to get quartered in one of the large, luxurious flats left by the Germans. These were usually reserved for Communist Party higher-ups. Yet Simha was handed the keys to a huge apartment that had once belonged to an aristocrat on Jerusalem Boulevard. (On the other hand, Boruch Spiegel, who had fought with the Home Army, had to share a room with two families in a partially destroyed tenement. "It had no electricity or running water," he recalled.)

Zuckerman quickly understood that the ZOB had the opportunity to gain much more than just spacious apartments from the new regime. He shrewdly set out to make himself as useful as possible to the new authorities. The Provisional Government was effectively starting from scratch, with little popular support and no administrative infrastructure. The ZOB's organizational skills and extensive contacts were useful. "A lot of our misfortunes were solved after the war because they remembered what we had done for them," Isaac said later in describing the payoff from that early assistance. Zuckerman did not conceal his agenda. He developed a close rapport with the secretary of the Communist Party in Warsaw, Alexander Kowalski. Kowalski had spent much of the war in Moscow. But he was an old ideologue, fascinated with movements like Zionism, and Isaac was frank with him. "We were firm friends," he recalled. "I never had to hide our situation from him. And I spoke as a Kibbutznik, a Halutz, on behalf of Eretz Israel"—in other words, about emigration.

At that time, an estimated 11,500 Warsaw Jews had survived the war. And many of those who had fled east in 1939 were beginning to trickle back from the USSR. Eventually, more than 150,000 Polish Jews returned from the Soviet Union, raising the total number of Jews in Poland to more than 200,000, peaking briefly in 1946 at nearly 300,000. The relationships Isaac Zuckerman was cultivating with Poland's new rulers had one goal: to get those Jews to Palestine.

Mark Edelman did not share Isaac's vision. "Why are you cooperating with those sons of bitches?" he lectured his colleague. The two had grown so close over the past several years that Edelman supplanted Tuvia Borzykowski as Isaac's most trusted confidant and sounding board. "They were best friends," said Simha Ratheiser. But a serious rift developed between them over Isaac's plan to win over the new authorities. "They really started fighting," Ratheiser recalled. "We had differences of opinion," Edelman curtly conceded. "Let's leave it at that."

The ideological divisions that had delayed the unification of the Jewish Resistance and prevented the ZOB from being formed earlier in the war now returned. To Bundists like Edelman and Spiegel, Communists were the enemy, and Zuckerman was now trading with the enemy. That he was doing so for the benefit of tens of thousands of ordinary Jews and not for personal gain was immaterial to Mark. The Bund had sworn allegiance to Poland—*der hoym*—and the Communists were foreign invaders. As for Zuckerman's Zionist goals, to Edelman, Eretz Israel was still nothing more than a pipe dream. The British had made that clear by clamping down on immigration to Palestine.

To Mark, Palestine was an illusion. What was happening in Poland was very real. A low-grade civil war was breaking out as the Communists tried to consolidate their tenuous grip on power. Some 15,000 Communist functionaries were killed in the immediate post-war period by right-wing organizations, particularly the quasi-fascist

National Armed Forces. The right itself suffered almost as many casualties in the political standoff. In the eastern parts of the country, ethnic violence between Poles and Ukrainians claimed an estimated fifty thousand lives. In the west, where boundaries were shifted as part of the war reparations and seven million Germans were expelled from newly Polish cities like Breslau and Stettin, six hundred thousand people died. Many, though not all, were murdered by the Red Army. Revenge killings were common in the lawless environment of 1945. Mass graves of German civilians, including the skeletal remains of many women and children, would continue to be unearthed for decades to come.

The value of life in Poland was severely cheapened by the war. People had become inured to death. More than 15 percent of the population perished, the equivalent in contemporary America of almost fifty million lives. The corpses that accumulated in 1945 made little impression on hardened Poles who had seen so much death. Robbery, murder, and rape were daily occurrences during the lawless postwar period, and the situation was aggravated by the residual stores of weapons that left almost everyone armed. Simha and Mark never left home without their revolvers.

The Soviet secret police and Jacob Berman's newly created Security Office were busy trying to stamp out political dissent. In the first six months of 1945, sixty thousand Home Army officers were arrested by the NKVD. Among those was Henry Iwanski, who claimed to have lost most of his family fighting alongside the Jewish Military Union during the Ghetto Uprising. He was sent to prison, as were countless others who had helped Jews. Not even the intervention of Adolf Berman could prevent his brother Jacob from jailing Wladyslaw Bartoszewski, the Auschwitz survivor and future Righteous Gentile and Solidarity foreign minister, for the crime of serving in the Home Army's Council to Aid Jews.

The newest terror campaign was ruthlessly implemented by Jacob Berman. But it was presided over by NKVD general Ivan Serov, who later became head of the KGB. His temporary office in Praga soon replaced the old Gestapo headquarters on Szuch Avenue as the most feared address in Warsaw. It was in the same student dormitory where Menachem Begin had lived while he studied law, and Isaac went there on a few occasions to meet with the "great Berman," as he cynically called Poland's newest villain. (Ironically, Jacob Berman was also a graduate of the University of Warsaw law faculty, though any similarity between him and Begin ended there.)

Edelman couldn't stomach the fact that his best friend was associating with people he considered traitors, like Berman, who had been personally trained by Stalin's chief butcher, Lavrenty Beria, to stamp out all opposition to the Soviet takeover of Poland. To Edelman, Zuckerman's Zionism was blinding him to all sorts of moral traps. "Isaac and Zivia had changed," Mark recalled. "I no longer knew what to talk to them about, they were so consumed with their burning obsession of getting people into Palestine."

Edelman felt betrayed. "I was alone and I didn't know what to do. My friends were engaged in activities I did not support. My party was gone"—the Bund had been wiped out by the Holocaust—"and there were Communists and Soviets everywhere." The few Bundists still around, people like Boruch Spiegel and Chaika Belchatowska, were not interested in reconstituting the Bund in Poland so much as "putting an ocean between them and the Russians. They wanted to run as far away as possible from Communism."

Indeed, Boruch and Chaika had decided not to stay in Communist Poland. "There was no future there for us," Spiegel felt. His entire family was dead. Not even photographs of his parents, his sisters, or his big brother Berl had survived. His only living relative was an uncle in Billings, Montana. Boruch sent him a telegram, hoping he could sponsor them. But the news on immigration to America was not encouraging. "The United States did nothing for Jews during the war," Spiegel concluded. For Boruch and Chaika, Palestine was not an option for ideological reasons, and Western Europe was teeming with refugees. That left Canada and Australia. Chaika's father had moved to Montreal long before the war. She did not know him well; his divorce from her mother had been bitter. But finding him was their best hope.

Edelman, on the other hand, had no intention of leaving. Poland, for all its glaring imperfections and bleak prospects, was home. Mark had no idea what he would do with his life now that the Bund was history. He did, however, still have one last duty to perform for the organization. Some Bundists had placed their children with Gentiles prior to joining the ZOB, often with nuns in convents. The money originally provided for the children's care had long run out. Had they survived? What had become of them? Government agencies were said to be handling such matters. But due to a sense of obligation to his deceased comrades, Mark set out to track down these lost children. One case in particular weighed heavily on his conscience. During the Ghetto Uprising he had promised Zalman Friedrich that he would find his daughter if anything ever happened to him. Friedrich was the Bund courier who had first uncovered the truth about Treblinka by following the railroad tracks. Zalman had fought tenaciuosly in the Brushmakers District alongside Simha and Edelman during the Ghetto Uprising, and he had been sent along with Simha to help Zuckerman organize a rescue mission. At the last moment he had begged not to join Ratheiser in the May 1943 sewer evacuation, because he had a premonition that he would never see his daughter again. He died senselessly a few weeks later when a German patrol stumbled on ZOB combatants hiding in the woods outside Warsaw. His daughter, Eliza, would be six years old now, if she was alive.

It took some work, but Edelman finally found his friend's daughter. She was with a Catholic family in a small town called Zyrardow, and like Joanna, she had forgotten about her real family and background. "Hide, hide, the Jews are coming for you," the other kids in the village cried when Edelman and another Bundist showed up. Eliza refused to see them, and the woman of the house would not give her up. Eliza now called her "mother." She spoke Polish rather than Yiddish. She made the sign of the cross when she prayed and considered Zyrardow her adoptive home. Edelman offered the woman a large sum of money: five hundred U.S. dollars collected in America by Jewish relief agencies. The woman was offended. Eliza was "not for sale," she said.

Edelman refused to give up. There were too many Elizas in postwar Poland: children who would never know who they were and where they came from, whose Jewish past had been swapped for a Catholic future. Often their identity was concealed from them for decades, and only in middle age, after the collapse of Communism in 1989, would many finally learn the truth about their real parents. Mark returned to the woman two more times, and still she would not relinquish the child. Only then did Edelman reluctantly cash in on the ZOB's connections with the Communist authorities. He offered the woman a trade. Her sixteen-year-old son had been caught in one of the secret police roundups of Home Army operatives and was in jail. If Edelman arranged his release, would the woman give up Eliza?

Eliza cried nonstop for two weeks while Mark made arrangements with Bundist contacts in the United States for the child to travel to America. A wealthy Jewish family in New York had agreed to adopt her. "In America she had a bicycle, a pony, a boat. She graduated from university, and got married," Edelman recounts. "Then on October 18, 1962, two months before her twenty-sixth birthday, she locked herself in a hotel room in Manhattan and swallowed a vial of poison." Mark did not know why Eliza killed herself. But the night before her death, she had met with another Holocaust orphan, the daughter of Michael Klepfish, the ZOB chief engineer responsible for the manufacture of homemade bombs and grenades in the Ghetto. Klepfish had died in the Brushmakers District while saving Edelman's life.

Every time a Jewish child was sent to the United States or Palestine by relief agencies, Edelman felt more alone, like the "last of the Mohicans," as he would put it. Despite his increasing despair and isolation, he found some comfort from a new person in his life, Alina Margolis. She was the young doctor who had led the "Red Cross" rescue mission to Jolie Bord. They became romantically involved while in Grodzik before the liberation, and after the Soviet takeover she helped nurse Mark through his depression. They fell in love and began living together.

Margolis wanted to leave the depressing capital. Her family was from Lodz, seventy-five miles west of Warsaw, where more Jews had lived before the war than in Berlin and Vienna combined. Only a few thousand remained, but the city was still relatively intact. Margolis had a town house in Lodz, in a prestigious enclave about a mile from the Central Station. Germans had appropriated the enclave during the war, but many budding artists and filmmakers were moving there, including Roman Polanski and Krzysztof Kieslowski.

Edelman agreed to go, arriving with nothing but the clothes on his back. The city in mid-1945 was still largely empty. When it had been incorporated into the Third Reich, all the Poles had been expelled. There were thousands of vacant apartments, and people from all over the country were arriving weekly to fill them: doctors, lawyers, engineers, and university professors. In Lodz everything was restarting from scratch, including institutes, universities, and factories. The Communist influence was not as prevalent as in Warsaw, and the new residents seemed freer, more energetic and hopeful. To Edelman, it seemed like a good place for a fresh start.

CHAPTER 42

NEXT YEAR IN JERUSALEM

A year had passed since the Red Army rolled into Warsaw, and the city remained largely uninhabitable. Boruch Spiegel's building was still without electricity or running water, and he and Chaika Belchatowska continued to wait for Canadian visas. Mark Edelman was in Lodz, finishing his first semester of medical school. After witnessing so much death, he had decided to devote himself to saving lives.

Most of the other surviving members of the ZOB were also still in Poland in early 1946. Only Simha Ratheiser and Zivia Lubetkin had gone abroad for any extended period since the Soviet takeover. Both went to Romania to scout discreet back channels to circumvent the British blockade of Palestine. The human smuggling network they were trying to help establish became known in Hebrew as the *Brikha*, or Flight. The *Brikha* was an illegal enterprise that initially moved Jews overland from Poland through Czechoslovakia and Hungary to the Romanian shores of the Black Sea. There, vessels chartered or purchased by Jewish relief agencies departed for the final and trickiest leg of the journey, trying to evade the British warships that patrolled the Mediterranean approaches to ports around Haifa. The operation was costly and complex and, in its early stages, frustratingly ineffective. In mid-1945, thousands of stranded Jews languished in Romania, which had become a refugee terminus, much as it had been for the Osnoses five years earlier. There were not enough boats. There was not enough money. And in world capitals there was not enough political will to overcome British opposition. While a steady trickle of refugees was getting through to Palestine, a far more organized method would be required to systematically move several hundred thousand people. And for that, tacit cooperation would be needed of various governments, Poland's and Britain's most of all.

Although her early smuggling efforts in Romania fell short, there was one pleasure in Zivia's return to Poland. In early 1946, Lubetkin discovered she was pregnant. Isaac wept with joy. For Holocaust survivors, every birth was a national rebirth, a rejoinder to genocide. Zuckerman immediately insisted that Zivia cease all conspiratorial activity to conserve her strength for the baby. He moved her to Lodz, where he thought she would be more comfortable, and asked Edelman to look after her.

In the meantime, Isaac continued to sweet-talk the new Polish authorities into facilitating emigration. Already, he had won permission from the Communists to purchase fishing trawlers in Gdansk, though the distant Baltic was hardly an ideal departure point for a lengthy seaborne operation to the Mediterranean. Isaac also persuaded his friends in the government to supply him with a plane so that he and other Polish delegates could attend a pan-Zionist conference in London. The event was hosted by David Ben-Gurion, and its purpose was partly to pressure Whitehall to relax its strict immigration policies to the Holy Land. The British were not swayed. They were under intense pressure from Arab leaders to restrict Jewish entry into Palestine. In the end, the conference served mostly to expose the rift within the Zionist camp between emaciated Holocaust survivors and the tanned, muscular emissaries from Palestine. There were clearly lingering resentments among the Polish delegates, who had felt abandoned during the war by their colleagues in Palestine. "I said bitter things at the conference," Zuckerman acknowledged, "and even then I hadn't said everything I felt because I knew there were attentive listeners and curious journalists." Privately, Isaac made a point of snubbing Ben-

Gurion, prompting the future Israeli leader to declare ruefully, "You despise me that much."

Zuckerman returned from England doubly convinced that the solution to mass emigration lay not in pointless congresses abroad, but in Poland with the new regime. The Provisional Government had already expressed its willingness to allow Jews to emigrate. Throughout 1945 and early 1946, the authorities had made no effort to stop Jewish citizens from leaving Poland. Very few did so, however, because they had nowhere to go: Destination countries either were not admitting Jews, or were dragging their feet on the documentation process and were therefore swamped with a backlog of applications. The net effect was that nearly three hundred thousand Jews were still stuck in Poland, even though a majority wanted out and the regime was willing to let them go.

Simha Ratheiser, as usual, was not content to leave his fate to distant powers. He was determined to make his own luck. After returning from Romania in 1945, Simha had drifted away from Isaac and Zivia's inner circle. The schism started in Bucharest, where Ratheiser met one of the founders of the *Brikha,* the poet-warrior Abba Kovner. Kovner was legendary in Jewish underground circles, the Mordechai Anielewicz of Vilna. He had commanded the resistance in the Vilna Ghetto and then led his followers into the forest to fight as partisans. Like Anielewicz, he was charismatic, emotional, at times rash, and far more militant than Isaac Zuckerman. In Bucharest, in addition to facilitating illegal emigration, Kovner had proposed forming Jewish revenge squads. The teams would fan out in Austria and Germany and assassinate Nazis. There was also talk of targeting ordinary civilians, poisoning wells, and planting bombs. Isaac and Zivia were vehemently opposed to such plans. There had been enough revenge killing already, Zivia argued with Kovner; their priority must be emigration. Simha, however, sided with Kovner. "I thought we still had something to do in Europe," he later wrote: "To settle our account with the Germans."

Whether the revenge squads were ever formed or unleashed is not completely clear. Simha himself had a change of heart along the way. At Kovner's request, he agreed to return to Poland and then to infiltrate Germany, but while in Warsaw he changed his mind. Simha had killed in self-defense, but he was not bloodthirsty. He lacked the assassin's temperament. Instead of joining a revenge squad, he volunteered to take forty refugees out of the country for Kovner's *Brikha*. This was another principal difference between Isaac and Kovner. Kovner was impatient, a man of continual action. To him, smuggling small groups was better than doing nothing. Zuckerman disdained this piecemeal approach. He wasn't interested in evacuating forty people at a time; he wanted to move forty thousand in one shot, even if that meant waiting, and patiently working the official channels.

Isaac decided to remain in Poland as long as necessary to coordinate the mass emigration. Ratheiser worried that it could take years. He wanted out now. So did Zivia. Her pregnancy had changed her outlook. It added a sense of personal urgency to her quest to reach Palestine. She wanted to give birth in Eretz Israel.

In the late spring of 1946, Simha bade his former comrades farewell and set out for the Polish-Czech border. His plan was to cross a mountainous stretch of the frontier under the cover of darkness. Unfortunately, the group he led included children and elderly Jews. The children were noisy and the elderly were slow-footed. A patrol apprehended them almost immediately. As they were brought to a border military garrison, Simha displayed the sort of quick thinking that had gotten him through so many scrapes during the war. As soon as an officer showed up to interrogate the group, Ratheiser feigned outrage. He flashed an International Red Cross identification card that he had procured for just such purposes and began to berate the officer for the behavior of his troops. They had stolen valuables from the refugees, Ratheiser charged, and had brought dishonor to the Polish Army. Simha was an accomplished liar and actor; he had been impersonating others for years, and, in his mock indignation, he grew so animated that he knocked over an inkwell by slamming his fists onto a table. The refugees were Hungarian survivors of Auschwitz, Ratheiser angrily lectured the Poles. After all that they had suffered, they simply wanted to go home.

Simha's performance must have been convincing, for the chastened district commander arranged for the group to be put on a train the next morning and called ahead to his Czech counterparts on the other side of the border to say that they had been precleared.

Once Simha was across the frontier, he made a rare selfish choice.

Ever since he had joined the ZOB, Ratheiser had worked for a collective good. The needs of the organization had always superseded his personal requirements. But now he decided to ditch his cumbersome followers at a *Brikha* checkpoint and continue alone. The chances of getting such a large and unwieldy group through Romania—or Austria and Italy, on a more direct route that *Brikha* was developing— were minimal. Traveling alone, he could get to Italy faster and find a boat.

The vessel that Simha eventually boarded in June 1946 was an old Greek tub called the *Biriya*. It was one of sixty-eight illegal emigration ships surreptitiously acquired and converted by the Haganah, the paramilitary self-defense force formed in the 1920s by Labor Zionist settlers in Palestine, to ferry Jews into the British Mandate. The ship was small compared to many others in the Haganah flotilla, and because of its relative stealth it was often used to make the final, most dangerous run to Palestine. When the Haganah's bigger passenger liners approached the coastline, refugees were transferred by lifeboat to the more nimble *Biriya* to better evade British destroyers. On Simha's voyage, unfortunately, a British corvette moved faster. He and all the other passengers were detained and shipped to the Altit Detention Camp, just south of Haifa. With its rail spur and barbed wire fences, its watchtowers and long wooden barracks, the camp looked familiar to Holocaust survivors. But peering past the fences and guard dogs, Simha saw palm trees and the future. He was not yet a free man, but he was in the Land of Israel.

By June 1946, Zivia Lubetkin had also left Poland forever. Isaac had mixed feelings about letting his pregnant wife undertake the perilous journey to Palestine by herself. But in the end he stayed in Poland to pursue his efforts on behalf of the wider Jewish community. Someone had to keep pushing the government, and Zuckerman was best positioned to fulfill that role.

On July 4, he was sitting in the office of Polish prime minister Edward Osobka-Morawski. He and Adolf Berman had come to talk to Poland's unelected leader about Palestine and the mass arrests of Jewish activists that had taken place there a few days earlier in a security sweep known as Black Saturday. Zuckerman and Berman wanted the Polish government to condemn Britain's crackdown against paramilitary Zionist organizations such as the Haganah, the Palmach, the Irgun, and the Stern Gang, whom the British were accusing of terrorism.

The prime minister nodded sympathetically, doubtless aware that Berman's brother outranked him in the regime's opaque hierarchy. As the head of the Soviet-established secret police, Jacob Berman was said to be the second most powerful man in Poland. "It was even said that he had a direct line to Stalin," Zuckerman recalled. In Poland, Jacob Berman answered only to Soviet NKVD general Ivan Serov. Serov took his orders from the infamous Soviet secret police chief Lavrenty Beria, who in turn answered only to Stalin. Key decisions on Polish matters of state were thus conveyed from Stalin to Beria to Serov, who then relayed the instructions to Berman. The prime minister was even farther down the chain.

Anxious not to offend his well-connected guests, the prime minister suggested that Isaac draft a statement for the Foreign Ministry to look at, but he cautioned that there were larger issues at stake and that Poland's situation vis-à-vis Britain was delicate. While the British had reluctantly recognized the new Provisional Government, they still held all of Poland's gold reserves. In London, former officials from the government in exile, who had shipped the gold to England during the war, were lobbying hard for the bullion to remain in British safes. So Poland was effectively bankrupt, the prime minister reminded Isaac. Children in Warsaw were required to spend one school day each week clearing rubble and cleaning bricks because there was so little money for rebuilding. The country desperately needed its gold, and could ill afford to cross the British.

Isaac sighed and said he understood. He was growing increasingly frustrated by his inability to push mass emigration through diplomacy. His work was not bearing fruit. Maybe Kovner and some of the other critics were right; maybe he was just wasting time, "pissing in the wind," as Mark Edelman once put it. After all, what did he have to show for eighteen months of slavish courtship of the Communists? For all those toasts to Stalin's health? In some respects, the whole emigration plan was losing steam. Much of the early momentum had been lost once the initial shock that accompanied the Allied discovery of death camps had waned in the West. To most Allied governments, the humanitarian crisis associated with the Holocaust was over. Now that Jews were no longer considered at risk in Eastern Europe, there was no great urgency to evacuate survivors. Priorities were shifting for Western policymakers: a new conflict, the Cold War, with a new menace, the Soviet Union, was becoming a more immediate concern.

The perception that Jews were now safe in Poland was, tragically, false. The defeat of Nazi Germany had done little to change the anti-Semitic views of the ONR, the Falanga, the Sword and the Plough, and the National Armed Forces. While these far-right groups had primarily turned to killing Communists—an estimated fifteen thousand in 1945 and 1946—they still murdered Jews when the opportunity arose. The greasers still robbed and raped, only now they were less disposed to leave witnesses. And a third, perhaps even more disturbing phenomenon also began to manifest itself: greed killings. During the early stages of the war, many Jews had left valuables with neighbors and acquaintances or arranged for Gentiles to assume nominal ownership of their businesses to prevent the Nazis from seizing them. After the Holocaust, many of the temporary custodians believed they were now entitled to the assets. When Jewish survivors began trickling home, they were not always welcomed. "People were shocked," Boruch Spiegel recalled. " 'Where are all these Jews coming from?' they asked. 'How could so many still be alive?' "

In some cases, particularly in small towns, peasants who had assumed control of Jewish mills or other small businesses opted to kill the returning owners rather than step back down to their previous status. What was most distressing was that the murderers were not hate-filled fascists motivated by warped ideology and nationalism, or career criminals like the greasers. They were outwardly ordinary citizens with no history of violence. This, more than any other indicator, showed how far the value of life—particularly Jewish life—had plunged in postwar Poland. It could be traded for a leg up on the socioeconomic ladder.

Since official records were not properly kept during this chaotic period, the total number of Jews murdered in 1945 and 1946 is not precisely known. Estimates by American scholars range from a low of five hundred to as many as fifteen hundred deaths. Historians and sociologists also struggle to explain the resergence in anti-Semitism in the immediate postwar period. The effects of five years of relentless Nazi propaganda are cited as one major contributor. Guilty consciences may also have played a role. For some Poles, the presence of Jewish survivors served as a reminder of their own less than honorable behavior during the war. They may have wanted the witnesses and victims of their shameless acts gone, out of sight and mind. Mark Edelman had a simpler explanation: In this Hobbesian period, the strong preyed on the weak—and Holocaust survivors were severely weakened. "Most of the attacks were pure and simple banditry, crimes of opportunity," he asserted. "They had nothing to do with anti-Semitism."

Edelman would not dispute, however, that hateful ideology underpinned some of the crimes. Jews were "victims of the atmosphere created by the National Armed Forces," he explained. "You'd hear in those days how Hitler didn't get a chance to finish his work because there were a few Jews left, and those Jews want to seize control of Poland." He was referring to the high-profile role that a tiny percentage of Jews were playing in the Soviet takeover. Some Jews were among the Polish Communists who had spent the war in Moscow being trained by the NKVD. Their numbers were relatively small, almost certainly fewer than a thousand officials, a tiny fraction of the nearly three hundred thousand surviving Polish Jews. Nonetheless, they occupied perhaps as much as half of the senior posts and almost all the top slots in the new Soviet-installed secret police agencies.

This was not accidental. Stalin had a policy of pitting ethnic groups against one another throughout his empire. In Lithuania, for instance, the Polish minority did much of the NKVD's dirty work. In Poland, Jewish survivors were sometimes recruited right out of the death camps by this new security apparatus. Told they would hunt Nazis and Gestapo collaborators, many eagerly signed on, thirsting for revenge. And part of the ministry's function was indeed to bring war criminals to justice; the SS general Jürgen Stroop, for instance, was in a Warsaw jail cell awaiting trial and execution for suppressing the Ghetto Uprising. The secret police, however, did not confine itself to hunting Nazis. Its primary role was to stamp out opposition to

Poland's annexation into the Soviet bloc, and Jacob Berman's agency rapidly became the country's most hated institution.

"It was already bad enough [for Jews after the war], but [Berman's agency] made the situation worse," Boruch Spiegel said. As Stalin possibly intended, his stratagem deflected popular anger away from the Soviet Union and channeled it internally toward an ethnic minority. Residual anti-Semitism stoked the political fires, and Jews with no role in the new regime were disproportionately targeted in Poland's low-grade civil war. The killings attracted little or no attention outside Poland because they occurred sporadically and individually against a persistently violent backdrop. Political and ethnic strife was also claiming the lives of thousands of Germans, Ukrainians, and Polish Gentiles. The continuing murders of Jews had not produced newspaper headlines in America or England, altered public opinion, or swayed Western policymakers. But as Isaac sat in the prime minister's office on July 4, 1946, discussing ways to pressure London into liberalizing Palestinian immigration, an event was unfolding that would change all that.

Their meeting was interrupted by the ringing of a telephone. "Gentlemen—a great catastrophe," the prime minister said after taking the call. "A pogrom in Kielce. A pogrom against Jews."

That night Isaac raced to Kielce, about a hundred miles southwest of Warsaw. The roads were in bad shape, and he did not arrive until early morning, by which time the streets were empty. "Kielce was a ghost town," he found. Zuckerman instructed his driver to take him to Planty Street, the epicenter of the violence, where he encountered a scene all too familiar from the Warsaw Ghetto. Feathers from ripped bedding covered the street. Furniture and pots and pans lay strewn on the sidewalks. Shards of glass were everywhere, along with dark pools of coagulated blood. And then there were the bodies: dozens of them, some hastily covered by newspapers, leaving bruised and battered limbs exposed.

Soldiers and militiamen milled around. Isaac approached an officer, demanding to see the ranking Security Office commander, who received him immediately and with great courtesy. It was obvious that the local secret police chief, Major Wladyslaw Sobczynski, knew of Isaac's impending arrival and had been instructed to cooperate.

Isaac started asking questions, trying to clarify details. The sequence of events was still murky, obscured by contradictory accounts. But Zuckerman quickly pieced together a rough picture of what had occurred. The trouble started when an eight-year-old Gentile boy failed to return home. He had gone to visit relatives in an outlying village without informing his parents, who notified the police that the boy was missing. Somehow a rumor spread that the child had been kidnapped by Jews and taken to Planty Street, where several hundred Jewish refugees were living in a large hostel. According to the rumor, the residents of the hostel were holding the boy in the basement and preparing to sacrifice him for a religious ritual. A crowd gathered on Planty Street, demanding the boy's return. The police arrived and discovered that the building had no basement at all. But the revelation only whipped the mob into a greater frenzy, and it steadily grew, attracting onlookers, passersby, and residents from throughout the neighborhood. The police sealed the building, keeping Jewish residents inside. Uniformed officers swept the hostel for weapons, confiscating pistols and a few rifles that members of a Zionist youth group had been using for target practice.

What happened next was less clear. According to Major Sobczynski, he called the local police chief, informed him that the kidnapping charges were nothing but a "provocation," and instructed him to withdraw his officers. The Security Office and the uniformed militia had a long-standing rivalry in Kielce, according to the Princeton historian Jan Gross, which allegedly began because Sobczynski's predecessor was Jewish. The militia had anti-Semitic members. After the call, Sobczynski dispatched one of his deputies, Albert Grynbaum, with two carloads of Security Office agents to remove the militia officers from Planty Street. A scuffle between the militiamen and the security agents broke out. By now the crowd was many hundred strong, and it sided with the militiamen. People started to hurl stones and insults at the Security Office men. Meanwhile, several truckloads of Polish soldiers showed up, and the mob began to shout for the military to search the hostel for the missing boy. Agent Grynbaum retreated inside the building. "I assembled about forty Jews in one room and didn't let the soldiers in. I told [the soldiers] that their task was to restore order in the street rather than carry out the search," he later testified. "A few minutes later two Jews came to tell me that the military were killing Jews and plundering their possessions. This was when I heard shots."

An orgy of violence then erupted. "Uniformed soldiers and a number of civilians forced their way into the building," Boruch Dorfman, a resident of the Jewish refugee hostel, recalled. "They told us to get out and form a line. Civilians, including women, were on the stairs. The soldiers hit us with their rifle butts. Civilians, men and women, also beat us. . . . We came down to the square. Others who were brought out with me were stabbed with bayonets and shot at. We were pelted with stones."

By the time the pogrom was over, more than forty Jews had been murdered, and many more were in critical condition. As Isaac listened to Major Sobczynski's report, he was fairly certain that he wasn't getting the full story. But his priority wasn't apportioning blame. Polish courts could do that later. His immediate concern was looking after the wounded and evacuating the survivors to safety. Isaac called Adolf Berman to arrange for a Red Cross train to be sent from Krakow. He also telephoned Mark Edelman. Although the two had drifted apart, Isaac needed someone he could trust. Mark had just finished his first full year of medical school, training that could be useful. Edelman immediately agreed to come to Kielce with the hospital train.

While Zuckerman waited for medical help to arrive, he supervised the collection of the corpses. They were scattered in staircases, in the street, in the square—even as far afield as the train stations of neighboring towns, where Jews had been forcibly removed from railcars and bludgeoned to death. Some of the pogrom victims had been mutilated. One pregnant woman had had her uterus ripped out. Another had been chased by a mob to a riverbank, where she was stoned to death. Shockingly, the perpetrators had been ordinary Poles: bakers and seamstresses, white-collar workers and carpenters, God-fearing Catholics who went to church on Sundays. How, after the tragedy of the Holocaust, something like this could occur in a supposedly civilized society, Isaac could not understand.

————

Newspaper editors around the world were asking the same question when, a few days later, Zuckerman received a call from a senior Security Office agent in Warsaw. Was Isaac free for coffee, the caller wanted to know. Two men met Zuckerman at a café. He didn't know their real names, but he recognized one as Jewish. They wanted to discuss emigration. If Jews were to leave Poland in large numbers, was there someone from the Jewish community who would take charge of the departure, they asked. "I said I personally would take responsibility," Zuckerman recalled. The second question was equally direct. How were Isaac's relations with Deputy Defense Minister Marian Spychalski? They were friends from Underground days, Isaac responded. Zuckerman should go see the minister, the Security Office men suggested.

Isaac and Adolf Berman called on Spychalski together. "We were accepted without delay. I'll never forget Spychalski's reaction," Isaac recalled. "The meeting with him was warm. Like us, he was shocked at the pogrom in Kielce." Not as shocked as he led Zuckerman and Berman to believe, however. Unbeknownst to the pair, Spychalski had issued orders during the pogrom for the military not to fire on Gentiles. He and other officials in Warsaw had feared "any action which might indicate that the authorities were siding with the Jews against 'the people,' " according to the historian Jan Gross. "In lieu of rushing to the defense of imperiled citizens—the Jews of Kielce who were being murdered—the guiding concern of the authorities was to persuade the public that they were not unduly preoccupied with safeguarding the Jews."

Spychalski did something in that meeting that stunned Isaac. He picked up the phone and called the Soviet general responsible for securing Poland's borders. "Do not under any circumstances use the northern borders," Spychalski instructed the general. "Use the southern route, across the Czech border." Zuckerman and Berman could not believe what they were hearing: The military was being conscripted in the *Brikha* illegal emigration campaign. The Polish government's involvement must be kept quiet, the two were told. The Foreign Ministry, in particular, could not publicly approve the enterprise, for fear of upsetting relations with the British. Berman and Zuckerman exchanged bewildered looks. Was this possible, Isaac wondered. "Could

Spychalski, who was acting as Minister of Defense, have decided such a thing on his own?" he asked himself. "Jacob Berman certainly didn't [take such a step] without asking Moscow." That meant the Soviets must have given their approval to the plan. "Perhaps 'high politics' was at work here," Isaac speculated. In light of the brewing Cold War, "the consideration might have been to make trouble for the British" by allowing several hundred thousand left-leaning Jews, many of whom had spent years in the Soviet Union and spoke fluent Russian, to destabilize Palestine. Maybe the Kremlin was hoping to gain a foothold in the Middle East. Whatever the reason, the decision to facilitate a sudden exodus was highly uncharacteristic of a regime that went to great lengths to imprison its subjects for the next half century.

For a few weeks, discussions of the logistics of the evacuation were kept tightly under wraps, and Zuckerman began to wonder whether the whole scheme had been just talk. Then events started moving quickly. In late July, the Polish authorities announced that they were building summer camps for Jews along the Czech border, and thousands began gathering at the "open-air resorts." Czechoslovakia's leader, Jan Masaryk, then declared that his country would open its border to Jewish refugees. In Washington, President Harry S Truman pronounced himself in favor of the establishment of a "Jewish National Home" in Palestine.

The floodgates had opened. By October 1946, seventy thousand Jews left Poland for Palestine through the unguarded border. By December, the number had risen to 115,500. Isaac Zuckerman surveyed the long, orderly columns of Jewish emigrants leaving Poland and knew that his work was done. At long last, he could join Zivia and his newborn child in Palestine.

He was going home.

AFTERWORD
Jerusalem, March 2009

"Don't be afraid," Simha Ratheiser reassured me, as a group of young Palestinians surrounded us. "It is enough that I'm afraid for all of us."

Simha didn't look particularly frightened. In fact, he looked as if he was enjoying himself. My wife, Roberta, and I, on the other hand, were somewhat rattled, bordering on terrified, and wondering with increasing anxiety what kind of a mess Simha had gotten us into.

Our excursion had started out innocently enough. We had been sitting in Simha's garden, sipping wine from his son's vineyard and discussing Hillary Clinton's first trip to Jerusalem as U.S. secretary of state—she had taken over the King David Hotel, where Roberta and I were staying—when Ratheiser suggested that we stretch our legs. He lived in a quiet residential neighborhood about a mile south of the King David and the Old City, on a leafy hilltop street along the 1949 armistice line—the pre-1967 border that once divided Jerusalem into Arab and Jewish halves.

Simha wanted us to see the gleaming condominium complexes that had been erected over the squatters' camps on the other side of the old demarcation line. "Don't go far," his wife, Dima, admonished.

"It's getting late." She was also a Polish Jew and a Holocaust survivor. Now she was an accomplished artist and a supporter of Peace Now, the group that advocated returning the occupied territories to Palestinian rule. "I'll show you why that's impossible," Simha said, as he grabbed a sweater and led us out the door.

"This is the old border," said Simha minutes later, as we walked past a series of large new single-family homes. "I remember the shooting here." The structures were crisp and modern, whitewashed and well tended, with dramatic views of the congested and far poorer Arab quarter that spread out below them. But aside from their intrusive vistas, staring down at the less fortunate, the big hillside homes were devoid of any outward signs of controversy. Without an old map, one could never tell that this expensive real estate perched on disputed land. "What's that?" my wife asked, pointing to a large forested tract that undulated over the barren ravines and valleys below. "That's a wonderful park," said Simha. "Come. I'll show it to you."

The former armistice line also ran through the sprawling park, and as we walked and talked and lost track of time, it became apparent—just after dusk—that we had crossed the pre-'67 border. You could tell because the park grounds, at first immaculate and manicured, with shiny plaques naming the American benefactors of benches and paths and lookouts, had gradually deteriorated as we headed east. Arabic graffiti appeared, then trash. The lights that had flickered brightly from ornate lampposts farther west seemed to dim, then went out completely as we went deeper into the park. I noticed that the bulbs had all been shattered, presumably by thrown rocks. There were no longer any joggers or people walking dogs now that night had fallen—just the three of us in this great big dark park. Then we heard music, pounding Arabic rap, and saw teens and young men in their early twenties milling around, smoking cigarettes and laughing loudly. They fell silent as Simha approached, Roberta and I nervously in tow. Venturing into a wooded public park after nightfall was not something we'd ever attempt back home in Washington, D.C., and it didn't seem like a good idea in conflict-torn Israel. But Simha was oblivious to any potential danger. "Don't worry!" he kept saying to my increasingly desperate pleas to turn around. Now in his eighties, his hair white, his frame still wiry and spry, his demeanor still mischievous, he parted the stunned crowd of Palestinian youths with the same fearless abandon he had displayed as a young man in World War II. The young Palestinians murmured what sounded like curses and glared at us with surly contempt. But they obediently stepped aside, letting us pass through the dark lane as if we were a heavily armed military patrol. "Are you hungry?" Simha cheerfully asked as we approached a United Nations compound on the Palestinian side of the park. "I know a good restaurant."

That walk, more than any of our conversations—about Poland, the war, the contemporary situation in Israel—showed me why Simha had beaten all the odds and survived. He was genuinely—perhaps genetically—fearless. The unnerving stroll had not been for my benefit, his wife complained. "I beg him not to walk at night," she sighed. "But he doesn't listen."

While Simha's wife had come to expect such risky behavior, she was surprised that her husband had spent so much time talking about his Holocaust experiences with me. For decades, he'd never uttered a word about the war or the Ghetto. But recently, he'd thought about those years a great deal, and even relished the opportunity to speak Polish again. This surprised Simha's wife the most. She apologized, but the language gave her the creeps. Her parents had died at Plaszow, the Krakow camp made famous by *Schindler's List,* and her one visit to Poland long after the war had made her physically ill. Simha, though, seemed to be approaching that stage of his life when he was reflecting back on his accomplishments—his marriage, his grown children, his career managing an Israeli supermarket chain—and perhaps he realized that nothing could ever surpass what he witnessed during World War II. For a long time he had suppressed those painful memories, but now, in his final years, he wanted the world to know what he saw and did as a young man.

"For years, Isaac hounded me to write a memoir and I kept putting him off," Simha recalled. He and Isaac had reconnected when Zuckerman finally joined Zivia in Israel in 1947, formalizing their marriage as soon he got off the boat. That same year, Isaac and Zivia started working on establishing a kibbutz to honor ZOB veterans, and they invited Simha to join. He declined because he didn't want to live with ghosts, which Isaac effectively did when he founded the Ghetto

Fighters' Kibbutz near Acre and the neighboring Ghetto Fighters' Museum. For the rest of his life, Isaac dedicated himself to those twin causes. Unfortunately, keeping memories of the Shoah alive took a toll on Zuckerman. He suffered bouts of depression, and he drank. As time went on, he shied away from politics and public appearances, tending his crops and archives, and he passed away at a relatively young age in Tel Aviv in 1981. Zivia had always been psychologically stronger than Isaac, and she coped better with post-traumatic stress disorder. She bore two sons and divided her time between the kibbutz and public life. She toured Israel, giving speeches in the early 1950s, and for a brief period headed the Jewish Agency's Aliya immigration bureau before retiring to tend chickens and raise her boys. In 1961, she was called as a witness at the trial of Adolf Eichmann. Despite her inner fortitude, she died at an even younger age than her husband—sixty-four—in 1978, leaving her feminist legacy in granddaughter Roni Zuckerman, who became the first female fighter pilot in the Israeli air force in 2001. "Zivia would have liked that," Simha said, smiling.

Unlike Simha, Mark Edelman was tired of talking about the Holocaust when I first visited him in Lodz in 2007. He still lived in the same townhouse he had moved into in 1945, a place filled with old furniture, cigarette smoke, and haunting paintings of train tracks disappearing into misty pine forests that reminded me eerily of Treblinka. Edelman was busy getting his car fixed and seemed impatient to be rid of me, another journalist posing the same "stupid questions" he'd answered "a hundred times before."

Mark had a reputation for being brusque and not suffering fools, and he clearly considered me one. "You don't understand anything" was a response I heard frequently from him. In time he softened a bit, but I always considered myself an intruder with Mark, rehashing the past when what he wanted was to be left in peace.

He had being doing these tiresome interviews out of a sense of duty for the past twenty years, and he was clearly tired of playing the role of Poland's last Jew. Mark had become famous following the collapse of Communism, not only as one of the country's leading heart surgeons and a Solidarity hero who fought Communists in the 1980s, but primarily as a living link to Poland's Jewish past, as an ambassador of history and a vanished culture. To legions of curious young Poles, Edelman was the embodiment of Judaism and the Holocaust—the only Jew they knew. His face was on billboards and on television. He had the name recognition of a major public figure, and he was the recipient of virtually all the nation's highest awards, the Polish equivalent of the Congressional Medal of Honor and the Presidential Medal of Freedom. And every time a historical controversy erupted, the national media descended on his doorstep, asking him to arbitrate. (Edelman's celebrity status did not, however, prevent someone from spray-painting a Star of David on the pillar of his front gate.)

Mark's health was failing, and I had to cancel several interviews because he was unwell. In 2008, a daughter of one of the Sawicki sisters took Edelman to live with her in Warsaw because he could no longer look after himself and was all alone. (Mark had married the doctor who had arranged the Red Cross rescue mission to Jolie Bord in 1944, but she had left him long ago, moving to France.)

Edelman spent his final days with the Sawicki family, dictating one last memoir: *And There Was Love in the Ghetto*. He died in 2009.

It was through Edelman that I found Boruch Spiegel, one of the least publicized veterans of the Jewish Fighting Organization. "I think he's in Toronto," Mark had said. Actually he was in Montreal, where he had moved with Chaika Belchatowska in the late 1940s, after a brief sojourn in Sweden. The two had married after the war, and Boruch had returned to his trade, managing a small leather goods factory until his retirement. Chaika was no longer alive when I first visited Boruch in the fall of 2007. By coincidence, his American son-in-law had been one of my professors at McGill University, though I had no idea we shared this connection. I did, however, immediately recognize the address of the assisted living facility where Spiegel was staying. It was two blocks from the medical center where my mother had established her practice after immigrating to Montreal, in a predominantly Jewish neighborhood that was one of the few places in Canada where a medical degree from the University of Warsaw meant something.

Her first patients were almost all Polish Jews, many of them Holocaust survivors, and I was startled to hear so much Polish and Yiddish in the elevators and lobby of the old age home where Boruch now lived. I probably met more Polish Jews in that one high-rise than in the three years I spent living in Warsaw, which struck me as terribly sad. In fact, it was from one of Boruch's fellow residents that I first heard the term "sound good." We were in the cafeteria having lunch and speaking Polish, when a woman at the next table, an Auschwitz survivor, volunteered the compliment. At the time I thought she was praising my linguistic skills. Only much later did I realize that she was referring to my non-Yiddish accent, and I was amazed by how deeply ingrained her survival instincts remained even after all these years.

Boruch had only recently moved into the facility, a converted apartment building across the street from a shopping mall, and he wasn't happy about the move, or about having to cope with a full-time nurse. But like Edelman, his health was failing him. He got around with a walker and only with great difficulty, and he was suffering from early-onset Alzheimer's, a condition from which I would see him deteriorating dramatically over an interval of a few short months. It was heartbreaking: Boruch, one of the kindest and gentlest men I ever met, could recall the slightest detail of events that had occurred seventy years earlier, but could not remember that we had talked the day before. His memory could be astonishingly vivid in one instant, and he could lapse into a prolonged silence the next, staring numbly at a framed photo of his granddaughter. (She looked just like Chaika, who was pictured in another framed photograph, shaking hands with Vice President Al Gore.)

At times I had to gently nudge Boruch when he drifted off, and I felt guilty for pushing him—for ghoulishly trying to extract every last bit of information before his mind went completely blank. My parting memory is of him dozing on a couch in the lobby of his building. He had fallen asleep during one of our talks, and I had waited for half an hour for him to wake up when his nurse intervened. "It is enough," she said. "Mr. Spiegel needs to rest."

The flame that Hitler had strived so maniacally to snuff out was slowly being extinguished by time. Joseph and Martha Osnos had passed away in New York, and their son Robert was retiring after a long career as a psychiatrist when I first reached out to him in 2008. Janine and Hanna Mortkowicz had died of old age in Poland, and Joanna was now a grandmother, living in Krakow, where the family had remained after the destruction of Warsaw. She kept the Mortkowicz legacy alive as a well-regarded author and screenwriter, and her 2001 family history had won Poland's equivalent of the National Book Award. She was finishing a biography of Janusz Korczak, the great children's writer and martyr whose statue stands at the foot of one the many new skyscrapers now rising in the former Warsaw Ghetto, when we met at her old bookstore. Joanna had not seen her family's former store since the war, and she was visibly astounded at its recent transformation into a high-end martini bar. "Everything is changing so quickly," she said of the economic boom that is throwing up glass towers in once dreary Warsaw at an almost Chinese pace.

Already all physical evidence of the Ghetto had been erased—first by hideous Communist edifices and now by shiny condominiums and office blocks that are replacing the Stalinist architecture. In a few more years the living memory of the Holocaust will also be gone. The final witnesses will pass away, closing one of the darkest chapters of human history. But the inspirational light of people like Simha and Isaac, or Boruch and Mark, or Joanna and Zivia, will burn on forever. Their courage and nobility transcend time. My life is richer for having made their acquaintance, and they have provided me with an answer to the question I posed at the outset of this tale: What would I have done in their place?

Before embarking on this narrative journey, I imagined myself valiantly fighting the Nazis. I now know that that would not have been the case, because of something Mark Edelman said. To join the Resistance, one had to leave one's family behind to face starvation, disease, and the roundups. It took less courage, in Mark's opinion, to pick up a gun than to stay with one's children and comfort them in the face of almost certain death. It was not a coincidence, he explained, that Resistance fighters were almost all young and unmarried. In fact, one of the bravest scenes Edelman witnessed during the war was the sight of a man entering the Umschlagplatz with his son on his shoulders. The boy was frightened and asking where they were going. "Not far," the father reassured him. "Soon it will all be over."

ACKNOWLEDGMENTS

This book would not have come into existence without the early support of Paul Golob and John Flicker, two of New York's finest editors. They opened up their hearts and purse strings for the project and I owe them both a lasting debt of gratitude. My agents Scott Waxman and Farley Chase, ably assisted by Beth Phelan, tugged and loosened those literary purse strings—both in the United States and abroad—and I am always in their debt.

At Random House the brilliant Will Murphy and Katie Donelan acted as surrogate parents, birthing and shaping the manuscript, which at times behaved like a difficult child. Emily DeHuff, Anna Bauer, and Jennifer Rodriguez all raised the book's standards through its unruly growth spurts, as did early readers Eric Rubin, Allen Feldman, and especially Alan Cooperman, whose trained eye rarely misses a beat.

In Warsaw, a few people made three long years pass more quickly: Jen and Michael Sessums, Esko Kilpinen, Marina Kotanska, and most of all Dagmara, Anya, and Zbigniew Roman, who give all Poles a good name. At home, Ari, Anna, and Lena heard more about Nazis and death camps than any seven-year-olds ever should, and when they are older I will apologize to them. And as always, the last acknowledgment is reserved for Roberta, my combative chief editor, muse, in-house censor, and designated adult. There is a lot of her in this book, and she reminds me of some of its characters.

NOTES

CHAPTER 1: HANNA'S TRIUMPH

3   **A comedy by the up-and-coming playwright Maria Pawlowska**   Czeslaw Grzelaka, ed., *Warszawa we Wrzesniu 1939 Roku: Obrona I Zycie Codzienne* (Warsaw Rytm, 2004), p. 480.

4   **addressed clients as "Your Excellency"**   Magdalena Dubrowska, *Gazeta Wyborcza*, April 26, 2008, p. 8.

4   **billed by its architect, Marcin Weinfeld**   Ewa Malkowska, "Stolica," *Warszawski Magazyn Ilustrowany*, no. 4, April, 2008, p. 28.

4   **Built by developers Karol Fritsche, Jacob Lowenberg, and Pinkus Loth**   Maria Irena Kwiatkowska and Marek Kwiatkowski, *Historia Warzawy XVII–XX Wieku: Architectura I Rzezba* (Warsaw: Panstowe Wydawnictwo Naukowe, 2006), pp. 106–11.

4   **Outside the PKO State Savings Bank**   Krzysztof Dunin-Wasowicz, *Warszawa W. Latach, 1939–1945* (Warsaw: Panstowe Wydawnictwo Naukowe, 1984), p. 24.

5   **"We reported to the officer"**   Isaac Zuckerman, *A Surplus of Memory: Chronicle of the Warsaw Ghetto Uprising* (Berkeley: University of California Press, 1993), p. 3.

6   **students at Public School Number 166 in upper Warka had raised 11.75 zlotys**   Martha Osnos, unpublished journal, p. 1.

6   "Not everyone understood what war with the Germans meant"   Zucker-
     man, *Surplus of Memory*, p. 4.

7   "blind people discussing colors"   Martha Osnos, unpublished journal,
     p. 1.

7   though pointedly not Yiddish   Robert Osnos, author interview, New York
     City, September 2008.

8   equivalent to around $100,000   Joanna Olczak-Ronikier, W. *Ogrodzie
     Pamieci* (Krakow: Znak, 2001), p. 216.

9   should send her eight-year-old son, Robert, to join little Joanna at the
     Mortkowicz country house   Joanna Olczak-Ronikier, author interview,
     November 2008.

9   "The entire Polish nation, blessed by God"   *Kurjer Warszawski*, no. 741,
     September 1, 1939, p. 1.

Chapter 2: Simha's First Day of School

10   far superior to models like Pfaff or Kempisty-Kasprzycki   Exhibition of
     Jewish crafts, attended by the author, Kazimierz, Krakow, August 2008.

11   Between them they could make five or six dozen pairs   Boruch Spiegel,
     author interview, Montreal, November 2007.

11   first cobbled in 1783   Kwiryna Handke, *Stolica: Warszawski Magazyn
     Ilustrowany*, p. 24.

11   two-thirds of Warsaw's prewar physicians were Jewish, as were 37 percent
     of its lawyers   Marian Fuks, *Mowia Wieki: Magazin Historyczni*, April
     2008, p. 14.

12   "we are strong, united and ready"   Stanislaw F. Ozimek, *Media Walczacej
     Warszawy* (Warsaw: Fundacja Walczacej Warszawy, 2007), p. 12.

12   tram line 17   Handke, *Stolica: Warszawski Magazyn Ilustrowany*, no. 4,
     April 2008, p. 24.

12   either sweet with "pure sugar" or bitter and "doubly saturated"   Jerzy
     Kasprzycki, *Korzenie Miasta*, vol. II (Warsaw: Veda, 2004), p. 158.

13   "Speculators who had money would walk in the courtyards"   Harold
     Werner, *Fighting Back: A Memoir of Jewish Resistance in World War II*
     (New York: Columbia University Press, 1992), p. 3.

14   "My father was an observant Jew"   Simha Ratheiser-Rotem, author in-
     terview, Jerusalem, March 2009.

15   "was never overly political"   Ibid.

16   where 40 percent of the residents were Jewish   Michal Pilich, *Warszawa
     Praga* (Warsaw: Center of Europe Foundation, 2006), p. 67.

16   3,870 workers streamed out of the Lilpop, Rau & Lowenstein
     plant   Marcin Jablonowski, *Polski Przemysl Wojenny z Perspektywy 1938*
     (Koszalin: PMTW, 1988), p. 48.

16   the three hundred workers of Samuel and Sender Ginsburg's BRAGE Rub-
     ber Works   Pilich, *Warszawa Praga*, p. 97.

18   "Today a total of 16 enemy airplanes were destroyed"   Grzelaka, *Warszawa we Wrzesniu 1939 Roku*, p. 377.

18   "My parents only associated with other assimilated Jews"   Robert Osnos, author interview, New York City, September 2008.

18   TO COMPLETE VICTORY   *Czas-7 Wiezcor*, September 1, 1939, no. 242, p. 1.

CHAPTER 3: WOLSKA STREET IS COVERED WITH BLOOD

19   "the firm resolve of returning once the war has been won"   Ozimek, *Media Walczacej Warszawy*, p. 22.

19   "Warsaw was going to surrender"   Boruch Spiegel, author interview, Montreal, November 2007.

20   the Bund "was about Jewish pride and dignity"   Ibid.

21   "the injustices and hatred of the Polish state against the Jews"   Zuckerman, *Surplus of Memory*, p. 5.

21   made Poland the world's eighth-largest producer of steel in 1939   Andrew Hempel, *Poland in World War II: An Illustrated Military History* (New York: Hippocrene Books, 2005), p. 6.

21   of children burned alive   Czeslaw Luczak, *Dzieje Polski 1939–1945* (Poznan: Wydawnictwo Poznanskie, 2007), pp. 12–14.

21   "Anti-Semitism has spread all over the nation"   Paul Johnson, *A History of the Jews* (New York: HarperPerennial, 1998), p. 470.

21   "We worked hard and the Poles were nice to us"   Zuckerman, *Surplus of Memory*, p. 6.

22   "It was crazy, it was chaos"   Boruch Spiegel, author interview, Motreal, November 2007.

23   "Go, I will stay with Robert"   Martha Osnos, unpublished journal, p. 3.

24   Simha felt frightened and helpless   Simha Ratheiser-Rotem, author interview, Jerusalem, March 2009.

24   "Wolska Street is covered with blood"   Dunin-Wasowicz, *Warszawa w latach 1939–1945*, p. 29.

CHAPTER 4: ROBERT'S PAPER AIRPLANES

25   "I don't know why they went off and left me"   Zuckerman, *Surplus of Memory*, p. 7.

26   "There would always be a dozen bodies lying on the road"   Boruch Spiegel, author interview, Montreal, November 2007.

26   flew at only half the speed of the far more advanced Messerschmitts   Hempel, *Poland in World War II*, p. 10.

26   the Warsaw Fighter Brigade had knocked out 72 German craft   Ibid.

27   "They began bombing the woods"   Zuckerman, *Surplus of Memory*, p. 8.

27   "I didn't know whether to walk at the head of the line"   Ibid., p. 9.

27   "No one gave any thought to serious fighting"   Marian Porwit, *Obrona*

Warszawy, Wrezesien, 1939 (Warsaw: Panstowe Wydawnicywo Naukowe, 1979), p. 51.

28   **82,000 civilian and military defenders**   Grzelaka, *Warszawa we Wrezesniu 1939 Roku*, p. 106.

28   **nearly one hundred battle-ready divisions sitting behind the Maginot Line. The Führer had only twenty-five divisions**   Richard C. Lukas, *Forgotten Holocaust: The Poles Under German Occupation 1939–1944* (New York: Hippocrene Books, 1997), p. 2.

28   **"a rain of bombs"**   Raul Hilberg, Stanislaw Staron, and Josef Kermisz, *The Warsaw Diary of Adam Czerniakow* (Chicago: Elephant Paperbacks, 1999), p. 73.

28   **"so urgent and important"**   Martha Osnos, unpublished journal.

28   **saw piles of books shaken from the shelves**   Olczak-Ronikier, *W Ogrodzie Pamieci*, p. 267.

29   **"This new reality offered certain attractions"**   Ibid.

29   **"I don't recall once being scared"**   Robert Osnos, author interview, New York City, September 2008.

29   **"The planes swooped so low over the Royal Gardens"**   Simha Ratheiser-Rotem, author interview, Jerusalem, March 2009.

29   **to her brother-in-law's spacious apartment**   Martha Osnos, unpublished journal, p. 2.

30   **five thousand shells fell on the Jewish Quarter and Midtown**   Grzelaka, *Warszawa we Wrezesniu 1939 Roku*, p. 488.

30   **astounding donation of $15 million by another Jewish philanthropist, Leopold Kronenberg**   Fuks, *Mowia Wieki*, p. 11.

30   **"an ocean of flames"**   Martha Osnos, unpublished journal, p. 5.

30   **"Young Poles and Jews performed miracles of heroism"**   Emmanuel Ringelblum, *Polish-Jewish Relations in the Second World War* (Evanston, Illinois: Northwestern University Press, 1992), p. 26.

31   **"There were no weapons"**   Boruch Spiegel, author interview, Montreal, November 2007.

31   **The town had had a prewar population of 33,000 and was half Jewish**   http://www.museumoftolerance.com/site/pp.asp?c=arLPK7PILqF&b= 249727.

31   **Poland's "railroad king"**   Fuks, *Mowia Wieki*, p. 11.

31   **"no one knew what to do, or where to go"**   Boruch Spiegel, author interview, Montreal, November 2007.

32   **too "junior, and not important" enough**   Ibid.

CHAPTER 5: HIS BROTHER'S HAND

33   **a million and a half soldiers and six thousand tanks**   Luczak, *Dzieje Polsk 1939–1945*, p. 24.

33 **"I wanted Warsaw to be great"** Dunin-Wasowicz, *Warszawa w latach
1939–1945*, p. 35.
34 **"She has the right to be stupid"** Olczak-Ronikier, *W Ogrodzie Pamieci*,
p. 263.
35 **Nine hundred howitzers and four hundred heavy bombers, mostly Junkers** Grzelaka, *Warszawa we Wrezesniu 1939 Roku*, p. 492.
35 **"there was dead silence"** Simha Ratheiser-Rotem, author interview, Jerusalem, March 2009.
35 **Nearly twenty thousand similar graves** Dunin-Wasowicz, *Warszawa w
latach 1939–1945*, p. 83.
36 **"I caught sight of a hand separated from a body"** Simha Ratheiser-
Rotem, *Kazik: Memoirs of a Ghetto Fighter* (New Haven: Yale University
Press, 1994), p. 9.

CHAPTER 6: WHERE IS YOUR HUSBAND?

37 **ceremonially cutting a white ribbon** *W Obiektywie Wroga: Niemiecy
Fotoreporterzy W Okupowanej Warsawie 1939–1945*, Nazi Propaganda
Photo and Film Exhibition, History Meeting House, Warsaw, September–
October 2008.
37 **propaganda footage of elderly men—their dark caftan frocks and beards
covered with pale dust** Ibid., Karl-Friedrich Schultze, Barch Bild 1011-
001-025143.
38 **the feminine qualities of Warsaw's newly inexpensive prostitutes** Dunin-
Wasowicz, *Warzsawa w Latach 1939–1945*, p. 45.
38 **Seventy-eight thousand apartment units had gone up in flames** Stefan
Korbonski, *Fighting Warsaw* (New York: Hippocrene Books, 2004), p. 263.
38 **Fifteen percent of all structures** *Katalog der Ausstellung Im Objektiv des
Feindes: Deutsche Bildberichterstatter im bessetzten Warschau 1939–1945*
(Warsaw: Dom Spotkan z Historia, 2008), p. 4.
38 **"The door was broken"** Martha Osnos, unpublished journal, p. 7.
39 **They even flanked the entrance to the Julius Meinl coffee shop** Kwiatkowski, *Historia Warszawy XVII–XX Wieku*, p. 76.
39 **the Starbucks of its day** www.meinl.com.
40 **ENGLAND! THIS IS YOUR DOING** Original poster on permanent exhibition
at Pawiak Prison Museum, Valiant Street, Warsaw.
40 **"Anyone approaching a window or the street will immediately be shot"**
Ksawery Swierkowski, *Hitler Widziany przez Szpare*, Stolica, 1971, no. 39,
p. 6.
40 **"They made an incredible impression on me"** Simha Ratheiser-Rotem,
author interview, Jerusalem, March 2009.
41 **"He passed right under our noses"** Jan Nowak Jezioranski, *Kurier z
Warszawy* (Krakow: Znak, 2005), p. 35.

41   ten thousand train-wagon loads of booty   Luczak, *Dzieje Polski 1939–1945*, p. 54.

41   "Where are you going?"   Martha Osnos, unpublished journal, p. 12.

42   "Where do you live?"   Ibid.

42   He selected the Art Deco mansion of industrialist Gustav Wertheim   *UKRaport: Gazeta Konstancinska*, no. 149, September 2008, p. 7.

43   her 14,000-square-foot home   Ibid.

43   resurfaced in 2007 at a garage sale in Lexington, Kentucky   Wlodzimierz Kalicki, *Gazeta Wyborcza*, April 28, 2008, p. 2.

43   a seventeenth-century canvas by the Dutch master Pieter de Grebber   Ibid., April 26, 2008, p. 1.

43   the impressionist collections of Jacob and Alina Glass   National Museum, author site visit, October 2008.

43   "It was one of the only times during the war that I can remember"   Robert Osnos, author interview, New York, November 2008.

43   "Don't be afraid"   Martha Osnos, unpublished journal, p. 12.

44   Jean-Antoine Houdon, whose works today are exhibited at the National Gallery of Art   www.getty.edu/art/exhibitions/houdon.

CHAPTER 7: MARK'S VOW

46   "It was terrible," he said, describing the once prosperous Jerusalem Boulevard   Witold Beres and Krzysztof Burnetko, *Marek Edelman: Zycie. Po Prostu* (Warsaw: Swiat Ksiaski, 2008), p. 40.

46   the Hilfzug Bayern "help trains"   Dunin-Wasowicz, *Warzsawa w Latach 1939–1945*, p. 44.

46   were marred by the grim faces of the recipients   Tomazs Szarota, *Okupowanej Warszawy Dzien Powszedni* (Warsaw: Stodium Historyczne, 1978), p. 78.

46   "*Sind Sie ein Jid?*"   Hilberg, Staron, and Kermisz, *Warsaw Diary of Adam Czerniakow*, p. 78.

46   "I saw a crowd on Iron Street"   Hanna Krall, *Shielding the Flame* (New York: Henry Holt, 1986), pp. 37–38.

47   "She had never even spoken to a Jewish person before she met me"   Martha Osnos, unpublished journal, p. 5.

48   (staged, as it turned out, by Arthur Grimm)   Prussian Cultural Picture Archives, Berlin, series 3001000 and 30032348, shown in W *Obiektywie Wroga: Niemiecy Fotoreporterzy W Okupowanej Warsawie 1939–1945*, Nazi Propaganda Photo and Film Exhibition, History Meeting House, Warsaw, September–October 2008.

48   "German propaganda agencies worked ceaselessly"   Marek Edelman, *The Ghetto Fights* (London: Bookmarks, 1990), p. 35.

48   "We also started hearing about how Jews were turning in Poles"   Beres and Burnetko, *Marek Edelman*, p. 40.

49   Electricity, gas, and water supplies had not yet been fully restored   Andrzej Szczypiorski, "Miezkania I ludnosc Warszawy w Czasie Wojny I Hitlerowshiej Okupacji," *Studia Demograficzne*, no. 46, 1976, p. 38.

49   "to overcome our own terrifying apathy"   Edelman, *Ghetto Fights*, p. 37.

49   "lazy"   Beres and Burnetko, *Marek Edelman: Zycie. Po Prostu*, p. 20.

50   They consisted of two small metal pots mounted over each other   Bernard Goldstein, *Five Years in the Warsaw Ghetto* (Edinburgh, West Virginia: AK Press, 2005), p. 34.

50   "Working by carbide light proved extremely strenuous"   Edelman, *Ghetto Fights*, p. 47.

51   It had a daily circulation of two hundred thousand copies   Ozimek, *Media Walczacej Warszawy*, p. 47.

51   ten people sentenced to death for tearing down a German flag   Luczak, *Dzieje Polski, 1939–1945*, p. 42.

51   "All Jews and Jewesses within the General Government"   *Nowy Kurjer Warszawski*, November 30, 1939, p. 1.

CHAPTER 8: JOANNA'S RHYME

53   "forbidden and invalid"   Yitzhak Arad, Yisrael Gutman, and Abraham Margaliot, eds., *Documents on the Holocaust* (Lincoln: University of Nebraska Press, 1999), p. 78.

53   "A Jew is a person descended from at least three grandparents"   Ibid., p. 80.

54   "In a corner of the great Warsaw there still stands a remnant of the medieval city"   Ellen D. Kellman, *Zydzi Warszawy* (Warsaw: Zydowski Instytut Historyczny, 2000), p. 105.

54   "Jew, Jew, crawl under your shack"   Olczak-Ronikier, *W Ogrodze Pamieci*, p. 270.

54   "It was then that I found out what was the real and macabre meaning of the rhyme"   Ibid.

55   "My grandfather wanted to be more Polish than the Poles"   Joanna Olczak-Ronikier, author interview, Warsaw, December 2008.

55   "He practiced pronunciation"   Ibid.

55   "the Hebraic-German garble"   Marci Shore, *Caviar and Ashes: A Warsaw Generation's Life and Death in Marxism, 1918–1968* (New Haven: Yale University Press, 2006), p. 2.

55   "It's not true!"   Olczak-Ronikier, *W Ogrodze Pamieci*, p. 270.

55   "She was a very proud and strong-willed woman"   Joanna Olczak-Ronikier, author interview, December 2008.

56   "I was so upset at being Jewish"   Ibid.

56   TUWIM AND SLONIMSKI ARE ONE HUNDRED PERCENT JEWS   Anthony Polonsky in Robert Blobaum, ed., *Antisemitism and Its Opponents in Modern Poland* (Ithaca: Cornell University Press, 2005), p. 198.

56 "I will never permit my Ladies" Olczakl-Ronikier, *W Ogrodze Pamieci,* p. 270.

CHAPTER 9: ISAAC ON MEMORY LANE

57 "321,700 Poles, 107,600 Jews, 75,200 Belarussians" Luczak, *Dzieje Polski, 1939–1945,* p. 41.

58 fifteen thousand Jewish refugees flooded into Vilna http://www.ushmm .org/wlc/media_cm.php?lang=en&ModuleId=10005173&MediaId=2580.

58 "Jews constituted at least 80% of every Bolshevik organization" Joseph W. Bendersky, *The "Jewish Threat": Anti-Semitic Politics of the American Army* (New York: Basic Books, 2000), pp. 84–85.

58 The experience remained "engraved" Zuckerman, *Surplus of Memory,* p. 14.

58 "What's new, *Dyedushka*?" Zuckerman, *Surplus of Memory,* p. 14.

59 "a rabbi who didn't want to make a living at it" Ibid., p. 13.

59 "Are you insane, where are you going?" Ben-cion Pinchuk, *Polish-Jewish Relations in Soviet-Occupied Eastern Poland,* http://www.electronic museum.ca/Poland-WW2/ethnic_minorities_occupation/Jews_15.html, p. 7.

60 "He would have understood if I had gone closer to Eretz Israel" Zuckerman, *Surplus of Memory,* p. 18.

60 "There were cases of members leaving the movement" Ibid., p. 19.

60 Of the 330,000 Galician Poles sent to Siberian camps in 1940, 21 percent were Jews Philipp Ther, "War Versus Peace," *Harvard Ukrainian Studies* 24 (1/4), pp. 265–66.

60 "Some day they'll probably lead me away like that too" Zuckerman, *Surplus of Memory,* p. 20.

60 "I was such a great conspirer" Ibid., p. 22.

61 paraded in nightgowns up the marble steps of the Opera Eyewitness account, Andrzej Roman, author interview, Warsaw, September 2008.

61 from 110,000 to 160,000 by year's end, so great was the flood of refugees Ther, *War Versus Peace,* p. 268.

61 The city itself was laid out like a landlocked San Francisco Author site visit, May 2009.

62 "They had more faith in the Soviet regime" Ibid., p. 26.

63 "like a captain who had been the first to leave his sinking ship" Arens, *Jewish Military Organization in the Warsaw Ghetto,* p. 7.

63 "Do you really believe that I did not have these thoughts?" Ibid., p. 8.

64 "We had a fight about it" Boruch Spiegel, author interview, Montreal, November 2007.

64 "Warsaw under the Nazis scared me to death" Zuckerman, *Surplus of Memory,* p. 29.

CHAPTER 10: ZIVIA

65 "unapproachable," cold, hard, and "tough"   Dina Rotem, author interview, Jerusalem, March 2009.

65 "Introverted and modest"   Abraham Raban, *The Promise, the Revolt, the Vow,* Histadrut/Lochamei Hagettaot Institute, Ghetto Fighter's House Museum brochure, n.d., p. 6.

65 "unproductive"—the endless chattering of "do-nothings" and "squares"   Ibid., p. 19.

66 "Zivia and Isaac only had two things in common"   Simha Ratheiser-Rotem, author interview, Jerusalem, March 2009.

66 "like living on a small Jewish island"   Raban, *The Promise, the Revolt, the Vow,* p. 6.

66 "In sociological terms, most of the Jews were middle class"   Ibid., p. 4.

66 "where Gentiles did the manual labor while Jews worked in the white-collar professions"   Ibid.

67 "Tell us, didn't they do anything to you?"   Ibid., p. 9.

67 "was terrified of what the Germans would do to me"   Zivia Lubetkin, *Zaglada I Powstanie* (Warsaw: Ksiaska I Wiedza / Zydowski Institut Historycny, 1999), p. 19.

68 "There were a few Jews cowering in one corner"   Ibid.

68 "Do I have the strength," she wondered, "to do this?"   Ibid.

CHAPTER 11: WHY DOES HITLER LIKE MRS. ZEROMSKA?

72 "We worshiped him"   Boruch Spiegel, author interview, Montreal, November 2007.

73 Goldstein had grown a thick tangled beard   Goldstein, *Five Years in the Warsaw Ghetto,* p. 25.

73 " a nobody and they were great men"   Marek Edelman, *I Byla Milosc w Getcie* (Warsaw: Swiat Ksiazki, 2009), p. 37.

73 "lightning reflexes and good nature"   Ibid., pp. 47–48.

74 one eyewitness put their numbers at around a thousand   Yisrael Gutman, *Jews of Warsaw 1939–1943* (Bloomington: Indiana University Press, 1982), p. 28.

74 "enraged by the pogrom in March"   Ibid.

74 "the fringe elements of Polish society"   Edelman, *Ghetto Fights,* p. 38.

74 "The guys in the Bund's Self-Defense Force were not shrinking violets"   Beres and Burnetko, *Marek Edelman: Zycie. Po Prostu,* p. 47.

75 "We decided to fight back with 'cold weapons'"   Goldstein, *Five Years in the Warsaw Ghetto,* p. 44.

75 "When the pogromists appeared in these sections"   Ibid., p. 45.
contracting by an estimated 40 percent   Szczypiorski, "Miezkania I ludnosc Warszawy w Czasie Wojny I Hitlerowshiej Okupacji," p. 47.

76 Some 270,000 men and 63,470 women   Ibid., p. 77.
76 "young men of land-owning families"   Korbonski, *Fighting Warsaw*, p. 12.
77 "I think she made more money than Father"   Simha Ratheiser-Rotem, author interview, Jerusalem, March 2009.
77 "We were not rich, but we were comfortable"   Ibid.
77 the day a Volksdeutsche walked into the store   Ibid.
78 seized 112,000 small businesses, 9,120 large enterprises, 76,000 small artisan shops   Leni Yahl, *Holocaust: The Fate of European Jewry 1932–1945* (Oxford: Oxford University Press, 1990), p. 158.
78 "The Volksdeutsche demanded the keys"   Simha Ratheiser-Rotem, author interview, Jerusalem, March 2009.
78 57.5 percent of all medium-sized and small enterprises and 40 percent of large industrial concerns   Fuks, *Mowia Wieki*, p. 12.
78 "I didn't realize that Mrs. Zeromska was really saving our lives"   Joanna Olczak-Ronikier, author interview, Warsaw, December 2008.
79 "I didn't understand why he left us behind"   Robert Osnos, author interview, New York, September 2008.
79 "We are going to get out"   Ibid.

Chapter 12: Am I Willing to Do This?

80 "to protect Jews against Polish excesses"   Barbara Engelking and Jacek Leociak, *Getto Warszawskie: Przewodnik po Niistniejacym Miescie* (Warsaw: IFiS/PAN, 2001), p. 75.
80 "spreaders of diseases"   Ibid.
80 88 among Jews and 5 among non-Jews   *Biuletyn ZIH*, no. 74 (Warsaw: Jewish Historical Institute, April 1970), p. 106.
80 a life expectancy that ranged between 7.5 years   Ibid.
81 and a full decade less   Johnson, *History of the Jews*, p. 356.
81 "I could not face Mama"   Boruch Spiegel, author interview, Montreal, October 2007.
81 "We could now only afford to eat one decent meal a day"   Ibid.
81 "We had to first and foremost provide the hungry with bread"   Lubetkin, *Zaglada I Powstanie*, p. 24.
82 totaled 669 calories for "Poles," 184 calories for Jews   Gutman, *Jews of Warsaw 1939–1943*, p. 66.
82 "I was amazed at Yehuda's senses"   Zuckerman, *Surplus of Memory*, p. 38.
82 "Now the German danger began"   Ibid., p. 39.
83 "Throw away your bundle"   Ibid., p. 40.
84 After climbing to 150 zlotys . . . it plunged to 90 zlotys in late May   Ringelblum, *Notes from the Warsaw Ghetto*, p. 41.
84 A specially prepared chemical was added to the lubricating oil   Tadeusz Bor-Komorowski, *Secret Army* (New York: Macmillan, 1951), p. 40.

84   "The Führer has awakened in me the consciousness of the German community"   Jan Karski, *Story of a Secret State* (Boston: Houghton Mifflin, 1944), p. 214.

84   "Their gait and their whole appearance seemed to proclaim"   Korbonski, *Fighting Warsaw*, p. 12.

85   from six thousand weekly copies in December 1939 to forty thousand   Ozimek, *Media Walczacej Warszawy*, p. 50.

85   "Horrifying night"   Ringelblum, *Notes from the Warsaw Ghetto*, p. 38.

85   "Some Poles are beginning to wear Jewish armbands"   Hilberg, Staron, and Kermisz, *Warsaw Diary of Adam Czerniakow*, p. 147.

86   sixty-five hundred were snatched from their Warsaw homes and places of work   Wladyslaw Bartoszewski, *Warszawski Pierscien Smierci 1939–1944* (Warsaw: Swiat Ksiazki, 2008), p. 60.

86   "Hundreds were lying in the sawdust"   Korbonski, *Fighting Warsaw*, p. 50.

86   designed in 1835 by Henry Marconi   Peacock Prison Museum exhibit, author site visit, August 2008.

86   "You could hear them calling"   Boruch Spiegel, author interview, Montreal, October 2007.

86   the hundred thousand Poles imprisoned at Peacock (almost all of them Christians)   Andrzej Stawarz, ed., *Pawiak 1835–1944* (Warsaw: Muzeum Niepodlegosci, 2002), p. 10.

86   thirty-seven thousand were shot on the spot or at Palmiry   Ibid.

87   the first Jews to settle there in 1564   Joram Kagan, *Polish-Jewish Landmarks* (New York: Hippocrene Books, 2001), p. 89.

CHAPTER 13: MARTHA AND ROBERT RUN

89   "Another elegant secretary took Joseph to the right place"   Martha Osnos, unpublished journal, p. 22.

90   "He looked like Mephisto himself"   Ibid., p. 13.

90   "One kitchen, one bathroom, and all those people just waiting for me to leave"   Ibid.

91   "By a miracle"   Ibid.

91   "I prepared a lot of vodka Wyborowa"   Ibid., p.14.

92   "Berlin was full of sunshine, flowers, decorated with flags"   This and all other quotes from the Berlin to Bucharest trip are from Martha Osnos, unpublished journal, pp. 15–18.

95   "We can delay and effectively stop for a temporary period"   Valery Bazarov, testimony before the U.S. House of Representatives Subcommittee on Immigration, Citizenship, Refugees, Border Security and International Law, March 19, 2009, http://judiciary.house.gov/hearings/pdf/bazarov090319.

95   "The Department received information from reliable confidential sources"   Ibid.

95   fell from 43,450 in 1939, to 23,737 in 1941, to 10,608 the following year
      Ibid., appendix I.

CHAPTER 14: HANNA AND JOANNA HIDE

97   "Nowhere else but Valiant Street could we seat forty people for
      classes"   Zuckerman, *Surplus of Memory,* p. 61.

98   the lives of 274 teachers and faculty members   Dunin-Wasowicz,
      Warszawa w Latach 1939–1945, pp. 157–61.

98   Enrollment quickly grew to 120 pupils   Zuckerman, *Surplus of Memory,*
      pp. 61–62.

98   "Holding a seminar next door to Peacock"   Ibid., p. 56.

98   The Young Guard had five hundred members in Warsaw, while Isaac had
      eight hundred   Ibid., p. 43.

98   "They intend to starve us"   Lubetkin, *Zaglada I Powstanie,* p. 30.

99   113,000 Gentiles and 138,000 Jews   Gutman, *Jews of Warsaw 1939–1943,*
      p. 60.

99   a fifty-kilogram suitcase for each adult and a thirty-kilo bag   Arad, Gut-
      man, and Margaliot, *Documents on the Holocaust,* p. 146.

99   "a) Open fires are to be extinguished; b) Water and gas supply is to be
      turned off"   Ibid.

99   "Reliable, discreet mediation in the exchange of all types"   *Nowy Kurjer
      Warszawski,* October 11, 1940.

99   Jews owned 40 percent of what was described as "Category A" property
      Fuks, *Mowia Wieki: Magazin Historyczni,* April 2008, p. 10.

100   "It was terrible"   Simha Ratheiser-Rotem, author interview, Jerusalem,
      March 2009.

100   fifty thousand inhabitants were spread out over an area more than twice
      that size   "Moja Dzielnica" (magazine insert to *Zycie Warszawy*), April
      2009, pp. 14, 18.

100   "If you are ever in trouble and need help"   Simha Ratheiser-Rotem,
      author interview, Jerusalem, March 2009.

101   "I don't think it ever crossed her mind to follow the [relocation]
      order"   Joanna Olczak-Ronikier, author interview, Warsaw, December
      2008.

101   The Germans issued 11,130 arrest warrants for Jews   Gunnar S. Pauls-
      son, *Secret City: The Hidden Jews of Warsaw 1940–1945* (New Haven:
      Yale University Press, 2002), p. 58.

101   "I don't know if there had been a family-wide discussion about it"
      Joanna Olczak-Ronikier, author interview, Warsaw, December 2008.

101   "As she was entering Gestapo headquarters"   Olczak-Ronikier, *W
      Ogrodzie Pamieci,* p. 273.

102   "As soon as the Poles were sent out we grabbed that job"   Zuckerman,
      Surplus of Memory, p. 132.

103 "We need to know what is happening to our brothers and sisters" Lubet-kin, *Zaglada I Powstanie*, p. 32.

103 seizing the 2,300 mostly Jewish-owned textile mills Leszek Skrzydlo, *Rody Fabrykanckie* (Lodz: Oficyna Bibliofilow, 2001), p. 7.

103 "They had to have an Aryan appearance, speak Polish well" Lubetkin, *Zaglada I Powstanie*, p. 49.

104 only 5 percent . . . classified themselves as native Polish speakers 19,300 of 353,000, per *Maly Roccznik Statystyczny* (Warsaw: Glowny Urzad Statistycczny, 1939), pp. 22–24.

104 "most Polish Jews could not speak Polish well" Nechama Tec, *When Light Pierced the Darkness: Christian Rescue of Jews in Nazi-Occupied Poland* (New York: Oxford University Press, 1986), p. 38.

104 "These differences permeated all aspects of life" Ibid.

104 "Your Aryan face is worth its weight in gold" Zuckerman, *Surplus of Memory*, p. 121.

104 Isaac's problem was his accent Simha Ratheiser-Rotem, author interview, Jerusalem, March 2009.

105 "Her Polish wasn't fluent" Ibid., p. 104.

CHAPTER 15: SIMHA AND BORUCH PAY THE BILLS

106 "There are long queues in front of every food store" Sloan, *Notes from the Warsaw Ghetto: The Journal of Emmanuel Ringelblum*, p. 86.

106 "On the first day after the Ghetto was closed" Ibid.

107 provided an estimated 80 to 90 percent of the food consumed in the Warsaw Ghetto Gutman, *Jews of Warsaw 1939–1943*, p. 67. See also Paulsson, *Secret City*, p. 61.

107 "It was not at all uncommon for ten- or twelve-year-olds to support entire families" Simha Ratheiser-Rotem, author interview, Jerusalem, March 2009.

107 "Getting out of the Ghetto was not that difficult" Ibid.

107 "At Goat Street smuggling is through a door in a wall" Sloan, *Notes from the Warsaw Ghetto: The Journal of Emmanuel Ringelblum*, p. 127.

108 Seventy to 80 percent of the food sold in Warsaw outside the Ghetto was already smuggled Dunin-Wasowicz, *Warszawa w Latach 1939–1945*, p. 113.

108 Ghetto residents were allotted a daily high of 400 calories Barbara Kroll, *Opieka I Samopomoc Spoleczna w Warszawie 1939–1945* (Warsaw: PAN, 1977), p. 89.

108 A kilogram of sugar, for instance, purchased with ration cards, retailed for 1.6 zlotys Wojciech Jastrzebowski, *Gospodarka Niemecka w Polsce 1939–1944* (Warsaw: publisher unknown, 1946), p. 367.

109 "I'd jump on and off moving trains to get there" Simha Ratheiser-Rotem, author interview, Jerusalem, March 2009.

109   "The other Jews would think I was a Polish smuggler"   Ibid.

109   798,000 Poles—all Christians—were already working as slave laborers in Germany   Lukas, *Forgotten Holocaust,* p. 33.

109   *don't* come with us to Germany   Korbonski, *Fighting Warsaw,* p. 226.

110   "I remember the smell of the huge round loaves, freshly baked"   Simha Ratheiser-Rotem, author interview, Jerusalem, March 2009.

110   "Apparently I was rather successful"   Ratheiser-Rotem, *Kazik,* p. 13.

111   Insurance companies offered policies on the safe delivery of goods   Perec Opoczynski, *Reportaze z Warszawskiego Getta* (Warsaw: ZIH, 2009), p. 21.

111   "The Zionists had theirs. We had ours. All the groups looked after their own"   Boruch Spiegel, author interview, Montreal, November 2007.

111   actually consumed 1,125 daily calories in early 1941   Paulsson, *Secret City,* p. 68.

112   "The innumerable confectionery stores that have sprung up lately"   Sloan, *Notes from the Warsaw Ghetto,* p. 106.

112   "It would take even a fluent Yiddish speaker coming from the more distant parts"   Ewa Geller in Eleonora Bergman and Olga Zienkiewicz, eds., *Zydzi Warszawy* (Warsaw: Zydowski Instute Historyczny, 2000), p. 115.

112   "Things were better"   Boruch Spiegel, author interview, Montreal, November 2007.

113   "Dating in the Ghetto was different"   Boruch Spiegel, author interview, Montreal, October 2007.

113   a musical comedy called *The Rabbi's Little Rebecca,* starring Regina Sugar   Ulrich Keller, ed., *The Warsaw Ghetto in Photographs: 206 Views Made in 1941* (New York: Dover Publications, 1984), p. 47.

113   The twelve-hundred-seat Yiddish Artistic Theater, built in 1913 . . . a new play, *Got Fun Nerume,* directed by and starring Adam Samberg   Anna Kuligowska-Korzeniewska, "Swiat Ktory Odszedl," *Stolica,* no. 4 (2193), April 2008, pp. 16, 17.

113   More than eighty former members of the Warsaw Philharmonic . . . two winners of the Chopin prize . . . and solo violinists like Ludwig Holtzman   Fuks, *Mowia Wieki,* p. 30.

CHAPTER 16: JOANNA CAUSES TROUBLE

115   Every few weeks Monika brought money from the store, which was doing shockingly well   Joanna Olczak-Ronikier, author interview, Warsaw, December 2008.

115   "I was mortally afraid of Mr. Glaser"   Olczak-Ronikier, *W Ogrodzie Pamieci,* p. 277.

115   "Conspirators, underground agents, and saboteurs used it"   Ibid., p. 279.

116   "Not bad for a hideout"   Ibid.

116 "help from God himself" Martha Osnos, unpublished journal, p. 24.

116 an earthquake that measured 7.7 on the Richter scale F. Wenzel, D. Lungu, and O. Novak, eds., *Vrancea Earthquakes,* Natural Hazards, vol. 19, no. 1, January 1999, p. 80.

117 Carlton Hotel, collapsed, killing 267 guests Ibid.

117 "Two days later we had a transit visa" Martha Osnos, unpublished journal, p. 24.

117 "It seemed impossible to accomplish in a few hours" Ibid., p. 25.

118 "known for all kinds of guides and *machers*" Ibid., p. 26.

119 "'Everyone is in mourning here'" Ibid., p. 27.

120 "the picture of bourgeois respectability" Hilberg, Staron, and Kermisz, *Warsaw Diary of Adam Czerniakow,* p. 26.

120 Most of the sixteen-hundred-strong force hailed from an upper-middle-class background Gutman, *Jews of Warsaw 1939–1943,* p. 87.

120 "Many used bribery and influential connections" Goldstein, *Five Years in the Warsaw Ghetto,* p. 59.

121 "I heard cries and shouts" Zuckerman, *Surplus of Memory,* p. 135.

121 a number that would peak at 1.6 million Lukas, *Forgotten Holocaust,* p. 33.

122 "These snatchings were done in streets and in houses" Zuckerman, *Surplus of Memory,* p. 134.

122 "Before dawn, we were led through the streets of Warsaw" Ibid., p. 136.

CHAPTER 17: ISAAC AND BORUCH GLIMPSE HELL

123 Czerniakow was "weak" Mark Edelman, author interview, Lodz, May 2007.

123 The *Judenrat* was rife with corruption and collaborators Goldstein, *Five Years in the Warsaw Ghetto,* p. 30.

123 "scoundrels, vipers, and louses" Hilberg, Staron, and Kermisz, *Warsaw Diary of Adam Czerniakow,* p. 46.

124 "He was in an impossible position" Boruch Spiegel, author interview, Montreal, November 2007.

124 "Vomiting at home" Hilberg, Staron, and Kermisz, *Warsaw Diary of Adam Czerniakow,* p. 85.

124 "At 2 a.m. I begin to fret" Ibid., p. 91.

124 "When they found out he wasn't there" Boruch Spiegel, author interview, Montreal, October 2007.

125 Ghetto entry for Christians was *Streng Verboten* Helena Balicka-Kozlowska, *Mur Mial Dwie Strony* (Warsaw: Dom Wydawniczy Bellona, 2002), p. 10.

125 "They remain all day on their filthy straw mattresses" Edelman, *Ghetto Fights,* p. 41.

126   "Very rapidly they started to die"   Boruch Spiegel, author interview, Montreal, October 2007.

126   "So they took me"   Ibid.

126   "Who was that woman?"   Zuckerman, *Surplus of Memory*, p. 138.

127   "For three days his body will hang as a warning"   Ibid., p. 193.

127   "I have only one explanation"   Ibid., p. 140.

128   a series of assisted "suicides" among the nine thousand Volks-deutsche   Wladyslaw Bartoszewski, *1859 Dni Warszawy* (Krakow: Znak, 2009), p. 202.

128   Bogus farewell notes were left at the scenes   Karski, *Story of a Secret State*, p. 226.

128   executing the customary one hundred Poles in retaliation   Lukas, *Forgotten Holocaust*, p. 35.

128   "I hinted that I would be willing to pay"   Zuckerman, *Surplus of Memory*, p. 141.

128   fifty-three died in camp, and another fifty died shortly after their release   Samuel D. Kassow, *Who Will Write Our History? Rediscovering a Hidden Archive from the Warsaw Ghetto* (London: Penguin, 2007), p. 133.

128   "They behaved wonderfully toward us"   Zuckerman, *Surplus of Memory*, p. 142.

128   "When you set up the gallows"   Ibid.

129   "I didn't understand what we were doing there"   Boruch Spiegel, author interview, Montreal, November 2007.

129   "They fed us a bowl of soup a day and two hundred grams of bread"   Ibid.

129   "It was awful"   Ibid.

130   "I thought the Blue Police was bad"   Ibid.

131   "when they finish with us, they'll move on to you"   Ibid.

131   "Don't faint. You can't faint"   Ibid.

CHAPTER 18: THEY DIDN'T DESERVE SUCH A PARTING

132   "the pampered child of Valiant" Street   Zuckerman, *Surplus of Memory*, p. 144.

132   "For the first time, I had seen with my own eyes"   Ibid.

133   Jews would enter from Forestry Boulevard   Paulsson, *Secret City*, p. 63.

133   "I saw how the Germans beat the Poles there at the station"   Zuckerman, *Surplus of Memory*, p. 122.

133   "We were sure of a quick victory by the Red Army"   Ibid., p. 146.

133   "barkers"   Ozimek, *Media Walczacej Warszawy*, p. 47.

134   "I left in a few minutes"   Zuckerman, *Surplus of Memory*, p. 122.

134   "We were shocked"   Lubetkin, *Zaglada I Powstanie*, p. 55.

134   "We must assume that this was an awful act of revenge"   Zuckerman, *Surplus of Memory*, p. 151.

135   "There was nowhere Lonka would not go"   Lubetkin, *Zaglada I Powstanie*, p. 52.

135   "The craziest rumors were circulating"   Mark Edelman, author interview, Lodz, May 2007.

135   "prone to childish bouts of fantasy and enthusiasm"   Beres and Burnetko, *Marek Edelman*, p. 59.

136   "We were ideological rivals"   Mark Edelman, author interview, Lodz, May 2007.

136   It would claim 14,449 lives by year's end   Beres and Burnetko, *Marek Edelman*, p. 71.

136   "Their organs were translucent"   Ibid.

136   "I instruct the entire population of the Warsaw District"   Bartoszewski, *1859 Dni Warszawy*, p. 290.

137   "Runge was smuggled into the ghetto with great care"   Goldstein, *Five Years in the Warsaw Ghetto*, p. 83.

137   a special pogrom unit of Lithuanians called the *Ipatingas*   Jean-Francois Steiner, *Treblinka* (New York: Signet Books, 1968), p. 18.

137   "rightful punishment to collaborators and traitors"   Richard Rhodes, *Masters of Death* (New York: Knopf, 2002), p. 41.

137   "On the concrete forecourt of the petrol station"   Ibid.

138   "from the reliable non-Communist elements among Ukrainians"   Ibid.

138   "Death to Jews, death to Communists"   Ibid., p. 59.

138   In the town of Radzilow, Germans incited Polish peasants to murder eight hundred Jewish inhabitants   Jan T. Gross, *Neighbors: The Destruction of the Jewish Community in Jedwabne, Poland* (New York: Penguin, 2002), p. 32.

138   "That was part of the German genius"   Mark Edelman, author interview, Lodz, May 2007.

139   "I didn't get out of bed for a month"   Boruch Spiegel, author interview, Montreal, November 2007.

139   suffering from *ascites* or the "wet form" of severe malnutrition: Myron Winick, *Final Stamp: The Jewish Doctors in the Warsaw Ghetto* (Bloomington, Indiana: Author House, 2007), p. 35.

140   This was known as the diuretic phase of starvation treatment   Ibid., p. 39.

140   "For her, everything was 'God's will'"   Boruch Spiegel, author interview, Montreal, November 2007.

140   "in the evening you could see well-dressed women, wearing lipstick and rouge"   Sloan, *Notes from the Warsaw Ghetto*, p. 222.

141   "He had had it for eight or nine years"   Boruch Spiegel, author interview, Montreal, November 2007.

141   "I didn't know if I could bring myself to swallow that bread"   Ibid.

141   "I watched him fade, day by day"   Ibid.

CHAPTER 19: SIMHA LEAVES ZIVIA TO HER PROPHECY

142   "bedsheets could be traded for half a kilo of bread"   Boruch Spiegel, author interview, Montreal, November 2007.

142   like Model Pienkert or Nathan Wittenberg's Final Journey Funeral Parlor   Photo exhibition, Jewish Historical Institute, Tlomackie Street, Warsaw.

142   forty-three thousand people had died of hunger and disease   Engelking and Leociak, *Getto Warszawskie*, p. 317.

142   "Dead bodies had become part of the landscape"   Simha Ratheiser-Rotem, author interview, Jerusalem, March 2009.

143   "I could only guess that this was a Jewish boy"   Paulsson, *Secret City*, p. 69.

143   "A little skeleton, four or five years old"   Ibid.

143   "I was almost seventeen and strong"   Simha Ratheiser-Rotem, author interview, Jerusalem, March 2009.

143   "My parents didn't like it"   Ratheiser-Rotem, *Kazik*, p. 13.

144   "My mom had relatives who lived in a tiny village deep in the countryside"   Simha Ratheiser-Rotem, author interview, Jerusalem, March 2009.

144   "I was very eager to leave"   Ibid.

145   "If international Jewry, in Europe and outside of Europe"   Lubetkin, *Zaglada I Powstanie*, p. 55.

145   "A fat German officer greeted them politely"   Ibid., p. 56.

146   "Nobody believed him"   Ibid., p. 57.

146   They had ample historic precedent   Laqueur, *History of Zionism*, p. 159.

146   "People were unable to believe that they could be killed like that"   Kerry P. Callahan, *Mordechai Anielewicz: Hero of the Warsaw Ghetto Rising* (New York: Rosen Publishing, 2001), p. 70.

146   "Something like this could never happen in the heart of Europe"   Lubetkin, *Zaglada I Powstanie*, p. 57.

147   "I closed my eyes"   Ibid.

147   "I remember sitting in silence"   Zuckerman, *Surplus of Memory*, p. 156.

148   "Those were the hardest weeks of my life"   Ibid., p. 157.

148   "It is better to die fighting like free men"   Yisrael Gutman, *Resistance: The Warsaw Ghetto Uprising* (Boston: Mariner Books, 1994), p. 103.

148   "Let's face facts"   Lubetkin, *Zaglada I Powstanie*, p. 59.

149   "We must make contact with other Jewish groups at all costs"   Ibid.

CHAPTER 20: JOANNA AND THE TERRIFYING MR. GLASER

151   She remained terrified of the mean and mysterious caretaker   Olczak-Ronikier, *W Ogrodzie Pamieci*, p. 277.

152   "My mother and grandmother would not have asked about it"   Joanna Olczak-Ronikier, author interview, Warsaw, December 2008.

152   "He's far away, traveling"   Ibid.

152 "In my next memory we are slogging through mud"   Olczak-Ronikier, *W Ogrodzie Pamieci*, p. 277.

153 "Was it for money? Out of servile loyalty to the occupiers?"   Ibid., p. 279.

153 "In my hazy recollection of events"   Ibid.

153 Auschwitz, which by 1942 had already claimed the lives of sixty thousand suspected Gentile rebels   Auschwitz Museum exhibit, author visit.

154 "So without shedding any tears I left Michael in a puddle"   Olczak-Ronikier, *W Ogrodzie Pamieci*, p. 279.

155 In total, fifty-two people were killed on April 17   Gutman, *Jews of Warsaw: 1939–1943*, p. 176.

155 deporting 461 suspected Resistance members to Auschwitz   Bartoszewski, *1859 Dni Warszawy*, p. 330.

156 where display windows were still stocked with wines and luxury goods   Balicka-Kozlowska, *Mur Mial Dwie Strony*, p. 11.

156 when the Germans extended the Cool Street corridor in January 1942   Engelking and Leociak, *Getto Warszawskie*, p. 143.

157 "We were accused of being dangerously irresponsible"   Lubetkin, *Zaglada I Powstanie*, p. 60.

157 "You are quite young," Isaac remembered him responding   Ibid.

157 "I was ready to kill my Bundist colleagues for their blindness"   Zuckerman, *Surplus of Memory*, p. 175.

158 "Many of us were not happy with the decision"   Boruch Spiegel, author interview, Montreal, November 2007.

158 "It was a mistake"   Mark Edelman, author interview, Lodz, May 2007.

158 "We had serious reservations"   Lubetkin, *Zaglada I Powstanie*, p. 62.

158 "This was after our great failure with the Bund"   Zuckerman, *Surplus of Memory*, p. 182.

158 "So we joined"   Lubetkin, *Zaglada I Powstanie*, p. 62.

CHAPTER 21: THE RIGHT OPTION

160 an elitist prewar organization called Brit Hechayal   Chaim Lazar, *Muranowska 7* (Tel Aviv: Massada Press, 1966), p. 126.

160 "well-off":   Marian Apfelbaum, *Two Flags: Return to the Warsaw Ghetto* (Jerusalem: Gefen Publishing, 2007), p. 23.

160 "We don't want to go to the *Oflag*"   Henryk Iwanski, *Kultura* 6, no. 16, April 1968, p. 254.

160 (and where a small square would be named in Apfelbaum's honor)   Dariusz Libionka and Laurence Weinbaum, "A Legendary Commander," Haaretz.com., news.haaretz.co.il/hasen/pages/ShArt.jhtml?itemNo=87401 7&contrassID=2&subContrassID=14&sbSubC.

161 "Hurray patriotism combined with primitive anti-Semitism"   Shore, *Caviar and Ashes*, p. 28.

161 "Anti-Semitism was not merely an addendum to the Endek program"   Jan

Engelgard, *Norodowa Demokracja I Okolice* (Warsaw: Wydawnictwo Prasy Lokalnej, 2006), p. 37.

161 "I must confess that I had never expected" Dan Kurzman, *The Bravest Battle: The 28 Days of the Warsaw Ghetto Uprising* (New York: Da Capo Press, 1976), p. 62.

161 "Help us organize the Jewish youth" Iwanski, *Mowi Major Bystry,* p. 254.

162 the Sanation regime helped train a radical offshoot Moshe Arens, *The Jewish Military Organization in the Warsaw Ghetto,* Oxford Journals, Holocaust and Genocide Studies, vol. 19, no. 2, p. 207.

162 "it is in your interest and in ours" Lazar, *Muranowska 7,* p. 42.

163 had found thirty-nine individuals Apfelbaum, *Two Flags,* p. 24.

163 "I receive thee among the soldiers of Freedom" Bor-Komorowski, *Secret Army,* p. 29.

163 supplied with twenty-nine handguns Apfelbaum, *Two Flags,* p. 24.

163 the first casualty of war Abraham Rabinovich, *Jerusalem Post,* April 20, 2006.

163 "almost to the point of total omission" Dazriuz Libionka and Laurence Weinbaum, *Deconstructing Memory and History,* Jewish Political Studies Review, 18:1–2 (Jerusalem: Jerusalem Center for Public Affairs, Spring 2006).

164 "what to make of the story of David Moryc Apfelbaum" Libionka and Weinbaum, *Haaretz,* June 22, 2007.

164 "They were smugglers and thieves backed by a bunch of [Polish] nationalists" Mark Edelman, author interview, Lodz, May 2007.

164 "elitist recruitment policies strongly weighted toward those better-off Jews" Apfelbaum, *Two Flags,* p. 45.

165 membership in the group soared to over 250 inductees Kalmen Mendelson, *Historia Powstania* ZZW.

165 "We became Fascists, Hitlerites" Wdowinski, *And We Are Not Saved,* p. 7.

165 "cannot serve two gods, Zionism and Socialism" Ibid., p. 5.

166 "Vladimir Hitler" Ibid., p. 10.

166 "was among the most beautiful, the most honest, the most modest people I have ever met" Wdowinski, *And We Are Not Saved,* p. 79.

167 "The [Polish Underground] became aware of this influx of volunteers and wanted to take advantage" Kalmen Mendelson, *Historia Powstania* ZZW, *Kronika,* no. 18, May 2, 1970.

167 By 1942, the JMU boasted nearly three hundred registered combatants Ibid.

167 A three-man general command staff presided over the secretive group Lazar, *Muranowska 7,* p. 139.

168 In two underground shooting galleries on Cordials and Franciscan Streets Apfelbaum, *Two Flags,* p. 62.

168   the JMU's Technical Department dug a tunnel in December 1941
      Tadeusz Bednarczyk, *Zycie Codzienne Warszawskiego Getta* (Warsaw:
      Goldpol, 1995), p. 67.

169   **"Bloody Friday has had strong repercussions"**   Sloan, *Notes from the
      Warsaw Ghetto*, p. 270.

169   **"I became a pariah"**   Zuckerman, *Surplus of Memory*, p. 179.

169   **"There were not many. . . . But they did a tremendous amount of damage"**
      Mark Edelman, author interview, Lodz, May 2007.

169   **"People don't like to hear that we had Jewish prostitutes, criminals, or col-
      laborators"**   Ibid.

169   **"The clientele of these places consisted principally of Jewish Gestapo
      agents"**   Goldstein, *Five Years in the Warsaw Ghetto*, p. 78.

170   **"Gancwajch is turning into a regular Maecenas"**   Sloan, *Notes from the
      Warsaw Ghetto: The Journal of Emmanuel Ringelblum*, p. 271.

170   **"The new arrivals would have nothing to do with Ghetto Jews"**   Gold-
      stein, *Five Years in the Warsaw Ghetto*, p. 88.

170   **"They still talk about *unser Fuehrer*"**   Sloan, *Notes from the Warsaw
      Ghetto*, p. 288.

CHAPTER 22: SIMHA PLAYS SHEPHERD AND EDELMAN PLAYS GOD

174   **"It was heaven on earth"**   Simha Ratheiser-Rotem, author interview, Jeru-
      salem, March 2009.

174   Its one-hundred-odd Jews were required to wear   Ibid.

174   **"My relatives were religious Jews"**   Ratheiser-Rotem, *Kazik*, p. 14.

174   **"Every morning I would go to the peasant's house, where I ate my
      fill"**   Ibid.

175   **"I was haunted by the idea that people in the Ghetto were suffer-
      ing"**   Simha Ratheiser-Rotem, author interview, Jerusalem, March 2009.

175   **"All Jewish persons living in Warsaw, regardless of age and sex"**   Pauls-
      son, *Secret City*, p. 73.

176   whose upper floors had traditionally housed dentists and denture manu-
      facturers   Engelking and Leociak, *Getto Warszawskie*, p. 474, annex.

176   Zamenhof in front of Teperman and Morgensztern's bakery   Ibid.

177   **"If they intended to kill us, they wouldn't feed us so much"**   Marek Edel-
      man, *I Juz nie Bylo jak Przedtem*, Gazeta Wyborcza, April 22, 1999.

177   **"When will we be given the bread?"**   Gutman, *Resistance*, p. 137.

177   **"In this way, even the most rebellious elements in the Ghetto"**   Edelman,
      I Juz nie Bylo jak Przedtem, Gazeta Wyborcza, April 22, 1999.

177   **"We didn't know where people were being taken"**   Mark Edelman,
      author interview, Lodz, May 2007.

177   **"He was a strong, well-built, athletic, handsome young man"**   Goldstein,
      Five Years in the Warsaw Ghetto, p. 101.

177   that ultimately damaged 6,930 locomotives and 19,058 railcars   Lukas, *Forgotten Holocaust*, p. 67.

178   held *Dienstausweis* identity papers   Michal Grynberg, ed., *Words to Outlive Us* (New York: Picador, 2003), p. 120.

178   some sixty to seventy thousand people   Gutman, *Jews of Warsaw 1939–1943*, p. 204.

178   "I had a hard rule. I only rescued those I knew"   Edelman, *I Juz nie Bylo jak Przedtem*, Gazeta Wyborcza, April 22, 1999.

179   "In order to pull someone out of the lines"   Krall, *Shielding the Flame*, p. 43.

179   "They weren't all sons of bitches"   Mark Edelman, author interview, Lodz, May 2007.

179   "People—your friends, your neighbors, your co-workers"   Boruch Spiegel, author interview, Montreal, October 2007.

179   "Mostly I was hiding on the roof"   Ibid.

179   "Street by street, building by building, they were emptying the Ghetto"   Ibid.

180   "Do not be deceived! You are being taken to death and extermination"   Goldstein, *Five Years in the Warsaw Ghetto*, p. 102.

180   "Everybody's eyes have a wild, crazy, fearful look"   Lennart Lindskog, *Living Testimony: Marek Edelman*, Torah.org, online at http://www.torah.org/features/firstperson/livingtestimony.html.

180   "They held her by the hands and legs"   Edelman, *I Byla Milosc w Getcie*, p. 98.

CHAPTER 23: ONE GUN

181   "I was accompanying Abraham Schneidmel"   Rudi Assuntino and Wlodek Goldkorn, *Straznik: Marek Edelman Opowida* (Krakow: Znak, 2006), p. 54.

182   "You can't shoot from two fingers"   Mark Edelman, author interview, Lodz, May 2007.

182   "He looked like a nobleman"   Ibid.

182   "didn't know the Zionists, didn't trust the Communists"   Ibid.

182   "I don't believe [it will be] a whole wagonload, but we'll get something out of this"   Beres and Burnetko, *Marek Edelman*, p. 105.

182   "He said that I should wait by a phone"   Assuntino and Goldkorn, *Straznik*, p. 55.

182   11-92-28   Ibid., p. 55.

183   "Suddenly I saw a large mob on the street below"   Assuntino and Goldkorn, *Straznik*, p. 55.

185   80 degrees even after dark   Engelking and Leociak, *Getto Warszawskie*, p. 683.

185 "There wasn't a single Jew on Valiant"   Zuckerman, *Surplus of Memory*, p. 200.

185 the bullet entered one cheek   Gutman, *Jews of Warsaw 1939–1943*, p. 239.

186 "It didn't occur to a Jew that Jews would use weapons"   Zuckerman, *Surplus of Memory*, p. 203.

186 he looked like a regular *"sheygetz"*   Adolf Berman, *Underground Days* (Tel Aviv: Hamenora, 1971), p. 191.

186 eight hand grenades and five handguns   Lubetkin, *Zaglada I Powstanie*, p. 73.

186 "I'll never forget the drinks in honor of that event"   Zuckerman, *Surplus of Memory*, p. 201.

187 "I gave orders to bring the weapons to us"   Ibid., p. 200.

CHAPTER 24: LITTLE ANGEL

188 "wet myself, I was so frightened"   Simha Ratheiser-Rotem, author interview, Jerusalem, March 2009.

189 "You are outside the area!"   Ratheiser-Rotem, *Kazik*, p. 15.

189 "I was standing ten feet away"   Simha Ratheiser-Rotem, author interview, Jerusalem, March 2009.

189 "I remember the blood pooling on the ground near my feet"   Simha Ratheiser-Rotem, author interview, Jerusalem, March 2009.

189 "was the first time that I really understood what was happening to my people"   Ibid.

190 "So many of our comrades were gone, and we were too ashamed"   Lubetkin, *Zaglada I Powstanie*, p. 75.

190 departed on September 21, 1942—Yom Kippur—carrying two thousand Jewish policemen   Engelking and Leociak, *Getto Warszawskie*, p. 689.

191 The shops housed the 34,969 Jewish slave laborers   Krzysztof Dunin-Wasowicz, ed., *Organizacja Wladz Niemieckich na Terenie Dystryku Warszawskiego 1939–1945: W Raporty Ludwiga Fischera* (Warsaw: PAN, 1987), p. 600.

191 the Wilfried Hoffman Works, where twelve hundred Jewish tailors sewed SS uniforms   Engelking and Leociak, *Getto Warszawskie*, p. 474, appendix.

191 "We were consumed with shame"   Lubetkin, *Zaglada I Powstanie*, p. 75.

191 Of 51,458 Jewish children under the age of ten in Warsaw, for instance, only 498 remained alive   Kassow, *Who Will Write Our History?* p. 308.

192 "We hid like mice in holes"   Zuckerman, *Surplus of Memory*, p. 213.

192 "I don't remember who spoke first": Yitzak Zuckerman, *In Ghetto and Uprising* (Tel Aviv: Ghetto Fighters House Ltd., 1986), pp. 80–81.

192   "Let's go out in the streets tomorrow"   Ibid.

193   "Ari must go back to the Aryan side. We must look for new contacts"
       Ibid.

193   "We started organizing again"   Zuckerman, *Surplus of Memory*, p. 215.

194   "Jews considered it the underworld suburb"   Ratheiser-Rotem, *Kazik*,
       p. 3.

195   the Rozenwein and Bromberg families had small shops down the street
       Kasprzycki, *Korzenie Miasta*, p. 330.

195   Mordechai's mother had a stall that sold fish, and she could not always
       afford to buy ice   Mark Edelman, author interview, Lodz, April 2007.

195   his younger brother Pinchas, a brawny wrestling champion   Kurzman,
       Bravest Battle, p. 32.

195   the P or Z bus lines . . . his thirty-groszy, or nickel, fare   Kasprzycki,
       Korzenie Miasta, p. 328.

195   his future nom de guerre, Aniolek, or Little Angel   Callahan, *Mordechai
       Anielewicz*, p. 19.

196   "That didn't fill me with pride"   Boruch Spiegel, author interview, Mon-
       treal, November 2007.

196   "It wasn't important to me that I was alive"   Ibid.

196   "Father, mother, sister all burned, my Zille in Majdanek"   Goldstein,
       Five Years in the Warsaw Ghetto, p. 158.

196   "They had misjudged the situation very badly"   Boruch Spiegel, author
       interview, Montreal, November 2007.

197   With only five hundred employees it was one of the smaller shops   Ibid.

197   Toebbens factories, which had a combined twelve thousand workers and
       supplied 60 percent of the winter clothing   Engelking and Leociak, *Getto
       Warszawskie*, p. 707.

197   "She was all I had left"   Boruch Spiegel, author interview, Montreal, No-
       vember 2007.

197   "Bernard didn't grasp the reality of the conditions in the Ghetto"   Edel-
       man, *I Byla Milosc w Getcie*, p. 47.

198   "As usual Mark was carelessly dressed"   Goldstein, *Five Years in the War-
       saw Ghetto*, p. 139.

198   "We saw eye to eye"   Mark Edelman, author interview, Lodz, May 2007.

199   "They were subordinate to fringe [Polish] ultranationalists"   Ibid.

199   "sharply opposed us and was especially virulent against the Soviet
       Union"   Ber Mark, *Powstanie W Getcie Warszawskim* (Warsaw:
       Wydawnictwo Idisz Bukh, 1953), p. 104.

199   "you didn't bring anyone in unless you knew them from child-
       hood"   Mark Edelman, author interview, Lodz, May 2007.

199   "Mordechai Anielewicz wanted to be commander"   Zuckerman, *Surplus
       of Memory*, p. 228.

200   "What is there to say?"   Mark Edelman, author interview, Lodz, May
       2007.

Chapter 25: Simha Returns and Joanna Flees

201 "I had a lot of confidence in my mother"   Simha Ratheiser-Rotem, author interview, Jerusalem, March 2009.

202 "He wasn't an anti-Semite, quite the opposite"   Zuckerman, *Surplus of Memory*, p. 75.

202 "We wanted to save the people"   Ibid., p. 76.

203 he recognized a familiar face: Rivka Pasmanik   Ratheiser-Rotem, *Kazik*, p. 17.

203 "Would you go on a mission to the Ghetto?"   Ibid.

204 the Piastow Rubber Works, which had 1,070 employees   Grzelaka, *Warszawa we Wrzesniu 1939 Roku*, p. 69.

204 Tudor Accumulator Systems, stood next door, spilling out 450 workers   Ibid., p. 42.

205 "We moved in at dusk"   Olczak-Ronilier, *W Ogrodzie Pamieci*, p. 280.

205 "At first we found the heavy traffic that passed through the house"   Ibid.

206 "Miss Irene was in the A.K."   Joanna Olczak-Ronikier, author interview, Warsaw, December 2008.

206 British officials thought the Poles seemed more intent on fighting one another than the Germans   Jan M. Ciechanowski, *Powstanie Warszawskie* (Warsaw: Bellona, 2009), p.118.

206 "If Irene sped off somewhere with a bag, she was sure to be taking supplies"   Olczak-Ronikier, *W Ogrodzie Pamieci*, pp. 280–81.

208 would result in the rescue of at least twelve hundred Jewish children   Ewa Kurek, *Gdy Klasztor Znaczyl Zycie* (Krakow: Znak, 1992), p. 102.

208 "Sister Wanda called us together"   Ringelblum, *Stosunki Polsko-Zydowskie w Czasie Drugiej Wojny Swiatowej* (Warsaw: Czytelnik, 1988), p. 83.

208 "I clearly remember my first encounter with that place"   Olczak-Ronikier, *W Ogrodzie Pamieci*, p. 281.

209 Breakfast and prayers followed punctually at eight. Between nine o'clock and noon, classes were held   Kurek, *Gdy Klasztor Znaczyl Zycie*, p. 71.

209 "This was the special skill of many occupation-era children"   Olczak-Ronikier, *W Ogrodzie Pamieci*, p. 282.

209 Referred to her torn undershirt as a *lejblik*   Kurek, *Gdy Klasztor Znaczyl Zycie*, p. 64.

210 One in five Polish priests died at the hands of the Germans during the war   Lukas, *Forgotten Holocaust*, p. 9.

210 "When an internal bell rang during lessons"   Olczak-Ronikier, *W Ogrodzie Pamieci*, pp. 282–93.

Chapter 26: Boruch and Robert Learn Different Lessons

212 "Because of the sun, the elegant people were housed on the shady, port side"   Robert Osnos, author interview, New York, April 2010.

213   "In Baghdad, my father had heard that if you had a transit visa"   Ibid.
213   "Phosphorescent like green gold fire and stars like we'd never seen them before"   Martha Osnos, unpublished journal, p. 32.
213   "didn't even know what they were or how to eat them"   Ibid.
214   "Money was never a problem in India"   Robert Osnos, author interview, New York, April 2010.
214   "My parents were very active socially in Bombay"   Ibid.
215   "My parents were borderline negligent in leaving me to my own devices" Ibid.
215   "He couldn't go swimming with us"   Ibid.
215   "Of course you're a Jew"   Ibid.
215   "What strikes me most in retrospect"   Ibid.
216   "700,000 Jews were reported slain in Poland"   New York Times, June 27, 1942.
217   "I was afraid it would go off accidentally"   Boruch Spiegel, author interview, Montreal, October 2007.
217   "It filled me with purpose and hope"   Ibid.
219   "As we walked, everything became increasingly unreal"   Karski, Story of a Secret State, pp. 330–33.
219   "They pretty much said you don't represent the Jews"   Zuckerman, Surplus of Memory, p. 220.
220   "What do you need—money?"   Kurzman, Bravest Battle, p. 47.
220   "Enemy Number One of the Third Reich"   Andrzej Krzystof Kunert and Jozef Szyrmer, Stefan Rowecki: Wspomnienia I Notatki (Warsaw: Czyelnik, 1988), p. 7.
220   "First Ally"   Norman Davies, Rising '44: The Battle for Warsaw (New York: Viking, 2003), p. 29.
220   "We must remember . . . that the position of the Anglo-Saxon world" Mark, Powstanie W Getcie Warszawskim, p. 107.
220   "I therefore plead with you"   Ibid., p. 108.
221   "Since we are citizens of Poland . . . the decisions of the Polish government"   Kurzman, Bravest Battle, p. 53.
221   "Jews from all sorts of communist groups"   Gutman, Resistance, p. 174.
221   "Instead of saying 'I hate you' it was easier for them to say 'I don't believe in you'"   Zuckerman, Surplus of Memory, p. 219.

CHAPTER 27: ISAAC'S NOT-SO-MERRY CHRISTMAS

222   "Nothing but trouble ever comes from that forsaken city"   Dunin-Wasowicz, Warszawa W Latach 1939–1945, p. 169.
223   "We were traveling openly. I looked like a rural Polish nobleman"   Zuckerman, Surplus of Memory, p. 235.
223   "He could keep his cool in any situation"   Lubetkin, Zaglada I Powstanie, p. 84.

223   "That night we got together to toast the success of the operation"   Zuckerman, *Surplus of Memory*, p. 236.

223   Thirteen Germans were dead and a dozen more were in the hospital Lubetkin, *Zaglada I Powstanie*, p. 85.

224   "After five steps, I began to feel warmth and a sharp pain"   Zuckerman, *Surplus of Memory*, p. 237.

224   "I said they could take me to the Gestapo in a cab, but I wasn't moving" Ibid., p. 238

225   "Hard times! . . . We are turning into wolves"   Ibid., p. 239.

225   "The station was full of Germans"   Ibid.

226   "Until the moment I entered the building I held up"   Ibid., p. 240.

226   "They found us. . . . An SS man, he had a whip"   Chaika Belchatowska, transcript of taped interview with Sandra Fishlinsky, November 29, 1993, Montreal, as part of the Contributions of Holocaust Survivors to the Cultural and Social Institutions of Montreal, in the digital archives of Concordia University (http://archives.concordia.ca/P007).

226   "In his shoe, in the sole of his shoe, he had a little saw"   Ibid.

227   "We started marching"   Ibid.

227   "They recognized that we were Jews"   Ibid.

227   "She had been taken on her birthday"   Boruch Spiegel, author interview, Montreal, October 2007.

227   "We felt certain the Germans were too busy with their roundups on the Aryan side"   Lubetkin, *Zaglada I Powstanie*, p. 87.

227   twelve thousand Varsovian Gentiles were arrested   Bartoszewski, *Warszawski Pierscien Smierci 1939–1945*, p. 228.

228   erased virtually every German street name in Midtown . . . and papered walls with forty thousand   Bartoszewski, *1851 Dni Warszawy*, p. 424.

228   such as Helgoland, Mitropa, and the Apollo Theater   Luczak, *Dzieje Polski 1939–1945*, p. 290.

228   "Even some Poles from the underground sought refuge in the abandoned sections of the Ghetto"   Lubetkin, *Zaglada I Powstanie*, p. 87.

228   minus twenty degrees Celsius   Bartoszewski, *1851 Dni Warszawy*, p. 425.

228   carrying two hundred SS troops and eight hundred Ukrainian and Latvian auxiliaries   Gutman, *Resistance*, p. 184.

229   "I don't think Isaac, at this stage, even knew who I was"   Simha Ratheiser-Rotem, author interview, Jerusalem, March 2009.

229   "We had three pistols and three grenades"   Tuvia Borzykowski, *Between Tumbling Walls* (Tel Aviv: Beit Lahomei Hagettoat, 1972), p. 23.

229   "My God, that's Angel"   Simha Ratheiser-Rotem, author interview, Jerusalem, March 2009.

229   "We've got to help him"   Lubetkin, *Zaglada I Powstanie*, p. 89.

CHAPTER 28: THE ORGANIZATION

231 "The doors suddenly burst open and in flew a band of Germans" Ibid., p. 90.

232 after liquidating a mere five thousand Jews Gutman, *Jews of Warsaw 1939–1943*, p. 311.

232 The Home Army counted 380,000 registered members across Poland Lukas, *Forgotten Holocaust*, p. 62.

232 greater than the French Resistance or any other insurgent group in Europe William Hitchcock, *Liberation: The Bitter Road to Freedom 1944–1945* (London: Faber and Faber, 2009), p. 155.

232 "The street was in the hands of Jewish fighters for fifteen to twenty minutes" *Biuletyn Informacjny*, no. 4, January 28, 1943.

232 "I doubt they will use them" Gutman, *Resistance*, p. 174.

233 "It changed everything" Boruch Spiegel, author interview, Montreal, November 2007.

233 "We are no longer in charge. A new authority now rules the Ghetto" Engelking and Leociak, *Getto Warszawskie*, p. 724.

233 "My assignment was to distract the [Jewish Police] guards" Simha Ratheiser-Rotem, author interview, Jerusalem, March 2009.

233 "word spread like wildfire that the operation had been commanded by a fighter from the Polish Underground" Ratheiser-Rotem, *Kazik*, p. 24.

234 "When others became nervous or agitated I got calmer" Simha Ratheiser-Rotem, author interview, Jerusalem, March 2009.

234 "Isaac [Zuckerman] would tell Hanoch who had been sentenced to death" Ibid.

234 "I wanted to drink, and I drank too much" Zuckerman, *Surplus of Memory*, p. 305.

234 "I'm sorry, I won't talk about that" Boruch Spiegel, author interview, Montreal, November 2007.

234 "A Jewish policeman, a real son of a bitch" Assuntino and Goldkorn, *Straznik*, p. 77.

235 "We would kidnap their children and ransom them" Simha Ratheiser-Rotem, author interview, Jerusalem, March 2009.

235 the nickname by which his Israeli grandchildren would address him, the nom de guerre on his email address Ibid.

235 "I put the barrel of my revolver near him" Ratheiser-Rotem, *Kazik*, pp. 28–29.

235 "They drew their guns, we also brought guns" Mark Edelman, author interview, Lodz, May 2007.

235 "In a low dark room where large amounts of ammunition" Arens, *The Jewish Military Organization in the Warsaw Ghetto*, pp. 15–16.

236 "It began in the cellar of number 7 Muranow and ended across the street in number 6" Ibid.

236 "In the command room was a first class radio that received news" Joseph Kermish, ed., *To Live with Honor and Die with Honor: Selected Documents from the Warsaw Ghetto Underground Archives Oneg Shabbath* (Jerusalem: Yad Vashem, 1986), p. 596.

237 "Nine squadrons were concentrated in the center of the ghetto, eight in the area of the Tobbens and Schultz workshops" Wladyslaw Bartoszewski, *The Warsaw Ghetto: A Christian's Testimony* (Boston: Beacon Press, 1987), p. 71.

237 "We did not want to be taken by surprise again" Simha Ratheiser-Rotem, author interview, Jerusalem, March 2009.

238 "We would aim and shout Bang, Bang" Boruch Spiegel, author interview, Montreal, November 2007.

238 "Allocating weapons without ammunition impresses us as being a bit of a mockery" Gutman, *Jews of Warsaw 1939–1943*, p. 358.

239 "a machine gun, a tommy gun, twenty pistols with magazines and ammunition, 100 hand grenades" Bartoszewski, *Warsaw Ghetto*, p. 71.

239 "the odor of the chemicals was overwhelming" Vladka Meed, *On Both Sides of the Wall* (New York: Schocken, 1979), p. 173.

239 "We would remove the pipes with a larger than normal diameter" Zuckerman, *Surplus of Memory*, pp. 293–94.

239 "One morning the entire ghetto shook to a mighty explosion" Borzykowski, *Between Tumbling Walls*, p. 39.

240 "this was a mistake" Engelking and Leociak, *Getto Warszawskie*, p. 726.

241 "not all of us were in such a hurry to die" Mark Edelman, author interview, Lodz, May 2007.

241 "I had not gotten to know him well because I didn't mix with Communists" Beres and Burnetko, *Marek Edelman*, p. 141.

241 "very emotional and sometimes acted rashly" Mark Edelman, author interview, Lodz, May 2007.

241 "After this incident the Coordinating Committee of the ZOB wanted to remove him from his post" Beres and Burnetko, *Marek Edelman*, p. 141.

242 "the Home Army had an iron-clad rule that if someone was burnt" Ibid., p. 136.

243 "He talked and looked like a typical Warsaw Pole" Zuckerman, *Surplus of Memory*, pp. 342.

CHAPTER 29: ZIVIA LETS LOOSE

245 (now couldn't sleep unless he had his trusted pistol under his pillow) Boruch Spiegel, author interview, Montreal, October 2007.

245 The ZOB's twenty-two fighting units had all been mobilized and deployed Gutman, *Resistance*, p. 197.

245 "In the bunkers, people push and shove and lie down on planks" Lubetkin, *Zaglada I Powstanie*, p. 105.

246   There were roughly 750 of them dispersed throughout the Jewish district's three remaining sections   Gutman, *Resistance*, p. 204.

246   "we would have a thousand warriors rather than five hundred"   Lubetkin, *Zaglada I Powstanie*, p. 105.

246   "The day of revenge is upon us"   Ibid., p. 104.

246   "Behind them were tanks, armored vehicles, light cannons and hundreds of Waffen-SS units"   Ratheiser-Rotem, *Kazik*, p. 33.

247   "We don't stand a chance"   Simha Ratheiser-Rotem, author interview, Jerusalem, March 2009.

248   only 850 Waffen-SS troops, drawn more or less equally from   Jürgen Stroop, progress report, April 19, 1943, translated in *The Stroop Report* (New York: Pantheon, 1979).

248   Deutsch-Negers   Kazimierz Moczarski, *Rozmowy z Katem* (Krakow: Znak, 2007), p. 177.

248   "Let them come"   Lubetkin, *Zaglada I Powstanie*, p. 106.

248   "I could see torn limbs flying through the air with my own eyes"   Ibid.

248   *Juden haben Waffen*   Haim Frymer in Gutman, *Resistance*, p. 207.

249   "We couldn't help ourselves"   Lubetkin, *Zaglada I Powstanie*, p. 106.

250   Anielewicz's groups had knocked out a tank on Zamenhof Street   Engelking and Leociak, *Getto Warszawskie*, p.734.

250   "We can't get into the Ghetto"   Kurzman, *Bravest Battle*, p. 105.

251   Twelve men were dead or wounded, a tank was wrecked, and two armored personnel carriers were burned beyond recognition   Stroop, *Stroop Report*, April 19, 1943.

251   "That idiot, Von Sammern-Frankenegg, drove a tank into those narrow streets"   Moczarski, *Rozmowy z Katem*, pp. 179–80.

251   picked out a four-hundred-acre parcel near Lvov   Ibid., p. 157.

252   "alcohol, parties, and loose women"   Ibid., p. 172.

252   "finest Egyptian tobacco in the world"   Ibid.

252   "I'm assuming command"   Ibid., p. 181.

CHAPTER 30: JOANNA PRAYS

253   "I don't really remember much beyond the fact"   Joanna Olczak-Ronikier, author interview, Warsaw, December 2009.

254   "They demanded an inspection of all the children"   Olczak-Ronikier, *W Ogrodzie Pamieci*, p. 286.

255   "I don't remember being especially frightened"   Joanna Olczak-Ronikier, author interview, Warsaw, December 2009.

255   "smell of ersatz coffee and slightly burned porridge"   Olczak-Ronikier, *W Ogrodzie Pamieci*, p. 285.

256   "Was it through mutual friends?"   Ibid., p. 284.

256   "Don't provoke the Poles"   Moczarski, *Rozmowy z Katem*, p. 181.

257 "Poland has to wait and gather its strength" Gutman, *Resistance,* pp. 212–13.

257 "a wide assortment of Hebrew dictionaries, textbooks, and self-teaching guides" Jewish Historical Institute, Warsaw, archival map exhibit, November 2009.

257 The famous Moskowicz Cheese Shop had been next door, along with Goldstein's Laundry Ibid.

259 "No sooner had he finished speaking than the house shook" Borzykowski, *Between Tumbling Walls,* p. 52.

259 "Afraid to stick their heads out, they fired blind" Ibid.

260 "We were beginning to feel the fire" Ibid., p. 53.

261 "It was a way so difficult" Ibid.

CHAPTER 31: GHETTOGRAD

266 "Damn you" Moczarski, *Rozmowy z Katem,* p. 186.

266 "Continue to play thus, Maestro" Ibid., p. 187.

267 thanks to the four submachine guns delivered by Security Corps Apfelbaum, *Two Flags,* p. 204.

267 "Get those flags down, Stroop" Ibid.

267 his finger on the trigger of an IED Simha Ratheiser-Rotem, author interview, Jerusalem, March 2009.

267 Many of the hundred German and Ukrainian soldiers in the assault party Edelman, *I Bila Milosc w Getcie,* p. 115.

268 a geyser of water shot straight upward Ibid.

268 most of the four thousand slave laborers hiding in cellars in the Brushmakers District Mark Edelman, author interview, Lodz, May 2007.

268 "Shoot them" Ibid.

269 "Hans, look, a woman!" Ratheiser-Rotem, *Kazik,* p. 34.

269 Four of the ten fighters in Simha's group were women Ibid., p. 33.

269 "These females fired pistols from both hands" Stroop, *Stroop Report,* p. 8.

270 "During the night the fires we had started earlier forced the Jews to appear" Ibid., p. 27.

270 "embark on the total destruction of the Jewish quarter" Ibid, p. 9.

271 "I'm not going down there" Boruch Spiegel, author interview, Montreal, November 2007.

271 As many as eighty ZOB members had participated in the opening battle Ibid.

272 "We are going to die" Krall, *Shielding the Flame,* p. 5.

272 "The sea of flames flooded houses and courtyards" Edelman, *Ghetto Fights,* p. 80.

272 "We didn't think of committing suicide" Boruch Spiegel, author interview, Montreal, November 2007.

273 the old Municipal Courts building with its soaring six-story columns Kasprzycki, *Korzenie Miasta*, vol. 2, p. 148.

274 But David Apfelbaum and Paul Frenkel . . . were reportedly refusing to use it Lazar, *Muranowska 7*, p. 281.

274 bringing their children to watch his artillerymen level the Ghetto Balicka-Koslowska, *Mur Mial Dwie Strony*, p. 26.

274 "It is impossible not to sympathize with and admire the Jewish population" *Dzien Warszawy*, April 20, 1943.

274 "The smoke clouds over Warsaw cannot disappear without a trace" *Polska, Zwyciezy*, April 30, 1943.

275 HORRIBLE CRIME COMMITTED BY JEWS FROM THE NKVD *Nowy Kurjer Warszawski*, April 18, 1943, p. 1.

275 "The Jews' struggle has nothing to do with Poland" Kurzman, *Bravest Battle*, p. 286.

275 Eighteen members of a Security Corps extraction squad were mobilized Lazar, *Muranowska 7*, p. 279.

275 "With Iwanski leading the way, the men plodded along in single file" Kurzman, *Bravest Battle*, p. 239.

275 The street had been one of the wealthiest in the poorer northern part of the Jewish district Opoczynski, *Reportaze z Warszawskiego Getta*, p. 20.

275 But there was nothing left of the Gdansk Café, Nathan Gershwin Pharmaceuticals, the Style hairdressing salon Kasprzycki, *Korzenie Miasta*, vol. II, p. 159.

275 "Thank God you've come" Kurzman, *Bravest Battle*, p. 240.

276 Three hundred and twenty German and Latvian SS troops Stroop, *Stroop Report*, p. 39.

276 Skeptical Polish and Israeli historians, however, would later cast doubt on many of the claims Libionka and Weinbaum, "Deconstructing Memory and History," *Jewish Political Studies Review* 18:1–2 (Spring 2006).

277 "Iron Cross 1st Class" Wdowinski, *And We Are Not Saved*, p. 203.

277 "The assault party discovered a gang of 120 men, heavily armed with pistols" Stroop, *Stroop Report*, p. 39.

277 "Polish terrorists were identified with certainty among the bandits" Ibid., p. 40.

277 Iwanski posthumously promoted him to major Apfelbaum, *Two Flags*, p. 227.

CHAPTER 32: FALLEN ANGEL

278 "The total number of Jews apprehended has risen to 40,237" Ibid., p. 49.

279 "You couldn't blame them" Mark Edelman, author interview, Lodz, May 2007.

279 "Anyone walking on top of the rubble would never have believed that only a few meters" Zivia Lubetkin, *Zaglada I Powstanie*, p. 118.

280   "Everyone out"   Mark Edelman, author interview, Lodz, May 2007.

280   "Mark was very cold, but he was also very brave"   Beres and Burnetko, *Marek Edelman*, p. 177.

280   "He was ruthless, but you felt safe around him"   Ibid., p. 178.

280   Mark's plan was to send them a distraction, a pretty young ZOB member   Kurzman, *Bravest Battle*, pp. 274–75.

280   Stroop's daily casualty rate had spiked to seven   Stroop, *Stroop Report*, p. 49.

281   a cramped and foul-smelling dugout that had been excavated by Ghetto garbage collectors   Mark Edelman, author interview, Lodz, May 2007.

281   By May 7, with the influx of Edelman's team, it was over three hundred   Lubetkin, *Zaglada I Powstanie*, p. 111.

281   "He behaves here in the bowels of the earth like king of the roost"   Ibid.

282   "He and his pals treated the Fighting Organization with great respect"   Ibid.

282   "We feared meeting the dead more than living Germans"   Ibid., p. 121.

282   "His face sagged with worry"   Ibid., p. 111.

283   By nine o'clock there was still no word and Edelman's patience had worn thin   Mark Edelman, author interview, Lodz, May 2007.

283   "Mark was always full of bravado, flouting safety regulations"   Zivia Lubetkin, *Zaglada I Powstanie*, p. 130.

283   She had fallen through a crevice   Mark Edelman, author interview, Lodz, May 2007.

283   "We started thinking about what practical jokes we could pull"   Lubetkin, *Zaglada I Powstanie*, p. 130.

284   "John." . . . "Warsaw"   Mark Edelman, author interview, Lodz, May 2007.

284   Eighty ZOB members were dead   Beres and Burnetko, *Marek Edelman*, p. 173.

284   "First Anielewicz shot Mira . . . then himself"   Ibid.

284   Historians would cite five   Mark, *Powstanie W Getcie Warszawskim*, p. 72.

284   "A leader has no right to commit suicide"   Beres and Burnetko, *Marek Edelman*, p. 174.

284   "He took the easy way out"   Mark Edelman, author interview, Lodz, May 2007.

284   Prostitutes had shared bagels and other food with him in the past   Krall, *Shielding the Flame*, p. 40.

CHAPTER 33: SIMHA THE SAVIOR

285   "The welcome of the two women whom I'd just met dazzled me"   Ratheiser-Rotem, *Kazik*, p. 46.

286   "I initially thought my job was to tell Isaac that the others were ready"   Simha Ratheiser-Rotem, author interview, Jerusalem, March 2009.

286 Every day, 180 trains loaded with soldiers   Piotr Rozwadowski and Aneta
     Ignatowicz, *Boje o Warszawe* (Warsaw: Fundacja Warszawa Walczy, 2007),
     p. 124.
287 "If you don't go, I'm going to go back in myself!"   Simha Ratheiser-
     Rotem, author interview, Jerusalem, March 2009.
287 "Fine!"   Ibid.
288 "You can keep leading us, or you can die right here"   Simha Ratheiser-
     Rotem, author interview, Jerusalem, March 2009.
288 "It took a few tries but we managed to get out of the Ghetto"   Boruch
     Spiegel, author interview, Montreal, November 2007.
289 "I spent three hours looking for my friends"   Simha Ratheiser-Rotem,
     author interview, Jerusalem, March 2009.
290 "I will never forget what I saw when I first descended into the sewer"
     Borzykowski, *Between Tumbling Walls*, p. 68.
290 "It was midnight"   Ibid., p. 101.
290 "We had been walking for several hours when we received a jolt"   Ibid.
291 "We were not accustomed to good news"   Borzykowski, *Between Tum-
     bling Walls,* p. 103.
292 "We drag[ged] them over the putrid water"   Lubetkin, *Zaglada I Powsta-
     nie,* p. 138.
292 "We lay in the sewage, body pressed to body, and counted the passing min-
     utes"   Borzykowski, *Between Tumbling Walls,* p. 104.
292 "Our despair grew from moment to moment"   Ibid., p.105.
293 Their paid-off gangster host, who called himself the King   Simha
     Ratheiser-Rotem, author interview, Jerusalem, March 2009.
294 "Drink this"   Kurzman, *Bravest Battle,* p. 322.
294 "Move, move" . . . "Hurry, hurry"   Lubetkin, *Zaglada I Powstanie,*
     p. 141.
294 "I told him this was a Home Army mission"   Simha Ratheiser-Rotem,
     author interview, Jerusalem, March 2009.
294 "We have to go"   Ibid.
294 "There are a lot of people down there"   Ibid.
294 "Stop! Stop!"   Kurzman, *Bravest Battle,* p. 325.
295 For Boruch, the virgin forest . . . had come as a shock   Boruch Spiegel,
     author interview, Montreal, November 2007.
296 "I could not believe that only a few hundred yards from the Ghetto ordi-
     nary life went on"   Mark Edelman, author interview, Lodz, May 2007.
296 "Mark has had a breakdown"   Edelman, *I Byla Milosc w Getcie,* p. 123.
296 "Go ahead . . . pull the trigger and we both die"   Simha Ratheiser-Rotem,
     author interview, Jerusalem, March 2009.
296 "Those people died because of me"   Ibid.
296 But for the eighty survivors of the Jewish Fighting Organization's original
     five hundred members   Lubetkin, *Zaglada I Powstanie,* p. 143.

CHAPTER 34: HOTEL POLAND

297   the Jews, as urbanites, had no idea how to live off the land   Boruch Spiegel, author interview, Montreal, November 2007.

298   "Life in the world of partisans in eastern Poland was extremely cruel" Lukas, *Forgotten Holocaust*, p. 81.

298   "it was dark and damp, like lying in a grave"   Werner, *Fighting Back*, p. 80.

298   Twenty-eight of the Soviet-made rifles had been distributed to the Jewish partisans   Zuckerman, *Surplus of Memory*, p. 398.

299   "From fifty people in our original group . . . we were down to around fifteen"   Boruch Spiegel, author interview, Montreal, November 2007.

299   arranging for a doctor to perform an abortion by candlelight   Simha Ratheiser-Rotem, author interview, Jerusalem, March 2009.

299   "the problem is too great for solution by the two governments here represented"   Kurzman, *Bravest Battle*, p. 132.

300   "Stop it, they're our people"   Ratheiser-Rotem, *Kazik*, p. 92.

300   "I pretended I was a big shot in the Underground"   Simha Ratheiser-Rotem, author interview, Jerusalem, March 2009.

300   "Miraculously, one of them had even gotten hold of a starched collar, cuffs, and tie"   Ratheiser-Rotem, *Kazik*, p. 92.

301   "I told him that the ZOB had to be left alone"   Simha Ratheiser-Rotem, author interview, Jerusalem, March 2009.

301   there were still an estimated twenty-eight thousand Jews hiding in and around the city   Paulsson, *Secret City*, p. 103.

302   the Gestapo had snared thirty-five hundred Jews with a single fiendishly clever trap   Ibid., p. 139.

304   "It was hard to rationalize that while some Jews were getting caught in the street, others were sitting comfortably in the Hotel Polski"   Zuckerman, *Surplus of Memory*, p. 441.

304   "I rode inside the tram and they stood on the platform constantly chanting 'Jew, Jew, Jew!'"   Ibid., p. 126.

305   Grabowski later estimated the total number of greasers in wartime Warsaw to be between five and ten thousand   Jan Grabowski, "Zrada, Agresja I Obojetny Tlum," *Newsweek Polska*, May 18, 2008, p. 94.

305   "The extent of their criminal behavior is difficult to measure"   Ibid.

305   "disapproving indifference rather than widespread condemnation"   Ibid.

306   "The problem was that the authors of the document had defined nationality on the basis of ethnicity"   Ibid.

306   "Polish is your mother tongue"   Ozimek, *Media Walczacej Warszawy*, p. 51.

306   His name was Jan Pilnik, and he appeared eighth on a list of ten individuals   Andrzej Krzysztof Kunert, ed., *Zegoda: Rada Pomocy Zydom 1942–1945* (Warsaw: Rada Ochrony Pamienci Walk I Meczenstwa, 2002), p. 114.

306   a dozen of the two hundred executions carried out by the Resistance in Warsaw   Korbonski, *Fighting Warsaw,* p. 126.

306   "When I got off the tram, they surrounded me"   Zuckerman, *Surplus of Memory,* p. 441.

307   1,400 men and 487 women, all Gentiles, were sent to Auschwitz on the first day alone   Bartoszewski, *Warszawski Perscien Smierci,* p. 284.

307   On October 16, for instance, twenty people were shot on Independence Street   Ibid., p. 288.

307   "You've brought this on yourselves. Why do you provoke us?"   Ibid., p. 292.

309   as Isaac's "right-hand man"   Simha Ratheiser-Rotem, author interview, Jerusalem, March 2009.

309   "Tuvia's Polish wasn't Polish"   Zuckerman, *Surplus of Memory,* p. 435.

309   a trusted Gentile by the name of Stephen Pokropek   Simha Ratheiser-Rotem, author interview, Jerusalem, March 2009.

310   "I told [Sheingut] there was no point in both of us hanging around"   Ibid.

310   "Bullets whizzed by my ear"   Ratheiser-Rotem, *Kazik,* p. 81.

310   "We were tormented by suspicion, and, naturally, it fell on Black"   Ibid., p. 82.

310   "I'm walking down the street and I see this big convertible"   Simha Ratheiser-Rotem, author interview, Jerusalem, March 2009.

CHAPTER 35: ROBERT'S AMERICAN PLEDGE

311   "Out of the blue my dad got a call that our papers were ready"   Robert Osnos, author interview, New York, April 2010.

312   "I don't know how, but my father guessed that there would be a backlash against colonialism after the war"   Ibid.

313   "He was accused of being a Peeping Tom"   Ibid.

313   "They thought it was some sort of codes"   Ibid.

314   "Hey buddy, you lose your pants or something"   Ibid.

314   "We were petrified that the Host would stick in throats"   Olczak-Ronikier, *W Ogrodzie Pamieci,* p. 290.

314   "On the commuter train a guy latched on to us, trying to make jokes"   Ibid., p. 291.

315   "Then I went back to the convent like a good girl"   Ibid., p. 292.

316   "You needed official permission to go out from your *melina*"   Boruch Spiegel, author interview, Montreal, November 2007.

316   "Even my eyes were Yiddish"   Ibid.

316   "He did everything to boost our morale"   Ibid.

317   Her grandmother translated *Dr. Dolittle's Return* into Polish   Joanna Olczak-Ronikier, author interview, Warsaw, December 2008.

317   "One day they would speak only in French"   Ibid.

317 "We had the feeling of being prisoners sentenced to an indefinite term" Borzykowski, *Between Tumbling Walls*, p. 133.

317 "You Poles are strange people"   Tec, *When Light Pierced the Darkness*, p. 51.

317 "it only takes one Pole to betray a hundred Jews, but it takes ten Poles to save one Jew"   Simha Ratheiser-Rotem, author interview, Jerusalem, March 2009.

317 Between forty thousand and sixty thousand Varsovians were actively involved in sheltering Jews   Emmanuel Ringelblum, *Polish-Jewish Relations During the Second World War* (Evanston, Illinois: Northwestern University Press, 1992), p. 247.

317 Some Western historians put the number as high as ninety thousand   Paulsson, *Secret City*, p. 129.

317 "These noble individuals face not only German terror but also the hostility of Polish fascists"   Ringelblum, *Polish-Jewish Relations During the Second World War*, p. 247.

318 "What a lot of people don't realize is that the Poles had it pretty bad too"   Boruch Spiegel, author interview, Montreal, November 2007.

318 "Once I was on the run and went to Marisa [Sawicka's] apartment"   Simha Ratheiser-Rotem, author interview, Jerusalem, March 2009.

318 The capital's non-Jewish population had shrunk by more than a fifth since 1939   Szarota, *Okupowanej Warszawy Dzien Powszedni*, p. 78.

319 The daily rate for boarding a Jewish child, for instance, was 100 zlotys   Ringelblum, *Polish-Jewish Relations During the Second World War*, p. 140.

319 "Death threatened for bacon and gold, for weapons and false papers"   Paulsson, *Secret City*, p. 129.

319 Wolski's ex girlfriend tipped off the authorities   Kassow, *Who Will Write Our History?* p. 383.

320 a translation of her book about Saint Francis of Assisi, *Blessed Are the Meek*, was a bestseller in the United States in 1944   Martin Gilbert, *The Righteous: The Unsung Heroes of the Holocaust* (New York: Henry Holt, 2003), p. 139.

320 Irene Sendler, who rescued three thousand Jewish children   Ibid., p. 142.

321 "I was so sure of myself, and the guard looks at my pass and says 'Where did you buy it?' "   Simha Ratheiser-Rotem, author interview, Jerusalem, March 2009.

321 "I was always calmest whenever I was in the most danger"   Ibid.

322 "It was filled with women wearing all kinds of creams, curlers"   Tec, *When Light Pierced the Darkness*, p. 34.

322 in 1944, its budget exceeded two million zlotys a month   Kunert, *Zegota*, p. 35.

322 The five-hundred-zloty monthly subsidy from the Council prevented eviction   Zuckerman, *Surplus of Memory*, p. 418.

323 "I contrived a system for myself for finding streets and people"
Ratheiser-Rotem, *Kazik*, p. 97.

323 "I was certain he had no chance" Simha Ratheiser-Rotem, author interview, Jerusalem, March 2009.

323 "He bandaged his face and pretended to be mute" Ibid.

323 He personally headed a cell that was sheltering 280 Jews Gilbert, *Righteous*, p. 143.

323 "I can testify only that a lot of money did arrive" Ratheiser-Rotem,
Kazik, p. 99.

324 "I was a bodyguard" Simha Ratheiser-Rotem, author interview, Jerusalem, March 2009.

324 In just one October 1943 cable to London, he acknowledges receipt of
$10,000 and £10,000 Mark, *Powstanie W Getcie Warszawskim*, p. 181.

324 "The only luxury on the menu was a glass of vodka" Ratheiser-Rotem,
Kazik, p. 99.

CHAPTER 36: ZIVIA GETS HER GUN

326 saplings . . . would grow into a dense, dark forest Author site visit,
March 2008.

326 Boruch Spiegel became convinced that Hitler was going to lose Boruch
Spiegel, author interview, Montreal, November 2007.

326 an astounding forty-seven thousand copies a day Ozimek, *Media Walczacej Warszawy*, p. 77.

326 In mid-May, German bureaucrats were issued handguns Bartoszewski,
1859 Dni Warszawy, p. 677.

327 "In the street markets . . . German military nurses are selling openly
watches and cigarette cases" Korbonski, *Fighting Warsaw*, p. 346.

327 UNSUCCESSFUL ATTEMPT ON ADOLF HITLER'S LIFE Ozimek, *Media Walczacej Warszawy*, p. 83.

328 "He played the great socialist with our bourgeois money" Joanna
Olczak-Ronikier, author interview, Warsaw, December 2008.

328 "People of the Capital! To Arms!" Zenczykowski, *Samotny Boj
Warszawy*, p. 26.

328 Twenty thousand troops still remained in Warsaw Bartoszewski, *1859
Dni Warszawy*, p. 711.

329 Mietek Pera, code name Frenchy, was in fact ferrying Sten guns Mieczyslaw Pera, oral testimony, Warsaw Uprising Museum, online at http://
ahm.1944.pl/Mieczyslaw_Pera.

329 "In the twinkling of an eye, the remaining civilians disappeared from the
street" Bor-Komorowski, *Secret Army*, p. 216.

329 Nearly forty thousand Home Army combatants had risen up Ibid.,
p. 208.

330 "Most Poles saw the [People's Army] as phraseologists or as aliens" Zuckerman, *Surplus of Memory*, p. 525.

330 "It was obvious to us that the insurrection had twin goals" Lubetkin, *Zaglada I Powstanie*, p. 149.

331 The Polish flag once again flew atop the Prudential Life Insurance Building Bor-Komorowski, *Secret Army*, p. 221.

331 In the first twenty-four hours of combat, the Home Army lost two thousand men Wladyslaw Bartoszweski, *Powstanie Warszawskie* (Warsaw: Swiat Ksiazki, 2009), p. 28.

331 "The People's Army knew of our contacts with the Home Army" Ratheiser-Rotem, *Kazik*, p. 66.

332 "They put me off with hemming and hawing" Zuckerman, *Surplus of Memory*, p. 523.

332 a brass plaque on the building informs visitors that double Nobel laureate Marie Curie had been born there Author site visit, January 2008.

332 "It would be too great a historical responsibility to send the few survivors of the Ghetto Uprising back to war" Zuckerman, *Surplus of Memory*, p. 534.

332 "Finally we can start living again" Edelman, *I Byla Milosc w Getcie*, p. 130.

332 "I hid in a store that was burning" Mark Edelman, author interview, Lodz, May 2007.

333 "'Jew, you set the building on fire'" Ibid.

333 delivering $40,000 in U.S. currency Edelman, *I Byla Milosc w Getcie*, p. 132.

333 The pariah National Armed Forces, with 72,439 members nationwide Sebastian Bojemski, *Narodowe Sile Zbrojne w Powstaniu Warszawskim* (Warsaw: Fronda, 2009), p. 32.

333 Only one in ten Home Army soldiers was properly armed Ciechanowski, *Powstanie Warszawskie*, pp. 116–17.

333 the Gestapo had seized a stockpile of 78,000 grenades Luczak, *Dzieje Polski 1939–1945*, p. 427.

334 "I wasn't going to fight with people trying to kill me" Beres and Burnetko, *Marek Edelman*, p. 208.

334 each intricately decorated with pastel murals and glass mosaics depicting folk tales Author site visit.

335 "It was twice her size" Ibid., p. 210.

335 The Home Army had only one thousand rifles in all of Warsaw Bartoszweski, *Powstanie Warszawskie*, p. 22.

335 "all the Gentiles knew that this was a Jewish unit" Zuckerman, *Surplus of Memory*, p. 535.

336 which enjoyed a seven-to-one numerical advantage over the retreating Germans Zenczykowski, *Samotny Boj Warszawy*, p. 56.

336   "Mein Führer . . . the action of the Poles is a blessing"   Norman Davies, *Rising '44: The Battle for Warsaw* (New York: Viking, 2004), p. 247.

CHAPTER 37: SIMHA'S SECOND SEWER RESCUE

342   That Saturday they murdered twenty thousand residents in Wola alone Bartoszweski, *Powstanie Warszawskie*, p. 38.

342   "If I changed the Polish names, it would sound like a Jewish story" Zuckerman, *Surplus of Memory*, p. 523.

342   "They drove us from the cellars"   Central Commission for Investigation of German Crimes in Poland, eyewitness testimony record no. 57, online at http://www.warsawuprising.com/witness/atrocities4.htm.

342   "Between 11 and 12 noon . . . the Germans ordered all of us to get out" Ibid., record no. 63.

344   was supposed to be fighting in the 6th District, third region, as platoon number 693   Oral testimony, Warsaw Uprising Museum, online at http://ahm.1944.pl/Mieczyslaw_Pera.

345   "To the credit of the Poles . . . they were brave people"   Zuckerman, *Surplus of Memory*, p. 538.

345   "I have been scared many times in my life"   Ibid.

345   the Home Army's *Information Bulletin* was receiving over one thousand new missing persons reports   Ozimek, *Media Walczacej Warszawy*, p. 145.

345   two million rounds of ammunition airlifted to Warsaw by converted RAF bombers   Davies, *Rising '44*, p. 311.

345   "Cinders were flying everywhere. You couldn't see the sun for all the ashes"   Ibid., p. 256.

346   including the Holy Sacrament Monastery in New Town, where a thousand people who had taken shelter all perished   Bartoszewski, *Powstanie Warszawskie*, p. 91.

346   Spam and Philip Morris cigarettes   Permanent exhibit, Warsaw Uprising Museum, Warsaw.

346   Gradually the two German forces were closing in on the five thousand defenders caught in the middle   Bor-Komorowski, *Secret Army*, p. 285.

346   "A single house could change hands several times a day"   Mark Edelman, author interview, Lodz, May 2007.

346   German losses during the latest push exceeded 1,570 men   Rozwadowski and Ignatowicz, *Boje o Warszawe*, p. 153.

347   a kilo of butter soared in cost to a staggering 2,400 zlotys   Bartoszweski, *1859 Dni Warszawy*, p. 781.

347   In fact, "the opposite was true"   Paulsson, *Secret City*, p. 171.

347   "I have to say that everyone, including the civilians, treated us cordially" Lubetkin, *Zaglada I Powstanie*, p. 150.

347   so-called Bear Cubs, Chevrolet Suburbans retrofitted   Permanent exhibit, Warsaw Uprising Museum, Warsaw.

348 "The carved oak beams in houses burned like matchsticks"   Bor-
Komorowski, *Secret Army*, p. 286.

348 The only food left was tinned tongue and wine   Ibid. p. 290.

348 "It became clear that no one was going to survive much longer"   Simha
Ratheiser-Rotem, author interview, Jerusalem, March 2009.

348 "I was placed in charge of a unit of mainly sergeants and officers"
Ratheiser-Rotem, *Kazik*, p. 125.

349 "My nostrils were assailed by a well-remembered repulsive odor"
Borzykowski, *Between Tumbling Walls*, pp. 179–80.

349 Tuvia grabbed her and pulled her by the hair   Ibid., p. 182.

350 Zivia, meanwhile, had fainted, and Isaac carried her on his shoulders
Zuckerman, *Surplus of Memory*, p. 543.

350 In all, some 5,200 people managed to escape Old Town   Bartoszewski,
Powstanie Warszawskie, p. 94.

350 "drunken soldiers practiced Caesarean sections with bayonets"   Davies,
Rising '44, p. 344.

CHAPTER 38: FOOLISH ERRANDS

351 the death toll in the Warsaw Uprising was approaching 150,000   Tadeusz
Sawicki, *Roskaz Zdlawic Powstanie* (Warsaw: Bellona, 2010), p. 190.

351 Marshal Rokossovsky's 3,360 tanks were now in Praga   Zenczykowski,
Samotny Boj Warszawy, p. 122.

351 "a purely adventuristic affair to which the Soviet government could not
lend a hand"   Rudy Abramson, *Spanning the Century: The Life of W.
Averell Harriman* (New York: William Morrow, 1992), p. 382.

351 "without the prior knowledge of Soviet military command"   Zenczykowski, *Samotny Boj Warszawy*, p. 118.

352 "They're pigs, not soldiers"   Cezary Gmyz, *Rzepospolita*, May 17, 2008,
p. 1.

352 "I've got used to the sight of male corpses"   Davies, *Rising '44*, p. 353.

352 "He took me and my mother by the hand"   This occurred to the author's
mother, Dr. Wanda Brzezinski.

353 A nearly mile-long trench separated the rebel and German positions
Piotr Basmajew, *Historia Zoliborskiego Powstanca* (Warsaw: PAX, 2008),
p. 90.

353 "all black and splattered with mud, reeking and covered in feces"   Ibid.,
p. 74.

353 "She ordered us to dunk our heads into it"   Edelman, *I Byla Milosc w
Getcie*, p. 141.

354 where half of the thirty documented murders of Jews by Gentile insurgents were committed   Paulsson, *Secret City*, p. 181.

354 "Part of the evidence was that Frenchy was frequently seen in the company
of a Jew"   Ibid., p. 176.

354 "Why endanger ourselves for papers? . . . For history" Ratheiser-Rotem, *Kazik*, p. 126.

355 historians estimate as many as 4,500 Paulsson, *Secret City*, p. 168.

355 "He immediately brought out a large sum and gave it to us" Zuckerman, *Surplus of Memory*, p. 546.

355 grains seized from the Haberbusch and Schiele breweries Goldstein, *Five Years in the Warsaw Ghetto*, p. 211.

356 one hundred and ten B-17 Flying Fortresses, escorted by 72 Mustangs Zenczykowski, *Samotny Boj Warszawy*, p. 119.

357 "Everything around going up in flames, walls caving in—and that music" Ratheiser-Rotem, *Kazik*, pp. 127–28.

357 "This river rat was always squirming his way everywhere" Edelman, *I Byla Milosc w Getcie*, p. 130.

357 They climbed inside, momentarily safe Simha Ratheiser-Rotem, author interview, Jerusalem, March 2009.

358 one hundred thousand people were already crammed behind the hastily strung barbed wire Davies, *Rising '44*, p. 386.

359 had permitted a two-hour cease-fire to evacuate nine thousand residents Sawicki, *Roskaz Zdlawicz Powstanie*, p. 154.

359 almost twenty-six thousand German casualties, including ten thousand dead Rozwadowski and Ignatowicz, *Boje o Warszawe*, p. 153.

359 "There were shiny new automatic weapons, tinned meat and milk" Borzykowski, *Between Tumbling Walls*, p. 186.

360 "Every house in the quarter was hit several times by shells" Ibid., p. 189.

360 had to be fired at very close range—less than fifty yards—to be effective Badmajew, *Historia Zoliborskiego Powstanca*, p. 66.

360 "The echo of that shooting made me completely deaf" Zuckerman, *Surplus of Memory*, p. 547.

360 "The whole unit had come back, except for Zivia" Ibid., p. 548.

360 "I asked one of the Gentiles to bring me some spirits" Ibid.

361 "Do you want to know what color a person who has taken a direct hit from a tank shell leaves on a wall?" Edelman, *I Byla Milosc w Getcie*, p. 144.

361 of the twenty-one people in his unit, he was the only one alive Assuntino and Goldkorn, *Straznik*, p. 105.

Chapter 39: Zivia's Cupboard

362 After sixty-three days and nearly two hundred thousand fatalities Lukas, *Forgotten Holocaust*, p. 219.

363 "You can't do this!" Simha Ratheiser-Rotem, author interview, Jerusalem, March 2009.

363 "Don't shoot, there are women down here" Ratheiser-Rotem, *Kazik*, p. 131.

363   to run fire hoses through coal chutes to drown everyone inside   This was experienced by the author's mother, who as an eight-year-old stood on her mother's shoulders in a cellar in Warsaw as water poured in. The flood stopped when the water pressure broke a door down.

363   "The ruins are exceptionally photogenic"   Stanislaw Kopf, *Wyrok na Miasto* (Warsaw: ASKON, 2001), p. 9.

364   "They were probably taking us there to rape the girls"   Simha Ratheiser-Rotem, author interview, Jerusalem, March 2009.

364   a Wehrmacht officer stopped the Ukrainians and asked where they were headed   Ibid.

364   its cemetery had been transformed by the SS into a makeshift crematorium   http://www.Swiety-wojciech.pl/historia.

364   "And how long have you had that name?"   Ratheiser-Rotem, *Kazik*, p. 133.

365   A total of 650,000 people would eventually pass through its gates   Kopf, *Wyrok na Miasto*, p. 28.

365   "Three hundred thousand people are now enjoying the fresh air"   Ibid., p. 27.

366   "Hundreds of human beings had to parade in front of German officers"   Ratheiser-Rotem, *Kazik*, p. 135.

366   along with 150,000 other able-bodied Varsovians   Paulsson, *Secret City*, p. 219.

366   "A mood of apathy descended on me"   Ratheiser-Rotem, *Kazik*, p. 135.

366   "I suppose fate had dictated that we should live"   Lubetkin, *Zaglada I Powstanie*, p. 151.

367   The spiteful omission affected four hundred combatants in Jolie Bord   Sawicki, *Zdlawic Powstanie*, p. 154.

367   "We didn't know what to do"   Lubetkin, *Zaglada I Powstanie*, p. 151.

368   "The women knew, and we knew, too, that our presence was not to their advantage"   Borzykowski, *Between Tumbling Walls*, p. 199.

368   He soon grew "very mad at Zivia," because "it seemed she pinched me the hardest"   Zuckerman, *Surplus of Memory*, p. 551.

369   "must completely disappear from the surface of the earth"   Ceiechanowski, *Powstanie Warszawskie*, p. 662.

CHAPTER 40: DESPICABLE YIDS

370   "Everything beneath us lies in ruin"   Kopf, *Wyrok na Miasto*, p. 100.

371   Pens filled with a few grams of explosive, enough to remove a hand   Ibid., p. 93.

372   "We budgeted the precious liquid with mathematical precision"   Borzykowski, *Between Tumbling Walls*, p. 203.

373   "Get us some help"   Ibid., p. 215.

374   "I had a feeling that Gestapo agents were everywhere"   Ratheiser-Rotem, *Kazik*, p. 140.

374   "I was sure the SS would be looking for me sooner or later"   Simha
       Ratheiser-Rotem, author interview, Jerusalem, March 2009.

374   "It seemed as if several platoons of soldiers had invaded the house"
       Borzykowski, *Between Tumbling Walls*, p. 215.

375   "We got to know the soldiers working around our house"   Ibid., p. 216.

375   "That night was a night of horrors"   Zuckerman, *Surplus of Memory*,
       p. 552.

376   "She had to be careful since she didn't know whom she was telling it to"
       Ibid., p. 553.

376   "Passing Germans looked at us with curiosity"   Borzykowski, *Between
       Tumbling Walls*, p. 220.

376   warning *"Achtung, Fleckfieber"*   Beres and Burnetko, *Marek Edelman*,
       p. 213.

376   "Despicable Yids"   Mark Edelman, author interview, Lodz, May 2007.

CHAPTER 41: MARK AND THE MOHICANS

378   "It was the saddest day of my life"   Mark Edelman, author interview,
       Lodz, May 2007.

379   "I finally realized that it was over"   Simha Ratheiser-Rotem, author inter-
       view, Jerusalem, March 2009.

379   "Are you crazy?"   Ibid.

380   "Give them everything they want, for after all, they are killing Germans"
       Abramson, *Spanning the Century*, p. 345.

380   Soviet losses were sixty-five times greater than America's   Hitchcock, *Lib-
       eration*, p. 132.

380   More than twenty million Soviet citizens had died fending off Hitler
       Ibid., p. 131.

380   "the barbarian invasion"   Abramson, *Spanning the Century*, p. 395.

381   "Harriman was never included in the private talks on Poland"   Ibid.,
       p. 376.

381   "He is a very sick man"   Conrad Black, *Franklin Delano Roosevelt:
       Champion of Freedom* (New York: Public Affairs, 2005), p. 1075.

381   On April 5, 1945 . . . the United States formally . . . recognized the new
       Provisional Government   Slawomir Cenkiewicz, *Sladami Bezpieki I Partii*
       (Lomianki: LTW, 2009), p. 37.

381   "his heart bled for them, but the brutal facts could not be overlooked"
       Hitchcock, *Liberation*, p. 155.

381   in Warsaw, the population had rebounded to 162,000   Luczak, *Dzieje Pol-
       ski*, p. 492.

381   "I cannot believe how fortunate I am to be alive"   Olczak-Ronikier, *W
       Ogrodzie Pamieci*, p. 298.

382   "I went crazy and almost killed them"   Simha Ratheiser-Rotem, author
       interview, Jerusalem, March 2009.

383 "She thought a tearful little girl with long plaits would fall into her arms"
Olczak-Ronikier, *W Ogrodzie Pamieci*, p. 297.

384 "A lot of our misfortunes were solved after the war because they remembered what we had done for them" Zuckerman, *Surplus of Memory*, p. 357.

385 "We were firm friends" Ibid.

385 an estimated 11,500 Warsaw Jews had survived the war Paulsson, *Secret City*, p. 198.

385 Eventually, more than 150,000 Polish Jews returned from the Soviet Union Jan T. Gross, *Fear: Anti-Semitism in Poland After Auschwitz* (New York: Random House, 2007), p. 43.

385 raising the total number of Jews in Poland to more than 200,000 Beres and Burnetko, *Marek Edelman*, p. 220.

385 "Why are you cooperating with those sons of bitches?" Simha Ratheiser-Rotem, author interview, Jerusalem, March 2009.

385 "They were best friends" Ibid.

385 "We had differences of opinion" Mark Edelman, author interview, Lodz, May 2007.

385 Some 15,000 Communist functionaries were killed in the immediate postwar Gross, *Fear*, p. 28.

386 In the west . . . six hundred thousand people died Timothy Snyder, "Holocaust: The Ignored Reality," *New York Review of Books*, July 16, 2009.

386 sixty thousand Home Army officers were arrested by the NKVD Zbigniew Blazynski, *Mowi Jozef Swiatlo: Za Kulisami Bezpieki I Partii 1940–1955* (Warsaw: LTW, 2003), p. 130.

387 "Isaac and Zivia had changed" Assuntino and Goldkorn, *Straznik*, p. 111.

387 "I was alone and I didn't know what to do" Ibid.

387 "There was no future there for us" Boruch Spiegel, author interview, Montreal, November 2007.

387 "The United States did nothing for Jews during the war" Ibid.

388 "Hide, hide, the Jews are coming for you" Beres and Burnetko, *Marek Edelman*, p. 235.

388 Eliza was "not for sale" Ibid.

389 "In America she had a bicycle, a pony, a boat" Ibid., p. 238.

CHAPTER 42: NEXT YEAR IN JERUSALEM

392 "I said bitter things at the conference" Zuckerman, *Surplus of Memory*, p. 601.

393 "I thought we still had something to do in Europe" Ratheiser-Rotem, *Kazik*, p. 150.

396 "It was even said that he had a direct line to Stalin" Zuckerman, *Surplus of Memory*, p. 673.

397   "People were shocked. 'Where are all these Jews coming from?' they asked"   Boruch Spiegel, author interview, Montreal, November 2007.

397   Estimates by American scholars   Gross, *Fear*, p. 28.

398   "Most of the attacks were pure and simple banditry"   Marek Edelman, author interview, Lodz, May 2007.

398   Jews were "victims of the atmosphere created by the National Armed Forces"   Assuntino and Goldkorn, *Straznik*, p. 116.

398   Nonetheless, they occupied perhaps as much as half of the senior posts   Gross, *Fear*, p. 228.

399   "It was already bad enough [for Jews after the war], but [Berman's agency] made the situation worse"   Boruch Spiegel, author interview, Montreal, November 2007.

399   "Gentlemen—a great catastrophe"   Zuckerman, *Surplus of Memory*, p. 660.

399   "Kielce was a ghost town"   Ibid., p. 661.

399   who received him immediately and with great courtesy   Ibid.

400   informed him that the kidnapping charges were nothing but a "provocation"   Gross, *Fear*, p. 85.

400   "I assembled about forty Jews in one room and didn't let the soldiers in"   http://www.Jewishvirtuallibrary.org/jsource/Holocaust/Kielce.html.

401   "Uniformed soldiers and a number of civilians forced their way into the building"   Ibid.

402   "I said I personally would take responsibility"   Zuckerman, *Surplus of Memory*, p. 666.

402   "We were accepted without delay. I'll never forget Spychalski's reaction"   Ibid., p. 667.

402   "any action which might indicate that the authorities were siding with the Jews"   Gross, *Fear*, p. 99.

402   "Do not under any circumstances use the northern borders"   Zuckerman, *Surplus of Memory*, p. 667.

402   "Could Spychalski, who was acting as Minister of Defense, have decided such a thing on his own?"   Ibid., p. 671.

403   "Perhaps 'high politics' was at work here"   Ibid., p. 675.

403   By October 1946, seventy thousand Jews left Poland for Palestine . . . By December, the number had risen to 115,500   http://www.Jewishvirtual library.org.

INDEX

ABOUT THE TYPE

This book was set in Sabon, a typeface designed by the well-known German typographer Jan Tschichold (1902-74). Sabon's design is based on the original letterforms of Claude Garamond and was created specifically to be used for three sources: foundry type for hand composition, Linotype, and Monotype. Tschichold named his typeface for the famous Frankfurt typefounder Jacques Sabon, who died in 1580.